Sailors in the Dock

Sailors in the Dock

NAVAL COURTS MARTIAL DOWN THE CENTURIES

PETER C. SMITH

Dedicated to the memory of the late Commander Douglas Gilbert, RN,
for his kindness, advice and encouragement during the birth pangs of this book

Uncharted the rocks that surround thee,
Take heed that the channels thou learn,
Lest thy name serve to buoy for another,
That shoal, the courts-martial return.
Though armoured the belt that protects her,
The ship wears a scar on her side,
It is well if the court shall acquit thee,
It were best hadst thou never been tried.

The Laws of the Navy, Admiral Hopwood

First published 2011

The History Press
The Mill, Brimscombe Port
Stroud, Gloucestershire, GL5 2QG
www.thehistorypress.co.uk

© Peter C. Smith, 2011

The right of Peter C. Smith to be identified as the Author
of this work has been asserted in accordance with the
Copyrights, Designs and Patents Act 1988.

British Library Cataloguing in Publication Data.
A catalogue record for this book is available from the British Library.

ISBN 978 0 7524 6562 3

Typesetting and origination by The History Press
Printed in the EU for The History Press

Contents

PART ONE: ORIGINS AND CUSTOMS   9

PART TWO: SOME FAMOUS CASES

1 A Little More Singeing (1587)   31

2 A Fleet in Being (1690)   36

3 The Abandoning of Benbow (1702)   41

4 An Incident Off Toulon (1744)   50

5 To Encourage the Others (1757)   57

6 Uncertainty Off Ushant (1778)   67

7 A Foundering at Spithead (1782)   76

8 Trouble with Breadfruit (1792)   85

9 'We Intend to be Masters' (1797)   94

10 Nelson at Naples (1799)   104

11 Action or Inaction (1805)   111

12 Indecision in the Basque Roads (1809)   120

13 Ships that Go Bump (1893)   129

14 'On the Knee' (1906)   137

15 Superior or Inferior (1914)   144

16 As The Sparks Fly Upward (1928)   155

17 Judgement or Conduct (1942)   164

PART THREE: POINTS FROM PROCEEDINGS

1 Mutiny and Desertion   175

2 Collision and Wreck   185

3 Losses in Action   208

4 Murder and Other Cases   218

5 Joining the Ladies   224

6 Unusual Cases and Verdicts   230

7 Peacetime Misdoings   242

8 Humour in Court   248

Appendix   253

Bibliography   259

Index   263

Part One

Origins and Customs

The origins of naval courts martial date back to the days of the Commonwealth. Prior to 1652, however, certain established 'laws and customs' of the sea, formulated piecemeal over centuries, provided a basis for the administration of justice afloat. The records are so imperfect, unfortunately, that it is impossible to be certain of when they came into being. Origination of law lay in the hands of the sovereign and, as it was often he who led his 'fleets' into combat, it can be assumed that it was from this source that the earliest regulations stemmed.

The 'Father of the Navy', King Alfred, laid the foundations of a tradition that endured until comparatively recent times. When he proclaimed dominion of the seas for himself and built the fleet to back it, he insisted that ships of other nations must lower their topsails and strike their flags on encountering a ship-of-war of his. Foreign powers continued to show this respect to the Royal Navy as late as the twentieth century.

This sovereignty was maintained by subsequent rulers; King Edgar's title was 'Sovereign Lords of all Albion, and of the maritime or insular kings inhabiting round about', and as Sovereign of the Narrow Seas, he took his fleet of 400 ships on a tour of the British Isles in AD 937. At Chester, eight kings and princes duly acknowledged that dominion by rowing his barge down the River Dee at noon, while he steered it in symbolic majesty.

Ethelred imposed the notorious Danegeld to pay for the guardianship of the seas and Cnut continued it. The Normans inherited this tradition, with King John imitating Edgar by sailing to Ireland with 500 ships to enforce the acknowledgement of his dominion over the waters. To administer justice the captains and admirals commanding the various assemblies of ships used their powers based on the accumulated 'Customs of the Sea'. The hardy sailor folk inhabiting the island of Oléron, off the French coast, gave their name to the medieval code of maritime law, '*La charte d'Oléron des jugements de la mer*', which was promulgated by Eleanor of Aquitaine. King Richard I adopted these laws on his return from the Crusades and decreed that they should govern English seamen and they became known as the 'laws of Oléron'.

Standing fleets as such did not exist; it was the merchants who provided the ships and the Cinque Ports the men themselves in time of war. Each captain administered justice to his own crew but was subject to the greater power of the embarked nobles who led the fighting. These knights held commissions from the sovereign to make their own ordinances and punish accordingly. These 'Generalls at Sea' often summoned Councils of War, before which the accused were brought to face the judgement of the peers. The trials were conducted for all offences against 'Articles or Ordinances of War' as each leader defined them at the time. Here we can see the germ of the courts martial concept.

The title 'Admiral' did not appear until the fourteenth century, but 100 years later a 'Lord High Admiral' had been permanently instituted and it was from him, under the auspices of his sovereign, that laws which governed the assemblies of men and ships he 'stayed' to the king's service were promulgated to the seagoing captain-admirals who administered it. Under King Richard I, this precedent had been set up for his fleet, which he took on the Crusade of 1190. He appointed justiciaries and gave them a set of rules concerning various crimes, laying down the punishments applicable. Murder, when proven, was dealt with by the guilty party being tied to the corpse of his victim and thrown overboard! Wounding or threatening to kill received equally pertinent justice, the felon having his sword arm cut off, while theft was, if anything, even less pleasant in its punishment – boiling pitch and feathers were administered and then the guilty party was marooned ashore at the first suitable spot. No doubt discipline was admirably maintained by such draconian methods.

Desertion in Richard II's day was punished with the loss of double any wages the sailor had received, topped with a one-year imprisonment, and an Act of Parliament was passed to confirm this. It was subsequently modified by other acts and became the first felony to be so treated, the accused being tried by the Lord High Admiral or his appointed generalls-at-sea. The latter still exercised their judgements and penalties as above on other criminal offences at this time. It will be noted that the definition between the generalls, or later admirals, at sea and the captains of the ships themselves was clear, and that the former still retained their overall power by custom and usage. This was not to survive the sixteenth century without challenge, however, as we shall see.

So, according to the prerogatives of appointed admirals commanding a fleet for their King or commanding a fleet for private venture, but with the sanction of His Majesty and always modified by the traditional 'Customs', was the law administered by martial courts up to the time of Charles I. The declaration by the Long Parliament that the prerogative of martial courts was unconstitutional removed all effective means of administrating justice in the fleet and had to be rescinded. In 1644, an ordinance was drafted by the House to re-establish control and this was passed by the Commons the year after, giving a general Council of War the power to hold courts martial and this was further strengthened in 1648.

With the arrival of Cromwell's Commonwealth in 1649, these ordinances remained the basis on which law at sea was administered. However, during the First Dutch War an unexpected defeat was suffered by the fleet under Generall-at-Sea Robert Blake, one of the greatest naval commanders of that time. This was the Battle of Dungeness, which took place on 10 December 1652 (30 November in the Julian calendar). The result of this was a sad testimony to the fighting power of the British fleet, which was defeated by Tromp in view of crowds of spectators ashore. Far worse, however, was the conduct of many of the ships' captains, both mercantile and regular navy. At least half of the forty-two vessels in the British fleet used the wind blatantly and shamefully to avoid becoming engaged in the fighting at all.

Such conduct was a humiliating experience to those whose long-claimed sovereignty of the seas that the Dutch had now made a mockery of. It did not need Tromp to hoist a broom at his masthead to prove to the new government that the long British mastery of the salt water had received a severe setback. To their credit, urgent and sensible measures were at once put in hand to restore both pride and power. But what of the culprits themselves, under the existing laws? Blake himself spelt out what he had in mind for them:

> In this account I am bound to let your Honours know in general that there was much baseness of spirit, not among the merchantmen only, but many of the State's ships, and therefore I make it my humble request that your Honours would be pleased to send down some gentlemen to take an impartial and strict examination of the deportment of several commanders, that you know who are to be confided in and who are not.

The commissioners did so, with some alacrity, and, as a result, five of the reluctant captains found themselves in the Tower of London. Captains Chapman, Saltonstall, Taylour, Wadsworth and Young were these worthies, and cowardice is not thought to have been the motivating force for their conduct, bribery or latent adherence to the Royalist cause being suspected. Even Blake's brother, Benjamin, was adjudged among the guilty on this black day and although he did not stand trial he was discharged from his command 'not again to be employed nor go forth in the service'.

So much for the immediate past, but the commissioners and parliament were much more concerned with the future. The existing rules were obviously inadequate in such an emergency and this was to be rectified with commendable speed. A committee was set up within two weeks, advised by judges of the Admiralty Court, which set to work to formulate a complete new set of laws for state ships. By December, these new regulations, the 'Laws' or 'Articles' of War, were passed by parliament and dispersed to the fleet. They were to form the basis of all subsequent laws and discipline for the fleet of Great Britain.

There were thirty-nine articles in total in the original 'Laws of War and Ordinance', ranging from daily worship to pillage, embezzlement to desertion, sedition to negligence, and in almost two-thirds of them the death penalty looms large, being either the only punishment or one of the alternatives. However, such was the rise in morale in the fleet brought about by other overdue reforms that this fierce list of dire facts did not have to be taken literally as an indication that error was always to merit execution. Indeed, few, if any, who fell foul of these new regulations received the death sentence in practice, not even those in the Tower whose conduct had brought them about. It was not until later that the hidden menace these new articles contained was translated into hideous reality for those found guilty.

What these laws did lead to – the following year – was the conferring upon the seagoing commanders the hitherto exclusive right of the Lord High Admiral to convene their own courts, at sea. The commissioners instructed their seagoing generalls on these courts martial, which could be held, in fleets or divisions of the fleets, by means of a Council of War comprising not less than three persons. Any sentence that meant loss of life or limb had to be referred to the commanders thus empowered, along with minutes and evidence, all of which had to be recorded by a Judge Advocate of the fleet, a title from the old Admiralty Court that ensured continuity from the Lord High Admiral's juris- diction. Nor could a captain be cashiered by court martial without reference to the empowered commanders, and so on, down the line to individual captains of ships.

It was a historic step for, as Michael Lewis wrote, 'that very concession of the power to punish delinquents at sea had conferred upon the Commander of the fleets just one important *droit of Admiralty*, so that, thereafter and for ever more, he assumed the *title* of Admiral'.

Not only did the empowering of these admirals give them powers never before legally convened over their officers and men, it also ensured that these same offic- ers and men had a legal framework in which to be judged, far fairer and less open to abuse than the old 'Customs of the Sea' had ever been. Of course, it was not perfect, but in the prevailing atmosphere afloat at that time it worked. The same laws also gave the generalls or admirals the authority to hold courts martial on offences committed by their men 'on shore in any place or harbour', which seemed to indicate that they were removed from the jurisdiction of normal English justice in these events instead of being subject to it as earlier.

With the restoration of the monarchy these laws were swept away again, the reinstatement of the office of Lord High Admiral cancelling out the powers afforded in 1652 to the seagoing commanders. The position went to the Duke of York (the future King James II), who reassumed his old powers of delegating what laws were to apply, as earlier. What this meant can be seen in a set of precise instructions he issued in June 1661 to Sir John Mennds, 'Vice-Admiral and Commander-in-Chief of His Majesty's Fleet in the Narrow Seas'.

They commanded him: 'First, above all things' to ensure that twice every day all the ships of his command must ensure that 'God be duly served' according to 'the usual prayers and liturgy of the Church of England'. Secondly, he was to make sure that all his men lived 'orderly and peaceably together' and that every officer in the fleet must faithfully perform his duty. If they did not, the duke's instructions were equally precise:

> … if any seaman or other in your ship shall commit murther or manslaughter, you shall send him in safe custody to the next goale, where he is to be received and kept in safety, as the keepers will answer the contrary at their perils, until he shall have his tryall according to law.

Anything else, and he listed tumult, conspiracy, drawing blood, swearing, blasphemy, drunkenness, theft, failing to keep his place clean, waste, absence without leave, insolence and disorder, was to be punished with '"due severity" according to the *known orders and customs of the seas*'.

Such a reversion could not stand for long in the aftermath of the order and obvious desirability of parliament's decrees. So, the new loyal parliament had little choice but to re-state these laws under an act of their own, duly modified to accord with the sensibilities of the monarchy. This they did with similar haste to the originals, but with far less care and thoughtfulness, especially in the drafting of the thirty-fourth article, which safeguarded the Lord High Admiral's place in the scheme of things. Until the Test Act debarred him from that office, the wishes of the king's brother had to be respected, hence this fatal article:

> And it is hereby further enacted, that the Lord High Admiral for the time being shall, by virtue of this act, have full power and authority to grant Commissions to inferior Vice Admirals or Commanders-in-Chief of any squadron of ships to call and assemble Court Martialls consisting of commanders and captains, and no Court Martiall where the pains of death shall be inflicted shall consist of less than five captains at least, the admiral's lieutenant to be as to this purpose esteemed as a captain; and in no case wherein sentence of death shall pass by virtue of the articles aforesaid or any of them (except in the case of mutiny) there shall be execution of such sentence of death without the leave of the Lord

High Admiral, if the offence be committed within the Narrow Seas. But in case any of the offences aforesaid be committed on any voyage beyond the Narrow Seas whereupon sentence of death shall be given in pursuance of the aforesaid articles, or of any of them, then execution shall not be done but by the order of the Commander-in-Chief of that Fleet or Squadron wherein sentence of death was passed.

This left grave loopholes. For example, by restricting the right to order courts martial only to the specially authorised commander-in-chief (C-in-C), they ignored the fact that fleets under such persons might be split into squadrons separated by hundreds of miles and for periods of many months or years. Or that the appointed C-in-C might be killed in action, die of illness or be incapacitated in any way, in which case nobody in that fleet could order a court martial, nor could the commander of a detached squadron do so. The further restriction, allowing only officers in 'actual service and pay', had no immediate effect but, when the new introduction of 'half-pay' officers came about later, this was read to de-bar them from serving on courts, although they were equally in the service of the king. Once a ship was wrecked or captured in action the crew's pay ceased forthwith and therefore none could be subject to court martial proceedings, as the famous *Wager* case, described later in these pages, showed up only too clearly. It omitted officers employed in the king's service on the civil side, but included others who sailed on their occasions with permission of the Lord High Admiral's commission, the East India Company men and the like. Nor were all the bolt-holes closed on some aspects of violence and fraud at sea.

Equally important, although it strictly imposed limits on the number of officers composing a 'death' board, it gave no directions as to how other tribunals were to be formed. All these oversights were to cause many headaches in the ninety years that followed and most of them had to be closed by special acts, as and when events occurred, which showed up the law to be an ass! We will be touching on a number of the most important of these in our narrative but much grief and trouble could have been saved if they had framed the new laws with a little more reference to those of 1652.

However, a number of the original laws were incorporated into the new 'Articles and Orders for the regulation and better government of His Majesty's Navies, Ships of War, and forces at Sea', as the new laws were titled (Act 13 of Charles II – 13 Chas. 2). Many were almost straight copies from the laws of 1652 with only slight differences in order and wording, but there were some omissions, false musters among them, and some additions, there being thirty-four in all.

Those that followed their predecessors closely were articles 1, daily worship; 2, blasphemy; 3, communing with the enemy or rebels; 4, communications from same to be reported to senior officers; 5, forbade succour to the same; 6, documents of prizes to be carefully preserved; 7, prizes not to be pillaged below the gun deck; 8, embezzlement of ships' gear; 9, prisoners not to be stripped of clothing unless they resisted (something, to the Royal Navy's credit, that was never done anyway); 10, failure of captains to encourage their crews, or asking for quarter, to be punished by death, or in such other way as the court martial shall decide; 11, men must obey orders to attack the enemy; 12, cowardice to be punished by death, or in other ways at discretion of the court; 13, condemned an officer protecting a convoy who did not defend his charge to the death; 14, condemned an officer who failed to pursue the enemy or help a friend in sight, punished by death; 16, rebellion punished by death; 18, spies punished by death; 19, sedition; 20, hiding others sedition; 21, striking a superior officer; 22, complaints of victual ling to be reported to senior officers; 23, private quarrels; 24, wasting ammunition; 25, negligent navigation; 26, burning of ships or gear other than enemy; 27, sleeping on watch; 28, murder; 29, robbery; 30, provost martial must take charge of prisoners and not allow them to escape; 31, apprehension of all offenders, whole crews duty; 33, all faults and misdemeanours not specified above to be punished by the Custom of the Sea; 34, as listed above setting up courts martial.

New articles were: 15, discouragement of crew in action forbidden; 17, desertion or enticement to desert, punished by death; 32, unnatural offences (sodomy etc.), to be punished by death 'without mercy'.

In 1714 came the first of the many acts passed to bring justice to those that these articles had omitted. This particular act gave powers over those ashore who committed acts of violence, quarrelling, assault on superiors and victualling racketeers, who had hitherto been subject to the jurisdiction of normal courts of law on land (which were often notoriously lax or lethargic), to the Navy Board, which could imprison of fine offenders. This still failed to include offences against the Articles of War, outside of these limitations, committed by personnel out of reach of seagoing admirals, but this was rectified by a clause inserted in 1720. For political reasons this clause was to come under severe criticism twenty-nine years later as an encroachment upon civil liberties. Another clause, of 1722, authorised the trial of captains found to have unauthorised merchandise aboard their vessels, and was an attempt to stamp out clandestine trade on behalf of the great companies being conducted by HM officers.

As mentioned earlier, although five officers was the limit of boards sitting to try murder or of cases requiring the death penalty, no limit was imposed on other cases and the custom of calling a Council of War led to a system whereby when a court martial was convened it was a case of 'one comes well all come' for the captains of all the ships of the fleet. This could lead to abuses whereby the C–in–C could order away the ships of those captains he did not wish to attend and then pack the court with his followers. This was in fact done in practice, which led to complaints, naturally enough, as to the partiality of courts martial at sea. The scandal of 'false musters' was another common abuse, crewmen 'loaned' to other ships still had their pay and rations drawn and claimed for by unscrupulous captains and became a blatant form of earning extra income for many. A temporary measure was the passing of an act in 1748 reinforcing the existing acts, but the time for a more drastic overhaul was upon them and it could be delayed no longer.

In 1749 came about the great reforming act, officially entitled 'An Act for amending, explaining and reducing into one Act of Parliament the Laws relating to the Government of His Majesty's ships, vessels and forces by Sea', or 22 George II. Attempts to subject half-pay officers to the act were strenuously resisted and were dropped.

Again, many of the original articles remained unchanged, save for wording and order; the cases where they differed or new articles were incorporated were as follows. Articles 1, 2, 3, 4, 11, 19, 20, 23, 24, 27 and 28 were the same. Changes in order were that 6 repeated 5 of the 1661 articles; likewise 7 repeated 6, 26 repeated 25, 32 repeated and combined 30 and 31. Article 5 provided punishment for spies; 8 forbade taking goods from prizes except for certain circumstances; 9 forbade ill treatment of prisoners; 18 was the anti-smuggling clause; 22 was in essence the same as the old 21; 30 a repeat of 29; 31, false musters; 33, cashiering of officers convicted of scandalous, infamous, cruel, oppressive or cruel conduct; 34, mutiny, desertion or disobedience committed ashore to be treated as hitherto at sea; 35, offences against articles ashore to be so also treated as at sea; 36 was a repeat of the old Article 33.

However, under stern King George, harsher penalties became the rule for most of the serious offences. The old spirit of discretion and leniency was displaced by the constant clamour for the death sentence for a whole host of offences. Thus we find Article 10 subjected officers of all ranks convicted of treacherous behaviour, cowardice or 'cries of quarter' to death without alternative. Article 12 called for those who held back in action to suffer death; the exercise of discretion held under the old Article 12 was taken away completely. Article 13: failing to pursue an enemy, death; 14: hanging back in action 'upon pretence of arrears of wages', death or other punishment the court thought fit; 15: desertion, death; 17: desertion and enticing to desert, death; 32: unnatural offences, death.

It was doubly unfortunate that these new, harsher articles coincided with the growth of ever more rigid 'Fighting Instructions' for regulating all aspects of battle at sea, so that commanders were hemmed in on both sides from straying from strictly ordained paths, and initiative was put into a crippling straitjacket for a considerable period. The effects of these manacles are reflected in many of the cases recorded in these pages. However, even though many of the bad omissions of the old act had been rectified, the articles were subject to continuing changes, some of them reflecting, happily, a less grim attitude of mind in the rulers of the nation as time went on, a process which, with accelerating speed, continues to this day.

For example, in 1779 an authorisation was enacted in 19 Geo. III to again lessen the penalty exacted for offences committed under Articles 10 and 12, many years too late to save one famous martyr, of course, but nonetheless welcomed. The obligation for members to remain aboard ship during the trial was challenged at this time, during the Keppel and Palliser fracas, as will be related. This too was rescinded under the above act. Further modifications were contained in 10 & 11 Vict. and, in addition, in the Queen's Regulations and Admiralty Instructions issued to the fleet in 1844. The Judge Advocate remained the prosecutor until 1884 when this duty was transferred to the captain or executive officer of the accused's ship. The Judge Advocate was then restricted to taking minutes of the proceedings, helping clear up doubtful points of law, drawing up the sentence and, under the President's direction, pronouncing that sentence.

The Articles of War were codified in the Naval Discipline Act of 1866, which made eligible all officers of or above the rank of lieutenant, providing they were 21 years of age, to sit on courts martial, but reduced the maximum number of sitting members allowed from thirteen back once more to the old limitation of no less than five nor more than nine. There remained no appeal from the death sentence, save by the sovereign, but the Admiralty had the right, which they exercised but rarely, to annul or amend a sentence if they so felt fit to do so. The number of offences gradually increased over the centuries; the rapid changes of the Victorian era – sail to steam, wood to iron – continued apace into the twentieth century and more had to be allowed for than could ever have been contemplated by the commissioners of 1661, but the death penalty was withdrawn from most of them as time went by, the last to be so sentenced and executed being a Royal Marine in 1860.

This act, to give it its full title 'An Act to make Provision for the Discipline of the Navy', dated 10 August 1866, was very important, for it formed the basis of all courts martial held up to the end of the First World War and, with the amendments contained in the Naval Discipline Act of 1922 (12 & 13 Geo. 5), right through the Second World War to the early 1950s. It contained fifty-one articles in part one and they may be summarised as follows:

1. Public Worship be 'solemnly, orderly and reverently performed' and that the 'Lord's Day be observed according to law'.
2. Misconduct in the presence of the enemy. Every officer who, upon signal of battle or on sight of the enemy, did not use 'utmost exertion' to bring his ship into action or failed to encourage others to fight or who would surrender his ship 'when capable of making a successful defence' or withdraw improperly was, if he acted traitorously, to suffer death; if from

cowardice – death or such other punishment as thought fit; if negligence – dismissed from the service, with or without disgrace.

3. Failure to pursue an enemy, pirate or rebel, beaten or flying, or not assist a friend or improperly forsake his station should suffer death if he acted traitorously; death or alternatives if cowardly; dismissal if negligence.

4. Any delay or discouragement to act in service or action, desertion in the face of the enemy, sleep on watch – to suffer death or such other punishment as deemed fitting.

5. The same penalties applied in the same circumstances to any misconduct by subordinate offices and men in action.

6. Spies to suffer death or such other punishment as seen fit.

7. Those convicted of corresponding with the enemy or providing intelligence to same, who fail to reveal information obtained from the enemy or who supply the enemy in any way – to suffer death or such other punishment as deemed fitting.

8. Improper communication with the enemy punished by dismissal with disgrace, etc.

9. Neglect of duty, desertion etc., punished by the same alternatives.

10. Mutiny with violence, failure to suppress such mutiny – to suffer death if traitorously or alternatives as above.

11. Mutiny with violence – the ringleader to suffer death, etc., all others imprisonment, etc.

12. Incitement to mutiny – death etc.

13. Civilians endeavour to incite mutiny – death etc. if aboard HM ship.

14. Sedition or mutinous assembly – penal servitude etc.

15. Concealing traitors – penal servitude etc.

16. Striking a superior officer – penal servitude etc.

17. Disobedience of orders, threatening or insulting language and contempt – dismissal with disgrace etc.

18. Quarrelling and fighting – imprisonment etc.

19. Desertion or absence without leave – if to the enemy the penalty to be death etc., other circumstances penal servitude etc. plus forfeiture of pay etc.

20. Inducement to desert – imprisonment etc.

21. Entertaining a deserter of any of the services – dismissal etc.

22. Breaking confinement – imprisonment etc. plus forfeiture of wages etc.

23. Absence without leave other than desertion etc. – in time of war, imprisonment etc., at other times detention not to exceed ten weeks etc., plus forfeiture of pay etc.

24. Absence without leave for a period of one month for any reason – forfeiture of effects at discretion of C-in-C.

25. Assisting desertion by civilians – summary conviction before civil courts.
26. Persuasion to desert by civilians – fined and as above.
27. Swearing, drunkenness, uncleanness 'or other scandalous action in derogation of God's honour and corruption of good manners' – dismissal with disgrace etc.
28. Officers committing acts of cruelty, oppression or frauds, dismissal with disgrace; conduct unbecoming an officer, dismissal with or without disgrace.
29. Negligence resulting in loss, stranding or hazard of ships (and later, aircraft) – dismissal etc.
30. Failure to protect convoys – reparation in damages as judged by the Court of Admiralty and also punished by death or alternatives.
31. Merchant skippers failing to obey orders of escort commanders – may be compelled to obey, force of arms being allowed, without liability.
32. Taking aboard goods (other than gold, silver or jewels) from merchant ships other than legitimate salvage – dismissal from service etc.
33. Embezzlement – imprisonment etc.
34. Arson at sea or ashore other than enemy property – dismissal etc.
35. False musters – dismissal with disgrace etc.
36. Misconduct in hospital – imprisonment etc.
37. Arousing unrest in connection with victualling etc. punishment as seen fit.
38. Failure to preserve captured documents etc. – dismissal etc.
39. Taking money etc. from prizes before so adjudged by Admiralty Court – dismissal etc.
40. Stripping enemy personnel of clothing etc. – dismissal with disgrace etc.
41. Collusion with enemy, ransoming etc. – dismissal with disgrace etc.
42. Breaking bulk on-board prize with view to embezzlement – dismissal with disgrace etc.
43. Other offences against naval discipline not particularly mentioned – dismissal with disgrace etc.
44. 'Any person subject to this Act committing any offence against this Act, such offence not being punishable with death or penal servitude, shall, save where this Act expressly otherwise provides, be proceeded against and punished according to the laws and customs in such cases used at sea.'

Therefore, almost right to the end, the 'Customs of the Sea' remained an integral part of Admiralty law. It can be seen at once that, save for treachery and traitorous behaviour, all the punishments that called for death were subject to alternatives. Equally, all offensive behaviour subject to courts martial proceedings were provided with one or more alternative punishments subject to the proviso that I have indicated by 'etc.': '… or suffer such other punishment as is hereinafter mentioned'. These were itemised in part three of the act.

Those offences that were punishable by ordinary law were covered by Articles 45, 46 and 46a. The first listed the following crimes and punishments: murder – death; manslaughter – penal servitude, etc.; sodomy – penal servitude; indecent assault – penal servitude; robbery or theft – penal servitude; other criminal offences – punishment under the first part of the act as an action to the prejudice of good order and naval discipline not otherwise specified, or subject to the same punishment awarded by ordinary criminal tribunal, according to English law.

In part two, Articles 47 to 51 made general provision on the power of court martial to find the intent with which offence was committed; to find the prisoner guilty on a lesser charge or greater charge; to deem rebels, armed mutineers and pirates as 'enemies' within the meaning of the act; to give power to arrest offenders and impose penalties on those not assisting in detection of prisoners.

The full list of punishments that could be inflicted were, in order of severity: death; penal servitude; dismissal with disgrace; imprisonment or corporal punishment; detention; dismissal; forfeiture of seniority; dismissal from ship only; severe reprimand or reprimand; disrating to subordinate or petty officer; forfeiture of pay, etc. and minor punishments.

The Admiralty reserved the right to suspend, annul or modify any sentence passed except in case of death, 'which shall only be remitted by His (or Her) Majesty'. The trial had to take place within three years of the offence being committed or one year of the offender returning to the United Kingdom. Corporal punishment was deemed to be equal in degree to imprisonment and applicable as a substitute (until it was first suspended and then abolished). Articles 56 to 57a defined the authorities having power to try offences, those empowered to impose punishments to adhere to provisions mentioned and covered trial of officers for disciplinary offences in time of war.

Part four covered the Constitution of Courts Martial and the Proceedings (Appendix 1) and the Proceedings (Appendix 2), while part five covered Penal Servitude and Prisons, and part six Supplemental Provisions. Part seven was the Saving Clauses:

> Nothing in this Act shall take away, abridge, or control, further or otherwise than as expressly provided by the Act, any right, power or prerogative of Her Majesty the Queen in right of Her Crown, or in right of Her Office of Admiralty or any right or power of the Admiralty. Nothing in this Act contained shall be deemed or taken to supersede or affect the authority or power of any court or tribunal or ordinary civil or criminal jurisdiction, or any officer thereof, in Her Majesty's dominions, in respect of any offence mentioned in the Act which may be punishable or cognisable by the common or statue law, or to prevent any person being proceeded against and punished in respect of any such offence otherwise than under this Act.

The next revolutionary change to the court martial system took place in the immediate aftermath of the Second World War. There was a great social upheaval at the time and National Service made many begin to look questioningly at the old order of law in the services. One catalyst to introduce change was the quashing of sentences imposed on British paratroops in Malaya following a 'mutiny' over living conditions. A committee under Mr Justice Lewis sat and recommended far-reaching changes in the court martial systems of the army and the RAF. Similar discontent had been brewing post-war among naval officers and ratings, of which we will mention later one of the most famous cases, the main import of which was a recommendation for the creation of a court martial appeal tribunal. In 1949, another committee was set up under Mr Justice Pilcher to look into the Royal Navy system and their findings were listed in great detail in the Pilcher Report a few years later.

As well as recommending an appeal tribunal, it looked hard at existing court martial procedures and found them, overall, satisfactory and fair. They did, however, suggest the following amendments, most of which were subsequently legislated for and approved. They considered that the captain of the accused's ship should not be included in the court; that the title 'Defending Officer' should be used instead of 'Prisoner's Friend', to bring courts martial more in line with civilian practice. One of the most revolutionary recommendations concerned the provision contained in the act of 1866 that surviving officers and crew of any warship lost, destroyed or captured could be brought to trials without specific charge. This was a hard condition for the Admiralty to swallow, not for any particularly vindictive grounds, but for the very pertinent fact that only by so doing could the survivors themselves be publically absolved of any blame for the loss. Furthermore, such trials were necessary to show up in details any defects in the construction of the ship, current orders in action and bad tactics, which could then be rectified to prevent similar losses taking place.

Yet another Select Committee was appointed in 1956, which was to examine and re-write the 1866 act and bring it in line with modern conditions in the fleet. Perhaps the most controversial of their subsequent modifications reflected the declining status of the Royal Navy itself in the eyes of parliament, if not in actual fact. The original preamble, penned when the Royal Navy was the greatest in the world, read proudly that 'Whereas it is expedient to amend the law relating to the government of the Navy, whereon, under the good Providence of God, the wealth, safety and strength of the kingdom chiefly depend'. In the mid-1950s, under strident lobbying from the RAF and the various anti-navy newspapers, like those owned by Lord Beaverbrook, this was deemed to no longer be true and so it was altered to read: 'so much depend'. In this twenty-first-century age of the nuclear submarine-borne Trident missile, perhaps the original deserves reinstating and maybe it would have been had the Admiralty itself survived the transition.

More relevant to our story were their other recommendations. The death option for all specifically naval offences was abolished outright, remaining only for treason and mutiny. Many other penalties were reduced or done away with, while others, relating mainly to the Fleet Air Arm, were introduced. A revised scale of punishments was introduced, which for the first time included the option of fines for officers. The WRNS had remained always outside the Naval Discipline Act, but no more. Today, of course, it is no longer considered that 'a code of discipline designed for service at sea was inappropriate to women'. It remained only to sever the connection between the application of naval discipline and 'Ships' Books'. Only those so entered on the pay ledgers had been subject to the 1866 act, but now every officer, whether on active duty or on the retired or Emergency Lists, and every rating, reserve or pensioner, whether borne on ships' books or not, became subject to the new act.

Finally, in 1971, the Naval Defence Act itself ceased to be a permanent statute as such. We have seen how, over the century, it had been constantly amended and how these amendments affected court martial procedures. It was decided under the new, all-embracing Ministry of Defence that henceforth the act should be reviewed by parliament at regular intervals of five years, thus ensuring that in future it would always be up to date and that changing circumstances would not bring the problems in interpretation of the law they had in the past.

This now governs the process and our story here ends prior to that date and watershed. The cases and events in this book therefore should be viewed as vignettes of a way of life now deemed so remote as to be almost curious. These are glimpses of the 'Old Navy', that force which served this nation so well down the centuries and kept us from those that would do us ill and enslave us – all now uncaringly tossed aside with progressive lack of understanding of their significance by our myopic rulers since 1946 and relegated to the limbo of history. We should not judge the verdicts herewith by today's standards, they are examples of their time. Nor should we be too swift to dismiss justice then as not as 'good' as justice now, for not all change is good.

In common with its civilian counterpart, Naval courts martial proceedings have always been awesome and daunting occasions, surrounded with pomp and ceremony. Although much of this has been swept away of late, for centuries established customs had lent it a special dignity and significance. Sharing the practice of civil courts, legal counsel must, in normal circumstances, appear in wig and gown. All members of the court itself had to wear their full dress, that is cocked hats, frock coats with epaulettes, adorned with their full orders, decorations and medals. Full dress belts and naval officers' swords completed the picture, which was the same whether the court sat aboard ship in Portsmouth harbour or sweltered under a tropical sun in the Pacific or Indian Oceans.

Except in the case of the loss of a ship, when there was no prosecutor and the charges were not specific but ordered directly by the Admiralty, the authority for convening such a court lay only, as from the beginning, with those commanders-in-chiefs whom had been issued the special Admiralty Warrant on their appointment. On receipt of the Circumstantial Letter from the accused's captain, containing the outlines of the case and which listed the charges separately, the C-in-C issued a warrant addressed to the designated President convening the court and then signed it. The President was always of as high a seniority as possible in the existing circumstances and at least twenty-four hours' notice was requested before he could convene the court, with the proviso that it had to be called at the earliest opportunity after that period of time.

At the same time similar summons were issued to the other members of the court, not less than five or more than nine it will be remembered, with at least two others to hold themselves in reserve in the case of the indisposition of the original members. With the duties of Judge Advocate confined, as we have seen, to that of combined usher, expert on procedure and overall secretarial adviser on a strictly impartial basis, an officer was selected for this important position. Usually, naturally enough, these were selected from the Supply and Secretariat branch (S-and-S). It was not uncommon for such an officer to be a barrister-at-law. He also received copies of all the papers relating to the case and it was his job to see to the attendance of all witnesses, furnishing the accused with all documents and, during the trial, recording the minutes and passing on his advice on matters of legal complexity.

According to the act, courts martial were to be held:

> … on board one of HM ships or vessels of war, unless the Admiralty or the officer who ordered the court martial in any particular case for reasons to be recorded on the proceedings otherwise direct, in which case the court martial shall be held at a port at such convenient place on shore as the Admiralty or the officer who ordered the court martial shall direct.

This was an amendment dating back to the 1770s and the Keppel trial. At that time it was not made permanent but had to be applied for, and so it remained. As the fleet shrank dramatically in the post-1945 years it was found increasingly necessary to hold courts marital at one of the 'stone frigates' that had sprung up in place of warships afloat, and of course HMS *Victory* dry-docked at Portsmouth provided an ideally historic and symbolic setting for such courts in later years, adding her own venerable dignity to the proceedings.

Once the Judge Advocate had made all the necessary arrangements, the President was duly informed and he then summoned the members of the court by a general signal not less than an hour before the opening. It was announced to the fleet, and the world at large, that a court was sitting by the hoisting of the court martial flag, the Union flag, at the yardarm, and the firing of the 'One-Gun Salute' once it had actually got under way. This was known in the old days as the firing of the 'Rogue's Gun', the lower deck, as always, adjudging anyone brought before a court as probably guilty of something, even if not the crime with which they were charged!

The members of the court, if arriving by boat, had their distinguishing pennant raised in her bows and, as they came aboard the ship in which the court was to be held, they were welcomed by the salute of the Boatswain's Pipe. The prosecutor, until the 1950s the accused's captain, usually took the stand and the Judge Advocate or Deputy Judge Advocate took his place. The officers of the court took their places, leaving their hats on their heads, and the Officer of the Court reported that the witnesses were all in attendance. This confirmed, the President formally declared the court open, and the Provost Marshal with drawn sword brought in the accused in hand.

The naval sword has been another casualty of post-war austerity, having since that time been made an optional, rather than compulsory, item of uniform, but they figured largely in the court martial ritual before they went the way of frock coats, gold-laced trousers and cocked hats. However, let us consider things as they were for the majority of the period covered by this book. In that event, the accused's sword, if an officer, was handed to the President and laid, still in its black leather scabbard with brass ferrules and hilt, across the table in front of him.

Except in times of war, courts martial were open to the public and special sections were roped off for both the press and more general visitors, and they were admitted at this stage of the proceedings. When certain parts of evidence were considered to be secret the courts had to be cleared and then this was heard in private and not reported upon.

The next step was for the Accused's Friend to be admitted and his name reported by the Judge Advocate to the President, whereupon the Judge Advocate then read out the warrant, the names of all the members of the court and asked the prosecutor formally if any were objected to. Even the President could be included in the list of objected to officers by either the prosecutor or, when next asked, the accused. Should the answer in either case have been yes, then a vote was taken and, if upheld, that officer was replaced. The Judge Advocate then asked the accused if he had any objection to the constitution of the court or, in later years, to the presence of a shorthand writer. All being well, the oath was then administered to all. Incidentally, there could be no objection to the Judge Advocate or the Deputy Judge Advocate.

The charge sheet and Circumstantial Letter were then read out and the Judge Advocate reported that the accused had been furnished with a copy of the same; he also informed him that he was not required to plead. If the accused did not plead guilty then the prosecution opened by putting his case and calling his witness. If the accused did plead guilty, then it was considered that he had admitted all the charges as being the truth and his plea was accepted. Any witnesses not called by the prosecution had to be called if the accused so desired it. When the prosecutor pronounced his case was closed the court had the discretion to call other witnesses or recall those already examined, if they so chose.

Both officers and men were allowed a 'Prisoner's Friend', or defending officer, if so wished and he could be just that, a friend, or even legal counsel, and he could, with the President's permission, conduct cross-examination of witnesses. Once evidence was taken, the witness had to leave the court. The accused could, of course, give evidence on his own behalf. The defence then opened. Wide latitude was allowed to the accused in order to be absolutely fair to him. He could retire beforehand to change his prepared defence in the light of evidence already heard. If this was done then the court adjourned. Again, as a result of earlier very long trials, it was the rule that compulsory adjournments were made after six or seven hours had elapsed at one sitting in order that the accused and the court should not be impaired by fatigue.

Once the defence had been completed, the defending officer was called upon to sum up by the Judge Advocate and then the prosecutor was invited to do likewise. The accused was then led out and the court was cleared while the members deliberated. Each member had to state his opinion orally in order of reverse seniority, the only exception to this being a case that was considering the death penalty. In the rare event of a vote split 50-50, the most favourable to the accused was accepted as the verdict, a practice that compared most favourably with civil law.

Once the decision was reached, it was written out by the Judge or Deputy Judge Advocate and signed by every member, whether in agreement or not. In ancient times the executioner indicated to the accused the court decision by turning the cutting edge of his axe either toward or away from him, thus clearly indicating his fate. This tradition survived in naval courts martial by the placing of the officer's sword, which had all through the proceedings lain on the table sheathed. Now, when the accused was re-admitted, he could tell equally quickly just how he had fared. If he had been acquitted the sword was to be found with its point turned away from him, the hilt, with its lion's head and mane, facing him; if found guilty, the point was turned accusingly toward him. Either way, before the court was re-opened the members replaced their cocked hats before judgement was pronounced.

If the findings of the court were guilty they were read out, followed by any good character references contained in certificates, logs and so on, and the accused could make a statement in mitigation of punishment. The court would call evidence on his character or qualifications at this stage. It then re-adjourned and considered the punishment, by which they were guided by the articles. This was then read out to the accused and he was removed from the court. If found not guilty, and the accused was honourably acquitted, then it was also customary for the President to pick up the sword and hand it back to its owner, personally congratulating him on his vindication.

Incidentally, the question of 'honourable' acquittal is an interesting point, it being only used in cases where the charges directly affected the personal honour of the accused. It should have been but rarely used for the very good reason that had it not been sparingly applied there might arise the feeling that an ordinary acquittal might leave a suspicion that the court was not totally satisfied as to the accused's innocence, whereas that finding should have been always regarded as complete and conclusive. As personal honour was a difficult thing to define, and the board usually left the matter to the discretion of the court. It had a long tradition behind it; otherwise the term 'honourable' acquittal might have been better abolished altogether.

Once the court had been dissolved the President would deliver to the C–in–C the findings and sentence for his approval and issue of warrant. When the court martial involved an officer the findings were also transmitted directly to the Admiralty. The minutes and a covering report were also sent to the Admiralty and were there examined in detail for a final check on fairness by the highest legal authority, the Judge Advocate of the Fleet. Should he have detected any illegality, error in procedure or misdirection, he made his views known and, as we have seen, Their Lordships had the power to alter the court's findings. In the event of this happening, the accused was notified and it was confirmed in the Quarterly Returns of Courts Martial by the line, rendered in italics in the original for particular emphasis, '*Their Lordships were pleased to dissent from the findings*'. Before the days of appeals being allowed this was the only hope for a convicted officer or man. Again, it did not happen often, but we shall record one such case in these pages.

Such were the proceedings of the traditional naval courts martial and, as in civil cases, there were many dramatic moments, twists of fate, startling revelations and surprises in evidence over the centuries which turned otherwise unremarkable cases into famous ones. The overall picture is one of great dignity and a certain awesomeness. However, we shall find all manner of variation to this overall theme in our study, for courts are about individuals and the Royal Navy has always been famed for its eccentrics as well as its heroes. We shall find in our pages murderers, a great many villains, some fools, some prigs and much humility. Some we may think harshly judged, others remarkably leniently. Treachery, bravery, cowardice, perception and yes, even humour, will come to us over the centuries in these absorbing documents.

To be summoned before a court martial was one of the most traumatic events in a sailor's career, be he admiral or pressed hand. Small wonder that many a great officer, fearless in battle and fearsome in authority, should shudder at the thought of it or sigh at the boredom of it. As Captain Rodney, aboard HMS *Monarch*, wrote to his wife on 30 July 1756: 'I suppose I shall be plagued with being one of his [Byng's] Judges next winter. You know I abhor Court Martial.'

The naval court martial of today is as fair as it can possibly be, every attempt being made to ensure that trials are conducted according to the law of the land. A staff legal adviser helps the convening authority to draw up a balanced court, the convening authority being a flag officer with the necessary warrant from the Admiralty Board of the Defence Council. Commanding officers no longer act as prosecutors, but the President still has to be of at least captain's rank or a flag officer when a higher rank is under trial. It is no longer necessary for the President to be an executive officer. Under the Armed Forces Act of 1967 the new sub-section (2) states only that members of a court must have held a commission in any of the armed forces of the Crown or have been an officer in the Queen Alexandra's Royal Naval Nursing Service or the appropriate reserve for three years.

Finally, to those who might condemn such a book out of hand as being only concerned with the worst side of life in the Royal Navy, let me say that even the most honourable and famous of our seamen came through such courts and went on to the highest offices and public renown. So, although such a hero as Lord Nelson might not be seen in a good light, another, like Benbow, made his whole reputation as a result of a court martial.

Let the reader judge the others recorded herein, both famous and unknown, with the same fairness and impartiality as the courts described. This is not a learned treatise on naval courts martial, but a general survey for the interested reader.

Part Two

Some Famous Cases

1 A LITTLE MORE SINGEING (1587)

Few would deny Sir Francis Drake (1540–96) his title of the foremost sea commander of the Elizabethan era. In an age noted for outstanding marines, Hawkins, Frobisher, Raleigh, Grenville and the like, he seemed paramount. He was, without doubt, a tough man to fall foul of. No gentleman he, but a hard, rough-edged sailor who would tolerate no disloyalty to himself, real or imagined.

The fleet of Elizabeth I owed its existence to the work of kings like Henry V, Henry VII and, most of all, Henry VIII. It was the latter who created by letters patent the body of commissioners under the Lord Admiral to administer a standing force of men-of-war. However, the bulk of the fleet was still called to service from the merchants, and the rules that governed those who led and those who served the various squadrons were merely general principles, the Customs of the Sea, unregulated by statute. As we have seen, it was for each commander to lay down his own rules within these guidelines every time he set sail.

As one set of customs might contradict another it was inevitable that sooner or later a clash of interest would take place, the result of which would set a precedent for future rulings just as cause modifies statute law. It was Drake himself who initiated one such precedent: the right of a captain or commander of a fleet to expect that his word at sea was final, although it was by no means the case in 1577 – for example, when Drake was captain-general of the expedition that set sail to harass the Spanish in the Pacific.

'Gentlemen' far outnumbered 'seamen' in command of the ships of Elizabeth's navy, and Seaman Drake was conscious of being in the minority. When medieval knights embarked upon ships they, and not the ships' masters, gave the orders and made the decisions, which were obeyed without question. The feeling was still strong that true-born Englishmen with titles and blue blood would still exercise this ancient right and this was backed up in general practice by the fact that masters still consulted with companies according to the Judgements of Oléron. That tradition was not to survive intact from Drake's circumnavigation of the globe.

With him on that expedition was his old friend Thomas Doughty, the antithesis of Drake's type of seaman, very much the gentleman. All might have been well despite this but for the disharmony in London between the declared intention of the voyage and the – very different – real aims of Drake and his companions. The latter could be summarised as exploring on the one hand, raiding and plundering on the other. Unofficially, the queen was in little doubt at all of what was in Drake's mind, but this could not openly be admitted. Lord Burghley, trying to preserve the fragile peace with the superior might of Spain, was strongly against anything that might upset the status quo. When Doughty had indiscreetly leaked the true purpose of the voyage to him, Burghley had strongly advised caution and asked Doughty to do what he could to limit the effects such a policy would have on relationships between the two countries.

That the circumnavigation of the globe, Drake's greatest achievement, should have started off with a potential clash of wills was therefore not surprising. That it succeeded so splendidly may be put down to not merely brilliant seamanship and navigation of their little cockleshell boats, but in Drake's firm handling of such an explosive situation before it got completely out of hand. The bickering between the two men finally came to the point of no return. One man had to give way and Drake, as commander, took the initiative when the little squadron reached San Julian.

Doughty was outright accused by Drake of mutinous talk. A trial was ordered and, in the face of nebulous evidence, this sentenced the unfortunate Doughty to death. Moreover, despite protest, that sentence was duly carried out in full and to the letter of the law. But what law? The law of Drake himself as sole arbiter of the company and its destiny. We can admire the firmness of that decision and we can deplore its harshness; we can doubt its strict legality and justness, but by making it Drake resolved any doubts about a sea commander's authority to administer a stern justice should the need arise. He sacked all the officers to ram the lesson firmly home and then, in an act of conciliation, reinstated them. Perhaps he had no choice, as his subsequent famous speech revealed, for they were dependent upon each other, but only one could lead:

> Here is such controversy between the sailors and the gentlemen and much stomaching between the gentlemen and the sailors, that it doth even make me mad to hear it. But, my masters, I must have it left. For I must have the gentlemen to haul and draw with the mariner, and the mariner with the gentlemen. What! Let us show ourselves all to be of a company, and let us not give occasion to the enemy to rejoice at our decay and overthrow.

To show them that he acted as he did for the greater good, and with some power-ful backing, he added: 'To say you come to serve me I will not give you thanks, for it is only Her Majesty that you serve.'

A decade later, and at the height of his fame, Drake found his authority being challenged again by the same attitude of 'them and us', although this time his adversary was one with almost as much knowledge of the sea as himself.

William Borough had served his apprenticeship in the harsh waters of the Barents Sea, opening up new trading routes with Russia and defending them. In this he had some measure of success, nothing as spectacular as Drake's epics to be sure, but sound achievement nonetheless. He was also knowledgeable in the art of navigation and was educated enough to express himself on the subject in words, while Drake was, by his own admission, not an educated man. Moreover, Borough had experience of high office to the Crown, having been clerk of the ships and subsequently holding down a series of important seagoing commands with the fleets.

He was, therefore, no novice and it may have hurt his pride somewhat to find himself only second-in-command to Drake when Queen Elizabeth had one of her periodic bursts of enthusiasm for humiliating King Philip of Spain. Drake had returned the year before from his sacking of the Spanish treasure ports and this had only strengthened Philip's resolve to once more 'liberate' England from the yoke of the Protestants by usurping her fickle ruler and destroying her power on land and sea finally. Enormous preparations were made to ready a mighty fleet that would land 1 million men on the coast of England and, in spite of the finan-cial strain this imposed on Spain's coffers, these preparations continued unabated, even though Elizabeth held her adventurers in check for a time in order not to provoke Philip further.

Then came the Babbington Plot and, in her fury at this direct threat to her life, the queen was stung into ordering a further lesson to be imparted. Drake was the man chosen for the job and he was ordered to take his squadron to Spanish waters 'to impeach the provisions of Spain' and to carry the war to the enemy ships 'within the havens themselves'. By a supreme effort Drake got his ships ready and away to sea by 1 April, ever fearful that the queen might have a change of heart. Indeed, orders for his recall arrived just as he slipped thankfully out of reach.

With him as he sailed away was William Borough, each man taking with him his own band of select followers, and here lay the seeds of trouble once more. Perhaps more conscious of his position relative to Drake (he was older), Borough was touched on raw nerves by the seeming lack of both courtesy and confidence shown in him. Perhaps also Drake was aware that Borough was his equal at sea while still being superior in other respects; whatever the reason, friction soon arose between the two factions, which quickly boiled over.

The campaign opened with the attack on Cadiz when the composite squadron of the English fleet boldly entered that harbour and soundly thrashed the
galleys of Spain, sinking and burning most of them and destroying much of the
great accumulation of stores and war materials assembled there. Next, the English
fleet sailed on to Lagos, which Drake proposed to take by landward assault after
subduing the castle of Segre guarding the seaward approaches to that town. All
this time Borough had been seething at the studied insolence shown him by his
commander-in-chief. It still remained customary for each action to be preceded
by a conference, but Drake treated this in a most cavalier fashion, calling the con-
ferences to be sure, but deciding the great issues by discussion between his own
followers only. A man of letters, Borough sought to put the less learned Drake to
shame by utilising his superiority in this skill to demolish completely Drake's plan
of attack, even to the extent of condemning the whole point of the operation.

This may have not been so bad, except that Borough could not resist levelling sneering accusations at the end of his reasoning (which in themselves were
quite sound criticisms), to the effect that the main purpose of the raid was to
enable Drake to boast of his actually having set foot on Philip II's territory, even
at the risk of possible defeat. Drake's reaction to this taunting epistle was violent. Borough was at once relieved of his command and replaced by a Captain
Marchaunt, one of Drake's most trusted confidants.

This was not the end of the affair. With Borough confined below as a prisoner in his own ship, the *Golden Lion*, further trouble broke out when the bulk
of the crew mutinied in protest at lack of rations, which they blamed on the
spite of Drake. Hopelessly outnumbered, Marchaunt and his few loyal followers
had the humiliation of having to ask Borough to intervene, which he curtly
refused to do. As the *Golden Lion* was out of reach of immediate aid from the
rest of the fleet, Marchaunt had to submit and was sent away. Borough then
sailed away and no longer took part in the expedition, in protest against his
'Superior's dictatorial attitude'.

When the crestfallen Marchaunt arrived back aboard Drake's flagship, the
Elizabeth Bonaventure, and confessed to his humiliation, the admiral exploded
in anger. Claiming to have unlimited authority to inflict punishment given to
him by the queen, a claimed later hotly disputed by Raleigh, Drake immediately
convened a 'general court holden for the service of Her Majesty'. As with the
Doughty trials, its legality was questionable; as to its verdict, if there was any doubt
it was not made apparent. Marchaunt stated the facts and Drake announced his
position unequivocally thus:

> Although I am not doubtful what to do in this case, nor yet want any authority,
> but myself have from her Majesty sufficient jurisdiction to correct and punish
> with all severity as to me in discretion shall be meet according to the quality of

the offences all those seditious persons which shall be in the whole fleet, yet for the confidence I have in your discretions, as also to witness our agreement in judgement in all matters, I pray you let me have your several opinions touching this fact which hath been declared in your hearing this day.

The meaning was clear, and nobody strayed out of line. The verdict was 'guilty'. Death sentence was announced on Borough and all his officers, with lesser punishment for the mutinous crew, save those who had stood by Marchaunt – just twelve in total.

Thus, the lesson imparted some ten years earlier was delivered afresh. Satisfied that Borough's fate was settled once and for all, Drake resumed his campaign. It was gloriously vindicated: the fortress of Sagres was taken, Spanish shipping off Cadiz and all along the coast was destroyed, while the Portuguese treasure ship *San Felipe* was captured by the fleet off the Azores. Drake returned in triumph to England.

However, this was not 1577. Borough was not Doughty, isolated thousands of miles from home and powerless. Borough was back in England long before Drake returned and had spent the time profitably ensuring that he got a far more comprehensive hearing than Doughty had been given the chance to receive. He shrewdly appealed directly to Burghley and made certain the case was brought before council.

Drake had therefore to produce definite charges against Borough, which he did at great length when the two men faced each other at Theobalds, before the commissioners. In them much is revealed of Drake's attitude to Borough and it seems that he may have thereby lost the sympathy of the committee. In fighting Borough with words, Drake was probably on a loser from the beginning. The commissioners appointed this committee, under Sir Amyas Paulet, to hear both sides and they, in turn, after listening carefully, concluded that Borough was more sinned against than sinner. No part of their findings was ever published unfortunately, but there is no doubt that they vindicated Borough.

Far from meeting death because of this trial, Borough, conversely, rose even higher in the queen's service, becoming a Sea Lord and comptroller of the navy in 1589. Drake's subsequent career ranged from his triumph over the Spanish Armada to his ghastly failure at Panama. His place in history is secure enough and his two extraordinary voyages into the Royal Navy's legal roots are equally famed.

Leslie Gardener's simplistic statement that this trial 'went down as the first naval Court Martial', is not factually true, for it was no such thing; not until some sixty years later were courts martial as such given sanction.

2 A FLEET IN BEING (1690)

Although the act of 1661 had been drawn up with considerable haste, it had worked well enough in practice with regard to court martial procedures, but it was inevitable that, as the year passed, legal loopholes were to be found in it by those who wished to find them. The closing of such gaps led to constant legislation, among the first of which was the passing of an act following the fracas that took place in the aftermath of the Battle of Beachy Head in 1690.

Arthur Herbert had commanded the English fleet in the Mediterranean in the 1680s, during the reign of Charles II. He was a firm Protestant, as was his contemporary and rival, Captain Edward Russell. By all accounts, he was a popular leader with the sailors he commanded but, with the accession of Catholic James II in 1685, he fell from favour. Initially the new monarch did much good for the navy, to which he was devoted and in which he himself had served with some distinction. He had commanded the fleet twice in action with the Dutch and had served for thirteen years as Lord High Admiral until the Test Act debarred him from that office because of his religion. He had also been Governor of Portsmouth.

With Samuel Pepys at his elbow, reforms to the service took place almost at once, four new appointments were made to commissioners and the rot left by his brother, Charles II, was gradually rectified. The debts were liquidated, stores properly purchased and stored, ships overhauled and Navy Estimates modernised and made more efficient. All this was excellent work. However, other legacies remained, in particular the odious one of favourites and, being a Catholic and determined to make his reluctant subjects Catholics also, James became his own worst enemy.

In this direction was one of his greatest blunders, the replacement of Herbert by the Catholic Sir Roger Strickland as commander-in-chief. Not only did this act cause uproar in the fleet when Strickland introduced priests to say Mass aboard the warships of his command, but both Herbert and Russell, perhaps not surprisingly, sped away to Holland and there laid their considerable expertise at the feet of William of Orange. The replacement of Strickland by Lord Dartmouth was too late, for the damage had already been done, and Protestants still in command of James' warships, including George Byng, kept close ties with the exiled Herbert and plotted to spread their influence still further.

Thus it was that when the Dutch fleet bore William down Channel on a 'Protestant wind' to initiate the revolution for which much of the nation then yearned, we find Herbert flying his admiral's flag in the Dutch warship *Leijden*, under the Dutch Admiral Evetsen the Younger, as she entered Torbay. There was no battle, Dartmouth awaited events and then wisely submitted to William. It is doubtful whether many of his captains would have backed him had it come to a trial of strength and the only victors would have been England's continental naval rivals.

However, James, with the willing backing of the French, made attempts to return to the throne. His religious backing in Ireland was substantial enough and it was there that he landed in turn, in 1689, to lay siege to Londonderry. Herbert, safely reinstated in his old position, sortied out to dispute control of the sea lanes from France and Ireland, sailing from Spithead and coming upon the enemy in Bantry Bay. The resulting skirmish, for it was no more than that, was hardly satisfactory and Herbert was back at Spithead in short order having achieved little or nothing. Despite the alliance with the Dutch, the British fleet was still outnumbered by the French, but that did not stop Commodore Rooke lifting the siege. By June 1690, the French were back in considerable strength to decide the issue. They had powerful ships, freshly rebuilt, and a strong army to put ashore. The position was serious indeed for the allies. Louis XIV had assembled his full strength by bringing the Toulon fleet round to Brest and thus the redoubtable Admiral Tourville had seventy men-of-war with which to give issue to the British and the Dutch, who between them could muster but fifty-five.

William was more of a statesman than James and, although he lacked the former's affinity for the sea, he recognised the value of the Royal Navy in the struggle that lay ahead. He made a special journey within months of assuming the throne to visit his fleet at Spithead in order to ensure the loyalty of its officers and men. He went aboard Herbert's flagship and distributed honours for the action at Bantry Bay far in excess of its results. Herbert himself was elevated to the peerage as the Earl of Torrington, Captains Ashby and Shovell received knighthoods and each man of the fleet was awarded 10 shillings. Despite this thinly veiled attempt at buying loyalty, there is little doubt that William would have had the backing of the fleet in any case, but it did him no little harm to make certain. He wished to have his back secure while he went off to war in Ireland. He left his consort in London with Admiral Russell as naval adviser, with unhappy consequences for Torrington.

Now Torrington was not a fool. He knew that his force was heavily outnumbered, but he reasoned that so long as the allied fleet was intact and capable of fighting and intervening at any time he chose, then the French would be reluctant to put their troops ashore anywhere in the British Isles where they might be cut off from supplies and reinforcements. His strategy was therefore to husband his strength, deliberately avoiding an eyeball-to-eyeball slugging match. For the first time was coined the phrase 'the fleet-in-being' and this by the British!

In the three centuries that followed 1690, this had become accepted naval policy for the weaker naval power to follow, and had been proven successful within certain limitations, with the Royal Navy – which before the headlong decline post-1945 had always been the superior navy – more often than not on the receiving end of it. The holding back of the German battleship *Tirpitz* at her Norwegian anchorage during the Second World War is a fairly recent example of this policy; a whole convoy was dispersed and largely destroyed on the mere

threat that she might have sailed. However, there was always the danger of such
a policy being misconstrued, by those at home without a full understanding of
the true position, as a lack of fire in the belly, of determination and even, perhaps,
cowardice. Nowadays an impatient and ignorant media is the most frequent cause
of such misunderstandings, in Torrington's day it was his peers. There was little
justification for this in Torrington's case, of course, but to the normal hazards of
misunderstanding were added other factors. The opportunism of Russell with the
ear of the court was one; the difficulty in explaining such a policy not only to his
own commanders but also to his allies was another.

It is evident from his subsequent conduct that, in this case, the Dutch admiral did not understand what was required of him, but it was from London that
Torrington's decision was first challenged. The French fleet was first sighted
off the Isle of Wight at the end of June 1690 but, in pursuance of his policy,
Torrington held off to secure the approaches to the Straits of Dover and nothing of great moment came to pass. However, Torrington's resolution was quickly
undermined by the receipt of strong instructions from the capital to stop backing
away and engage the enemy boldly forthwith.

Bowing to these instructions Torrington endeavoured to do the best he could.
That best was, unfortunately, not good enough! His plan, as explained beforehand,
was for the Dutch under Evetsen to lead the line, but, instead of concentrating on
the enemy van in the traditional manner, should instead hold off and thus merely
contain the bulk of the French fleet, while Torrington himself would close the
action with his ships against the French rear.

Whether, in fact, Evetsen misunderstood or whether his natural aggression was
just too much to contain in the heat of battle cannot be certain now but, which-
ever it was, the result was disaster. Instead of holding back, the Dutchman closed
and engaged the French van ship to ship and this left Tourville free to use his
superior numbers to double back on the British line thus catching Torrington in
his own trap. Things began to go ill for the allies but, fortunately for them, the tide
turned, literally, and carried the French fleet out of range. This gave Torrington
time to save his most damaged ships and destroy those too badly damaged to succour, before making a withdrawal to the safety of the Thames Estuary.

The whole of the English Channel was now open to the French to do as they
wished; they could have landed on the Isle of Wight and held it. Nevertheless,
perhaps Torrington's strategy was proven, if only by Tourville's subsequent indecision. Instead of seizing his opportunity he kept his eye over his shoulder and
contented himself with useless diversions; he burnt Teignmouth and then meekly
sailed back home to France. This tame endeavour reflected more upon Tourville
than Torrington but it was upon the latter that the wrath of an indignant nation
fell to an unusual extent. Within a short time, Torrington found himself a prisoner
in the Tower of London awaiting his court martial.

As well as being a seaman, as a peer Torrington had many friends still in government circles and a determined effort was made to prevent the trial taking place at all. The king was wrathful when the man he so recently honoured had failed to, as the king saw it, justify his trust. As the rumblings grew, Torrington demanded the right to be tried by his peers instead, where, it was assumed, he would receive more favourable treatment. The line taken by his supporters questioned the very power of the Admiralty itself in this respect. This proved both a provocative and dangerous way to go.

The battle raged in both Houses and prominent lawyers were called in to give their opinions on the matter. They finally decided that such authority was indeed vested in the commissioners to issue the commission to try him, earl or no earl, but his supporters pressed the point still further. Hannay described this contention as 'absurd' and stated that this attempt could not be explained 'except by faction pushed to folly'. He added that 'Nothing would have been heard of it if the accused had not been a member of the House of Lords, and a party man'.

To put the question beyond further doubt an act was drafted, a bill being introduced vesting in the commissioners of the Admiralty the same power in regard to granting commissions, which was already vested by law in the Lord High Admiral of England. After stormy sessions in the House, it was finally passed on its third reading by a majority of two. That Torrington was then to be tried by court martial under this act was then hotly disputed by many of the lords. Their arguments included the point that:

> … whereby the Earl of Torrington may come to be tried for his life, for facts committed several months before this power was given or desired; we think it reasonable that every man should be tried by that law that was known to be in force when the crime was committed.

It was all to no avail, for the king was determined. He appointed a new Board of Admiralty composed of seven members instead of the previous five, and the act gave them the power of appointing courts martial 'for the trial of any officer of what rank whatsoever, as a Lord High Admiral might do'.

The lords on the earl's side considered this 'unprecedented and of dangerous consequence, that the jurisdiction exercised by the Lord High Admiral, should by a law be declared to be in the Commissioners of the Admiralty, whereby an unknown and therefore unlimited power may be established in them'.

Nonetheless, a court martial Torrington had to face and the charges brought against him were most serious. The king, and the public at large, had not understood his strategy; to them he had not only held back until ordered not to do so, but had let down his allies who had fought hard and almost lost most of his fleet in doing so, while still leaving the country open to invasion. Ignorant and scared people do not behave rationally, they wanted somebody's head, and, as usual, the man on the spot was the obvious target. In vain did more rational observers like the Bishop of Salisbury comment on the affair that 'Both the Admirals were equally blamed – ours for not fighting and the French for not pursuing' – the general public felt that the nation had survived more by luck than by any skill or judgement on the part of their admiral.

The charges read that Torrington, 'through treachery or cowardice, misbehave in his office, drawn dishonour on the English nation, and sacrificed our good allies the Dutch'.

While it is true to say that the crisis of 1690 was a grave one, invasion had rarely seemed so imminent or inevitable as then. Torrington was by no means disloyal to William, nor was he a schemer like Russell. His tactics were 'skilful, but were ruined by a subordinate who came from a different country and spoke a different language', according to a recent naval historian. He might have added that he was harassed from the start by a monarch with exactly the same deficiencies as the Dutch admiral.

That there was more on Torrington's side than had been revealed came out in the court martial itself, for the verdict was one of honourable acquittal. The evidence revealed to the court's satisfaction that the allied preparations were made too late (a common enough English failing which will appear many times in this chronicle) and that our fleet was too weak (similarly to be endlessly repeated down the centuries), our ships were ill-manned and that Torrington had been provided with no intelligence of the French movements or intentions.

It seemed from this verdict that Torrington was totally vindicated, but William, with his land victories behind him, had appointed the wily Russell to command the fleet (a man who had little compunction in secretly advising James and even considering supporting him) and determined that Torrington, and all who stood with him, should be firmly put in their place.

Torrington's command remained suspended, he was never employed again, and thus he passed into history. The vengeful William also dispensed with the services of several members of the court itself and broke some forty officers who had spoken up for their old leader. Fortunately for the navy, his fury seems to have spent itself after this and the naval victories of Barfleur and La Hogue, which followed the vacillating Russell's change of heart in 1692, decided events at sea firmly in England's favour. Torrington's undeserved fate, however, may have influenced others from trying anything too revolutionary in the manner of sea warfare for some considerable time.

In considering William's harshness over this incident we should, perhaps, to be fair, consider the other side of the coin regarding acquittals from court martial at this period, and for insight into this we can turn to the indispensable Pepys. When the fourth-rate *St David* foundered in Portsmouth harbour a court martial was held on 11 November 1689 to apportion blame. Her captain, John Gaydon, pointed out certain rotten timbers to Admiral Sir Richard Haddock, who advised him to have her heeled over so that dockyard workers might effect repairs.

This order Gaydon, who lodged ashore at the time, passed on to his first lieutenant, Lumley, and his master, Parker. Work was in progress when the captain boarded her next morning, but the ship's carpenter had failed to secure the ship's ports and water began to enter. He breezily replied, on hearing this news, that it could be pumped out again once the repairs had been done, but the dockyard gang was later aboard. When Gaydon finally put in a passing appearance to watch the work being done, he suddenly realised that his command had an alarming list. Too late he gave orders for the heel to be righted, and within short order the *St David* filled and went down, leaving Gaydon, his crew and the dockyard mates swimming – those that could!

Final responsibility for anything done in the ship belonged to Gaydon and the other two officers, but at the court martial the captain was exonerated completely while Lumley was jailed and the master and carpenter heavily fined.

Pepys' comments on this episode contain wry remarks on the obvious partiality of the proceedings. Recording the conversation between one of the members of the court to Gaydon, as the court rose: 'God damme, Jack, we had made shift to bring you off, but by God you must remember to do the like by any of us when it comes to our turn!'

Whether Dutch William felt the same about Torrington's acquittal or not, he certainly acted in a very arbitrary way towards both the findings and the court itself, so much so as to virtually invalidate this particular court's verdict completely.

3 THE ABANDONING OF BENBOW (1702)

Although very little is known about the career of Vice Admiral Sir John Benbow, he has come down through history as the epitome of the rough, bluff, no-nonsense British sea dog, coarseness redeemed by fearlessness. Born the son of a Shrewsbury tanner in 1653, he ran away to sea as a youth and no doubt earned his experience in the school of hard knocks. No gentleman adventurer was he, to be sure, but a self-made man, no doubt abrasive and rude in manner but seaman enough to have become master's mate aboard the third-rate *Rupert* by the age of 25.

It was on 30 April 1678 that he sailed from Portsmouth in this vessel under the command of Captain Philip Herbert, later Earl of Torrington, and quickly won his spurs in the navy, his previous sea service having been with the merchant fleet. In action against the Barbary pirates in the Mediterranean, he so conducted himself in Herbert's eyes that in June of the following year he was given command of the fourth-rate *Nonsuch* on that station, serving under Admirals Sir George Rooke and Sir Clowdisley Shovel, who were both equally impressed with his work.

Unfortunately for Benbow, his success was not matched by his tact. In 1681 he captured an Algerian pirate raider, which had previously been attacked by the *Adventure*, commanded by a Captain Booth, and survived. No doubt elated by their prowess, the crew of the *Nonsuch* was not backward in comparing their victory with *Adventure*'s failure. One can imagine the banter and bragging that has always been part and parcel of rival ships of the same squadron, but in this case the boasting seems to have gone too far and Captain Booth took exception to what he took as a personal slur both on his own honour and that of his crew.

Booth made a formal complaint and Benbow was brought to a court martial, it being alleged that he was among the foremost of Booth's taunters. Benbow's plea in self-defence stated that he had merely repeated what had already been said before. Although this plea was accepted, it was still not considered gentlemanly to publicly criticise a fellow officer's misfortune in this way. The board found a satisfactory way of emphasising this point. Benbow was fined three months' pay, which was used to comfort the wounded of the *Adventure*, and he had to make a public apology to Captain Booth.

How Benbow felt about this we cannot now know; he probably thought it was a lot of fuss about nothing, but within a short period *Nonsuch* was paid off and, unemployed and maybe slightly bitter, Benbow reverted to the merchant marine once more. He began trading in the Levant with his own ship, the frigate *Benbow*, in 1686, about which other legends of his toughness grew, true or not, including the famous incident of his beheading thirteen Moorish corsairs and taking their heads to Cadiz as trophies of war. Bullocke attributes this story, and many of the others, to the over-fertile imagination of his son-in-law, a certain Mr Calton, but, whether fact or fiction, there seems little doubt that to have survived for so long in the that area Benbow must have been more than a little ruthless, accepting his background and the circumstances he found himself in.

On 1 June 1689, Benbow entered the Royal Navy once more, as a third lieutenant aboard the third-rate, seventy-gun *Elizabeth*. Here the patronage of Torrington and others became manifest and his promotion was rapid, becoming captain of the seventy-gun *York* the same year and then moving on to command first the *Bonaventure* and then the *Britannia*. He finally became master of Torrington's flagship, *Sovereign of the Seas*, and, as we have seen, came forward to give evidence in support of his mentor at the latter's court martial after the Beachy Head fiasco, the outcome of which, strangely enough, left his own reputation unscathed.

By 1692 Benbow was master of the fleet under Admiral Edward Russell aboard the *Britannia* once more and was present at the victories of Barfleur and La Hogue. Under Admiral Shovell again by 1693, he commanded a flotilla of five bomb vessels which made repeated harassing attacks on the French Channel ports for the next two years, seeing action at Dunkirk, Granville and St Malo. His continued abrasiveness is reflected in the court-martialling of one of his captains in 1693 for what he considered lack of initiative, a charge which failed to stick. His fame was widespread, the newsheets (the garish and sensationalist tabloids of their day) calling him 'the famous Captain Benbow', which might have increased his conceit. It certainly caused certain coolness between him and his then C-in-C, Lord Berkeley, in 1695.

Nonetheless, Benbow continued to flourish, his cutting edge not dulled, and the following year he was promoted to rear admiral, commanding the squadron instituting the blockade of Dunkirk and chasing the elusive French squadron commanded by Jean Bart, this time without success. After the Treaty of Ryswick things became quieter at sea, but Benbow, appointed C-in-C of a West Indian squadron, managed to keep things astir during the years 1696 to 1700. His own lower-deck background made him particularly appreciative of conditions aboard his ships. The notorious death rate on that station he attributed to bad management at home in fitting out the vessels and keeping sufficient supplies of fresh food and water on board. Needless to say, the civil servants of the victualling department did little or nothing to implement his suggested reforms.

Benbow had, meanwhile, made life very unpleasant for the Spanish authorities on the Main, threatening to blockade Cartagna, Porto Bello and San Domingo, quarrelling with Colonel Collingwood and ranging as far afield as Newfoundland in his search for action. He returned to England in 1700 and served briefly again under Admiral Rooke. Benbow found that in the Grand Fleet opportunities for glory were considerably less and he soon volunteered to return to the West Indies on the resumption of hostilities with France, this time as commander-in-chief, where he almost immediately became involved in a dispute with the Governor of Jamaica.

By the early summer of 1702, news arrived of the attempted reinforcement of Cartagna by the French Commodore Ducasse, and Benbow made preparations to intercept that fleet. The French had 1,500 soldiers embarked in a transport vessel which was protected by five ships-of-the-line, *Heureux* (69), *Phénix* (60), *Agréable* (50), *Apollon* (50) and *Prince de Frise* (30), along with four frigates. On the evening of 19 August they sighted Benbow lying in wait for them off Cartagna. Ducasse, however, having no wish to engage him in combat, made every attempt to avoid battle.

Benbow's squadron comprised seven ships-of-the-line: his flagship, the third-rate *Breda* (70), commanded by Captain Christopher Fogg, *Defiance* (64) (Captain Richard Kirkby), *Greenwich* (54) (Captain Cooper Wade), *Windsor* (60) (Captain John Constable), *Falmouth* (48) (Captain Samuel Vincent), *Pendennis* (48) (Captain Thomas Hudson) and *Ruby* (48) (Captain George Walton). Again, little is known of these men, their subsequent conduct condemning them to be blackguard forever more. Speculation that they may have been 'gentlemen' who resented Benbow's manner towards them earlier, who might have resented the man for what he was, can only remain just that – speculation. What can be in no doubt, however, is that there was considerable ill feeling among them and that Kirkby was the instigator of the whole affair. There was a willing complaisance from the others, to be sure, in an attempt to discredit their admiral in combat and so bring him down to suit their own ends. Officers versus 'Tarpaulins' again!

On sighting the enemy, Benbow, having a superior force and being between them and their destination, was elated and gave orders for battle. His squadron was somewhat dispersed at the time and in order to form line of battle in the order *Defiance, Pendennis, Windsor, Breda, Greenwich, Ruby* and *Falmouth*, Benbow marked time to enable the ships 5 miles astern of him to come up into this formation before commencing his attack.

It was at 1300hrs that the order was given, but it soon became apparent that Kirkby was in no mood to comply with his commander's wishes. It required the dispatch of a lieutenant, with instructions to him to make more sail and come up abreast of the French van, before *Defiance* took up her appointed position and by this time three vital hours had elapsed.

At 1600hrs the action finally commenced but, again, with a half-heartedness on the part of most of the British captains. *Pendennis* remained out of position throughout and was never engaged. Of the three leading ships remaining, the *Windsor* took no part of any significance, although the range was point-blank. Meanwhile, *Defiance* lived up to her name, at least with regard to Benbow's orders, for after firing but three broadsides at the enemy, and totally undamaged in return, she retired out of range, leaving the *Breda* alone to continue the action with two of the Frenchmen.

Contact was maintained through the night and the battle was resumed the next day, the 20th. However, dawn revealed that, alone of his companions, only the *Ruby*, whose Captain Walton was evidently ashamed by the previous day's doings, was up in support of the *Breda*. The rest of the British squadron hung back some 4 miles astern of this pair, even though they were reputed to have been better sailing vessels than the flagship.

Benbow, as a fighting seaman, therefore decided to lead by example and signalled that the line of battle was to be changed to become *Breda, Defiance, Windsor, Greenwich, Ruby, Pendennis* and *Falmouth*. He gave particular emphasis in signals to Kirkby to ensure he take up his appointed place in line. It was all to no avail. *Breda* and *Ruby* were left together to face the enemy alone all day, the French heading off westward under full sail when they could well have turned on and annihilated both unsupported British warships.

So the sorry tale continued throughout the 21st. Finding himself in a position to cut off the rearmost enemy ship, Benbow attempted to do so, but before this manoeuvre could be accomplished he was forced to go to the aid of the *Ruby*, which was getting much the worst of it in direct combat with a far more heavily armed Frenchman. Sending his boats to tow the battered *Ruby* out of range, Benbow then engaged her assailant broadside to broadside for two hours, during which time both *Defiance* and *Windsor* had ample opportunity to finish off the rear French ship, but declined even to open fire on her.

With the damaged *Ruby* left astern Benbow again went off in pursuit of the Frenchmen, with the rest of his line following well astern. The *Breda* again engaged the two rear ships of the French squadron, but once more, although within shot of the enemy, his subordinate captains failed to follow his example before night fell.

During the night, Captain Vincent, perhaps stricken with the same remorse as the captain of the *Ruby* had been the night before, closed up some and dawn found the *Falmouth* out of her station and up with the *Breda*. Vincent sent his lieutenant across asking permission to maintain this position instead of his allotted place, in order to support his commander, as nobody else seemed inclined to do so. Benbow warmly accepted this offer. Of the remaining fit British ships, the *Defiance* led most of them some 4 miles astern of the flagship, but the *Greenwich* was some 9 miles adrift.

Not until late afternoon on the 22nd did *Breda* and *Falmouth* manage to come up with the rear of the French line and darkness came before anything more than a few exchanges of fire had taken place. Once more Benbow hung on grimly to the enemy coattails and on the 23rd they finally closed the gap and were rewarded by the capture of the galley *Anne*, a prize taken by Ducasse earlier on the other side of the Atlantic. This was small reward for all their efforts, but it was something. For the rest, however, being 4 miles astern of Benbow at dawn, they too had come up by evening but again made no contribution to the fighting.

Breda and *Falmouth* resumed the battle early on the 24th, *Defiance* and the rest lagging 4 miles behind, and Benbow engaged the rearmost French warship in the pre-dawn darkness for several hours. During the course of this last exchange, around 0300hrs, Benbow himself, an inspiration to those that followed him, had his right leg lacerated by chain shot and was taken below. But not for him such an insipid end to all his endeavours: he ordered that he be taken up to the quarterdeck in his cot, where he continued to direct the action.

The rearmost enemy ship, having borne the brunt of *Breda* and *Falmouth*'s fire, was seriously disabled and Benbow attempted to board her and carry her as a prize. Unfortunately, observing the plight of their companion now it was daylight, the remaining French vessels turned back to her aid. The predicament of the two British ships was now dire, but with a little enterprise their erstwhile companions could have come up and turned this into a decisive British advantage.

Needless to say they behaved in their usual way and one by one they passed the struggling enemy ship to leeward, fired a few ineffectual broadsides and then sailed away, leaving Benbow to whatever fate Ducasse deemed fit. Fortunately he was as unenterprising as they, and contented himself with rescuing his cripple, firing a few broadside into *Breda's* rigging and then resuming his flight. *Falmouth* and *Breda* set off in pursuit once more but were delayed by the arrival of Captain Wade of the *Greenwich*, who came aboard the *Breda*, possibly to explain his conduct, possibly to see whether Benbow was still alive, but more likely to try to persuade him to give up the chase.

One can only imagine Benbow's feelings at this juncture. Never an easy man, he must have been totally outraged at any such suggestion from one who had done nothing at all during the battle. Whatever the argument then, Benbow made one last attempt to bring his subordinates to a sense of their duty. He told Captain Fogg to send a message to each ship imploring them to obey his original signal and to 'behave themselves like Englishmen'. Delivered to Kirkby by Wade, this stirring exhortation had no effect other than to harden their resolve to avoid further combat and Kirkby himself went aboard the *Breda*.

Ignoring his leader's condition, Kirkby threw himself into impassioned pleadings that the fight be broken off at once, stating that the enemy was too strong and the battle had gone on too long. Benbow angrily dismissed such faintheartedness and ordered the rest of his captains to come aboard to give their opinions. All the time the British ships were to the windward of the French in an ideal position to carry the fight to a victorious conclusion. Due to Ducasse having shown no great aggressiveness himself, there was little doubt in Benbow's mind as to the probable outcome of renewed battle.

Kirkby, meanwhile, had not been idle in pursuing a lesser cause; he drew up a document stating his case and persuaded the others as to the correctness of his attitude. Benbow retorted that such a document 'would ruin them all'. Unabashed, Kirkby drew up a another, saying they would defer the fighting ''til a better opportunity', to which Benbow, all this time in considerable pain from his wound it must be remembered, replied defiantly that there would never be a better opportunity than right now, since the enemy were outnumbered, the English had the weather gauge and, apart from *Breda*, had suffered almost no casualties.

Despite this, every captain signed the document, including Vincent and Fogg surprisingly enough. This disgraceful piece of paper stated that, for the various reasons listed, none of which stood up to the most casual examination, 'Wee [sic] think it not fit to Ingage [sic] the Enemy at this time'.

Resigned to their attitude and weak from loss of blood, Benbow could only accept and the squadron returned to Jamaica, where his leg was amputated. A supposed letter from his recent French opponent expressed the sentiment: 'As for those cowardly captains who deserted you, hang them up; for by God, they deserve it.' Nevertheless, whether or not Ducasse sent such an epistle, the view expressed admirably reflected Benbow's own feeling on the matter. He issued orders to his newly arrived second-in-command, Rear Admiral Whetstone, commissioning him, several captains and a lawyer, Arnold Browne, to convene a court martial on all the captains of his squadron, with the honourable exception of Walton of the *Ruby*. Captain Hudson of the *Pendennis* avoided this trial by dying by his own hand shortly after the ships returned to Jamaica – no doubt his was judged by a higher tribunal, while Benbow's own captain, Fogg, and the captain of the *Falmouth*, who had made honourable amends, were only to be tried on the actual signing of the document calling off the battle.

The rest were not so fortunate. No doubt they hoped that Benbow would not be alive to initiate such proceedings and somehow hoped to cover their tracks by their unanimity of opinion. In this, if such was the case, they were thwarted by the tough old sailor, who, though he died from his wounds on 4 November at Port Royal, had already set in train the course of justice from which were was to be no escape, no lagging astern or tardy avoidance. He lived long enough to give evidence himself against them, there being no legal objection to either the competence of the witness or the admissibility of his evidence or that he was the prosecutor, although of course he could not have presided, even had his medical condition made this possible.

The court was assembled aboard the *Breda* at Port Royal on 8 October and, not surprisingly considering the number of persons on trial, lasted four days. Kirkby was the first to be summoned and the catalogue of charges against him was like a broadside in itself and included cowardice, neglect of duty and breach of orders, among other things. Witnesses included, other than Benbow himself, Fogg and Vincent, along with eighteen other officers.

The cowardice charge was more explicit than might have been expected. It was not merely his reluctance to close the enemy that he was accused of, but of cowardice of the most basic kind in battle, that of flinging himself on the deck and hiding behind the mizzen mast when the fighting became fierce. It was alleged that he had withheld shot and powder to his guns crews when they could have made the enemy pay on the rare occasions *Defiance* came within range, and that he had altered his Master's Journal during the battle for his own ends.

Whatever the clashes of character between Kirkby and Benbow, it is on record that the former did not conduct himself in the courtroom as befitting one born 'above the salt', his attitude being described as 'unbecoming a gentleman'. Indeed, there may be something in the theory that his personal feud with Benbow had made him slightly insane, either before the battle or after it. Certainly he had not acted the part of the coward on earlier service.

Some of Kirkby's replies to questions would seem to back up such a theory; although, of course, a theory alone it is. When asked why he did not open fire on the enemy when he found himself, on the third day, within point-blank range, his answer was 'because they did not fire at him but that they had a respect for him'. Perhaps by this answer he was trying to convey that the mere presence of the *Defiance* was enough to overawe the French, but this is hardly recommended conduct for a full-scale naval engagement.

Kirkby totally rejected charges of personal cowardice and brought witnesses to back him up, but these seemed to have little to say in mitigation of his conduct and were dismissed as 'insignificant'. Later he was to protest at the whole trial, railing against the appointment of Browne as Judge Advocate, 'a common lawyer, who knew nothing of Civil Law', who 'proceeded contrary (in all respects) to the methods of naval trials, rejecting my defence and … discountenanced my officers in giving their evidence to the truth'.

One of Kirkby's arguments merits closer study, in that it will appear again in these pages with totally different results and be the cause of many of the courts martial we describe relating to commanders-in-chief at this period. Describing how he had been asked by the court why he did not open fire at certain times during the battle when he might have done so, Kirkby wrote that 'the enemy sheered off from us and the admiral having taken the lead upon himself would lead me no nearer so that by our usual distant fight Her Majesty's ammunition was spent to no purpose'.

In other words Kirkby held that he had complied strictly to the Fighting Instructions (drawn up by Admiral Russell and not superseded by Admiral Rook's version until a year later), whereby it was rigidly laid down that line of battle must be formed 'conterminous with that of the enemy'. This meant that the English van must engage that of the enemy and likewise the rearmost ship engage her opposite number. As, Kirkby is arguing, Benbow was engaging the rearmost ship himself, although he was in the English van, the other British ships could not engage without breaking Fighting Instructions themselves, as Articles 17 and 18 were understood. He further vindicated his lassitude by adherence to Article 19, by which no ship was to open fire until the range was point-blank, and Article 20, which stated that the main part of the enemy fleet must have been disposed of before pursuit of small numbers could take place.

In Kirkby's case his allegations that it was Benbow who was at fault by not keeping to the instructions are absurd and, indeed, counteract one of Kirkby's own defences whereby he stated that while within point-blank range he did not open fire because the enemy 'respected' him. Benbow, as we have seen, was left with no choice in the matter due to Kirkby, and most of the others, not forming the ordered line of battle in the first place. Still, this obsession with the rigid compliance with Fighting Instructions was fast taking hold on the fleet, as will become only too evident.

For all his wild accusations and cries of 'unfair', Kirkby could not evade his just deserts. Guilty was the verdict on every one of the charges and the sentence, also laid down in the Articles of War, which he continually cited, was death. He was duly ordered to be shot but was detained awaiting the queen's pleasure. Some at home stood up for him, he was apparently not without influence, but Her Majesty was no more impressed than the court had been with his conduct. The warrant for his execution was duly issued.

Although it is not following the strict order of proceedings, it is convenient next to consider Captain Cooper Wade of the *Greenwich*; the vessel, it will be remembered, was more conspicuous by her absence than presence throughout most of the battle. The charges against Wade also included cowardice, although it was by keeping well clear of the action rather than in the more dramatic gestures of Kirkby that was implied. On the rare occasions that his ship did open fire, it was alleged, it was at such a range as to make his shot useless. It was maintained that when his own officers had remonstrated with him on this, he had replied that, nonetheless, they should continue firing or else Benbow 'would not believe that they had fought'. Benbow most certainly didn't believe this and nor did the court. Despite the fact that, seemingly in some kind of attempt at making amends or belated realisation of what he had done or, mayhap, merely to ingratiate himself (although the latter is doubtful), he praised Benbow's conduct throughout the battle as courageous and well conducted. Wade also received the death sentence and, like Kirkby's, it was upheld.

Captain John Constable was, in fact, the second to be tried and the charges were breach of orders and neglect of duty. In the evidence it transpired that so much a puppet of Kirkby was this worthy that he had twice been summoned by the firing of a gun aboard the *Breda* to take his place in line, but, upon being told by Kirkby to remain where he was, he ignored Benbow's summons. Again, in his defence, it was argued that he was also complying with the strict order of battle as laid down and that had he taken his place as instructed it would have meant taking his vessel ahead of *Defiance*, which could not be done. It will not have escaped notice that even Captain Vincent of the *Falmouth* had felt obliged to request of Benbow that he might break line in order to join him in the fight.

Nonetheless, even more damaging evidence was placed before the court. Lieutenant Langridge had twice been sent over to deliver a message to Constable, ordering him to keep within half a cable's length of his next ahead, and both times he had failed to comply. Witnesses were also produced who swore that Constable was the worse for liquor during the battle, which, if he were struggling against his conscience, well may have been the case. The defendant's argument was that he had issued rum to the men to keep their spirits up and that the only reason he had signed the notorious documents was because of the damage his ship had suffered.

It made no difference to the court's findings. Although he escaped the death penalty, Constable was sentenced to be immediately cashiered, kept under lock and key, and sent home in disgrace.

Having signed the letter which had caused the battle to be broken off prematurely, there was no evading the issue for either Fogg or Vincent, but in their cases Benbow himself spoke up for them, attesting to Fogg's 'courage, bravery and conduct' and stating that, had not Vincent come to his aid when he did, the *Breda* would have been lost. This did the trick. Their own defence was that they only signed the document because, in view of the way the other captains had behaved earlier, had they continued the action alone they might have been deserted once more (an opinion with which it is hard to disagree) and that to continue in such circumstances was to invite capture and defeat.

They were found guilty, of course – they had put their names to the paper – but the sentence of suspension was to await the pleasure of Prince George, Lord High Admiral. The Admiralty, in their wisdom, left the decision to Benbow, but he died, although not before writing a letter in their favour, and in the end they were never suspended and continued in service.

The British public at large were in no doubt about the only possible outcome of such behaviour and were duly rewarded when, on 16 July 1703, Kirkby and Wade arrived at Plymouth aboard the *Bristol* and were shot there and then. They met their ignoble ends with more aplomb than they had shown during the battle itself, it should be said. Constable, Fogg and Vincent vanished into the limbo of history, while the gallant Walton later became Sir George Walton, Admiral of the Blue.

As for Benbow himself, his last action became his most notable claim to fame and he has been immortalised ever since: three battleships and a naval shore base were named after him in the centuries that followed. Sir Henry Newbolt included him amongst the honoured in his *Admirals All*. It was argued by some that Benbow should have dismissed his captains when they first showed their true colours and replaced them with their lieutenants. Whether or not that would have been practical in the midst of a battle, or if it would have led to a worse incident with ship against ship, cannot be stated with any degree of certainty, but, as one of the most infamous incidents concerning Royal Navy officers in the face of a fleeing enemy, the abandonment of Admiral Benbow will always be a page of shame in the navy's long and glorious history.

4 AN INCIDENT OFF TOULON (1744)

Strict adherence to the Fighting Instructions had been partially cited in the Benbow case as we have seen, but this excuse was to predominate in what was to be the largest series of courts martial in the history of the Royal Navy, which took place some forty years later. As with all large organisations, a continued period of growth leads to unwieldy bulk. Therefore, in the expanded navy constraints upon all aspects of sea fighting, introduced in order to institute some control over large numbers of vessels, gradually became an act of faith among the more pedantic-minded at the Admiralty.

The old free-for-all system as applied to the stately concourse of the fleet in the eighteenth century, coupled with the primitive signalling arrangements of the period, obviously called for some degree of organisation. Unfortunately, commencing with the rules initiated by James, Duke of York, later King James II, gradually the old fire and natural ability of the British seaman was stifled.

More and more rules began to be applied for every conceivable eventuality and impossible task in the days of sail, and were repeatedly shown to be as futile in the age of steam as the 'Buggins' Turn' attitude was at the Battle of Jutland in 1916. With the best intentions, slowly but surely the initiative, which had won England command of the seas, was buried under a mass of paper rules. The abandonment of these, for whatever reason, was, in theory, punishable by death, or at best, dishonour. Many individuals fought against this monolithic structure as it grew, but the trend could not be reversed. By 1744 the courts martial of captains and flag officers of the fleet, en masse, showed very firmly to those who sought to re-assert the old values of daring and individualism, just what their fate might be.

We have seen how Articles 17 and 18 had already impressed themselves on the minds of officers at the turn of the century. The introduction of Sir George Rooke's Permanent Fighting Instructions of 1704 had, in Michael Lewis' words, driven 'the last nails into the coffin of initiative at sea'. If this was indeed the case, and it is thus generally accepted, then the Toulon courts martial series of trials lowered the coffin into its grave.

Even more of a British tradition than either the Royal Navy or its Fighting Instructions is the neglect of its armed forces in times of peace. Cutting the navy to the bone and paying the price later in lives and needless sacrifice has ever been paramount in the policy of those that govern these isles, and parsimony did not originate in the 1950s or the 1980s. The outbreak of the War of the Austrian Succession in 1744 found the fleet in a state of some neglect. Meanwhile, the talk was of the fleets of Spain and France combining to make common cause against us once more. To ascertain the truth of this, and to deal with it accordingly, the Mediterranean Fleet was dispatched to 'look into' Toulon harbour.

In theory this fleet, which comprised twenty-eight ships-of-the-line, was a formidable force. However, it contained among its respective captains the normal wide diversity of talent and incompetence that a long period of peace brings. In command was Admiral Thomas Mathews, a venerable officer of wide experience dating back to the first decade of the century, when he was a post-captain.

As with most of our admirals, Mathews was an individualist, not of the Whig persuasion, which may have helped seal his fate in the intricate in-fighting of the politics of the day. Mathews was also possessed of a volatile temperament and given to self-importance and an acute awareness of his position. Not for nothing was his nickname in the fleet '*Il Furibondo*' and he seemingly enjoyed neither the affection of his men nor the complete trust of those at home. Despite all this, he was a fighter, and brooked no delay in seeking to come to grips with the situation as soon as possible.

It was regrettable that his second-in-command was not only an equally combustible character but also one of the opposite political persuasion. This worthy was Rear Admiral Richard Lestock, and he and Mathews seemingly saw eye to eye on very little. The seeds for another Benbow-Kirkby scenario appear to have thus been well sown, and this was indeed how things turned out, although Lestock does not seem to have such a vindictive objective as Kirkby in his mind. Nonetheless, Lestock was to utilise those rigid Fighting Instructions to bring about the downfall of his C-in-C far more effectively than Kirkby in practice.

On 11 February 1744, the Mediterranean Fleet sighted the combined enemy fleets, which, by chance, exactly equalled them in number, and Mathews at once made to engage. The enemy were on a southerly course heading for the Straits of Gibraltar and Mathews succeeded in bringing the British fleet to the windward of them. Unfortunately, despite his best efforts, Mathews found himself out of position with regard to his dispositions for battle, according to the rules that is, and he was not allowed to fight any kind of battle in any other way!

Mathews now found himself in a similar predicament to Benbow, but, in his case, it was the weather gauge and not reluctant captains that placed him on the horns of a dilemma. Try as he might, he could not advance his line to match the van of the enemy. His own van was abreast the enemy centre, his centre the enemy rear, and his rear faced nothing but open sea. Even this position was only held with difficulty due to the rising wind and worsening sea conditions.

What was Mathews to do? He could continue the hopeless attempt against all the rules and persist in the futile attempt to line his fleet up according to the book. In so doing, it was quite likely that the enemy would merely take advantage of his manoeuvring to make their escape without any loss at all. As usual with British fleets throughout history, they found themselves trying to bring a reluctant enemy to battle, for the 80-year-old French admiral, despite the equality of numbers, was no more willing to fight the British than Ducasse had been in 1702 or Scheer would in 1916.

This was always where the carefully thought out instructions fell down: drafted by English seamen who rarely conceived any fleet wishing to avoid a battle, it made no provision for enemy fleets which all too often had nothing else but avoidance in their minds. Van to van was fine, if the enemy played by the same game, but the enemy, more often than not, refused to do so.

The day was well drawn on by now and the coming winds and deteriorating weather would very soon end the game of chase for both fleets and leave Mathews with nothing to show for his efforts. He therefore made a momentous decision. It was, in the circumstances, the right thing to do to force the issue; it was perhaps the only positive thing he could have done, but it was also very rash. Abandoning his efforts to pull into line, Mathews turned his flagship straight at the enemy closest to him, intending to engage.

Now, if the rest of his captains had without hesitation followed their leader in his daring action, it might well have been that the centre and rear of the enemy would have been annihilated. At the very least, all would have been engaged and thus given time for the rear of the English line, under the abrasive Lestock and still some mile astern, to come up to complete the rout. Had the enemy van turned back to succour their companions, a general action might well have followed, which would have certainly suited the English.

Unfortunately for Mathews no such thing happened, instead he got the worst of both worlds. For a start only a few of his ships followed his example, among them – to be sure – his next ahead and next astern, but their example was followed by just one other, the gallant and brave Edward Hawke, who, by so doing, showed his mettle early on in what would be a distinguished career. But the other captains were not of the same mould as Hawke, or as bold in disobeying hallowed laws as Mathews.

The decision that these worthies came to was that they would support their leader without breaking the instructions. This they did by opening fire, but holding their positions, which meant that the action was conducted at such long a range as to be futile. By contrast, Mathews and his few followers closed to within 'pistol shot' of their selected opponents and engaged them in a furious cannonade.

The action of the four British ships so engaged had the welcome effect of slowing down the fleets and thus Lestock's division, which Mathews had earlier exhorted by signal to make more sail and close the gap, finally had the opportunity to do so. No doubt Mathews welcomed the sight of these reinforcements bearing up bravely from astern, but if he expected Lestock to throw himself whole-heartedly into the combat in his support he was to be sorely disappointed.

The rear division complied with Fighting Instructions and held their line, thus contributing nothing to the real fighting. The onset of darkness hid the final debacle in its welcoming shroud. By dawn, such fighting as there was had reached its conclusion. There was damage to ships on both sides, with some vessels disabled. The advantage still lay with the English, for one Spanish battleship had blown up and another had been captured. The rest made good their escape, however, and the general result was an indecisive draw.

On reaching harbour Mathews' temper took its normal course; Lestock was summarily dismissed and sent packing back to London. Once there he no doubt took advantage to stress his side of the case, with the result that the Admiralty stepped in to assert itself and ordered Mathews himself to resign his command. Courts martial were authorised on both principals and, for good measure, most of the other senior officers involved.

Lestock was the first of the two admirals to be brought to trial, but many other lesser officers preceded him. Sir Chaloner Ogle, Admiral of the Blue, presided over the court, together with Rear Admiral Perry Mayne and Commodore William Smith, along with no less than twenty-one captains, among them Rodney and Spragge. On 23 September 1745, four lieutenants of the *Dorsetshire*, David, Griffiths, Page and Smelt, were acquitted of having advised their captain, George Burrish, 'not to bear down upon the enemy'. Two days later Burrish himself was accused on five counts, each count having several sections, including 'not engaging within point blank range', 'withdrawing from the fight', 'not keeping proper station', not backing his admiral or helping his next ship, the *Marlborough*, and so on.

Captain Burrish pleaded that he had no powder filled to enable him to do so, this in spite of the fact that the battle had been expected for several days prior to the action. On 9 October sentence was passed on him that he was to be cashiered and forever rendered incapable of being an officer in His Majesty's navy. Next, the court, sitting aboard HMS *London* at Chatham, proceeded with the trial of Captain Edmund Williams of the *Royal Oak*. The charges were similar, that he did not bear down and engage the enemy, 'but kept back from the fight to windward of his station in line'; that he wasted ammunition by firing out of range; that he failed to help the *Namur* and *Marlborough* when they were hard pressed; and disobedience of his admiral's signals. On almost all these points the court found him guilty. However, the court tempered justice with mercy, 'in regard of his long services, and his eyesight being very defective'. He was judged unfit to be employed at sea any more (a trifle overdue conclusion one would have thought). It was recommended that he continue on the 'half-pay list' according to his seniority. This was done and Williams was appointed a superannuated rear admiral the following year.

After a rest, the court re-convened on 18 October to try Captain John Ambrose of the *Rupert* on similar charges to Williams, added to which was the charge that he failed to cover and protect the galley fire ship *Ann*, while she was endeavouring to come to grips with the *Real*. The court found him guilty of failing in his duty and not engaging more closely when he had the opportunity to do so. But again, in considering his conduct both before and after the battle, they deemed his errors 'a mistake in judgement'. He was cashiered 'during His Majesty's pleasure'. His rank was restored by a generous sovereign and he was appointed a rear admiral in 1747. Exactly the same charges and sentence were received by Captain Dilk of the *Chichester*.

Captain Frogmore of the *Boyne* was accused, but died before reaching England, while Captain Norris of the *Essex* resigned his command shortly after the battle on the grounds of ill health. He had intended returning home, but angry at talk of his own conduct during the battle he asked Vice Admiral Rowley, then in command in the Mediterranean, if he might be tried by court martial in order to clear himself. As he had resigned, it was not within Rowley's power to comply with this request, so Norris petitioned the Admiralty and they duly commissioned Rowley to proceed. This court martial took place aboard the *Torbay* at Mahon, with Rowley himself as President and twenty-five captains, including Dilk. The accuser was the second lieutenant of the *Essex*, Edward Jekyl, who refused to be sworn. After sitting for several days, a motion was carried on 5 February questioning whether '… the court had a right, or ought to come to any determination on the matter before them, as Captain Norris was not then in His Majesty's service or on full pay'.

The court finally decided to pass the buck back to the Admiralty and duly sent the minutes to London. Jekyl himself complained of the treatment he had received and fellow lieutenants from the *Essex*, Gower, Palliser and Peyton, also wrote in his support. The matter ended up in the House of Commons, which pronounced the whole proceedings 'partial, arbitrary and illegal'. Captain Norris was accused of bad conduct and a vote in the Commons requested he be tried. Norris evaded the fate of his contemporaries, however, by the simple expedient of nipping over the border from Gibraltar into Spain, changing his name and thus he 'remained for ever in obscurity'.

The full glare of publicity had been turned on the whole unhappy episode with a vengeance, but there were lots more of the same to follow. The courts martial continued. Lestock himself accused a whole bevy of captains, Thomas Cooper, James Lloyd, Robert Pett, George Sclater and Temple West, of misconduct on several charges. Pett and Sclater were acquitted, the others cashiered, although once more these sentences were 'deemed extremely hard, and reprobated as sever and bearing no proportion to the faults proved against them'. They were restored to the former ranks.

Now it was Lestock's turn to face a court martial. The court assembled aboard the *Prince of Orange* at Deptford, under the presidency of Rear Admiral Perry Mayne, Admiral Ogle being ill. One Rear Admiral of the Blue, John Byng, was also in attendance, along with fourteen captains. Lestock's trial was a long, drawn-out affair, not made any simpler by the enormous number of witnesses examined. It lasted the whole month of May, from the 6th, and the sentence was not read out until 3 June. What Brian Tunstall termed the 'extraordinary verdict' was worded as follows, and Byng, to his later discomfiture, concurred fully with it:

The court were of opinion, that the information the charge was founded upon was not true, and that the evidence in support of the charge was not sufficient to make it good; and that many witnesses in support of the charge, as likewise those in the admiral's defence, had refuted the whole; therefore the court unanimously acquitted Vice Admiral Lestock of the whole and every part of the charge.

In other words, by sanctimoniously sticking to the point that he had 'obeyed the Instructions', Lestock came out of the whole thing without a mark against him. Having cleared the decks, as it were, Lestock rounded upon his commander-in-chief and laid no less than fifteen charges against him. In sum, they amounted to the charge that, through Mathews' misconduct, by which he meant the failure to follow 'the instructions', the whole sorry outcome of the battle was due.

The last round in this messy and unedifying business now took place. The court reassembled on 16 June, with the same principals and fourteen of the same captains who had exonerated Lestock himself on board. One might be forgiven if one feels that, having come to one conclusion, these officers were unlikely to have much choice in the ultimate verdict they passed on the unfortunate Mathews. The admiral himself raised objections to only three of the officers sitting, on the grounds that they were 'not captains of ships, within the districts and limits of the command of the flag officer or commander-in-chief, who preside at such court martial; and second, that the said captains, objected to, were then captains or commanders of ships, that were out of the district or limits of the commander-in-chief'.

The court, in effect, overruled these objections, but delayed the trial until the Admiralty gave a ruling. They ruled that the Act of Parliament 13 Charles II, 'which is the foundation of martial law, and for trying offences committed at sea, mentions no such restrictions as are contained in Admiral Mathew's first objection' and that the absence of captains from their ship to attend courts martial was only a temporary measure that did not invalidate their rank.

This technicality dealt with, the case proceeded. Again, the number of witnesses called was legion, and there were many more adjournments. The trial dragged on, ensuring that the washing of dirty linen in public was prolonged to the fullest extent. The reputation of the Royal Navy suffered accordingly. It was not until 22 October that sentence was finally passed. Not surprisingly, considering the circumstances and political pressures, Mathews took the full force of injured pride. Again, the verdict deserves to be seen in full:

> The Court, having examined the witnesses produced, as well in support of the charge as in behalf of the prisoner, and having thoroughly considered their evidence, do unanimously resolve, that it appears thereby, that Thomas Mathews, esq, by divers breaches of duty, was a principal cause of the miscarriage of His Majesty's fleet in the Mediterranean, in the month of February 1844, and that he falls under the 14th article of an act of the 13 Charles II for establishing articles and orders for the regulating the better government of His Majesty's

navies, ships of war, and forces by sea; and the Court do unanimously think fit to adjudge the said Thomas Mathews to be cashiered, and rendered incapable of any employ, in His Majesty's service.

Lestock was victorious! His whole case rested on his insistence that Mathews had hoisted the signal to engage the enemy without hauling down his earlier signal to form line ahead. As he could not obey the second without disobeying the first, his conscience was clear, and with this the court agreed. Little wonder that these verdicts made a lasting impression on Byng; they had a similar effect on every other serving officer. Henceforth they would think long and hard before taking any risk, even if that meant losing touch with the enemy.

Mathews, not surprisingly, was most indignant that his attempts to give battle should have brought such a fate down upon his head, while his reluctant junior should be praised for not closing with the enemy. The general public was of a vastly different opinion, they tended to see things more simply and to them an admiral who tried, and at least partially succeeded, was a better man than one who did nothing but stick to the rules. However, despite public opinion, the Admiralty, in their wisdom, remained adamant. Having made their decision, they refused to go back on it or admit that their instructions might be too rigid. Mathews was not granted the charity shown to his lesser captains; he was never reinstated nor was he ever employed again. Lestock, by contrast, continued to enjoy Their Lordships' full confidence.

Ironic though it may have been, there was a loophole that Mathews might have employed, and indeed people like the audacious Hawke later exploited to the full. This was the ruling in those self-same instructions that authorised a commander-in-chief to use his discretion if he felt certain that the enemy was not offering battle but was taking to his heels. In such a case, the C-in-C could order a 'General Chase', without sticking to the rigid formality of the line of battle. Poor Mathews was too honest, or too hidebound, to himself resort to such subterfuge off Toulon in 1744. Indeed, it required a smashing victory even to get away with such a deception, no matter how worthy the motive.

Mathews was not the first, neither was he the last, to be caught in this vicious trap. Nor was he by any means the last admiral of the Royal Navy to be caught up in the web of political intrigue and left floundering out of his depth.

5 TO ENCOURAGE THE OTHERS (1757)

Poor Admiral Byng! His fate was no more deserved than that of Mathews, a confused victim of the same inflexible system of rules and muddling government, and Voltaire's telling lines, so often quoted out of context, mirror the sympathy his death was to arouse from the same people who had earlier called for his blood. He is deserving of our sympathy to be sure, but how ironic that he, who had helped terminate Mathews' career twelve years earlier, should be hoisted so cruelly by the same petard.

Born in 1704, a son of Admiral Sir George Byng, later Admiral of the Fleet Lord Torrington and Treasurer of the Navy, then First Lord, John Byng entered the Royal Navy in 1718 where, aboard the *Superb* (60), he was present at his father's great victory of Cape Passaro. After serving in a number of ships, he eventually rejoined this vessel in 1724 as second lieutenant. Further service up the Straits followed until, on 8 August 1727, he was appointed captain of the frigate *Gibraltar* (20). Commands followed at regular intervals and, at the time of the War of the Austrian Succession, he commanded the *Sutherland* (50) at Newfoundland and later the *Winchester* (50) in the Channel. He became flag captain of Sir Charles Hardy in the *St George* (90), before returning to the Channel Fleet in 1745.

Despite this long period of service at sea, Byng himself had seen little action but, due no doubt to his distinguished connections, he was made Rear Admiral of the Blue in August 1745 at the early age of 41. His service at the court martial proceedings of Lestock and Mathews has been recounted already and the impression that it made upon him has also been noted. One biographer stated that it 'would seem impossible to have devised a better method of turning an officer into a hidebound formalist than by making him sit on two such courts'.

As second-in-command to Admiral Medley in the Mediterranean, his lack of confidence in himself became very apparent, but the loss of the Lerins Islands, which his squadron was supposed to prevent, did not stop him being upgraded to Vice Admiral of the Blue in July 1847. He succeeded to the position of commander-in-chief on the death of Medley shortly afterward. Within a year another promotion followed, to Vice Admiral of the Red and, still without experiencing much shock or shot, he returned home on the conclusion of hostilities.

The outbreak of the conflict that was to become known as the Seven Years War was preceded by ominous rumblings and clear warnings, to which, true to form, the government of the day turned a blind eye until it was too late. Nor were they any less pusillanimous in their attitude to either the preparations for the war or the means of waging it than their counterparts in office before or since. Thus, despite the strivings of Anson, the fleet was, yet again, not in the best condition to face up to what soon developed into a worldwide struggle that raged from the wilderness of Canada to the Mediterranean. The problems then became the usual ones, how to hold on with what was available and again, as always, whether we could do so or not depended mainly on the Royal Navy and the admirals in charge of its far-flung squadrons.

Thus, although it was common knowledge that the French were making war-like preparations to their fleet at Toulon some six months before they acted, little or nothing was done to improve our own defences. Therefore, when the inevitable took place, and a strong naval force under the Marquis de la Galissonière landed an army of some 16,000 men on the island of Minorca and laid siege to the small British garrison at Port Mahon, all was atwitter in Whitehall. It was correctly anticipated that such a move might merely be a feint to draw away the main body of the fleet and thus leave the home islands in peril of invasion. Equally, something had to be done to hold our possessions in the Mediterranean, and so an entirely inadequate fleet was sent out there to do what it could and so ease the political puppet-masters' consciences.

In these inauspicious circumstances, the always hesitant Byng was not to be envied when it fell to his lot to be appointed commander of that fleet. Nor were his considerable doubts as to his chances of success made any lighter by the fears and forebodings of his friends and advisers, few of whom could detect any ray of hope in the undertaking he was launched upon. Nor were his military compatriots any more helpful. The Governor of Gibraltar refused to allow Byng the marines he was expecting to add to his force on the way out. Byng's second-in-command was the same Temple West who had been cashiered and then restored after the Mathews-Lestock contretemps, although that worthy might have redeemed himself fully since then at the First Battle of Finisterre. He was now a rear admiral, but it hardly required yet another reminder of Mathews' fate to inspire Byng in the same waters. West flew his flag aboard the *Buckingham* (68), Byng in the *Ramillies* (90), the fleet being divided into two divisions.

Two other factors might be counted in Byng's favour. The first was that the French ships, being not long out of dock, were in better shape than many of his own, which badly needed cleaning. The second was the French tactic, then relatively new but soon to become wearisomely familiar, to surrender the wind gauge and rely on long-range gunnery directed at the English rigging while avoiding by every means any attempt to get within point-blank range. Such a policy, although quite reasonable from the French viewpoint, did not make a decisive encounter, as dictated by the Articles of War, any easier for Byng to achieve. For, by utilising this method, Galissonière was still, by the rules, offering battle, thus ruling out the 'General Chase' option, even if Byng had wished to take advantage of it.

The French admiral flew his flag in the *Foudroyant* (84), his subordinate flag officers in the *Redoubtable* and *Couvonne* respectively. When first sighted by the English fleet, on the morning of 19 May 1756, south of Minorca, the French ships were under sail, while Byng's ships were almost becalmed on a lee shore. In consequence, no action was forthcoming that day, although by evening the two fleets were within a couple of leagues of each other. Byng, having served in those waters before, was unperturbed by this and slipped inshore to await the morning wind and, by 0300hrs of the 20th, was making ready to form the line of battle.

After a great deal of intricate sailing Byng worked his squadrons between the enemy and the island and, at 1000hrs, the two lines approached each other vying desperately for the weather gauge, a race which, due to a shift in the wind, Byng was able to win. However, as we have seen, this by no means daunted Galissonière with his new tactics up his sleeve. According to Article 17 of the Fighting Instructions, as soon as his van was level with the enemy rear, the situation reached by 1320hrs, Byng could tack and bring his ships abreast the enemy on a converging course ready for close-range action.

However, Byng was not without knowledge of French methods. He appreciated the dangers of their long-range fire during the period of approach, during which they would concentrate their fire on the English ships' rigging. To this fire, the English fleet would not be able to reply effectively until they could come into line ahead and engage their full broadsides. He decided to hold on longer and then make his approach by 'Lasking', making a more diagonal approach, which, as he subsequently explained 'would give an opportunity to every ship to lead slanting down on the one she was to engage, and they would not be so liable to be raked by the enemy's fire'. This was highly commendable but proved unduly complicated when the French reacted to what they thought was a concentrated attack upon their rear.

The French order of battle was *Orphee, Hippopotame, Redoubtable, Sage, Guerrier, Fier, Foudroyant, Temeraire, Content, Lion, Couvonne* and *Triton*, with the commander-in-chief placed in the centre of his three squadrons. The English line, approaching them at a tangent, was led by *Defiance*, followed by *Portland, Lancaster, Buckingham, Captain, Intrepid, Revenge, Princess Louisa, Trident, Ramillies, Culloden* and *Kingston*, giving equal numbers, both fleets having attendant frigates on their disengaged sides. However, Byng was well astern of the actual initial point of contact and badly placed to make any signals to control matters should, as was possible, anything go awry.

Go wrong they did, almost at once! Captain Thomas Andrews of the *Defiance* assumed that Byng's manoeuvre was, in fact, a mistaken late turn and made hard for his opposite number the *Orphee*. Worse was to come, for one by one his compatriots astern of him followed suit, thus wrecking Byng's careful deployment plans, which no amount of subsequent frantic signalling and gun firing could rectify.

The French fire now began to take effect on West's ship aloft, but, nothing daunted, he pressed on and began to inflict what he took to be severe punishment on his opposite number. By 1520 the Frenchmen were seen to be retiring and West felt elated, but it was only the pre-arranged plan and the enemy reformed in line, firing heavily again as they did so, the gallant, if mistaken, Captain Andrews being among the many Englishmen to fall to their shot.

Heavily knocked about in turn, West's squadron was now threatened with worse, for the French centre now loomed up. Looking for Byng and the others to support them, the Englishmen in the van saw nothing at all. Why was this? Simply because Captain James Young of the *Intrepid* had also charged in guns blazing upon the *Fier* and had, in turn, become victim of the French gunners, losing her foretopmast. The *Intrepid* came up into the wind and was taken aback. Behind her, the English line was thrown into confusion.

The *Revenge* ran to leeward of the crippled *Intrepid* to cover her, and when, in turn, *Princess Louisa* was similarly discomforted, the *Trident* made the same gesture of aid and succour. Very soon the English line had a great gap in it and was in danger of being destroyed piecemeal. In the midst of this misfortune, the vision of Mathews rose before Byng's eyes and ended his one chance of salvaging something from the wreckage of his plan.

The fatal gap could be closed by *Ramillies* setting more sail and, breaking the line, steering to overtake the struggling mass of ships ahead of her. This Byng just would not authorise, despite the urging of his captain, Arthur Gardiner. Long-range firing by the English rear soon broke out all along the line. Meanwhile, Galissonière was seeking to pass his squadron through that gap and thus close the trap around West. The destruction of the English van appeared imminent.

Thankfully, before this movement by the French could be effected, *Revenge*, *Trident* and *Ramillies* finally came up, reinforced by the *Deptford*, which had earlier been detached to leeward. Seeing himself thwarted, the French commander now made off rapidly to the north-west and all further attempts by Byng to close them before nightfall came to naught.

The French had retreated but they inflicted much damage on the English van and Byng was therefore at a disadvantage should conflict resume. Fortunately, the French seemed content with their achievement of avoiding serious battle and did not seek to press home their advantage. The lack of French enterprise yet again saved our fleet, but it was not to save the commander. Byng now convened the fateful Council of War to decide what he should do next.

In fact, he had already decided what he must do, and that was retire at once. He thought that Minorca was doomed anyway (and nobody at the time disagreed with him) and that he must therefore fall back to protect Gibraltar. According to the facts, as they were known at the time, he felt justified in this course of action. He had no forebodings, for once, that he had not acted correctly. His report of the battle, though hardly a model of clarity, was expressed with a quiet satisfaction of having done his best. Alas for him, this report did not reach London until after the French admiral's description of the battle, which, needless to say, announced a victory. By the time Byng's account lay on the desks of the government the mob was howling for a scapegoat and there was an almost indecent haste in higher circles to lay that particular honour upon Byng himself.

On 3 July the frigate *Antelope* arrived at Gibraltar where Byng was all a-bustle preparing his fleet for sea once more to resume hostilities. The *Antelope* anchored and revealed herself to be carrying a new commander-in-chief, Hawke, and a letter from the Admiralty notifying Byng of the fact that he was relieved owing to His Majesty's dissatisfaction with his conduct in that 'the French (though inferior to you in force) kept before the harbour, and obliged you to retreat'. They also thoughtfully enclosed a copy of Galissonière's report for Byng to read, on which they had based this decision, even though they had not yet even read Byng's own account.

Quite naturally Byng was indignant, to say the least, but sailed for home in the *Antelope*, full of fight and expecting an apology once the facts became known. Instead, he found himself placed under arrest and, in due course, facing a court martial.

It was not until 14 December that the Admiralty issued an order for the trial to Vice Admiral Thomas Smith, a distant relation of Byng and known as 'Tom of Ten Thousand', to try Byng on the charge that 'he did withdraw, or keep back, and did not do his utmost to take, seize, and destroy the ships of the French king'. Furthermore that 'he did not do his utmost to relieve St Philip's Castle in His Majesty's island of Minorca'. Of the first part of the charge there was, of course, little evidence to support the allegation, other than small breaches of the Fighting Instructions. It was the second charge that really applied, in order to assuage public outcry at home and cover up the government's embarrassment. But Byng could only be tried for his conduct in the battle itself, and thus paragraph 12 of the Articles of War was applied.

Unfortunately, since the Toulon affair, those found guilty of breaking this article found themselves without the option of mercy that earlier forms had contained. Thus, whereas up to the War of the Austrian Succession the sentence had read 'shall suffer death, or such other punishment as the circumstances of the offense [sic] shall deserve, and the court martial shall judge fit', now every word after 'death' had been suppressed. Death remained the only option open to the court should the charge be proven. Only the traditional intervention of the Crown's mercy could alter that.

The court assembled aboard the *Prince George* in Portsmouth harbour on 28 December 1756 and sat for a month (other than Sundays). Three rear admirals, Holbourne, Norris and Broderick, and nine captains formed the court. Among the latter were names that were to become well known in the years ahead, Holmes, Bentley and a certain Keppel. However much the baying of the mob and the machinations of the politicians trying to clear their yardarms of any guilt or the recent Admiralty Board re-shuffle and changes in government might have affected the national opinion, there was never any doubt about the impartiality of the court itself. However, they were tied strictly to the rules as they stood.

Temple West was the first witness and his testimony was more noticeable for his own trumpet blowing than any attempt to vindicate Byng. He completely ignored the error made by Captain Andrews, which had so spoilt Byng's approach plan, and held out stoutly that his van had beaten that of the enemy unaided. He made no concession that the enemy turn-away might have been a pre-arranged plan. More damaging to Byng, he did not commit himself to commenting on any reasons why he was not immediately supported. The question put to him that most hurt was on whether he felt that the wind and the weather were such at that critical juncture that Byng could have supported him. His reply was, 'Yes, it appeared to me so: I saw no impediment', although he immediately qualified that statement by adding, 'I beg leave to observe that I don't say there was none, but that none appeared to me'. While no doubt strictly the truth, this was hardly helpful. The question was put to him again later, and he once more replied, this time without qualification, 'I know of nothing to prevent their doing so'.

Byng conducted his own cross-examination and obtained West's backing to most of the major decisions, including the reasons for the delay at Gibraltar and the unsatisfactory condition of most of his ships, but he overplayed his hand when framing his clincher. Although West admitted that owing to the superiority of the French in sailing power pursuit was out of the question, Byng pressed him further on a finer point of the battle itself, whereupon West again refused to back him.

Next in dock was General Blakeney, the defender of the fortress. When asked questions on the practicality of aid being landed from the fleet, he replied to good effect that it could have done. Under questioning later, he held fast to the opinion he could have held out until forced to admit by Byng that he had since publically stated the reverse.

On the actual battle itself, the captains were paraded before the court and the questions flew across the dock toward them, but their replies were as obscure in many cases as had been the field of battle on the day. Everitt of the *Buckingham* backed West in saying he saw no reason why the rear could not have made more sail and supported them, and lieutenants from the same ship made similar statements. Captain Harvey of the *Defiance* was slightly more forthcoming, being ideally placed to witness the reasons for many of the decisions made. He confirmed that the French could out sail our fleet and that their withdrawal seemed to be in response to a signal from the French flagship, rather than due to any damage inflicted by the English van. However, even though he described the hold-up caused by *Intrepid*, he stoutly held to his opinion that 'this could have been nullified by the rear running to leeward of her', which was something the court could judge and that to press him for opinions was not in accordance with correct procedures of the court. All true, and the court was out of line in attempting to force him thus, but it was of no help to Byng.

Captain Lloyd of the *Chesterfield* also made the statement that the British rear could have closed if more sail had been set. However, under questioning by Byng, Lloyd was forced to concede that it was *Revenge's* sluggish clearing of *Intrepid* and likewise by *Trident* of *Princess Louisa* that had caused most of the delay. Captain Baird of the *Portland* conceded that the turn-way by the French van was due more to their wishing to avoid action than from any damage inflicted by West's squadron and Byng's case began to look good.

Having thus established that it was the obstructions caused by the *Intrepid* and *Princess Louisa* that Byng's case for not closing the enemy rested upon (they accepted his method of approach without criticism as it was concentration of the van as per the book), the evidence of the commanding officers of these two vessels was awaited with considerable interest.

First up was Captain Young of *Intrepid*. Right from the start he refused to admit that it was through any fault of his that the rear had been delayed. Indeed, he refuted any damage at all to his command until after she had turned broadside to the enemy. Asked whether he noticed his ship was causing an 'impediment' to Byng's division, he seemed to evade the issue. He implied, if nothing else, that he was too busy doing his duty to wonder why others were not doing theirs. When asked how long it was after his ship had been damaged that the other ships astern of him passed him to leeward, he replied: 'Not much above three-quarters of an hour, I believe. It can't be much above.' He also stated that Byng could have closed despite this, had he set more sail, but that they were never closely engaged. He did admit that 'some of our ships' opened fire later.

Young's subsequent answers were no less tinged with sarcasm, and he felt more could have been done to close the range. Asked about signals at the height of the crisis, he revealed much of himself by stating flatly, 'I took no notice of any signals after the signal for battle was made'. A Nelsonic touch? Perhaps, but he seemed aloof to the fact that the reason why the rear could not close was because he was in the way. 'I did not see the ship astern. I did not look for her', was another gem. How then, asked Byng, if that was the case, could he judge that he was not causing an impediment to the rest of the fleet? The reply was enlightening: 'I answer for my own ship, that I made no impediment to any other ship's closing'.

The captain of the *Revenge*, when questioned on why it had taken so long for him to clear the *Intrepid*, replied that there had been no signal he could see giving him permission to quit the line so he had sent a boat over to Young asking such permission, but he denied that this had held up the rest. He could not to leeward without permission; why then did he not pass to windward? 'I could not think of withdrawing from the enemy', was Cornwall's reply. If then he was so hidebound by the rules and regulations, why did he not apply them, pressed Byng, asking him directly: 'What does the twenty-fourth Article of the Fighting Instructions direct a captain to do?' Cornwall then read out the article in full to justify his actions.

Thus it continued. It became more and more evident from the answers that nobody was going to admit to hanging back from battle, but, equally, nobody was prepared on the day to take any risks by breaking the line of battle, no matter what the justification, certainly not Byng himself. This was brought out by the testimony of Captain Gardiner. Upon sail being shortened at the first delay, *Intrepid*'s dithering, he had turned to his admiral with the suggestion that instead more sail should be made to set an example to those astern and thus quickly close the enemy. Byng's reply was illumination itself:

> You see, Captain Gardiner, that the signal for the line is out, and that I am ahead of the *Princess Louisa* and Durell, and you would not have me, as Admiral of the Fleet, run down as if I was going to engage a single ship. It was Mr Matthew's misfortune to be prejudiced by not carrying his force down together, which I shall endeavour to avoid.

In his final summing up, delivered by the Judge Advocate, the same attitude of mind is revealed in his two prefacing observations, which included the line: 'no commander of a particular ship has a right to deviate from the established discipline and rules of the Navy, contained in the Fighting Instructions.' Byng also excused any delay in making more sail to clear the obstructing ships by stating that as the French showed willingness to fight at first there was 'no occasion to hazard a disorder by crowding too much sail and making the attack with precipitation, contrary to the invariable practice of every prudent, good or great officer, heretofore in similar cases'.

Byng himself called but two witnesses, Gardiner and his secretary, George Lawrence. The defence concentrated on proving Byng was innocent on four main points: needless delay at Gibraltar; proving he could not have landed troops to reinforce the garrison; that he showed no 'backwardness or criminal misconduct' during the battle itself; and that it was impossible for him to have followed up with another attack afterwards. On 21 January, the court retired to consider their verdict and took six days of deliberations to do so.

How the court resolved the dilemma was torturous. They could not deem it possible to acquit him of all blame for the loss of Minorca, but they had to sentence him on his conduct at the battle itself. Cowardice and treachery were obviously unthinkable charges to level against Byng, so it had to be negligence or nothing. Negligence, under the Article 12, as we have seen, now meant death, but death was not what they had in mind at all. What to do? Their answer was to pass sentence but to enter a strong plea to the king for mercy, which, all assumed, would be forthcoming.

So it was done, the verdict delivered being that the court 'do therefore unanimously adjudge the said Admiral John Byng to be shot to death, at such time and on board such ship as the Lords Commissioners shall direct'. However, then they added their important rider, by which they hoped all would be set right:

> ... they did not perceive any backwardness in him during the action, or any mark of fear of confusion, ether from his countenance or behaviour, but that he seemed to give his orders coolly and distinctly, and did not seem wanting in personal courage and from other circumstances, the court do not believe that his misconduct arose either from cowardice or disaffection, and do therefore unanimously think it their duty most earnestly to recommend him as a proper object of mercy.

On 27 January the court composed a document sent to the Lords Commissioners of the Admiralty, setting out in full their problem and their recommendations thus:

> We the underwritten, the president and members of the court martial, assembled for the trial of Admiral Byng, believe it unnecessary to inform your lordships, that in the whole course of this long trial, we have done our utmost endeavour to come at truths, and to do the strictest justice to our country and the prisoner; but we cannot help laying the distresses of our minds before your lordships on this occasion, in finding ourselves under a necessity of condemning a man to death, from the great severity of the 12th article of war, part of which he falls under, and which admits of no mitigation, even if it should be committed by an error in judgement only, and therefore for our consciences sake, as well as in justice to the prisoner, we pray your lordships, in the most earnest manner, to recommend him to His Majesty's clemency.

However, both the Admiralty and the king felt resentful that the court should have shifted the blame in this manner. On Byng's side, many felt that the whole thing was illegal, both Lord Temple and Admiral Forbes expressing this opinion, while against him was Admiral Boscawen, who was vehement in his argument that the verdict should stand. Even the French expressed horror at the sentence, but George closed his harsh mind to all pleadings and petitions, as did Lord Anson. The Admiralty, divided as it was, passed the whole thing along to the king on 9 February, along with a 'Memorial' in which their doubts on the legality of the sentence were noted. They appealed to the sovereign's 'wisdom and determination'. His Majesty showed ample of the latter quality but none of the former.

Angry that the buck had finally stopped with him, wanting no part of it, he decided to play the part of the autocrat. Although one cannot condone his decision one can perhaps understand his vexation at being served by men in both government and Admiralty who would not make any decisions of their own. Nor, under the constitution, did he have the power to alter the sentence passed by parliament. What he could do, all he could do, was either confirm or exercise the Royal Pardon. The question of legality might prove a possible loophole and so a panel of twelve judges was assembled under Lord Chief Justice Baron Mansfield. Most of them owed their power and position to the former Newcastle adminis-tration and, not surprisingly, they delivered their findings in short order, declaring them perfectly legal. There was no way out of the dilemma that way.

Members of the court were by now horrified at the way things were developing and several times tried to intercede with the king to grant the necessary pardon. The wording of Article 12 was attacked in parliament as being 'Blundering and absurd'. Its repeal and alteration was sought. All too late! Keppel, a Member of Parliament himself, asked to be absolved from his oath of secrecy so that he might speak freely on the deliberations of the court itself. Pitt, in an audience with the king, expressed the view that the House was in favour of a pardon. Temple added his voice. To all of which the king replied sourly, 'that he thought him guilty of cowardice in the action, and therefore could not break his word, they had forced him to give to his people, to pardon no delinquents'.

The execution was now postponed while parliament wrangled to and fro over a bill to release the members of the court from their oaths of secrecy; the mem-bers themselves got cold feet and in the end the bill was rejected by the House of Lords. Byng's fate was now finally decided; the maze of alternatives had been explored and found to be but cul-de-sacs.

On 14 March 1757, John Byng was made to kneel on the quarterdeck of the French prize *Monarque* (Captain John Montague) in Portsmouth harbour. He was blindfolded and, at midday, a party of Royal Marines in three ranks faced him at point-blank range. He uttered a brief prayer and his conduct throughout was calm and dignified. It made a great impression on all those who witnessed it. Byng dropped his handkerchief, and the front two ranks fired.

6 UNCERTAINTY OFF USHANT (1778)

It will come as no surprise to the reader that when the French decided to take advantage of our commitment in North America to enter the war against us in 1778, British preparations were once more found wanting. As previously, the danger had long been recognised, by Lord Sandwich among others. Regrettably, the king's friends, under the leadership of Lord North, held all the high offices and were reluctant to precipitate events by early mobilisation of the fleet. Not until March, when the Franco-American alliance was announced, did the man-ning of the fleet receive serious consideration. By that date, the French had sixty battleships ready for combat, well backed up with supplies and very ably led. In the moment of crisis the man chosen to lead the fleet was Admiral of the Blue Augustus Keppel and, as his third-in-command, Vice Admiral Sir Hugh Palliser, a member of the Board of Admiralty, was appointed. This was a not uncommon practice at that period.

Although assured that the state of the fleet was satisfactory, Keppel found that only twenty from a total of forty-two battleships at his disposal were in fact ready for sea. The condition of the remainder left a great deal to be desired. Indeed, of those twenty, only half a dozen were, in his opinion, 'fit to meet a seaman's eye'. Keppel himself had been reluctant to take command of the fleet when his political opponents held the government, but was finally persuaded to do so by Sandwich. Keppel was a staunch Whig and, although a Member of Parliament himself, held that naval affairs should be above political squabbles. Unfortunately, Palliser was of opposite persuasion, not only a Tory but also an active one. Surrounded as he was by the king's men, it can be seen that right from the start the position of Keppel was a delicate one, should all not go well.

Augustus Keppel was born in 1725, and had enjoyed a distinguished career at sea up to the time of his appointment as C-in-C. As captain of the *Torbay* during the Seven Years War in the Western Squadron, and particularly for his conduct at the Battle of Quiberon, he had shone. He was commodore of the squadron that had captured Belleisle and had commanded, with distinction, the Inshore Squadron during the capture of Havana in 1762. The king had chosen him as a commander-in-chief elect in 1776, just in case France should enter the lists against us, and his appointment was held to be popular by both the nation and the fleet. Although his political persuasion was to the extremes of the Whig party (he backed Rockingham), he swallowed his prejudices enough to conduct a long exchange of letters with Sandwich, pointing out the many deficiencies in his fleet. In rectifying these faults, he received the backing of the Admiralty in most of them, as that body seemed anxious to make amends for their previous neglect.

Sir Hugh Palliser was two years Keppel's junior. The son of an army officer, Palliser had been a captain under Saunders at Quebec and had served in the Mediterranean during the Seven Years War. After a period as Governor of Newfoundland, he had been appointed comptroller of the navy in 1770 and was made a baronet by the king three years later. His other claim to fame was as the patron of Captain James Cook, but it was just prior to the rebellion in the American colonies that he had replaced Lord Bristol at the Admiralty, where he worked closely with Sandwich. He had a quick temper coupled with strong political views. However, his loyalty to Keppel was initially beyond dispute, and he was a brave and able commander in action.

Keppel's second-in-command was Sir Robert Harland, who had been in command of the East Indies squadron until relieved by Commodore Sir Edward Hughes in 1774, but he must play only a subsidiary role in the story as here related.

By dint of much labour, Keppel contrived to get twenty ships in a good state or order by June with which to face the French, manning the vessels being the major problem as always. This force duly put to sea, but the Admiralty, aware of the strength of their opponents, gave strict instructions to Keppel that he was in no way to become involved in a naval battle if he found himself outnumbered. It would appear that, having appointed him in command of what few ships there were, they feared his reputation as a fighter and thought that he might accept odds that would result only in destruction of the fleet before other ships could be made ready to reinforce him. It was an overdue admission of Torrington's 'Fleet-in-being' doctrine, forced upon the Royal Navy by their own neglect. Such a policy naturally did not commend itself to Keppel, but, when he found himself up against a fleet of thirty-two battleships soon afterwards off Ushant, he curbed his own feelings and obeyed orders. He refused combat and returned to Portsmouth. It must have been gall and wormwood to such a fighter.

Keppel determined never again to back off from a battle in this way; his decision was helped by the further reinforcing of his fleet and then he again put to sea. His tactical retreat, although approved by the Admiralty, of course, found no more favour with either His Majesty or his loyal subjects in 1778 than it had in 1690, and this may well have reinforced Keppel's resolve. Palliser himself did much to cool down the feelings that the first withdrawal had blown up between Keppel and Sandwich.

Meantime, the French fleet, under the Comte d'Orvilliers, had again thrown down the challenge and when first sighted, on 23 July, some 25 leagues west of Ushant, the French fleet totalled thirty-two ships. In fact, two of the French battleships never got into the fight, so the opponents were equally matched, with a slight advantage in weight of ordnance on the British side. Seeing that his previous superiority in numbers had gone in this second encounter, d'Orvilliers was no longer eager to become involved and attempted to escape out into the Atlantic. A long chase now followed, which lasted four days, during which time the British ships gradually overhauled the fleeing enemy. Ushant was now left far behind. It had been noon on the 23rd when the French had first been sighted by the *Valiant* and, despite crowding on full sail, Keppel was unable to close with his hull-down opponent until the 27th. This was due to a change of wind and d'Orvilliers realised that he must make some stand, even only briefly, to postpone the inevitable.

The French plan was by now usual French response. Observing Keppel's line was straggled out from the long chase, d'Orvilliers planned to turn briefly on his British tormentor by turning downwind and taking the British van from the windward. The French admiral planned thus to engage the leading British ships on an opposite tack and hope that his broadsides into the rigging of his opposite numbers would so cripple them as to make his ultimate escape a certainty. The

Frenchman had no intention of obliging Keppel in the latter's desire for a prolonged combat at close quarters, much as the British would have desired it.

The disposition of the fleets before the French fleet wore was as follows. In
the British van was Sir Robert Harland's squadron: *Monarch* (74), *Hector* (74),
Centaur (74), *Exeter* (64), *Duke* (90), *Queen* (flag) (90), *Shrewsbury* (74),
Cumberland (74), *Berwick* (74) and *Stirling Castle* (64). The British centre, with
Keppel flying his flag in the *Victory* (100) was formed by the *Courageux* (74),
Thunderer (74), *Vigilant* (64), *Sandwich* (90), *Valiant* (74), *Foudroyant* (80), *Prince
George* (90), *Bienfaisant* (64) and *Vengeance* (74), with the flagship ahead of the
Foudroyant. Finally came Sir Hugh Palliser with the *Worcester* (64), *Elizabeth* (74),
Defiance (64), *Robust* (74), *Formidable* (flag) (90), *Ocean* (90), *America* (64),
Terrible (74), *Egmont* (74) and *Ramillies* (74). The French van under the Comte du
Chaffault comprised the *Dauphin Royal* (70), *Duc de Bourgogne* (80), *Alexandre* (64),
Bien-Aime (74), *Couneonne* (flag) (80), *Palmier* (74), *Saint-Michel* (64), *Indien* (64),
Glorieux (74), *Amphion* (50) and *Vengeur* (64). The French centre, with the Comte
d'Orvilliers with his flag in *Bretagne* (110), was formed by the *Reflechi* (64), *Ville
de Paris* (90), *Actif* (74), *Magnifique* (74), *Fendant* (74), *Eveille* (64), *Actionnaire* (64),
Orient (74) and *Artesien* (64). Finally, the French rear, under the Duc de Chartres,
consisted of the *Sphinx* (64), *Robuste* (74), *Roland* (64), *Fier* (50), *Zodiaque* (74),
Saint-Esprit (flag) (84), *Intrepide* (74), *Triton* (64), *Solitaire* (64), *Conquerant* (74) and
Diademe (74). Of the French ships both the *Duc de Bourgogne* and *Alexandre* of the
van failed to get into action. Both sides had numerous frigates present and in the
field the French outnumbered the British by nine to four.

With such a formidable order of battle a daunting struggle might have well
been expected, but such was far from the case. As Lord Robert Manners was to
write later, 'It was more a skirmish than an action', and Palliser confirmed this,
although his squadron was more heavily involved than anyone else and had as
many casualties as both the other two British squadrons combined. Palliser wrote
that 'we at last were only able to skirmish with them, for it can't be called a battle
as we could not bring them to general engagement'.

Nonetheless, it was hot for a while and, in the initial stages, the fleets passed
by each other on opposite courses at close range. While the heavy Atlantic swell
made it impossible for the French to open their lower gun ports and deploy their
heaviest artillery, they plied the British rigging to good effect. Keppel wrote that
'The object of the French was at the masts and rigging, and they have crippled
the fleet in that respect beyond any degree I ever before saw'. In reply, the British
gunners wrought some execution upon the hulls and upper works of their opponents sufficiently to dispel any faint thoughts d'Orvilliers might have entertained
to linger too long on the field of battle.

After the first pass, it was the British rear, Palliser, that had borne the brunt of
the enemy fire in this respect, being engaged in turn with the French centre and

rear as well as the van. The flagship of Palliser's squadron, *Formidable*, was one of the hardest hit but the admiral refused to leave his men. By contrast, the British van was in good order and Sir Robert Harland sought to come to grips with the enemy and finish the job by turning into the wind and following them on the same tack. In this intent he was stopped by Keppel, who wished to re-concentrate his force, and this left the French able to draw clear as they had all along planned. This should have been the end of the action had not the sight of crippled British ships drifting out of line to leeward proved too much of a temptation for the French commander-in-chief.

When the French fleet again wore, intent now on annihilating Palliser's damaged ships, Keppel signalled for line ahead, turning downwind himself. If these instructions had been followed the British fleet would once again have been formed 'Conterminous with the enemy', and the French would again have been faced with the set-piece battle for which they had no stomach. While Harland in the van quickly complied, Palliser, with his squadron in some disarray, merely acknowledged and made no move to drop back into place once more. Keppel's move had thwarted d'Orvilliers, but unless line was again formed the approaching dusk would frustrate the British chance of a decisive action.

Increasingly puzzled by Palliser's inaction, as he saw it, Keppel did not perhaps realise just how damaged some his ships were. Keppel repeated his signal, twice, but still with no visible result. Seeing his chance slipping away, Keppel then made individual signals to each ship in Palliser's squadron, ordering them to join his flag. Only then was the line again re-formed, but by then night had fallen. When last seen, though, the French were to leeward and forming themselves into a parallel line, so hopes were raised that the battle would, after all, be continued the next day. Alas, when dawn came only three of the enemy were in sight and these immediately made off to the south-east.

Keppel commented:

It is uncertain whether those three ships had not observed the motions of the rest of their fleet during the night, or whether they were left to lie to leeward of us, and, by showing lights, to make us believe they waited for us in line to leeward as at dusk and thereby deceived us and covered their retreat.

Keppel's frustration and indignation at such tactics was shown in his comments to Sandwich after the battle. 'That I have beat the French there cannot be a doubt, and their retreat in the night is shameful and disgraceful to them as a nation after the fair opportunity I gave them to form their line.' Familiar sentiments to students of British naval history, it might have been Jellicoe so lamenting after Jutland in 1916 or Cunningham the morning after Calabria in 1940. But then, as ever, the chance to destroy the enemy had passed never to recur.

The British fleet returned to harbour disappointed, but not ashamed. They had done their utmost, for, as Admiral Jervis observed, equal fleets cannot produce decisive actions unless they are both determined to fight it out or one of the commanders misconducts his line. In his report on the action, Keppel was ample in his praise, not a word about Palliser's seemingly strange behaviour. There was no note of censure, instead Keppel noted that 'the spirited conduct of Sir Robert Harland, Sir Hugh Palliser and the Captain of the Fleet deserves much commendation'. That they were heroes all can now be doubted; indeed, it was subsequently proven that the captain of the *Duke*, William Brereton, was drunk on both the day before and the day of the battle. Keppel, it seemed, was not looking for any scapegoats at this time as the disappointment he blamed, correctly, chiefly on a reluctant enemy.

All may then have been well had not a article appeared in *The General Advertiser and Morning Intelligencer*, an anti-government newspaper, signed 'E', which violently criticised Palliser's conduct and blamed him for the failure to renew the battle the next day. Although the offending article was not published until 15 October, Palliser reacted strongly. He cornered Keppel in London and asked him to sign a complete denial of the allegation and, when Keppel demurred, he wrote his own version of the battle, which was published in many leading newspapers between 3 and 6 November. Nor was Palliser merely satisfied with defending his own conduct thus; enraged, he had gone on to criticise Keppel. Palliser wrote, 'I have only favour to hope for, that is that I may not be out of the way when Parliament meets.'

Palliser was as good as his threat. The result was a slanging match in the House, which took matters out of control. Finally, in full self-righteous flow, Palliser wrote a letter on 9 December, demanding that Keppel be brought before court martial for misconduct and neglect of duty. This was not only a stupid and vainglorious step to take, but it was to prove his undoing.

Had Palliser merely wished to clear his own name, as he all along stated, the correct way to go about it was to ask for a court martial on himself. He was to be granted this eventually, but by then everything that had happened on that day, including his disobedience to the signals, would have come out. There was never much doubt that Keppel would emerge with honour, for the public mood was with him. No doubt Palliser was bolstered by the knowledge that the king was on his side, the latter having written to Sandwich that 'This must make an eternal breach between the two Admirals, and occasion much ill-humour among those concerned in that day; but Palliser could not avoid the step he has been drove to without the greatest blame'.

There were other factors that locked these two famous seamen into needless conflict, apart from their political followings and the rabble of pressmen determined – as always – to make cheap capital out of the situation. Palliser may have stood on his offended dignity more than usual because he was, in the main, a self-made man who rose to the heights largely by his own efforts. He had achieved his promotions in rank later than Keppel, the aristocrat, and may have resented that fact. In the aftermath of the battle, Sandwich appointed Palliser lieutenant-general of marines, which Keppel deeply resented. Although Palliser was to resign that appointment in 1779, this may have caused Keppel's change of attitude, which hitherto had been to play the whole affair down. Palliser, also, had been a Roman Catholic and this might have made him over-sensitive to public opinion.

Thus, the whole affair moved to a climax with the inevitability of a Greek tragedy. Palliser's charges were specific. Keppel was accused of attacking in disorder, failing to support his hard-pressed rear immediately after the first pass, calling off the battle prematurely, turning away from the enemy and not pursuing them finally. Palliser's best friends could have told him that such charges could not possibly withstand close examination; indeed several of them did so, but to no avail.

Efforts were made in the House to question whether the Admiralty itself could nullify the whole thing and, during the course of these debates, the whole basis of the court martial procedure was itself questioned. This was but the first of several unprecedented events surrounding these trials, which made them unique and really relegated the question of guilt or innocence of the two parties to a subsidiary importance as far as the historian is concerned.

When, in December 1779, the point was raised of whether the Admiralty could simply just refuse to accept the charges at all, and whether they could with any officer thus accused, the Admiralty replied that they had no choice in the matter whatsoever. Once charges were made and correctly framed they could only receive them and give necessary directions for the trial. However, it was then admitted that if the charges were loosely worded, frivolous or inaccurately drawn up, then Their Lordships could examine in case, for these reasons, no proper defence could be made or any positive conclusion reached. Nevertheless, they point out that in this case none of these conditions applied as Palliser had made specific charges, correctly framed. They could therefore either prejudge the truth, which was out of the question, or admit them to be fit to send for constituting a court martial.

Wait a minute, replied the opposition in effect; Their Lordships could not have it both ways! They claimed that this would establish a principle which would henceforth leave every superior officer at the mercy of a junior who might be motivated by reason of malice, rage or folly (a hint perhaps that these might be Palliser's movers). The Admiralty could not elect to prejudge some cases as fitting of court martial procedures and others not and then claim that they could not prejudge at all. Either everything was fit or everything must be examined. There was much scratching of heads and learned Crown lawyers pored over the mess, finally backing the Admiralty's ambiguous viewpoint.

The age and health of Keppel brought about another precedent, for it was felt that the customary practice of always holding the court aboard a warship might prove too taxing for him. On 16 December a special bill was enacted that allowed the trial to be held ashore instead and this, nowadays, is more the rule than the exception, if only for lack of ships. It was unfortunate in Keppel's case, for his supporters swarmed into Portsmouth and during the proceedings they then influenced the judges by their conduct, openly hissing and booing, or applauding, according to how the evidence was going.

The court assembled initially aboard the *Britannia* on 7 January and was then adjourned to the governor's house at Portsmouth. The President was Admiral of the White Sir Thomas Pye and comprised four other admirals, Buckle, Montague, Arbuthnot and Roddam, along with eight captains – the Judge Advocate, George Jackson, calling out their names in rank and seniority until enough had answered from those assembled. This meant that several who had been summoned to give evidence were passed over. When Captain Walsingham objected to this, another huddle was gone into and reached the conclusion that 'if any officer, entitled by his rank to sit, is either prosecutor, party, or witness, the person next in authority must supply his place'.

Nor was the end to the technicality wrangle thrown up. Palliser claimed the right to reply to Keppel's submitted defence and again the court had to be cleared while the legality of this point was looked into. Once more they found against Palliser, the court's opinion being that a prisoner may submit his defence either verbally or in writing and a prosecutor had no right to reply. Furthermore, many questions of opinion were submitted during the trial, a point on which, it may be recalled, Captain Harvey of the *Defiance* had been adamant in refusing during Byng's trial, but here it was held to have numerous precedents and was allowed.

Finally, to run ahead of ourselves a little, the inconvenience caused by the length of the proceedings led the officers to submit a letter to the Admiralty calling for periods of adjournment; hitherto the rule had been that once the trial commenced the officers of the court were to remain 'aboard' until it terminated. The request was agreed to.

The trial itself was full of accusation and hint, all of which was duly played upon, and the washing of the navy's dirty linen in public was done in a very complete manner. Keppel requested that the ships' logs should be produced in evidence; Palliser said that after they had given their evidence it should suffice that the logs be left for examination to save time, which was agreed to. On 8 January, this was done and each master had to swear that the logs were exactly as they had stood during the course of the battle. Quite a sensation was caused when one of them, the master of the *Robust*, refused to swear, stating that his captain had altered the entries concerned since that time. In the event Captain Hood was cleared of deliberately falsifying the log to influence the court, but it did Palliser's cause no good at the time.

Sandwich himself was present on 28 January, to submit letters written to him by Keppel and Palliser, at the latter's request, but these were refused by the court as inadmissible and so Sandwich did not actually give evidence.

Keppel's reply to the charges was in the main the assertion that it was Palliser's failure to comply with his repeated signals to reform the line, which was really to blame for the enemy's escape. Thus, as expected, the fat was in the fire and it was not long before Sandwich was warning Palliser that moves were afoot in parliament by Keppel's friends for his own court martial. This satisfaction Palliser belatedly determined to deny them by requesting it himself. He was already resigned, by the antics of the mob and the press as well as the court, to the verdict expected on Keppel, 'from the very beginning, everything has been heard which was offered by the accused at any time, so almost everything which I have offered at any time has been refused'.

Indeed, the verdict was as predicted, the court finding on 11 February:

> ... that the charge is malicious and ill-founded, it having appeared that the said admiral, so far from having, by misconduct and neglect of duty, on the days therein alluded to, lost opportunity of rendering essential service to the state, and thereby tarnishing the honour of the British Navy, behaved as became a judicious, brave and experienced officer. The court do therefore unanimously and honourably acquit the said Augustus Keppel of the several articles contained in the charge against him, and he is hereby fully and honourable acquitted accordingly.

There was much public rejoicing by Keppel's self-appointed champions and a mob stoned Palliser's London home. Worse, many of the captains of the fleet signed a memorial calling on the king to remove Palliser from his posts. That worthy bowed to the public clamour and resigned them but, meantime, Keppel had in turn struck postures about his future as C-in-C. The Admiralty gladly used this as an excuse to dispense with him also. With some dignity, however, Keppel refused to prefer any charges against Palliser. Nevertheless, there was no avoiding the issue and the Admiralty therefore had to resort to the dubious practice of ordering a court in order to enquire into Palliser's behaviour on points arising from Keppel's trial. Jackson, the Judge Advocate of the Fleet, was appointed to conduct the trial and Palliser was so notified of their decision.

This court duly assembled aboard the *Sandwich* at Portsmouth on 12 April. Vice Admiral George Darby was President, with Rear Admiral Robert Digby and eleven captains, including two, Duncan and Cranston, who had sat on Keppel's court. They duly sat for another three interminable weeks; by this time most people were fed up with the whole issue. Eventually they acquitted Palliser, but the sting in the tails revealed how much they had resented the whole business. The court found that 'conduct and behaviour on those days were in many respects highly exemplary and meritorious; at the same time they cannot help thinking it was incumbent on him to have made know to his Commander-in-Chief the disabled state of the *Formidable*'. In other words, they accepted his excuse as to why he did not comply with his orders, but felt he had acted less than sensibly in not explaining matters at the time instead of months later. In truth, he hoped not to have to explain it at all, but had brought it all down upon himself.

These courts martial marked the end of the seagoing service of both men, and this at a time when Britain was hard-pressed at sea. Keppel spent the rest of his days at the Admiralty, becoming First Sea Lord with the departure of his arch-enemy North from government in March 1782. He died in 1786. Palliser had to make do with the governorship of Greenwich Hospital, and even this lowly post was opposed in parliament. He took the chance to speak on all the things that had vexed him about the trial, including omissions to the published version of the evidence, and did something to repair his tattered reputation. He died, unforgiving, ten years after his old C-in-C, a bitter old man.

Not until more than 150 years later did a Keppel and a Palliser serve together in the Royal Navy in perfect harmony once more. In the mid-1950s a new class of small frigates were built, which bore the names of famous officers. Some wag at the Admiralty decided to name one of these ships *Keppel* and another *Palliser*. Whether this was done in genuine ignorance of this odd juxtaposition, as some long-delayed conciliatory gesture or as a very private joke is uncertain, but the two names were again briefly united in the service of their country.

7 A FOUNDERING AT SPITHEAD (1782)

There have been many great disasters in the history of the Royal Navy, both in times of peace and of war. When great fighting ships, so invulnerable to the layman's eye, so extruding pride and power to the seamen that know them, are suddenly stricken, they leave huge gaps. The gaps are not just in the sea as it closes over such ships, not just in the immaculate formation of which they have formed a vital part, but also in the hearts of those who have known and loved them. Dramatic endings to famous warships are numerous and to each generation the shock comes fresh and anew. The destruction of the 'Mighty *Hood*' after a brief exchange of gunfire numbed the nation in the last war, just as did the sudden demise of the *Prince of Wales* and *Repulse* to aerial torpedo attack, an event which Churchill, whose unwise policies had contributed to their demise, confessed gave him the greatest shock of the entire war. More elderly people would have equated these wartime disasters with the similar blowing up of three British battlecruisers at the Battle of Jutland in 1916, or the mysterious explosions that sank the *Vanguard* and the *Natal* at their moorings in the same conflict. The loss of an earlier *Vanguard* and another great battleship, the *Captain*, will be touched upon later in these pages. At the time, these were all considered national disasters. Nonetheless, most of these could be explained away as hazards of war or nature, albeit with human elements contributing.

However, never has any great warship sunk so quickly, with such an enormous loss of life, much of it civilian, women and children, in such unlikely circumstances and conditions as did the *Royal George* in 1782. So great was the disaster, so complete and so unexpected, that it can still excite controversy to this day. Just how was it possible for a great three-deck ship-of-the-line, lying at anchor in the calm waters of Spithead, surrounded by a great fleet and with hardly a breath of wind to disturb her, plummet to the depths so fast and with such a grievous death list?

Launched in 1756, the *Royal George* was old, but not exceptionally so. Far older ships served with the fleets of all nations and others then present at the calamity went on to perform great deeds at a much greater antiquity. She was a 100-gun first rate, long used to serving as a flagship to many of the most distinguished admirals of her era. She had a long and honourable career with the fleet since she had first hoisted her colours. She was the largest ship of her time when first completed and one of only three such ships built for the Royal Navy, the others being the *Britannia* and the *Victory*, the smaller but handier 74s being more favoured.

The *Royal George* had first seen action under Admiral Hawke at his memorable victory at Quiberon Bay when he drove her in among the shoals and rocks in a full gale to destroy the French fleet cowering there in the winter of 1759. In 1762, she was laid up in ordinary at Plymouth with the ending of that war and here she remained for fifteen years.

During this period of idleness, the *Royal George* was overhauled just once, in 1768, but for the rest of the time she swung round her moorings in neglect. It was not until July 1778 that she was hastily re-commissioned with the renewal of the conflict with the succeeding defection of the American colonies and the preparations for intervention by the old enemy France becoming increasingly apparent.

We have seen, in the cases of Keppel and Palliser, to what low ebb the Royal navy had been allowed to lapse under the corrupt and inefficient Admiralty of Sandwich. Acting far too late, the number of ships that could be made ready and their condition was a national disgrace. It took a good nine months to get the *Royal George* ready to face the enemy again, and she was twice involved in minor accidents after that. With the refusal of Keppel to command again the Admiralty had to scrape the bottom of the barrel to find a seagoing commander to lead the shadow of a fleet into action. The name they came up with was Sir Charles

Hardy, but he had no option but to retreat in the face of the combined French and Spanish fleets when they appeared in the Channel, and thus *Royal George* saw no action in 1779.

In the following January, however, she was present at Rodney's relief of Gibraltar. Two of the Spanish Admiral de Langara's ships struck to her during the preceding action off Cape St Vincent. The *Royal George* thus further added to her reputation first gained at Quiberon when she had sunk an enemy battleship with a single broadside. Her next action was her last, capturing the *Courier* on 18 June in the Atlantic. She was then docked in 1780 to be copper-sheathed as protection against the ravages of the sea and the teredo worm. This could not disguise her growing list of defects, as she was well past her youth. On 9 October, for example, her rudder dropped from her sternpost and it had to be replaced by one cannibalised from another ship. In January she was damaged again, this time in a collision with the *Warwick* and later a merchantman also gave her a hard knock.

The records of Portsmouth dockyard registered that the *Royal George* at this time was 'in very bad condition'. Nothing had been done by October when it was recorded that she was making a lot of water. A month later Sandwich himself was noting that 'she must be docked'. This long overdue refit finally took place in March 1782, at Plymouth. How well was it done? It is common knowledge that at this time there was a great shortage of timber in the dockyards and that repairs to other ships had been less than fully or efficiently carried out. Was this the case with the *Royal George*?

Lewis records that 'it had been known to most officers, executive and dockyard alike, that she was in need of a major refit'. Was the attention she received at Plymouth such an overhaul? It seems unlikely, in the time allocated to her, but she was nonetheless pronounced 'fit for service'. Vice Admiral Milbanke was to state, quite positively, that:

> When she was docked at Plymouth I went over her. I saw her opened – there was not a sound timber in her. The officers of the yard said they would be able to *make her last the season*. They could scarce find fastenings for the repairs she underwent.

It sounds very much like a promise to patch up the old ship for the time being, which is hardly a major refit. George Aynon, the shipwright, confirmed this belief: 'the timbers were rotten ... the holes were eighteen inches apart. The timbers of both were rotten, and the trunnels.' With the best will in the world then, how could the dockyard have corrected such faults completely in the time allowed? They made no pretence at trying, as their statement to Milbanke indicated.

Nonetheless, she was pronounced fit for service, and duly took her place among the great concourse of ships assembled under Lord Howe at Spithead, in readiness to sail once more to the relief of Gibraltar, then five years under siege. Over thirty battleships, an equal number of frigates and more than 200 merchant vessels lay around her on 29 August 1782, all within sight of land. This great assembly made a brave sight and many ashore stopped more than once to gaze at such a concentration of British sea power. At the masthead of one of the largest battleships, the *Royal George* herself flew the flag of a much-loved and worthy officer, Rear Admiral Richard Kempenfelt. He was a brilliant officer, born in 1718, who had initiated many lasting reforms in the service, the most well known being his revolutionary system of signalling.

One other thing might have attracted the eye of any watcher on that calm day: the *Royal George* lay heeled over at an angle of more than 8 degrees. Why was this, was she in some kind of difficulty? Any sailor could have assured otherwise. She was deliberately heeled over thus in order to carry out some sort of repair below the waterline on one side. The method known as a 'Parliamentary Heel' was being employed to do this. It was an easy method, much favoured because of that, against the more complicated method of careening on a suitable sandbar. It might be thought that, with the knowledge of the vessel's condition, a docking might have been more prudent. It appears that the attention required was of so minor a nature that this was not thought worthwhile, if at all.

There were two ways this method could be carried out. The first was by hanging heavy casks of seawater from the ship's spars and along her sides. The second by running out the heavy guns on one side as far as they would go and shifting others over to add to the tilt. The former was known as the 'old, safe method', for, should any sudden squall strike the ship while thus vulnerable, the weights could quickly be cut free.

This first method, however, took a greater time to prepare, while running out the guns was faster and simpler, and not a great deal of extra time would be taken in hauling them back inboard, should the need arise. It was, without doubt, marginally more risky. In the circumstances then prevailing, with the ship preparing for sea, with barges and boats alongside and with the weather fair and the sea smooth, this risk was accepted by the *Royal George's* captain, Martin Waghorn. Admiral Kempenfelt did not interfere, even though he had been warned of the dangers by his old friend and companion, William Nichelson, master attendant at Portsmouth, who he had just visited on shore.

The cause of the trouble that had necessitated this attention was the minor problem of a blocked cistern pipe on the ship's starboard side, which had become fouled up. Its solution required that the water-cock, as it was termed, be replaced with a new one. To effect this repair there needed to be a heel on the ship of just a small angle, so the dockyard workers then employed could easily access it. The whole port battery was therefore run out while the guns of the starboard battery were hauled in amidships and secured.

Work then proceeded and two factors combined to make this simple and easy operation dangerous. For one thing, the *Royal George*, already heavily laden with stores for the pending voyage and carrying a crew of over 800 officers and men, was thronged with over 300 extra souls. These were the wives, sweethearts and children of the crew, plus a large number of 'ladies of the streets' come to bid farewell, in their various ways, to the men of the *Royal George*. It was common practice for such an influx to be permitted on the eve of sailing and the extra burden of all these supernumeraries added significantly to the displacement of the old ship.

Secondly, the angle of heel, although not in itself excessive to the eye, was dangerously close in fact to the critical mark, and brought the water level right up to the bottom ports on the lower gun deck, so that it steadily lapped into the ship. This was aggravated by the comings and goings of the many small boats alongside, which set up a localised chop that added to the influx. So much water indeed had come aboard that sailors were seen giving children boat rides in tubs inside the ship.

Nobody seemed seriously alarmed at first. Kempenfelt was in his cabin writing, a large group of officers was on deck supervising the loading, among them the officer of the watch Lieutenant John McKillop and the first lieutenant, George Saunders. The master, the gunner and the boatswain, despite instructions to the contrary, were all ashore. Had the ports on the heeled side of the ship been properly supervised they could have been closed, but they remained open to facilitate the loading of provisions. Nor were the scuppers plugged.

The angle of heel at the time was, in fact, less than a normal roll at sea, but there would have been very few occasions when the lower ports would have been open in such circumstances. The water continued to enter, the weight of newly loaded casks that had not been stowed away adding to the danger. Around 0900hrs alarm finally registered among some of those working below and the ship's carpenter, Thomas Williams, quickly went to the quarterdeck to raise a warning. Once there he was initially unable to make out which officer was in control, so he addressed his remarks to Lieutenant Monins Hollingbery. This worthy, with a reputation for ill temper, sent him below again with a flea in his ear.

Williams was so alarmed by what he now found there that, despite his earlier curt dismissal, returned to the quarterdeck and begged that the ship be immediately righted. The alleged response this time was, 'Dammne, Sir, if you can manage the ship better than I can you had better take command!' This remark was overheard by several of the seamen nearby. Nevertheless, the warning was finally taken, if not from the carpenter then from the master who was just arriving alongside in a small boat. He, Richard Searle, noticed all was far from well as he drew near and shouted out, 'She will sink! Give way!' Thus urging the boatman alongside he went up on deck and warned the captain that there was 'a great deal of water in the ship'.

By now the time was 0918hrs and the indefatigable carpenter again appeared on the quarterdeck at the same time as Searle and told Waghorn bluntly that the ship was settling. At once the alarm drum was sounded to right the ship, but, before anything much could be done to move the guns (although some of the crew had anticipated this order, but not enough), the end came with awesome suddenness.

Down below John Smart, gunners' yeoman, heard 'a great crack' below him and knew the ship had had her day. He quickly leapt from one of the after gun ports as the ship went down at 0920hrs. When she went, it was with such speed that most of her crew and visitors were caught completely by surprise. Very few managed to follow Smart's example. Most were trapped below – men, women and children – with no hope of survival. Of those fortunate few who managed to jump to safety, or who were swept out of the ship in her final convulsions as the air was forced out of her by the inrush of the sea, many were caught up in her great death sworl and sucked down. Others struggled in great masses, the non-swimmers pulling down those who could. Some managed at last to find a temporary sanctuary on one of her topmasts which still protruded from the water after she had settled almost upright on the bottom mud.

How many died will never be known for certain. For days afterward bodies were being washed up ashore in groups of thirty to forty at a time. Some 821 officers and men were recorded on the *Royal George*'s muster book but, as we have seen, a few of them were ashore, although not many for it had been forbidden. Of the visitors nobody has ever been able to do more than make a guess at the numbers. At least 300 women and children was accepted as a general figure. Of the total aboard that day, 255 seamen were recorded as being saved, as well as forty-seven Royal Marines. Captain Waghorn, Second Lieutenant Hollingbery, five other lieutenants, twelve midshipmen, two Royal Marine officers, the gunner, purser, boatswain and clerk were among those saved. Among those who went down with the *Royal George* were Kempenfelt himself, the first lieutenant, Saunders, the fifth lieutenant, McKillop, twelve midshipmen, six Royal Marine officers, the gallant Searle, the surgeon and the poor carpenter, whose warnings had so repeatedly fallen on deaf ears. Also among the dead was Waghorn's son.

The completeness of the tragedy was self-evident. The responsibility for so great a mishap was left for the court martial to ascertain. This court duly assembled aboard the *Warspite* in Portsmouth harbour on 7 September 1782. The President was Vice Admiral the Hon. Samuel Barrington, who had only recently struck his flag aboard the stricken ship, shortly before the disaster befell her. The members of the court were a distinguished company indeed: Vice Admirals Evans and Milbanke, Rear Admirals Hood and Hughes, Commodores Hotham and Leveson-Gower and Captains Allen, Moutray, Dalrymple, Duncan, John Jervis K.B. and Robert Faulknor. Despite the reputations of many of the officers there assembled, some historians have indicated the feeling that this court was both partial and corrupt. This author finds this allegation very hard to believe. The Judge Advocate was Williams Bettesworth.

The opening proceedings of the court were unusual in that, instead of being asked to plead guilty or not guilty to the charge, Captain Waghorn was asked the question: 'Do you know of any impropriety or negligence in the conduct of the officers or the ship's company of His Majesty's late ship *Royal George*, to occasion the loss of the *Royal George*?' Waghorn's reply was 'None at all'. The court then asked the collective assembly of ships' officers and men. 'Do you know of any impropriety or negligence in the conduct of Captain Waghorn to occasion the loss of that ship?' An unnamed representative replied for them all, 'None in the world'.

Captain Waghorn's narrative was then read out to the assembly. In it he revealed that the initial heel had proved insufficient and that to raise the side sufficiently for the carpenter to do his job he had shot rolled over. He wanted the job done quickly and in such a way that the offloading of supply vessels would not be hindered. He warned the carpenter not to 'bore too many holes in the old ship's bottom'. He had breakfast with Kempenfelt, who made no comment on the heel of the ship whatsoever.

On returning to deck he had been advised by Lieutenant McKillop that '…the water don't come up to any of the ports by a foot or more, and no water comes in at all'. Waghorn did not refer to the early visits to the quarterdeck by the carpenter until the last dire warning direct to himself, so presumably McKillop had remained mute on these. As neither man had survived the foundering, they could not be cross-examined. Midshipman Power was asked, 'Did she appear to have any such heel as to make you think her in danger?' Power replied, 'No, indeed she did not.'

George Aynon, the dockyard shipwright, gave a graphic picture of how things appeared to those doing the work:

> When we were boring these holes, a man came to us and said there was a deal of water in the hold. We asked him how much, and he said, 32 inches. My brother and I were observing to one another there must be a deal of water in the bilge if there was so much in the hold.
>
> The Carpenter, when his attention was called to the rotten timbers, observed that next time she came home she must go into dock to be repaired, for they had tied her up with riders as much as they could. My brother asked me whether I was afraid or not. I told him I was not afraid, but I should like to go up upon deck. I stopt [sic], and he immediately found the tier cable going from under him. I took up my cloathes [sic], carrying them on my back, and a man helped me out of the port.

Aynon was then asked whether he had heard anything crack when the ship went down and he replied that he did not, but added 'there was such a great cry of the people and noise of things rolling about, that it was impossible to distinguish anything else'.

One witness who did hear the old timbers giving way through gross overstraining of her rotten framing was the gunner's yeoman, who was in the lower gun deck gunroom on the starboard side of the ship. He, John Smart, was in a perfect place to attest to such an incident, and, being a responsible person (or he would not have held such a position), was able to state the facts quite clearly to the court. He was asked the question: 'Did you continue in the gunroom?' He replied, 'I did until I heard a great crack.' 'What crack did it appear to be?' 'It appeared to be a bodily crack.' 'Was it above or below?' 'Below.' 'What do you mean by a bodily crack?' 'She gave a great jerk or crack first, and, within a moment, another, and sent down. I jumped out of the starboard stern port.'

Now, there is an important difference between the implications of the words 'crack' and 'jerk'. A 'crack' would seem to indicate that timbers, rotten through and ancient, had finally given up the ghost and her bottom had fractured. By qualifying this with the words 'or jerk', Smart might have implied a sudden motion, which could have been caused by a final inrush of water into an already well-filled ship which thus brought about the final last plunge of the *Royal George*. If the latter was the case, then the heel of the ship would have suddenly increased and the court put this point to him. 'Did you observe the heel to be increased?' He replied, 'No, not in the least.' This answer apparently satisfied the court, for they did not examine him further on this vital point.

Lieutenant Durham was asked about the earlier reports of the carpenter. Did he appear to be alarmed at the time? Durham answered, 'Yes, very much so; but he was apt to be so, and as soon as I saw him come up on deck I said he was as much alarmed now as when the tiller was broke.' Was it then a case of him 'crying wolf' once too often that made the officers ignore his first warnings?

William Murray, a quarter gunner on the lower deck, stated: 'I was in the hold till half after eight. I saw no water coming up through the bottom. There was no water in the hold while I was there. The water was now within a few inches of the ports amidships.' He was asked, 'Did you look out?' 'No, I could not, for the water in the inside was almost level with the water out … Two ports had been lowered, abreast of the lighter, but not secured.' He commented to his mates that if the ship was not righted within a few minutes they would never right her.

Murray was then questioned on whether he had heard any shock, crack or indeed any noise just before the ship went down, and he replied that he did not, only the noise of the people and of the guns and shot shifting on the middle deck. He stated, firmly, that the water 'came in at no leak, but from the scuppers and the ports'. He also added the fact that the heel was increased more than normal because the provisions unloaded from the lighter were stacked on the port side and not struck down into the main hold.

The findings of the court were duly pronounced. They found that the ship had not been over heeled and that the captain, officers and company had used every exertion to right the ship as soon as the alarm was given. They continued:

> … the Court is of the opinion, from the short space of time between the alarm being given and the sinking of the ship, that some material part of her frame gave way, which can only be accounted for by the general state of decay of her timbers, as appears upon the minutes. The Captain, Officers and Ship's Company are acquitted of all blame.

That ended the court martial, but many centuries later it has not ended the arguments as to whether or not this was the true reason for the *Royal George*'s sudden demise. Brigadier Johnson made a minute study of all the available evidence and came to the conclusion that it was the steady flooding of the ship over a period of time that brought about a final critical condition in which a little extra water brought about the final catastrophe. He totally dismisses the evidence of Smart and points to many things that support his own view.

In particular, Johnson points out that when years later attempts were made to raise the wreck, the hull was moved bodily forward for a considerable distance without it breaking up. He contends that this would not have been possible had her bottom fallen out at the time of the disaster. Johnson also puts forward a variety of reasons why the court, in his view, should have preferred to attribute the blame to other sources than negligence by flooding. Cited thus are the disgust felt by serving officers at the inefficient Navy Board; an unwillingness to blame Waghorn for a disaster that had brought about the death of his son; and so on. Nobody, Johnson contends, other than Smart had heard 'a great crack' just before she went down. There are many other points he makes to forward his argument.

Against this viewpoint must be set the fact that there was ample evidence that the ship's timbers were in a terrible state. Johnson argues that so were the timbers of other ships but they survived for many years afterwards. Michael Lewis put forward the hypothesis of the last straw breaking the camel's back, pointing out that the great weight of the extra people aboard, plus her heel, 'perfectly safe in a normally safe ship, but highly hazardous in one whose bottom was on the point of giving out anyway', set in motion an inevitable train of events.

Who is right? The argument will no doubt go on forever. It can only be said with any certainty that both cases are, and will probably remain, not completely satisfactory. The verdict of the court martial, however, was final and stood. Waghorn and his officers, including the irascible Hollingbery, were fully exonerated.

8 TROUBLE WITH BREADFRUIT (1792)

Captain William Bligh of the *Bounty*; who does not know of him and his ship? What schoolboy has not had firmly implanted in his mind the vision of the ogre of the waves, arch-villain and demigod who ruled his unfortunate crew with a rod of iron and flogged them within an inch of their lives for the slightest display of spirit? Beginning with the infamous Sir John Barrow book of 1831, and taken to extremes by the usual factual distortions of Hollywood, Bligh has been accorded an 'honoured' place in the Villains' Hall of Fame the world over down the years.

Thankfully, Bligh's reputation has been somewhat modified more recently by the more thorough and accurate research of Bullocke, Danielsson and others, and the picture that emerges is no longer that of the implacable tyrant but more of a stubborn, insensitive man, a product of his age and the system. No harsher than many of his fellow officers, in surprising ways less so in his concern for his men. However, still, for all that, not a loveable character in the least.

Bligh was born in September 1754, the son of a Plymouth customs inspector. He was marked down early on for a naval career, his name being entered on the ships' books when he was 8, according to the practice of the time. However, before taking his allotted place in the service, he had a good local education. He was considered to be above average in this grounding compared to most of his fellow officers. The fact that his name was down as a captain's servant in the *Monmouth* at the tender age of 7 misled several early biographers, but it was not until 1770, when he was aged 16, that he actually joined HMS *Hunter* as an able seaman.

Bligh was promoted to full midshipman six months later, a post not a rank, and subsequently served in that position for five more years until 1776, including a three-year stint aboard the frigate *Crescent*. Bligh had no 'sponsor' in the service, and would have remained unremarkable but for the offer of a position as master aboard the *Resolution* in March of that year. This proved a major feather in his cap and set him on course for a distinguished career. The *Resolution* sailed with Captain Cook and the *Discovery* on that worthy's third voyage of exploration to find the North-West Passage, a voyage that took Bligh for the first time to the exotic world of the Pacific.

Already Bligh must have made his mark as a navigator of some merit or else Cook would not have chosen him, but this voyage gave him great scope and the opportunity to learn and improve these skills under the guidance of the master. After Cook had been killed by natives, the expedition returned to England in 1780, where Bligh married. Up until that time he had experienced no combat action at sea. This omission was rectified when, as warrant officer aboard the frigate *Belle Poule*, he fought in Admiral Hyde Parker's bloody action with the Dutch at the Dogger Bank in 1781.

Bligh's long sought-after promotion followed this battle, an indication that he had acquitted himself in combat. In September he became a lieutenant and served in a succession of frigates, but saw no further action other than being present at Lord Howe's relief of Gibraltar in 1782. With the end of the war Bligh found himself 'on the beach', but was given employment by his wife's uncle, Duncan Campbell, who ran a few trading ships to the West Indies. As commander and agent, he remained in this employ until the spring of 1787, although he had always wished to return to the service of the Crown if he was able. In this he had to thank Campbell once more, for, while he was away, that worthy used his considerable influence to have Bligh appointed captain of the *Berthia*.

Bligh's West Indian and Pacific connections had come together. To feed the plantation workers a more stable and cheaper diet, it had long been recommended that the South Sea breadfruit should be transplanted in the Caribbean, as growing conditions there were similar. The Royal Society offered a medal to anyone bringing this desirable state of affairs about, and the West Indian merchants raised the money to offer a bounty to go with it. Sir Joseph Banks, Cook's old patron, was involved in this scheme and thus the strands came together to give Bligh his big opportunity. Although Bligh received no promotion for his services, even though his experience was acknowledged, he considered the idea too good a chance to pass up. Bligh returned home to find the brand-new vessel, *Berthia*, fitting out at Hull. Taking command, Bligh lost no time in renaming her His Majesty's Armed Vessel *Bounty*.

Bligh was allocated a forty-five-man crew, a botanist and a gardener. A few of his crew Bligh, to his later misfortune, hand picked himself, among them a certain Mr Fletcher Christian. This worthy came from a similar background to Bligh, being a son of landed gentry. Christian had served as ship's boy on the *Cambridge* when Bligh had been a lieutenant aboard her and had later sailed with him to the West Indies. This friendship grew and Christian owed his later promotion to gunner to Bligh. Christian was selected, along with others from Bligh's West Indian or Pacific days, but the majority of the crew were unknown to him.

The *Bounty* finally sailed on 23 December, her original departure date having been delayed for three weeks by bad weather. This did nothing to improve Bligh's already notorious short temper. Many of his men described him as 'passionate' and it cannot be doubted that patience and tolerance were not among the captain's virtues. Nevertheless, he showed concern for his crew's well-being on the outward voyage, splitting the watches into three to give them more rest in the appalling weather conditions that they encountered and employing a fiddler at his own expense to entertain them.

Despite this, Bligh's abrasiveness and stickling for discipline soon sowed the seeds of unrest aboard the little ex-collier. For example, when two men objected to dancing, Bligh stopped their grog, a petty enough thing no doubt but so was their 'offence'. It was not until 11 March that he enforced harsher punishment. A seaman, Matthew Quintal, behaved insolently to him and the master and was duly rewarded with two dozen lashes. According to his own journal, Bligh appeared to regret that this step had to be taken. In his log Bligh wrote: '... and I had hopes I could have performed this voyage without punishment to anyone.' Justified it might have been, resented by the recipient it certainly was and from then onward Quintal nursed a brooding resentment.

Even prior to this episode there had occurred several instances of Bligh's inability to control his fierce temper at the most trivial of things. A cask of cheese was brought up on deck to be aired and, upon being opened, two were found to be missing. Hillbrant, the ship's cooper, reminded Bligh that two cheeses had, in fact, been sent to his house on orders of his clerk while the *Bounty* was in the Thames. Bligh's response to this simple, plain statement of fact was to fly into a rage. He threatened to flog the unfortunate Hillbrant if he so much as mentioned it again, and stopped the issue of cheese for both officers and men until the deficiency was made good.

Shortly after the *Bounty* had left Tenerife, Bligh decided to limit the biscuit ration in order to eke it out in case they were delayed later on in the long voyage. He issued two-thirds of the ration, making up the deficiency with pumpkin, but only 1 pound's worth, instead of 2 pounds of biscuits. He explained this to the men in a reasonable way, but pointed out that, as the pumpkins would not last long, they had to be consumed quickly. Nothing upsets sailors more than a suspicion that they are being short-changed on their rations. Some of the crew were unwise enough to voice their disapproval, upon which Bligh went off the deep end once more. 'You damned infernal scoundrels, I'll make you eat grass or anything you can snatch before I've done with you.'

It is probable that these measures, along with the care he took about the men's personal hygiene and their quarters (being introduced by Bligh from his past experience as things to help the men stay healthy), on being disputed, served to rouse his ire even further. There is nothing worse than ingratitude to upset the misunderstood benefactor.

The rounding of Cape Horn proved to be a terrible experience which, for a time, put a stop to such petty feuding and forced the whole ship's company to work together for their own survival. From 23 March to 11 April the *Bounty* tried, but failed, to make headway against the elements. In the end Bligh was forced to abandon the attempt and to try the Cape of Good Hope route instead; so they finally arrived at Simon's Bay on 22 May to refit.

The next major dissension took place when the *Bounty* reached Adventure Bay, off Tasmania on Brunei Island. A party had been sent ashore under Christian for fresh water and wood but, when Bligh followed them on land later to check on progress, he found that a row had broken out among them. William Purcell, the ship's carpenter, had refused to help in the carrying of the water, arguing with the master, John Fryer, that it was not his duty. Nor, it turned out, had Purcell done his own job fast enough, and Bligh threatened to withhold Purcell's provisions until he had done so. This did not change Purcell's attitude much, but at least the threat got the work done. Bligh also lost patience with Fryer, who several times received the rough edge of his captain's tongue. So, it was again an unhappy ship that set sail on 4 September.

Having now quarrelled with two of the most important of the ship's company, Bligh compounded affairs by falling out with the ship's surgeon, Thomas Huggan. A seaman named Valentine underwent treatment for asthma and, upon being bled, had subsequently died of septic poisoning. The news of his demise was brought to Bligh by the master's mate, Elphinstone, and not by the surgeon himself. Huggan proved himself a complete incompetent, being drunk most of the time. Although Bligh tried alternately reasoning with the surgeon and berating him, Huggan did not improve. The already sullen Fryer took Huggan's side in this, from his own discontent, and yet another clique was formed against the captain.

Fryer's resentment came to a head over another small incident, the signing of the ship's account books. On 9 October Fryer refused to do this unless Bligh gave him a certificate stating that 'he had been doing nothing remiss'. The captain would not accept conditions of this nature being dictated to him and, turning out all hands, read the Articles of War to the master. Fryer eventually signed: '… in obedience to your Orders, and this may be cancelled hereafter.'

Eventually, the *Bounty* reached her destination, Tahiti, in the Society Islands, where she dropped anchor on 26 October. Before allowing any of his crew ashore Bligh issued them with another set of instructions to govern their conduct in order that the friendship of the native islands should not be in any way marred or ruined. This was perfectly reasonable: Bligh had to keep the locals' trust to succeed in his mission, but soon these simple rules became yet another cause of grievance among his crew.

Relations between visitors and hosts were indeed very good, the natural warm-heartedness of the natives, both men and women, making the island appear something like paradise to the crew. However, the natives were in many ways childlike and were soon pilfering from the ship on a large scale. In this the natives were frequently helped by members of the crew, with whom they had struck up warm relationships. This, of course, led to further arguments and more floggings, the ship's butcher, for example, receiving twelve lashes for allowing his cleaver to be stolen.

The gifts showered upon the men also caused a major upset. These included live pigs and Bligh wished to salt as much pork away as possible for the long voyage home. He therefore confiscated these animals as they came aboard. The natives then began presenting the pigs to the men ashore but Bligh intercepted them here also and, when Fryer protested, Bligh declared, with complete lack of tact, that 'everything was his, as soon as it was on board, and that he would taken nine-tenths of any man's property'. The effect of this rash statement can be readily imagined.

The longer the *Bounty* remained in this idyllic setting, the more lax the men became, which naturally infuriated Bligh to the *n*th degree. Men were found asleep at their post on 5 January 1789, while others had taken arms and a boat and deserted. They were not brought back until the 23rd and then were duly flogged, the master-at-arms, Charles Churchill, receiving twelve lashes, his two seamen accomplices, Muspratt and Millward, two dozen apiece. Midshipman Hayward was punished for his laxity in allowing the desertion.

Still more incidents followed. When seaman Martin struck a native caught stealing, Bligh ordered him to receive nineteen lashes. Yet again, on 2 March, natives stole a water cask and a compass and Bligh berated Christian for slackness and flogged one of the thieves 400 times. Bligh was eventually forced to issue all orders in writing through trusted subordinates to get anything done at all. It must have been with considerable relief that Bligh finally set sail for home again on 4 April with his cargo of 1,015 breadfruit plants.

The crew of the *Bounty* were, on the whole, less happy to be leaving the island. They had nothing to look forward to now but a long and miserable voyage, more punishment and no hope of ever attaining such a delightful living again. At Aitutaki, John Sumner was flogged for neglect of duty and at Annamooka, on 25 April, a repetition of the Adventure Bay incident took place. A landing party under Christian had their implements stolen by natives and were roundly tongue-lashed by a furious Bligh. The captain stormed at Christian that he was 'a cowardly rascal' and asked if he was afraid of natives when he had guns. Christian replied, with some justice, that 'arms are no use while your orders prevent them from being used'.

When Fryer protested that such small items were of no great importance anyway, Bligh rounded on him in turn. 'Not great, Sir! By God, if it is not great to you, it is great to me!' Bligh mustered the crew and pointed a loaded pistol at one of them, William McCoy, for not paying sufficient attention to his words.

The final straw came on the 27th and again the reason was, in itself, seemingly as trivial as many of the others before it. A pile of coconuts stacked on board caught Bligh's eye and he convinced himself that it was not as large as it ought to have been. Someone, he felt sure, had been stealing again. He called for his officers, all of whom swore that they had not touched them. Fletcher Christian answered the question on how many he had brought aboard with the words, 'I do not know, Sir, but I hope you don't think me so mean as be guilt of stealing yours?' 'Yes, you damned Hound, I do', was Bligh's alleged response. 'You must have stolen them from me or you would give a better account of them.' Bligh then accused his officers of being 'all thieves alike, and combined with the men to rob me'. The captain ordered that their grog be cut and the issue of yams cut in half, 'and if they steal *them* I'll reduce them to a quarter.'

These accusations were later reported by the boatswain's mate, James Morrison, and may well have been invented in large part. There is, however, no doubt that the incidents referred to did take place, and, for many of the officers and men, this last affair, coupled with their depression at having to leave the South Seas, was just too much. Christian himself proposed to desert there and then, and began to build a raft. Other like-minded members of the crew joined him and these soon came to a more startling decision, to seize the ship. Among the ringleaders were familiar names, Quintal, Martin, Churchill, McCoy and others. What occurred next was later described by Bligh thuswise:

> Just before sunrising, while I was yet asleep, Mr Christian, with the Master at Arms, gunner's mate, and Thomas Burkitt, seaman, came into my cabin, and seizing me, tied my hands with a cord behind my back, threatening me with instant death, if I spoke or made the least noise. I, however, called as loud as I could, in hopes of assistance; but they had already secured the officers who were not of their party, by placing centinels [sic] at their doors ...

It was all over very quickly indeed. So quickly that Bligh, not surprisingly, was confused about just who was with the mutineers and who was not. Bligh attempted to reason with Christian, but failed. Eventually, the captain, with eighteen others, was put into the ship's cutter and cast adrift. Of the twenty-five who remained aboard the *Bounty*, however, by no means all were mutineers, some were detained against their will, others stayed out of fear. Those that Bligh knew were not involved but remained aboard the ship were Coleman, Macintosh, Norman, Martin and Byrne, and he later advised that these were 'deserving of mercy'. Nevertheless, others, Morrison claimed that he was one such, were also reluctant mutineers.

We can leave them all at this juncture. Of the subsequent adventures and misadventures of the plotters and of their various fates on Pitcairn and other islands, much has already been written. Of their subsequent capture and return home in circumstances both vile and dangerous, again we must, perforce, draw a veil. Likewise, the epic voyage of Bligh and his companions to reach safety, overcoming incredible odds, does not come into our story. Suffice it to say that, whatever his many other faults as a man and a leader, by this achievement William Bligh proved himself to be an outstanding navigator and the possessor of abundant courage. We will take up the story again three and a half years later, when the then surviving men accused of mutiny, which the long arm of the Royal Navy's vengeance had reached out for and found, stood before their judges aboard HMS *Duke* in Portsmouth harbour.

The court martial sat under the presidency of Vice Admiral Lord Hood, C-in-C Portsmouth and consisted of eleven full captains. Nor was Captain Bligh among those present to see justice done or to speak for the prosecution, for Their Lordships had contented themselves with accepting his own description of the mutiny and had sent him off again on a second voyage for breadfruit. Bligh was therefore half a world away from the events as they unfolded. Bligh's statement was duly read out in full. That it contained some gross errors and also some unfounded assumptions is clear. Bligh maintained that the mutiny was planned long in advance, when, in fact, it was hardly 'planned' at all. Bligh's statement left out references to many of the incidents that had led up to the final explosion, but, as these were fully detailed by Morrison and others, these omissions were rectified. He exonerated Coleman, Macintosh, Byrne and Norman and these men were duly dismissed. However, both Heywood and Morrison were named as active mutineers, much to their horror.

In all, the courts martial lasted from 12 to 18 September. The prosecution called Lieutenants Hallett and Hayward, Master Fryer, Boatswain Cole, Gunner Peckover and carpenter Purcell as witnesses, as well as some from the *Pandora*, the warship that had been wrecked bringing the accused home for trial. With the four men vouched for by Bligh duly found not guilty and acquitted, the case concentrated on the remainder. Of these, verdicts of guilty were just as much a foregone conclusion and of these so found Burkett, Ellison and Millward were soon adjudged active mutineers.

While all sought to justify their actions, Ellison on the grounds of youth (he had been 16 when the mutiny took place), the rest that they had been forced to comply by others, the findings were 'guilty' upon them all. Muspratt had a good case and clever lawyer. He argued that he had only taken up arms when he thought Fryer was going to lead a counter-revolt. He asked that the verdicts of the court on Norman and Byrne could be pronounced then and there so they would be able to speak up on his behalf that he was not involved. This the court refused to do.

Heywood had good family connections, who provided top legal advice to him in drawing up his case. Bligh's words were damning enough: 'His baseness is beyond all description', he had written to the man's mother. Still both Heywood and Morrison fought the charges, and each other, with considerable skill. Fryer was the initial witness and he was questioned by the court on Morrison's behaviour during the mutiny.

Fryer said he had spoken to Morrison in the after hatchway and had asked him if he had anything to do with it, to which Morrison had replied emphatically, 'No'. Convinced by this that he was loyal, Fryer had whispered to him to hold himself ready to retake the ship, upon which, he alleged, Morrison had replied, 'Go down to your cabin, Sir, it is too late.' Under cross-examination by the accused, Fryer denied that Morrison had himself indicated that he wished to retake the ship. The intervention of the court, however, brought about a more favourable response from Fryer. He admitted that Morrison's advice might not have been a threat but a friendly warning to get out of the way until a better opportunity arose, that he did not speak to him in a threatening tone and that he later acted in a way to assist Bligh, 'and giving him a better chance of his life'.

Of Heywood, Fryer had no knowledge at all, not having seen him during the course of the mutiny. Cole took the stand next, and he too stated that he had not seen Heywood take any active part in those proceedings, that the accused had been in his bunk when things started. Furthermore, said Cole, when Heywood later went below deck he had heard Churchill order two men to 'keep them down there', which surely showed that they were under guard and not active mutineers.

When the trial recommenced again on the 13th, Morrison was naturally anxious to obtain the same kind of backing from Cole, and he asked him if he recalled a conversation that they had held during which he had explained that as the boat was overloaded he would take his chances on the ship and that Cole understood and vouched to speak for him. Cole answered that he could not recall the incident in full but that 'I remember shaking hands with him and he telling me that he would take his chance in the ship. I had not other reason to believe but that he was intending to quit the ship.'

Asked by the accused if he considered his conduct gave him reason to suspect he was implicated, Cole replied, 'I have no reason to suppose it.' However, under examination by the court he was asked whether Morrison had expressed any desire to join Bligh's party in the boat or if he was prevented from so doing, to which Cole answered: 'He did not express a desire to me, nor was he prevented that I know.'

The other witnesses called all stated Heywood had taken no active part in these proceedings, although Purcell, in recalling that he had seen that worthy with his hand on the hilt of his cutlass while the boat was being lowered, caused some upset. Despite later amplifying this as an indication of helplessness on the part of Heywood to do anything positive, the statement had muddied the clean sheet that he had received so far. Morrison was likewise cleared by all four of taking an active part, although, on the other hand, they declared he had done precious little in the way of opposing things either.

On the 14th Hayward and Hallett were called again and both were very hostile to both Heywood and Morrison, as they had been before. However, Hayward's testimony was shaken on several occasions by pertinent questioning by Morrison and, in endeavouring to extradite himself, he only became more tongue-tied. Eventually the President of the court became irritable and intervened, showing him up still further. At the end of it all, however, Hayward refused to name either of the accused as being held against their will aboard the *Bounty*.

Hallett went even further, stating that he had seen Morrison holding a musket when the boat pulled away and that he had shouted, 'If my friends enquire after me, tell them I am somewhere in the South Seas'. Hallett stuck to this story under questioning by Morrison. He was equally as damning of Heywood. Bligh had spoken directly to him, Hallett said, and the reply the accused gave was to laugh in his face and then turn his back upon him.

On the 17th both men gave their defences. Heywood's was a rambling statement, containing all manner and parcel of excuses: his age and lack of experience, his fear of joining an already overladen boat with little hope of survival, that he had changed his mind and wished to join Bligh but that Churchill and Thompson had stopped him. Morrison was likewise long-winded, claiming that there was no room in the boat anyway, and that he had remained because Bligh said he must do so.

On the final day, Heywood produced his old certificate of baptism to prove he was only 16 on the day of the mutiny. It was a last pathetic gesture. The names of those found guilty were then read out: Heywood, Morrison, Ellison, Burkett, Millward and Muspratt. All six were sentenced:

> … to suffer Death by being hanged by the neck, on board such of His Majesty's ship or ships of War, at such Time or Times and such Place or Places as the Commissioners for executing the Office of Lord High Admiral of Great Britain and Ireland, etc, or any three of them, for the time being, should in writing, under their hands, direct.

The President then continued to show how the court had distinguished between active and passive mutiny, 'that in consideration of various circumstances the court did humbly and most earnestly recommend the said Peter Heywood and James Morrison to His Majesty's Mercy'.

That royal prerogative was exercised on 24 October and both men continued to serve in the Royal Navy, Heywood becoming a post-captain in 1803 and dying in 1831. Morrison, to his lasting credit, kept those condemned to die company on their last night on earth. These worthies, Burkett, Ellison and Millward, met their end together at midday on 29 October, all three being hung from the yardarms of HMS *Brunswick* in Portsmouth harbour, Millward making full confession before he died, addressing the assembled company and acknowledging the justice of his sentence.

There remained Muspratt – from the point of view of our subject, the most interesting of those condemned. He was not for accepting his fate. His legal adviser immediately claimed that Norman and Byrne should have been tried separately so that they could have been called as witnesses on his behalf, as had been asked for and refused. That being so, he declared, the sentence on Muspratt should be declared null and void on a technicality. Muspratt petitioned the

Admiralty accordingly and they, apparently nonplussed by such an unexpected turn of events, passed this hot potato on to the Attorney General, Solicitor General and counsel for the affairs of the Admiralty and navy, for their joint or separate opinions.

The Attorney General, Macdonald, and the Solicitor General, Eldon, both reached similar opinions on the complex issues involved. Both concluded that, in this case, perhaps the prisoner should be given the benefit of the doubt, although both conceded that civilian practice was not all of one mind on the issue. Mr Broderick for the counsel came down in favour of Muspratt, concluding that the case appeared to him deserving of great consideration because vital evidence was denied to the defendant even though it was correctly applied for in writing to the court. The twelve judges were also consulted and Muspratt duly received the Royal Pardon.

Morrison, like Heywood, prospered in the service after this close call. He joined HMS *Victory* as quartermaster and gunner's mate under Lord Hood himself. He saw service in the Mediterranean, being later promoted for 'his exemplary good conduct'. He became gunner aboard the frigate *Lutine*, famous for when she was subsequently wrecked off Vlieland in 1799; her ship's bell was salvaged and now hangs at Lloyds and is rung whenever there is a shipwreck, for she carried a great treasure when she went down.

What of Bligh? Public opinion was firmly with him at the time of the trial, but later veered sharply in the opposite direction. This mutiny was not the last that this officer was to undergo and we shall meet him again in trying circumstances in later pages. Brilliant navigator or ogre, his name has become immortal, but whether for the right reasons or not is still very much a matter of opinion.

9 'WE INTEND TO BE MASTERS' (1797)

Unhappy is the lot of the misfit, the man who 'means well', the go-between who, from the best of motives, finds himself representing a group for which he has little affinity against another group from whom he receives nothing but disdain. The road to hell is truly paved with good intentions. Such was destined to be the fate of Richard Parker, confined by history to the role of arch-villain of the Nore mutiny and duly hanged for his crimes. Such people often seemed dogged by ill luck from birth, the fruits of their endeavours always being snatched from them by the last-minute intervention of cruel fate, and such was Parker's unfortunate lot. Falling between two stools, he was condemned by both sides and mourned by neither. There are always those willing enough to load the bullets for others to fire and Parker eventually found himself holding the trigger of discontent and paying the price of the front man.

Parker was born in 1767 at Exeter, the son of a successful baker. His future seemed set fair by the standards of the day. He received education at the grammar school run by the Rev. Marshall and studied navigation under the keymaster at Topsham in Devon. By 1782, he had volunteered for the Royal Navy, joining his first ship, the *Mediator*, where his cousin was a lieutenant, and following her captain, Luttrell, into the *Ganges* in 1783 as a midshipman. Service followed aboard the *Bulldog* off East Africa. On her return home the following year Parker was discharged sick to Haslar Hospital, rejoining his ship briefly before once more being hospitalised at Plymouth in July. Upon his full recovery Parker joined the *Blenheim*, but shortly afterwards resigned from the service and entered the merchant marine to further his career.

According to his own statements, Parker seemed to alternate between commercial shipping and brief periods in the Royal Navy, serving in the Mediterranean and in Indian waters. He married the daughter of a Scottish farmer at Braemar in 1791. That he was a man of some worth and ability seems evident from the fact that he was invited to join the *Sphynx* by her commanding officer, Captain Lucas, in 1793 and was promised promotion to lieutenant under the eye Sir Alexander Hood no less. All seemed well up to then, but then Parker blotted his copybook.

That Parker's temper was as uncertain as his health was clear; one earlier story (without much proof to back it up) held that, during the American War, he once challenged his captain to a duel. True or not, his spirit soon showed when he was unable to join the *Sphynx* and was instead sent to the *Assurance*, pending suitable opportunity to transfer to Captain Lucas' command. He was far from happy with this situation as a supernumerary and, when the *Assurance* was ordered to sail, asked for a transfer to the *Sandwich* to await the return of the *Sphynx*. Here he was given cause for complaint, for he was denied this request as 'he was too useful to the *Assurance*' and when the ship of his choice finally arrived back in port he was refused permission to communicate with her.

Parker addressed a protest at his treatment to Admiral Dalrymple, seeing his hopes of advancement fast vanishing, but this plea was likewise ignored, and he sailed with the *Assurance*. It was cruel usage, but no more so than that of hundreds of others in similar circumstances. Perhaps we can sympathise with Parker's anger and understand that, at the first opportunity, he should vent his wrath. This opportunity soon presented itself with a dispute over the tidiness of the hammocks with Lieutenant Richards of the *Assurance*. Parker refused to take up his own hammock when so ordered, claiming that he 'was an officer in this ship and will not disgrace myself'. Richards applied to his captain, stating that Parker had been 'contemptuous and disobedient' and Parker duly found himself facing court martial aboard the *Royal William* on 12 December 1793.

Parker was found guilty, dis-rated and ordered to serve on any ship the C-in-C thought fit to send him. Even so, there were still some who rated his services, as the captain of the *Hebe* asked for him, but even this second chance to redeem himself was dashed by reoccurrence of illness. Thus, Parker found himself once more in Haslar Hospital with rheumatism. Here he remained from April to August, before finally being discharged from the *Royal William* on 26 November.

Parker tried to settle down ashore with his wife for a time, first at Exeter and then at Braemar, but he found life away from the sea difficult to adjust to. Parker followed the career of a schoolmaster, fell into the debt for which that profession was noted, found himself before the Edinburgh magistrates and was jailed. In order to pay off the sum owing he accepted the king's bounty of £20 and rejoined the navy, despite the fact that his wife claimed he was deranged at the time. Indeed, both he and his sister had a record of mental instability.

And so, with all his bright hopes gone, Parker found himself back at the very bottom of the navy again – a quota man. He was decamped in due course into the floating stench pit that was the *Sandwich*, an unseaworthy, verminous and rotting hulk that disgraced her title of line-of-battle ship, barely afloat, cramped and seething with discontent. Parker, who had experienced a higher station in the service, must have thought his life was done with. Raging inside and full of illness, mental disturbance and misery at this fate, Parker had touched rock bottom and there seemed to be no way out. Then, on 12 May 1797, while Parker was working below in the carpenter's mate's berth, there came the sound of wild cheering. He ran swiftly up on deck to see what it was all about and found, to his astonishment, for he had not been in on the plot at all, that the forecastle guns were pointing aft. His moment, though even then he did not realise it, had come!

Much has been said on the mutinies in the fleet that took place at Spithead, at the Nore and at Yarmouth. Of the rank injustices that prevailed and of the complete indifference of the Admiralty and parliament, not to mention the nation at large, to the conditions of the seamen who were defending England from invasion and worse, much has been written. Mutiny, it is said, is never justified, but it is doubtful whether any mutiny was more justified than this one. It is to the eternal shame of the leaders in high places that they not only were themselves unaware of the harshness and total unfairness of life aboard the ships of the fleet, but that, when appraised by responsible officers of those conditions, they chose to ignore them. Politicians, of course, never change their spots and never learn anything other than how to count the latest votes, but there were those at the Admiralty itself who should have known better and acted with more urgency to the situation. Old Lord Howe himself cannot escape censure on this point, although it is to his credit that, once roused, he did more than any man to rectify matters, crowning his efforts with the accordment reached at Spithead, which promised the men that all their demands would be met and a free pardon from the king would also be granted.

There is substantial agreement on this point then, but not on the subsequent and far more serious outbreak at the Nore, to which the ships at Yarmouth, after some hesitation, joined for a time. The general train of thought is that this second outbreak was not necessary, all the men's demands having been met in full. This was most certainly the Admiralty's response at the time, and is the opinion of many since. Though partly true, it cannot be denied that the men had heard these promises before, and nothing had actually been done. The men at Spithead had got rid of their bullying officers and retained the good ones; the men at the Nore were given no such opportunity. The men at Spithead had remained largely an anonymous group, in their wisdom; the men at the Nore took the fatal step of appointing leaders and these leaders were rash enough to fully identify themselves. Some revelled in the brief glory of it all, short-lived fame; others had the position thrust upon them and were marked men from the start. Richard Parker was one of the latter.

As the Spithead men had fought the fight and won, it was perhaps inevitable that the Nore men had to go further. They had risen when it was almost done and over with in the south. To meekly submit at once was asking too much of human nature that had suffered too much. An outlet for the years of anger had to be found and so they had to make yet further demands to justify their actions; they were, in effect, pushed to extremes by the tardiness in taking up the cause. It was equally predictable that, having given way once, the Admiralty would give no further. Therefore, the immovable object met the irresistible force with a crash that shook the navy and the nation to the core.

The earliest actions of the Nore mutineers had been to follow the example of the Spithead men and clear their ships of the officers they considered either brutal, incompetent or plain offensive. They had taken advantage of the fact that aboard the *Sandwich*, which was acting as a depot ship, the commander-in-chief, Vice Admiral Charles Buckner, was absent at a court martial, along with Captain Mosse. The former elected not to return but took up his residence at Sheerness. Mosse, however, was made of sterner stuff and remonstrated with the men, but to little effect. The first lieutenant had already been 'seen off' by the *Sandwich's* crew and from the two other battleships present, *Inflexible* and *Director*, unpopular officers were also on their way ashore by boat. Of the eight frigates also present, most complied with the mutineers; any that showed a disinclination to join in no doubt took heed of the *San Fiorenzo*. This frigate had arrived the next day from Spithead where the mutiny was just about done, but she was fired upon by the rest of the fleet until she agreed to join them.

By this act the Nore men had already gone further than their brothers in the south and their continual parades ashore, jibing and cheering the local garrison and populace, harassing the surgeons at the hospital and their 'regattas' around the fleet to musical accompaniment, showed that they were just getting into their stride. They dispatched a delegation to Portsmouth to what would today be termed 'show their solidarity', and when the remnant of that party returned with evidence that it was all finished with down there, there was some feeling of anticlimax.

Parker himself had at first expressed the opinion that things were out of hand. There was too much violence for his liking, he confided to the carpenter's mate, Simms, and that worthy agreed that clearer heads were required. That statement led to Parker being invited to join the delegates aboard *Sandwich* and soon he, being a man of education and a former officer, was being asked to chair the meetings. From that it was but a short step to becoming their President. Parker had preached moderation, now he had to exercise it against the rabble-rousers and wilder spirits aboard, fire-eaters, troublemakers, even Irish Nationalists as eager to add to the confusion. These unruly elements, seeking to promote their own diffuse causes as is their want while the going was good, did not receive support from the men as whole, despite their ranting, but it did not make Parker's position an enviable one.

One can imagine, maybe, Parker's feelings at this time. Here was his chance! He would guide the men, rejecting overt violence, producing just and reasonable demands, in excess of the Spithead men to be sure, but still 'reasonable' as far as the Nore mutineers were concerned. Parker could thus present himself as a moderating influence on the one hand and as a leader of a just cause on the other. Alas for Parker, he found instead that he was unable to achieve either of these worthy aspirations.

Thus Parker criticised the emissaries returned from Portsmouth, denouncing them as having done no more than brought 'two or three pennyworth of ballads of twenty pounds' and sought to frame yet further demands of the Admiralty. Parker argued that the act for increasing their pay was only an Order in Council and, although proved legally incorrect on that point, only grudgingly admitted it. Parker stated that, in that case, the act was only valid for one year and worthless. That unpopular officers might be removed was a signal to continue with that work and the unfortunate Captain William Bligh, then in command of the *Director*, was given his marching orders. Bligh had evidently learned absolutely nothing from the *Bounty* affair. Floggings had been frequent aboard the *Director*, even after the negotiations at Spithead. Three officers had been dismissed ashore on the 12th and Bligh followed them on the 19th, splutteringly indignant as ever. The Admiralty quickly found work for him to do. (In passing, it should be mentioned that he continued to lack comprehension on how to treat men: his third and most humiliating mutiny was to take place in Australia, when he was usurped as Governor of New South Wales during the so-called 'rum rebellion'.)

On the same day, the delegates called Vice Admiral Buckner ashore to present their demands, which he, mistakenly, thought he had already talked them out of. Next day Buckner set out to visit them aboard the *Sandwich*. It was not an auspicious end to his career. Parker was not even there when the admiral arrived on board; he was shown no honours as he went aboard his own flagship. When he did finally deem to put in an appearance Parker pointedly kept his own hat firmly on his head when confronting the admiral. Buckner was presented by Parker with the demands on the quarterdeck with scant formality, and, in so many words, was told that he was of no use to them. Parker coldly informed the admiral that they wanted to speak to someone higher up, more competent or, to use the admiral's own indignant words later, 'the personal attendance of a Board of Their Lordships here, which, they insisted they have a right to expect, there having been a precedent for it at Spithead'.

With that, Buckner was dismissed. When the admiral forwarded these demands to the London the reaction of the board was one of anger. The Admiralty had expected the Nore mutineers to fall gracefully into line with the Spithead agreement; instead they had got further demands. Their Lordships immediately instructed Buckner to refuse all new demands. London also dispatched troop reinforcements, which further put the backs of the delegates up. Parker, writing to Buckner, remarked that such conduct was 'an insult to the peaceable behaviour of the seamen'. Parker added that he considered 'the Lords of Admiralty have been remiss in their duty in not attending when their appearance could have given satisfaction'.

In other words, Parker was looking for a show by which to persuade the men to fall into line, and the Admiralty, now fully on their dignity, were in no way prepared to provide one. All hopes of a peaceful and early termination to the affair now faded as both sides dug their heels in.

Thus, while the ships at the Nore hoisted the red flag, Their Lordships prepared for sterner measures. The mutineers concentrated the fleet, bringing the rest of the ships into line. The Admiralty reiterated the letter of pardon, but again refused to come to Sheerness to discuss it any further. Parker wrote, on 25 May, that 'no accommodation can take place until the appearance of the Lords of the Admiralty at the Nore'. Parker was later to state that, in writing thus, he was merely reflecting the wishes of the delegates and not expressing his own viewpoint. In fact, Parker was by now just a hapless pawn, as he later stated: 'It is well known what authority the seamen had over the Delegates, and in what a ferocious manner the Delegates were frequently treated for not according with every wild scheme which the sailors proposed to carry into practice.'

The stand-off therefore continued, but, behind the scenes, some were seeking a way out of the impasse. The Lord Chancellor, Lord Loughborough, suggested to the First Lord, Lord Spencer, that perhaps it would be as well to meet with the men and settle the affair, a suggestion that was not well received. Nonetheless, on 28 May down they all went, but only to present the new pardon in person. The board would do that much but no more, as a sop to the men's demands. Parker arrived at their lodging as the head of the delegates that same evening. Spencer refused to see him at all, so Admiral Young spoke with him, asking, 'What do you wish to see the Board for?'

Parker, excitable as ever, gave the admiral a sharp rejoinder: 'You are a man of sense, and know what is due to us; you know what we want.' Young did indeed, but the delegates' demands to speak with the board were refused and, finally, they presented their much watered-down demands again, asking only that the Spithead agreement and Royal Pardon be applied to them and their new demands 'considered'. Spencer refused to contemplate it; he wanted total submission first, only then would he grant the pardon.

There was much dissention in the fleet and all the next day arguments raged back and forth on whether to call the mutiny off or not. Finally, it was decided to keep going, and that evening Parker made a pitiful attempt to renegotiate alone in one last desperate attempt. The scene has been described thus:

> Already he appears as a lonely figure: he could not be of the men; he was not among the rulers. On being told there was no answer he said nothing; he made a low bow and walked away …

That was the end of the 'negotiations'. The mutiny had to run its long and increasingly bloody course. The tide turned dramatically each way: the arrival of the Yarmouth ships, the escape of the *San Fiorenzo*, the firing into the grounded *Repulse*, crisis following crisis, with Parker torn between two minds on how to act for the best.

The latter incident is a good indication of just how split Parker was at this time. On witnessing the attempted escape of the *Repulse*, he shouted wildly that he was going aboard the *Director* and, as for the *Repulse* and her crew, he 'would send her and them to the Devil!' Once aboard the battleship, and finding her guns loaded and ready to fire on their former colleagues, Parker had a change of heart. He called for the *Director's* crew not to fire upon their brother men. The men ignored him and, seemingly not being able to bear their rejection, he changed tack yet again. Now Parker ordered them to open fire, which they did, and then he took himself to the *Monmouth* in a frenzy of action. Here he helped load the guns and yelled to her mutineer captain, 'slip your bowers and go alongside the *Repulse*, and send her to hell where she belongs, and show her no quarter in the least'. The man was demented. He could see both the mutiny and his chance of glory steadily slipping away from him. Once more, it seemed to him, fate was ruining his opportunity to make his mark on history, and for the last time.

When the mutiny crumbled at last, yet another change came over Parker, he seemed resigned to his fate and revelled in the picture of himself as a martyr.

Unfortunately for him, the picture that Their Lordships, the government and the nation in general had of him was that of a despicable, seditious, opportunist, the ringleader, for whom no punishment was bad enough.

Parker skulked aboard the *Sandwich* to the end, she being one of the last ships to hold out before surrendering. While other mutineers tried to escape their fate in small boats bound for France, Parker remained. When the crew finally opted for surrender, he cheered their decision. Perhaps he still felt he might avoid the hangman's noose by skilful argument, if so he was to be quickly disillusioned. He handed over the keys of the ship's magazine to Lieutenant Flatt with the words: 'I give up the charge of the ship to you.' For his pains he then asked Flatt to confine him, changed his mind and refused to go below and instead helped man the capstan and was finally confined below under guard. Later, he was put in irons and sent ashore.

There was a great deal of hurrying and scurrying among officialdom now to get their revenge on the man they believed to be the originator of the whole affair. With blatant partiality, Evan Nepean, secretary to the Admiralty, wrote to Admiral Sir Thomas Pasley, President Elect of the court martial which was to judge Parker, that:

> You may prove almost anything you like against him, for he has been guilty of everything that's bad. Admiral Buckner will be a material evidence to state the proceedings which took place on his visit to the *Sandwich*, and which, indeed, of itself appears to be enough to dispose of a dozen scoundrels of Parker's description.

To his credit, the President Elect wrote back, with withering scorn: 'The conviction of the villain Parker must have been so very dear to you at the Admiralty that the place and time of his execution might have been previously settled.' However, Pasley added the rider that he hoped Parker's body would be hung in chains, which also showed a streak of vengefulness. However, this later statement was after the trial.

The court martial itself sat aboard the *Neptune* in Long Reach on 22 June. Captain Mosse was the prosecutor. Right from the start there was never any doubt that they would find him guilty, but the trial was as fair as it could possibly be, notwithstanding Nepean's communication. The accused was allowed every chance to call as many witnesses as he wished. The court even advised Parker to withdraw damaging questions, even though he had received the answers. Parker was allowed extra time to prepare the best defence possible and the court also called witnesses to give defence of his character, Knight and Northesk.

The accused must have known what his fate was to be, but, for his last appearance at the centre of events, he maintained a dignity that became him well. He based his defence on his moderating influence, stressing how but for that the wild men would have gone further than they did. He weakened his case by also claiming again that to a large extent he was in their power, only doing what they ordered him to do. While both these claims held elements of truth, he really could not have it both ways. It was the testimony of witnesses during the *Repulse* incident that damned him without redemption, for here he had acted in a more extreme manner than anyone.

In his final summing up, Parker stressed his background and his honour:

> As I have been at sea from my youth, to the knowledge of one of the honourable members of this court, I hope nothing can be expected from me but plain facts. I cannot be expected to dress up my defence in that pompous language which a lawyer might have done could I have procured a lawyer's constant attendance.

Parker continued in much the same vein:

> Nothing but a consciousness of the integrity of my intentions, and a knowledge that I only entered into it after it had commenced, with a view to endeavouring to stop the fatal spirit I saw predominant in the Fleet, could have supported me during the examination of so many witnesses against me … Conscious that I have prevented a number of evil consequences which would have insued, at the frequent hazard of my life, I can wait with calmness the decision of this honourable Court.

The decision of that honourable court was to find him guilty and sentence him to death. Parker received even this verdict with certain calmness, telling his judges:

> I have heard your sentence – I shall submit to it without a struggle – I feel thus because I am sensible of the rectitude of my intentions. Whatever offences may have been committed, I hope my life will be the only sacrifice. I trust it will be though a sufficient atonement. Pardon, I beseech you, the other men; they will return with alacrity to their duty.

Alas for his pleadings, the Admiralty having got the blood of the chief culprit were by no means satisfied or sated with only that. They determined to break all thought of further rebellion among the men by stern example. Courts martial were held on more than 400 other mutineers and the sentences were savage. Fifty-nine men were sentenced to death, nine to severe floggings and twenty-nine to imprisonment. Although the death sentence was commuted on thirty of the men, the others duly paid the supreme penalty. Others languished for years in the living death of the Marshalsea or the Coldbath Fields prison at Clerkenwell. Death, for many of these, might have been kinder.

The king, whose Royal Pardon had been so freely offered when things looked black, joined in the call for the last dregs of vengeance to be exacted, writing that:

> The offence of which Richard Parker has been convicted is of so heinous and dangerous a nature that I can scarcely suppose there can be any legal objection, after confirming the sentence for his being hanged, to order his body to be hung in chains on the most conspicuous land in sight of the ships of the Nore.

Fortunately, the court was more civilised in this instance than his most gracious Majesty, and Parker was spared this final indignity. His execution date was fixed for the 30th and Parker, confined once more aboard the *Sandwich*, addressed his last testimony to posterity. It was a long, rambling document, in which he strove to justify himself as a moderate man beset by circumstances over which he had no control, and that he would consider himself always a martyr. It contained some bitterness at those he had represented, but also, surprisingly perhaps, touches of humour:

> A little while and I must depart from this world, and for ever close my eyes upon its vanity, deceitfulness, and ingratitude. My passage through it has been short, but chequered. My departure from it will be extremely boisterous, but I seriously assure you, upon my part, by no means unwilling.

Parker had all along maintained that he acted for the sailors following his conscience, but, although he still considered it right for that reason, he confessed that it lacked prudence:

> The latter consideration is the only compunction which I feel under my doleful calamity. Yes, prudence urges that *I ought to have known mankind better*, than blindfold, to have plunged into certain destruction. Long since I had leant that the miseries under which the lower classes groan are imputable in a great measure to their ignorance, cowardice, and duplicity, and that nothing short of a miracle could ever afford them any relief.

It was not only the lower classes that he fatally misjudged, of course, but the middle classes to which he aspired so unsuccessfully. The blockade of the Thames and London, to which the mutineers' hunger eventually drove them, although vigorously maintained, scared and turned the merchants and moneyed classes against them more than any threat of invasion could have done. Even though the money-lenders and traders were quite content to let the men live in conditions of utter degradation at sea, while depending on them to defend them, when these self-same sailors sought to hinder the steady flow of goods and profit into the City, they rose in awful wrath as one man against them. It is ever thus.

Parker made one last attack on the establishment that had broken him time and time again:

> I have reason to think the Civil Power would have acquitted me, but by the Articles of War my destruction was irremidiable [sic], and of this the Government was well aware, or I should not have been tried by a Court Martial. By the Laws of War I acknowledge myself to be legally convicted, but the Laws of Humanity, which should be the basis of all laws, I die illegally.

So, on 30 October, aboard the *Sandwich*, Richard Parker partook of a last glass of wine, shook hands with Captain Mosse, toasted the 'salvation of my soul and the forgiveness of all my enemies' and was led to the scaffold on the forecastle. He was masked, walked steadily to the end, thrust his hands into his pockets and jumped. The gun was fired as he dropped and the reeved rope caught his body, which was hoisted to the yardarm. His wife was not allowed aboard to see her husband in his last hours, but after he had hung an hour, she was allowed to take the body ashore. He was buried in Whitechapel, not too far from the City whose wrath had been his final downfall.

10 NELSON AT NAPLES (1799)

In the proud history of the Royal Navy, Lord Nelson's place is both supreme and secure; he is, in fact, *the* hero. It is not the intention of this study to lessen in any way the fully justified image of such a leader, but in viewing him, one must review the whole man, not just the legend. Nelson had the faults as well as the virtues of all men. One of the most unusual episodes of his life was the unfortunate Caracciolo affair at Naples in 1799. It was unusual in that it seemed to reflect upon Nelson in a most untypical light. In short, he appeared to act out of character. Therefore, this case is more interesting for the reasons and possible motivation of Nelson's role in it, rather than as a cause célèbre.

After Nelson's crushing victory at the Battle of the Nile, honours were heaped upon him and, on his return to Naples, and the beguiling charms of Emma Hamilton, his judgement appears to have been influenced by the adulation. Nelson's patriotic fervour had not been assuaged by his triumph, and he set about seeking new ways to inconvenience the French. The little admiral judged that the enemy lines of communication in the Roman Republic were dangerously extended, which was true. With the newly won command of the Mediterranean

Sea, Great Britain could exert telling pressure in support of military operations ashore against the stretched French armies. It was the traditional British strategy, usually successful and only abandoned at a horrendous cost in lives during the First World War.

Had troops been available from the second coalition to make a concerted attack, no doubt Nelson's strategy would have worked well enough. However, Nelson advised the local monarch, King Ferdinand of Naples, that his own army would suffice to do the job on its own, and in this bizarre belief he had the backing of both Lady Hamilton and the queen herself, Marie Antoinette's sister, both beautiful women but hardly military strategists.

The Neapolitan Government therefore concluded an alliance with Austria and declared war on France, but, in fact, the only material assistance they received from the new ally was the dispatch of General Mack to command their army. Nelson was appointed commander-in-chief of the Neapolitan navy and instructed to make Naples his headquarters for watching the coast. This the admiral did not find too inconvenient to his other campaign, the siege of the lady, nor to his plans to reduce the French occupation forces at Malta by close blockade. To both these courses of action, Nelson duly applied himself, dispatching the *Alexander* on 4 October and following himself aboard the *Vanguard*, with the *Goliath*, *Audacious*, *Terpsichore* and the fire ship *Incendiary*. However, although only a short period was envisaged before Malta fell, the French garrison there had been so well provisioned that two years were to pass before they finally surrendered the island.

Nelson himself returned in his flagship to Naples on 5 November, leaving Captain Alexander Ball to continue the blockade with the assistance of a newly arrived Portuguese squadron commanded by the Marquis de Niza. Nelson was very angry at the failure of ministers to supply the Maltese themselves with arms and ammunition, as they had promised to do, and he set about goading them into more warlike activity against Napoleon's forces. Nor did the admiral fail to succumb to the blandishments of the ladies, writing that same day: 'I am, I fear, drawn into a promise that Naples Bay shall never be left with an English man of war ... Who could withstand the request of such a Queen?'

Nelson also attended a mock battle as the Austrian general put the Neapolitan army through its paces in all its glittering finery. The results were not auspicious and revealed Mack to be devoid of both 'ability or professional knowledge'. Nevertheless, the army duly marched out with a great fanfare towards Rome, 'an army of 40–50,000 men ... under incompetent, if not traitorous, officers'.

As a second prong to the offensive, Nelson sailed for Leghorn on 22 November with 5,000 additional troops embarked aboard his squadron's warships. This force arrived off that city three days later and took its surrender the same night without resistance. Leaving Troubridge to keep watch there, Nelson returned once more to Naples on 5 December. Here the admiral found his ally had not matched his

own easy victory. Indeed, the reverse was the case. Nelson was given the astound-
ing news that the king's glittering army had met a French force half its size and
had fled after the first exchange of shots. The Neapolitan army had instantly
broken up into a disorganised rabble and was fleeing pell-mell back to Naples
as fast as it could run. On 11 December, Nelson wrote bitterly: 'The Neapolitan
officers did not lose much honour for, God knows, they had not much to lose;
but they lost all they had.'

For the loss of just forty men, the army of Naples had disintegrated, abandoning cannon and baggage, which helped the advancing French army enormously.
Naples itself was now threatened and a hasty dispatch brought Troubridge back
post haste to help prepare an evacuation. All the English residents were taken
aboard three transports and, on 21 December, the royal family was taken aboard
the *Vanguard*. All these refugees were landed at Palermo on the 27th and Naples
was abandoned for a time to its fate.

Not surprisingly then, those thus left offered little or no resistance to the
enemy and indeed many, Neapolitan Jacobins, welcomed the occupation with
open arms and co-operated fully in setting up the Vesuvian, or Parthenopeian,
Republic. Part of the Neapolitan navy was involved in this change of sides and all
that Nelson could do was to institute a close blockade of the city from his new
headquarters. The first act of the farce was over.

With regard to history, the period that followed was probably the nadir
of Nelson's career. The blockade was left to Captain Edward James Foote of
the frigate *Seahorse*, who was told to co-operate as best he could with what
remained of the royal forces ashore, under Cardinal de Ruffo. In the meantime,
Nelson anchored the *Vanguard* at Palermo and, except for brief periods, here he
remained, his gambling and his wooing of Lady Hamilton filling the air with
delighted scandal.

Thus it remained throughout the early months of 1799, but in April came a
change. A French squadron of twenty-five battleships and five frigates took the
brief opportunity to evade the blockade off Brest and, under the command of
Admiral Bruix, entered the Mediterranean on 4 May. This fleet arrived at Toulon
eight days later unchallenged. They were joined up the straits by a Spanish fleet
of seventeen battleships, which also reached Cartagena safely. Earl St Vincent
now moved with commendable speed to rectify this dangerous situation. The
earl dispatched Keith to watch Toulon and he also reinforced Nelson's squadron,
which had concentrated, and ordered him to assemble at Rosas Bay in order to
prevent the French and Spanish ships from joining up. Nelson, however, seemed
unable or unwilling to drag himself away from the fleshpots of Palermo and its
many charms. He cruised for a short time in the Sicilian Channel to block the
way east, but was still obsessed with his Naples adventure. Nelson thought that it
was the enemy intention to sail there and he was determined to retake the city

and forestall them. Nelson therefore returned to Palermo once again, 'to offer myself for the service of Naples where I knew the French fleet was going'.

In the interim, a great deal had been occurring at Naples. A message reached Nelson in April, which informed him that only about 2,000 French troops remained in the city. True, an equal number of the civil guard were present, but they would not offer serious opposition and would join whosoever was in control. The guard had already stated that their job was merely to keep the peace and not to fight. The heady promises of the rump republic had already been shown to be hollow to all but the most dedicated Jacobins and the city appeared ripe for counter-revolution. Much plotting was taking place in the usual Italian manner, and the whole situation was confused and ready for exploitation by the allies.

Troubridge had already re-occupied several of the outlying islands before being called away, and the main French garrison was concentrated at St Elmo. A great many of the fellow travellers had seen the writing on the wall and had left with the bulk of the French forces to save their skins. Many of those that had remained fled to the forts of Vovo and Nuovo and prepared to resist. The larger part of the populace, however, merely switched allegiance once more from the republic back to Ferdinand and awaited events.

For his part, the king, sensing victory again, gave strict instructions to Ruffo not to enter into any negotiations with the republicans. Ruffo, the man on the spot, elected to turn a Nelsonic blind eye to these orders. On his own initiative Ruffo commenced talks with the republican leaders. No doubt Ruffo was motivated by many factors in so doing, perhaps the most worthy of which was to save unnecessary bloodshed, although there were other intrigues without doubt. Whatever his reasons, Ruffo took it upon himself to grant terms to the republicans, which they, knowing their position was hopeless, were only too eager to accept. Ruffo offered these republicans safe conduct and free pass to France, if they surrendered the forts to the allies.

Captain Foote, a junior officer, was placed in a very difficult position. Foote had been told to fully co-operate with Ruffo, but Ruffo was acting contrary to the king's and Nelson's wishes, although Foote could not be certain of the latter. In the end Foote decided to accept the fait accompli and also put his own name to the capitulation document, thus binding British honour to the illegal promises made. All was in train for the surrender, but nothing had actually been done to effect it, when Nelson returned in person.

Nelson arrived aboard his new flagship, the *Foudroyant*, on 24 June, along with his whole squadron, to find only the French garrison at St Elmo was still offering resistance. The admiral was aware of the armistice and was furious at the turn of events. On seeing the truce flags flying from the republican forts and the *Seahorse*, Nelson at once made a signal annulling it. Upon anchoring Nelson found that the capitulation had not yet actually taken effect, even though agreed to. His reaction was swift and he issued a declaration that the truce was null and void. No safe conduct was forthcoming, Nelson informed the republicans in the two forts. They must either surrender absolutely and throw themselves on the mercy of the king or face the consequences.

The dismayed defenders had no choice but to comply and, on the 26th, they gave themselves up and were made prisoners of war. Those fortunate enough to be ashore at the time made efforts to flee to safety in the mountains, but by now the whole country was up in arms against them. Many were caught and brought back into captivity.

One such unfortunate was Commodore Prince Caracciolo, who was found hiding in a well in a mountain village and brought back by the peasants to face his fate on the 29th. Caracciolo had joined the republican cause and had opened fire on several of the king's ships back in December. Now the prince was taken aboard the *Foudroyant* and Nelson, as commander-in-chief of the Neapolitan navy, ordered that the commodore face a court martial at the hands of the senior officers of the king's fleet.

This court was hastily convened and Caracciolo was charged with 'rebellion against his lawful sovereign' and of 'firing on the King's colours hoisted on board the King's frigate *Minerva*'. The court was presided over by Commodore Count Thurn, and consisted of seven Neapolitan officers aboard *Foudroyant*. It was an open court and several British officers who attended later commented favourably on the accused's bearing. He was found wearing peasant clothes and was grimy and weary from his escape attempt, but his 'distinguished appearance' was much noted upon. One officer thought he was 'about seventy', whereas his true age was 47, a reflection, no doubt, of his dreadful experiences. Nevertheless, Caracciolo conducted his own defence with some dignity and made no attempt to evade his responsibilities. The accused pleaded guilty to the charge but put forward mitigating circumstances.

During the two-hour trial Caracciolo claimed that, although guilty, he had been coerced into the action he had taken. This cut no ice with the court whatsoever and, after the short proceedings, the vote was taken, all the officers finding him guilty as charged. When it came to the sentence they were slightly split, five officers voting for his death by hanging, two, perhaps compassionate or thinking of what they would have done had they found themselves in his position the previous December, voted against. All the accused could do on the passing of this sentence was to plead for a more dignified form of execution, as became a nobleman. There was some feeling for him in this; both Count Thurn and Sir William Hamilton were moved to ask Nelson for at least a twenty-four-hour stay of grace on his behalf. These requests were refused outright.

At five o'clock that same afternoon Caracciolo was duly hanged at the fore yardarm of the *Minerva*.

Even at the time, there was a considerable body of opinion that the whole matter had been conducted with undue haste and motivated by feelings of revenge. The Jacobin sympathisers and their friends, who raised a great outcry at the sentence and the manner in which it was carried out, swelled this feeling later. Naturally, their wrath was not directed solely at the sentence on the unfortunate commodore. They also accused Nelson of obtaining possession of the two forts by treachery and of breaking a solemn agreement entered into in good faith on their part with the representatives of both the King of Naples and the British Government. Caracciolo was by no means the only Jacobin to be executed in the aftermath of this sorry affair, but the unseemly haste in which he had been dealt with and his undignified end made a lasting impression on friend and foe alike. Nor was it only the erstwhile republicans who expressed dismay at the sentence and the execution. Captain Foote felt deeply about the whole affair. He wrote:

> Nothing can be more evident than the fact that a solemn capitulation had been agreed upon, formally signed by the chief commander of the forces of the King of Naples, by the Russian commander, and by myself, all duly authorised to sign any capitulation in the absence of superior powers. This was not a treaty of peace subject to ratification, it was not a truce liable to be broken, it was a serious agreement for surrender upon terms which involved the lives and properties of men, which might have chosen to forfeit those lives and properties, had they not relied principally upon the faith of a British officer. Parts of this agreement were performed, and actual advantage was afterwards taken of those parts of the capitulation that had been thus executed, to seize the unhappy men who, having been thus deceived by a sacred pledge, were sacrificed in a cruel and despotic manner.

Cruel and despotic, that is hardly the picture of Nelson we all have. How far can his conduct be condoned in this matter has been the subject of acute controversy ever since. Let us examine the legality of the business first. Here there can be little doubt that Nelson acted according to his strictly legal rights. Nelson had been appointed commander-in-chief of the Neapolitan navy and was therefore correct in ordering the court martial of an officer under his command known to have committed mutiny, desertion and rebellion. The written authority of Pitt to enforce an unconditional surrender of the enemy further backed up Nelson's position. On whether or not the terms of the capitulation had been carried out, we are in territory that is more contentious. That they had not been fully carried out is clear, and on that point, as C-in-C, Nelson had every right to refute them. However, if, as Foote claimed, they had been partly carried out and those parts were duly taken advantage of, the position is murkier.

Nelson himself dismissed Ruffo as 'a worthless fool', and he may well have been correct in judging the man's moral character, but does that clear his own?

Foote could not make such sweeping moral judgements; to him Ruffo was the accredited representative of the King of Naples who he was told to co-operate with to the full. Foote had accordingly done so and, in so doing, pledged the word of his nation, a fact that carried more weight at the time with the republicans than any promise by Ruffo himself. In addition, of the latter it has been said that, as a native of the country, he had more reason to harbour feelings of hatred and vengeance than Nelson. Yet, Ruffo saw fit to grant the republicans immunity for the greater cause. Caracciolo had stated to the court his own situation with regard to loyalty. The king and his hangers-on had fled the sinking ship, what were those left to face the music to do?

Finally, the whole speed and manner of Caracciolo's trial had left a bad taste in the mouth of many. Caracciolo was, after all, a nobleman and a flag officer of a navy. To terminate his life, no matter what his crimes by stringing him up at the yardarm of the British man-of-war like a common murderer, smacked strongly of vindictiveness and partiality, and did not reflect the common humanity for which Nelson had hitherto been famed.

One cannot help feeling, rightly or wrongly, that at this period of his life Nelson's dalliance with Emma Hamilton had allowed his heart to overrule his head. He displayed a hard and ruthless side of his character, almost as if he wished to play the iron man to impress his ladylove. Her friendship with the king and Queen of Naples, the adoration of the most popular hero of the hour, were all too much for her, a common trollop and adulteress after all, and she would appear to have allowed the allure she had for Nelson to lead him amiss in order to please her passing whim. Lest this be thought unfair and harsh, let it be mentioned that the Caracciolo episode was followed, almost immediately, by an even greater indiscretion on Nelson's part.

While the admiral had been engrossed with the Naples affair, even greater events had been occurring in the western Mediterranean, which, in more normal circumstances, would have brought out the true naval commander that he was. However, they did not, for the same reasons mentioned above. Admiral Bruix had slipped out of Toulon with his fleet and set course to join the Spanish squadron under Massaredo. Keith duly gave chase but, fearful lest the true French intentions were to double back and attack Minorca, he sent word to Nelson to detach part of his squadron to cover that island. Everybody still remembered Byng.

Nelson, however, was so engrossed in the Naples adventure that he decided to ignore this request and so, for a time, the whole of the western basin was left without a single British warship to defend it. Luckily, the French sailed back into the Atlantic, achieving nothing, while the Spanish warships were in too poor a condition to bestir themselves either. Still, it had been a gamble for Nelson to so ignore his superior's orders in this manner and it showed just how much the comparatively trivial affair at Naples was distracting him.

That Prince Caracciolo had fought with Nelson at the Battle of Genoa in 1795, counted for naught. The prince's plea, that he be tried by British officers, was turned down, his request for a second trial was rejected, he was not allowed to produce evidence to show he had been coerced and his final request, for death by shooting, was ignored. All in all it was a far from creditable performance on Nelson's part. Perhaps the best that can be said in closing this sad episode is that stress of war, or love, brought about a decision that was entirely alien to his normal character. But there, love does indeed make fools of us all.

11 ACTION OR INACTION (1805)

We have already seen how the rigid compliance with Fighting Instructions had become something of a fetish for many naval commanders. When others, with either frustration or initiative as their spur, attempted to modify them and had failed, retribution had been swift. However, times were changing, and gradually the daring and more resourceful admirals overcame the stifling limitations by hoisting 'General Chase' when appropriate. Such tactics brought victories for Anson, Hawke and Byron respectively at the battles of Finisterre, Quiberon and Grenada. Lifted by such examples of unorthodoxy, others sought new solutions to the sterile doctrine of battle on a parallel course. Boscawen and Rodney both achieved victories by abandoning this straitjacket. In addition, the evolution of improved signalling facilities enabled bolder strokes to be made by the likes of Howe, Kempenfelt and Duncan, where, instead of cannonading away ship-to-ship, they had boldly steered through the enemy line, cutting off parts of it and annihilating them piecemeal.

These were the pioneers who were rewarded with success, but there would always remain naval leaders, adequate and brave men in themselves, who would feel themselves bound by the rules as laid down, conformers rather than innovators. Such a man was Sir Robert Calder. It was his unfortunate fate to have decided to stick to what he thought were the wishes of his superiors only to find that he had misjudged the temper of the moment. He was not the first, and by no means the last, to find out too late that the Admiralty allowed themselves a certain ambiguity in how it framed its orders and how it expected them to be carried out. Admiral Sir Dudley North in the Second World War is another famous example of a victim of this kind of trap.

Robert Calder was born in 1745 and joined the Royal Navy in 1759, serving under Captain Sawyer in the *Chesterfield*. Robert later followed his patron to the *Active* and received early reward with success when that vessel captured what was one of the richest prizes ever recorded, the *Hermione*, in May 1762. Even as lowly a person as a midshipman received prize money of £1,800 for that feat. The same year he was promoted to lieutenant, but he then had to wait until August 1780 before he achieved advancement to post-captain. As such, Calder served on the home station in HM ships *Buffalo*, *Diana* and *Thalia*.

This service was followed by a long period without employment which lasted until the outbreak of the Revolutionary War, when Calder was rescued from half pay and given command of the *Theseus* (74) in the Channel, and here he remained for three years. His next step was an important one for his career, being appointed captain of the fleet to Admiral Jervis in the Mediterranean in 1796. Calder was present at the Battle of Cape St Vincent, where his services were rewarded with a knighthood in 1797.

Much was made by some of the fact that Calder had expressed open disapproval of Nelson's conduct during this famous victory. Calder certainly revealed himself at that time as not a man to whom unconventional deeds commended themselves in any way. Indeed, Calder quoted Fighting Instructions to Jervis in censuring the way the *Captain* had been handled. That worthy's response should have crushed such an attitude in his subordinate ('It certainly was so, and if ever you commit such a breach ... I will forgive you also'), but subsequent events were to prove that it did not. Robert Calder remained wedded to 'correctness'. It was alleged that when Calder was sent home with dispatches of the battle, he so altered them as to omit reference to Nelson's bold conduct and that there was a long feud between the two men, but this has never been fully proven. Certainly, Nelson's own attitude later seems to dispel this rumour as merely that.

What can be stated is that there never were two commanders more dissimilar than Nelson and Calder, and their subsequent different fates in 1805 cannot come as much of a surprise. In 1799, Calder was promoted to rear admiral and hoisted his flag in the *Prince of Wales* (98), part of the Channel Fleet. In 1801, Calder made a bad error of judgement that led him to take his squadron of seven battleships and three frigates in an abortive hunt right across to the West Indies in search of a French squadron. Despite this gaffe he continued to serve under Cornwallis in the Channel and, in 1804, he was made vice admiral, once more flying his flag in the *Prince of Wales*, blockading Brest. By February 1805, Calder was commanding a squadron of five battleships keeping watch off Ferrol, wherein lay ten Franco-Spanish battleships fitting out for battle. Meanwhile, Nelson had been led the same merry dance by Villeneuve as Calder had been by Ganteaume.

When word reached Lord Barham that Villeneuve was on the way back across the Atlantic to join his fleet with those now ready in the Spanish ports, he immediately ordered the concentration of the British squadrons on blockade duties and told them to intercept the enemy at all cost. Admiral Cornwallis was to patrol off Ushant with part of the Channel Fleet, while Calder was to be reinforced by Rear Admiral Stirling's five battleships and, with a combined strength of fifteen ships-of-the-line, Calder was to spread his ships west of Cape Finisterre. The enemy fleet, he was assured, was but sixteen or seventeen battleships. The risk was accepted that the enemy ships the British had been watching for so long might take the opportunity to slip out and try to join Villeneuve, but the destruction of the latter's command was deemed the greater priority.

Thus, initially, it fell out. Stirling joined Calder on 15 July and the combined fleet took up a position 90–120 miles west of Cape Finisterre. On the 22nd Villeneuve obligingly sailed into the trap.

The day had dawned fine, but with patches of thick fog and little wind. As the morning wore on a slight breeze commenced from the west-north-west and, as the mist dispersed, the French fleet was clearly seen to the south. It was not the sixteen sail as forecast but twenty battleships and six frigates, against which Calder could pit but fifteen battleships and two frigates. Not daunted, Calder decided to engage forthwith. The time was 1100hrs when the French first hove into view, and, an hour later, the signal to clear for action was made and the British fleet steadily closed the enemy on the starboard tack.

At 1300hrs, Calder hoisted the signal for line ahead, close order, strictly according to the book. The question now, as so often before, was would the enemy also play according to the rules? That they should stand fight, having a marked superiority in numbers, seemed obvious to the approaching British captains, but would they? Initially there was some uncertainty. Villeneuve's instructions were those given to many of his French predecessors: he was not to go in and fight with any British fleet. Napoleon's orders were very clear on this point: he expected his admiral to avoid any such action until he had joined forces with the ships bottled up in harbour. Only then, with Nelson decoyed out of the way, and with the Franco-Spanish fleet in overwhelming strength, could Villeneuve fall upon any British squadron with impunity and thus clear the Channel for the Grand Army to cross for the final reckoning with Great Britain.

However, the French admiral was a fighting seaman and, orders or no orders, he saw he held the card of superior numbers now and he had the weather gauge. After some pondering of this situation (who, after all, would willingly disobey the emperor?), Villeneuve accepted battle and, also forming his ships into line, steered north to meet Calder.

The composition of the two fleets at this juncture was as follows: the British fleet had the *Hero* (74), Captain the Hon. A.H. Gardner; *Ajax* (74), Captain W. Brown; *Triumph* (74), Captain H. Inman; *Barfleur* (98), Captain G. Martin; *Agamemnon* (64), Captain J. Harvey; *Windsor Castle* (98), Captain C. Boyles; *Defiance* (74), Captain P.C. Durham; *Prince of Wales* (98), Captain W. Cuming, flagship of Vice Admiral Calder; *Repulse* (74), Captain the Hon. A.K. Legge; *Raisonnable* (64), Captain J. Rowley; *Dragon* (74), Captain E. Griffith; *Glory* (98), Captain S. Warren, flag of

Rear Admiral Charles Stirling; *Warrior* (74), Captain S.H. Linzee; *Thunderer* (74), Captain W. Lechmer; and *Malta* (80), Captain E. Buller.

The French and Spanish fleet consisted of *Argonauta* (90), flagship of Vice Admiral Don F. Gravina; *Terrible* (74); *America* (64); *Espana* (64); *San Rafael* (80); *Firme* (74); *Pluton* (74); *Mont Blanc* (74); *Atlas* (74); *Berwick* (74); *Neptune* (80); *Bucentaure* (80), flagship of Vice Admiral Pierre Villeneuve; *Formidable* (80) flagship of Rear Admiral Dumanoir le Pelley; *Intrepide* (74); *Scipion* (74); *Swiftsure* (74); *Indomptable* (80); *Aigle* (74); *Achille* (74); and *Algesiras* (74).

Due to the light airs prevailing it was 1520hrs before the two fleets were finally abeam each other, some 7 miles apart, with the French and Spanish ships in the unusual position, for them, of being to the windward of their opponents and in greater force. Calder did not flinch and signalled his ships, 'Engage the Enemy'. Due to the range, the British battleships could not immediately comply. Nevertheless, the enemy had accepted the challenge and confidence was high. Calder instructed his van to make all possible sail and, painstakingly slowly, the two fleets converged, with the two British frigates, *Egyptienne* and *Sirius*, out ahead to report on the enemy movements.

Although the gap between the two fleets, still on opposite courses, had narrowed, there appeared, by 1620hrs, a distinct chance that if both held their course the French might sail straight past the British line and, using the advantage of the wind, win clear away before they could be brought under fire. To rectify this Calder ordered his ships to tack in succession on a northerly course. This would have taken a long time to achieve – tacking in succession meant that each ship followed her next ahead, keeping the line intact and following a leisurely U-turn. At best it might have left the British van only abreast the French centre on completion, a familiar situation we have noted before. If the order had been given for the British ships to tack together this would have much reduced the time lag, but such a course did not commend itself to Calder's strictly orthodox thinking.

Then the whole picture was altered by chance. The *Sirius* (Captain W. Prowse) had sighted the French frigate *Sirene* astern of their line and she was observed to have in tow a captured galleon, the *Matilda*. Sensing rich pickings if she could be cut out, the *Sirius* steered to engage and the *Sirene* fired warning shots, which brought the French admiral's attention to the situation astern of him. Villeneuve immediately ordered his fleet to wear to the south in succession. So it came about that both fleets simultaneously turned in line ahead back toward each other, again on opposite courses. The British fleet remained to leeward, but with the range now down sufficiently for action to be certain, if brief.

It must be remembered that, during all these complex and stately evolutions, visibility had remained indifferent and so, when the leading British battleship sighted the leading enemy vessel, neither admiral was fully aware of the true overall situation. Captain Garner of the *Hero*, in the British van, fully appreciated this, and, showing far more initiative than his commander-in-chief was to do that day, took advantage of Calder's 1709hrs signal to engage the enemy as close as possible. *Hero* turned sharply to port and placed herself broadside on the *Argonauta* and a fierce duel commenced at close quarters between these two battleships.

More by accident than design, therefore, the much-sought 'ideal' position had been achieved with the fleets in place to line up conterminous to each other. Again, not all the captains in the British fleet were endowed with the same spirit as Gardner. The second in line, Captain Brown of the *Ajax*, sought to contact Calder and explain what was happening up ahead, rather than immediately conforming to *Hero*'s manoeuvre and supporting her. Instead of turning to port, therefore, the *Ajax* wore round leaving *Hero* on her own at a critical time.

It was fortunate for the *Hero* that the remaining British captains showed a more ready appreciation of what was required and, one by one, the *Triumph*, *Barfleur*, *Agamemnon* and the others of the van complied with Gardner's new course and the action became general. Calder, with the information from the *Ajax* taken in, and with that vessel reallocated a place back in line astern of his own flagship, followed the leaders' example. Thus, by 1800hrs, the majority of the British battleships were engaged with one or more of the enemy line. The action was particularly hot in the van, but gradually the true victor, it became obvious, was to be the weather. The mist remained patchy and the visibility poor, conditions not enhanced by the volumes of smoke drifting over the field of battle.

In this confused situation, both battle lines became ragged and the battle broke up into individual actions, some of which were pressed home hard, while others were conducted at long range and to little material effect; some ships, indeed, hardly came into action at all. As always, the British shot low when they could and the enemy shot high. Again, as usual, the damage inflicted naturally reflected this. By the time that the coming dusk had forced Calder to break off the fight, the Franco-Spanish fleet had clearly suffered a telling reverse, receiving some 650 casualties against but a third of that number among the British ships. Two enemy battleships had been dismasted and had struck their colours, the *San Rafael* and the *Firme*, while three more had been badly knocked about and were in difficulties, the *Espana*, *Pluton* and *Atlas*.

On the British side, the *Agamemnon*, *Prince of Wales* and *Defiance* had suffered some damage, the *Ajax* and *Malta* severe damage, while the *Windsor Castle* had come off worst of all and had to be taken in tow by the *Dragon*. Despite this, Calder had given the enemy a bloody nose for all their advantage of wind and numbers and could well be satisfied with how things had gone thus far.

The night was spent by both fleets in repairs to their damage in readiness for the next day, when a resumption of the fight was expected. The two captured enemy battleships were taken in tow by the British frigates and steered clear of the battle zone, along with the *Windsor Castle.*

Dawn on the 23rd was greeted with some expectancy. The day proved still a misty one, but this cleared away quickly, the wind remained light and the enemy fleet was in view some 17 miles off, and still to windward. If the battle was to recommence then it must depend on Villeneuve once more. Despite his losses, he still outnumbered Calder eighteen to fourteen; moreover, the British fleet had become split up in the darkness and one squadron, the *Barfleur, Hero, Triumph* and *Agamemnon,* were found to be within 6 miles of an enemy squadron of four ships, with the main fleets of both sides almost as far away again and unable to immediately support either.

While these two advanced squadrons remained in sight of each other throughout the initial period, both commanders appeared hesitant to come to grips again. At 0800hrs Calder recalled these battleships to his line and concentrated his fleet. Calder still lay between the enemy and his base, and seemed quite content to remain thus without forcing the issue further. Calder's considerations at this juncture, he was later to state, were threefold: the protection of his two prizes, the protection of the *Windsor Castle* and, last but not least, his knowledge that the French and Spanish fleet, already superior to his own, might at any time be reinforced by the fifteen ships in Ferrol and the five in Rochefort, which would have given the British a hopeless inferiority in numbers.

A bolder man might have grasped the nettle and closed to inflict as much damage as he could before this possibility came about, but Calder determined that he had done enough for the moment. If the British admiral hesitated, what of the French? Villeneuve soon became aware of Calder's stand-off policy and his initial reaction was to feel that he had his enemy on the ropes. Villeneuve decided to risk Napoleon's wrath and take advantage of this rare situation to present his emperor with a crushing victory. The French admiral therefore signalled to his commanders that he was going to engage. By midday the Franco-Spanish fleet had formed up and was approaching the British line intent on battle. Due to the conditions of the wind, this charge was more in the form of a funeral procession and it was not until mid-afternoon that Calder became aware of the enemy's decision to force the issue. Calder at once instructed his warships to haul closer to the wind and clear for action.

Then there came yet another turnabout in this game of nautical musical chairs. As the two fleets drew close on converging courses Villeneuve had a change of heart. Instead of running the British were preparing to stand fight – maybe he had been a little too hasty. At 1600hrs, therefore, the French came about on to a parallel course and the fleets were stalemated once more. Now it was Calder's turn to change his mind, and he steered to close the enemy. Again, at this critical moment, as before, the weather frustrated that intention. The wind changed, the

British could make no progress and night fell with both fleets in sight of each other, but still out of range.

Calder still remained to the east of Villeneuve and both fleets continued to the south-east during the night, Calder slightly in advance of the enemy. By first light on the 24th, a gap of 15 miles had opened up. At 0800hrs the Franco-Spanish fleet decided that their chance to reach their rendezvous had come and they turned back. Calder let them go. By 1800hrs the enemy had disappeared over the horizon. It was an extraordinary and tame anticlimax, which did neither admiral much credit. However, both men felt justified in their actions by their orders.

The subsequent movements of both fleets after the 24th become academic to our story, although of course they were the prelude to the great victory at Trafalgar some months later. Villeneuve steered for Vigo Bay, anchored there on the 26th and then, five days later, sailed for Ferrol. Calder, on his part, escorted his prizes and the cripple back to toward England and then turned back with thirteen ships. After looking into Ferrol and finding little there, Calder resumed his original blockade. Three of his battleships were then detached to resume the watch on Rochefort, and *Dragon* was set to scout Ferrol once more on 9 August after a storm had driven Calder off station. The *Dragon* found the enemy had, as Calder had feared they might, joined up and now numbered twenty-nine against his reduced force of just nine battleships. There was nothing the British could do against such odds and they withdrew, Calder joining Cornwallis off Ushant on the 14th, where the squadron remained, guarding the southern approaches to the English Channel until the arrival of Nelson's ships.

Secure in his own mind that he had done his best as conditions and orders had permitted, Calder had no hint of the coming storm. News of the indecisive action and the subsequent lifting of the blockade was received with incredulity at the Admiralty and fury in the streets. When word reached him of these expressions of opinion, Calder at once applied for a court martial in order to clear himself, but the Admiralty, who had already dispatched instructions for his return home via Nelson himself, had forestalled him in this.

When Nelson joined the fleet off Cadiz on the 28th he appraised Calder of the situation. Lord Barham had been most put out at Calder's seeming lack of resolution and had deleted sections of Calder's report that had justified his actions when the document had been published, thus contributing to the criticism. Nelson was more sympathetic, stating that, 'I should have fought the enemy, as did my friend Calder; but who can say that he will be more successful than another?' Further, Nelson sought to lessen the mortification of Calder on being recalled at such a time, by allowing Calder to proceed in his flagship, even though every major ship was vital to him at this time. How could he have done otherwise, Nelson was to write, he might well be criticised for such a gesture, 'but I trust I shall be considered to have done right as a man, and to a brother officer in affliction – my heart could not stand it'.

Noble sentiments indeed. Nelson also sent home those officers who were willing to speak up for Calder, Captains Brown and Lechmere, but others refused to go. Some, like Harvey, did not wish to be absent when the final showdown with the enemy came at sea; others, like Durham, because they just did not like the man. (Durham had had been upset because Calder had not given him credit for being the first to sight the enemy on 22 July.)

The court martial of Calder did not finally get under way until December, and was held aboard the *Prince of Wales* at Portsmouth. In his defence, Calder stressed the importance he attached to the preservation of his two prizes and to protecting *Windsor Castle*. This, Calder felt, justified his decision not to force combat in the succeeding days. 'Circumstanced as I was, it appeared to me to be impracticable to force the enemy to action with such advantage as would justify me, even if I had nothing to apprehend but the opposing squadron.'

However, it was the possibility of the enemy ships at Ferrol and elsewhere, coming out to reinforce Villeneuve, that most weighed with Calder at that time:

But when I reflected that sixteen sails were at Ferrol, who might have come out to the assistance of the combined fleet, or ... be pushing to England, the invasion of which was an event daily expected, I felt that by renewing the action I should run too great a hazard and put my fleet in a state of danger which I could not have been justified for doing. I therefore thought it best to keep my squadron together and not to force the enemy to a sever engagement till a more favourable opportunity.

Again, Calder comes back to this possibility. 'Had I then been defeated it is impossible to say what the consequences would have been. They might have gone to Ireland.' To which Nelson remarked that 'He appears to have had the ships at Ferrol more in his head than the squadron in sight'. And so it appeared to the Admiralty!

The charges of cowardice or disaffection against Calder were totally absurd, of course, and he was duly quickly acquitted on both counts but, on the 23rd, the court found him 'guilty of an error of judgement' and he was sentenced to be severely reprimanded. In truth, Barham and the board judged him yet more harshly, for it marked the end of his career. Calder was never to be employed again. The accused lived quietly, becoming, by virtue of his seniority, a full admiral in 1810 and was a KCB in 1815. The last years of his life were further marred by his wife's mental disorders and he finally died in August 1818.

History has also been hard on Calder. Perhaps this was inevitable, Calder's conduct being contrasted unfavourably with Nelson at Trafalgar and naturally showing him in a very poor light. Very few modern historians have tempered their judgement with the charity of Nelson himself. One of these gentlemen wrote, 'these obstacles do not excuse his failure to issue instructions designed to gain a decisive victory, such as those already mentioned as having been issued by Nelson, or, indeed, for failing to conceive any plan for doing so'. Another historian stated that Lord Barham had wanted to 'establish an abiding dread that though hostile squadrons might slip out of their blockaded ports, the penalty of their success would be never to return. At the cost of a sacrifice … he had placed Calder in a position to secure that end, and Calder had not secured it.' On Calder's obsession with his prizes, a third such judgement was equally scathing:

> Considering the little value of these vessels, the *San Rafael*, as hip of 34 guns, and the *Firme*, a ship fifty-one years old, and both battered to pieces, their destruction would have been not only a justifiable measure, but under the circumstances, the most eligible that could have been devised.

John Terraine is kinder in assessing the character of the man and what was asked of him, or others, what was tacitly hinted at in his orders. '… Calder was expendable …' He added, 'It must be remarked, however, that it requires a special temperament to be able to regard oneself as expendable without being explicitly told so, and Calder should not be blamed too much for not having it.' Villeneuve himself was critical of the conduct of his own officers. 'In the fog, our captains, without experience of an action or of fleet tactics, had no better idea than to follow their second ahead, and here we are the laughing-stock of Europe.' Such self-criticism perhaps suggests that Calder did not fail completely, in that he lowered Franco-Spanish morale and self-esteem yet another notch. Even when they were superior, and having the advantage of the wind and a hesitant opponent, they could not win.

Nearer to his own day, Calder found at least one historian to stand up for him. The Rev. L.H. Halloran, a naval chaplain, made this telling judgement on the critics:

> I cannot but deem an officer, who, though of unquestionable bravery, and having gained an important advantage over a superior force, is yet severely criticised for an error of judgement! – sentence which, it might be presumed a court, composed of men, themselves weak and fallible, would have paused, and seriously deliberated upon, before they thus indelibly placed upon record, what may hereafter sanction their own condemnation! Byng was sacrificed, and Calder censured, because they were not exempted from human Fallibility!

If he had been asked to give up his life and sacrifice his fleet, no doubt Calder would have done so; his failing then was that he was too hidebound by those cursed rules to gain a decisive victory and not astute enough to grasp that the situation at the time called for more than total obedience and a paper victory.

12 INDECISION IN THE BASQUE ROADS (1809)

Long after Trafalgar had been fought and won, and Calder had been sentenced and forgotten, the naval war at sea continued, with the French and their allies once again building up their strength and the Royal Navy patiently resuming watch over all the major ports in close blockade. From time to time the enemy timidly ventured forth, taking advantage of weather conditions, but their periods spent at sea were few, and resulted either in the defeat of their squadrons piecemeal if caught or a hasty retreat back into harbour again if not. Such a situation was to be found in 1809. James, Lord Gambier, commanded one such British squadron blockading Brest, but his ships were driven off station during a February gale and the French took the opportunity to escape.

Following his previous orders, Gambier therefore detached Vice Admiral John Duckworth with eight battleships and a frigate to search for them, while he withdrew to Cawsand Bay to await orders in his flagship, the *Caledonia*. On the way there, word came from the frigate *Naiad* that enemy ships from Brest, eight battleships and two frigates, had taken refuge in the Basque Roads on 24 February, where they had been joined by another force of four battleships and two frigates from the Aix Roads. The combined French fleet lay at anchor, secure, they felt, from the British behind the sandbanks and shallows, and under the protection of the gun batteries on the Isle D'Aix, with the Charente Estuary at their backs.

Gambier at once set sail again on 3 March, with *Caledonia, Tonnant, Illustrious, Resolution* and *Bellona* to join Rear Admiral Stopford blockading Rochefort with the *Caesar, Defiance, Donegal* and four frigates. If no enemy were found, then the combined force was to proceed to the Basque Roads to deal with any enemy ships they might find there. The rendezvous was effected on 7 March, when it was found that reinforcements under Captain Beresford awaited them, *Theseus, Triumph, Valiant, Revenge* and *Hero*. The news was the enemy had anchored in the Aix Roads with eleven battleships and four frigates. Such were the hazards of this part of their own coastline that the French, in making this simple move, had lost one of their own battleships, *Jean Bart*, wrecked on the Pallas Shoal.

Gambier duly took up his blockading position in the Basque Roads off La Rochelle, and considered his next move. He could attack straight away. The inherent dangers of such an approach was that, threading their way slowly through the uncertain waters off the Isle of Oleron, with charts they did not trust and with turncoat French pilots who were incompetent, the British ships might go aground or be picked off one at a time as they made such an approach. Gambier decided that the best way of dealing with the enemy was by use of fire ships.

Gambier also discovered that the French on the Boyart Sand were readying another battery, but that it was either damaged or not yet complete. The British admiral therefore decided to repeat the attempt of Admiral Strachan some years earlier and burn the enemy at their moorings. Gambier duly wrote to the Admiralty to this effect on 11 March. The Admiralty had anticipated his wishes and had ordered that twelve old transports be fitted out as fire ships to join. The *Cleveland*, another converted transport, containing a marine rocket detachment as well as this weapon's inventor, Mr Congreve himself, to try their luck. The Admiralty also sent Gambier five bomb vessels (*Etna*, *Fury*, *Hound*, *Thunder* and *Vesuvius*) whose shallow draught made them suitable for penetrating the maze of shoals and sand, so they might engage the enemy close inshore. All this was well anticipated and welcomed. Additional transports containing combustibles and several gun brigs also joined Gambier's force around this time. The preliminary action taken by the British was to destroy the works under construction at Boyart.

On 3 April the frigate *Imperieuse* arrived to join the fleet. She carried Lord Cochrane, whom the Admiralty had ordered to command the actual fire boat attack in person, much to the consternation of some of the officers of the fleet who had expected that honour themselves. Nonetheless, ample volunteers were found for this dangerous work and the plans began to be laid.

The French fleet, commanded by Admiral Allemande, was anchored in two lines some 250 yards apart, protected at that time by the Aix batteries and by a chain boom half a mile long. The British attack took place on the night of 11 April, with the fire ships and three explosion vessels designed to blow up among the enemy. These latter vessels were included at Cochrane's insistence and he commanded one of them, the *Mediator*, in person. Conditions of wind and tide were favourable for their approach but little chance was afforded for any of their gallant crews to make a successful escape afterward. In the event, two of the explosion ships were to detonate prematurely, thus alerting the enemy, who scrambled to get clear and find safety. Several of the fire ships were ignited too soon and were wasted, but the *Mediator* broke the boom and the remaining fire ships were put to their work most efficiently.

The French were now thrown into considerable panic and disarray. The *Regulus* (74) and *Ocean* (120) cut their cables to avoid the fire ships, but the latter immediately went aground and was attacked by one of them. The great three-decker quickly took fire and burnt out completely. Two further battle-ships, *Tonnerre* and *Patriote*, collided with the blazing *Ocean*. Daybreak revealed the extent of the devastation. The wreck of the *Ocean* lay on a nearby mud bank, gutted. Some 500 yards off lay the *Varsovie* (80), *Aquilon* (74), *Regulus* (74) and *Jemappes* (74), all hard aground on the rocks. The *Tonnerre* (74) had thrown her guns overboard but was still hard fast and bilged, while the *Patriote*, *Tourville*, *Calcutta* and four frigates were also ashore.

Observing the pitiful condition of the French fleet, Cochrane felt the chance should be seized to finish the job. Accordingly, he signalled to Gambier, 'Eleven on shore, only two afloat', and a little later as another hint, 'Half the fleet can destroy the enemy'. The British fleet duly weighed and stood in toward shore, but re-anchored again before noon, still some 6 miles from the stranded enemy. Gambier was convinced that to send in his own battleships to carry out the bombardment was to risk losing them on the shoals. Gambier considered the job could be just as effectively carried out, and with far less risk, by the shallow-draught gunboats. The *Etna* and three brigs were therefore sent in to attack.

The only two French ships still afloat, *Foudroyant* and *Cassard*, on seeing these vessels approaching, cut their own cables and made a run for the Charente, but they, in turn, ran aground at its entrance on another shoal. The French ships began dumping their guns and one of them got afloat again. The *Calcutta, Varsovie* and *Aquilon* were also seen adopting the same desperate measures to try to escape their fate. Cochrane was aghast at the thought of these hapless enemy ships slipping away to safety from under his very nose and he took the *Imperieuse* in boldly through the twisting shallow, trusting implicitly in his French charts and ignoring the fire from the protecting French batteries.

By 1400hrs, Cochrane had anchored on the starboard quarter of the *Calcutta* and the little British frigate began single-handedly to engage the three enemy battleships as they struggled to get free of the mud. Meanwhile, Gambier had detached the frigates *Aigle, Emerald, Indefatigable, Pallas* and *Unicorn* to support Cochrane, and, once the tide turned enough to give them sufficient depth of water beneath their keels, he also sent in the battleships *Valiant* and *Revenge*. The *Calcutta* had taken the brunt of Cochrane's fire, and she was abandoned and then blown up by her crew. After a short time under fire by the whole British squadron, her two compatriots followed her example and were abandoned, the *Tonnerre* also being blown up.

Five further enemy ships remained aground and Rear Admiral Stopford in the *Caesar* led in three transports, hastily converted to fire ships, to deal with them. The *Caesar* quickly ran aground, showing Gambier's fears on that score to be well founded, as did some of the transports. All that could be accomplished was the burning of the *Aquilon* and *Varsovie*, which finished them off. The main fleet now withdrew out to sea again, but Cochrane remained inshore with the *Imperieuse, Pallas*, the shallow-draught gun brigs and the *Etna*, and renewed the assault. The *Beagle* engaged the *Ocean* from astern but, before her destruction could be completed, the tide and wind turned against the British and they were forced to withdraw on the 14th. By ditching their guns and equipment, all the enemy ships, save the frigate *Indienne*, were ultimately refloated and took refuge in the Charente at Rochefort.

Initially this affair appeared a substantial achievement for, without the loss of single ship, the British fleet had destroyed a good part of the French fleet in very difficult conditions. Lord Cochrane received the Order of the Bath for his gallant part in the proceedings. However, his aggression toward the enemy (at one time in order to spur Gambier into action he had hoisted the signal in *Imperieuse*,

'This ship is in distress and requires to be assisted immediately') now spilt over in his frustration at not being able to finish the job totally. Cochrane had made no comment at the time, although he complained to Gambier that he had been let down by many of the fire ship's officers, but later he made it very plain how he felt toward Gambier himself.

The First Lord of the Admiralty, Lord Mulgrave, had proposed that a vote of thanks be carried in the next session of parliament. Cochrane, an MP himself, replied that he could not agree to this – if it included Gambier. In other words, the men had done well but Cochrane did not consider that the C-in-C had. On learning of this comment, Lord Gambier, deeply offended, applied for his own court martial in order to clear his name, and this the Admiralty agreed to.

The court sat aboard HMS *Gladiator* in Portsmouth harbour from 26 July to 4 August 1809. The President was Admiral Sir Roger Curtis, and no less than six admirals, Young, Stanhope, Campbell, Duckworth, Douglas and Sutton, and four captains, Irwin, Dickson, Hall and Dunn, comprised the court, with Mr Moses Greetham as Judge Advocate.

After the letters and dispatches had been read out, and the logs and charts produced, the proceedings opened with the first witness, Thomas Stokes, master of the *Caledonia*, who produced a chart showing the position of the French fleet at the time of the attack. Robert Hockings, the signals officer of the flagship, who produced her signal log, followed Stokes. Much was to be made of these two documents later on. The master of the *Imperieuse* was closely questioned about entries in that ship's log. It transpired that, after the battle was over, Cochrane had instructed him to make soundings of the anchorage with a view to proving that the battleships could have been sent in with safety to engage the enemy. The master, John Spurling, established that he had filled in these details later and that he had confirmed various entries with a check against those of the *Indefatigable*'s on return to port. The master of the *Beagle*, who was similarly questioned on some late entries, followed Spurling.

This groundwork completed, Cochrane himself was called. He proved to be a difficult customer for the court to deal with. Did it appear, Cochrane was asked, that the admiral gave every assistance in his power toward carrying into effect 'such propositions as your Lordship made to him, for preparing, arranging, and sending fire ships against the enemy?' Cochrane replied, 'Every possible assistance.' And were the frigates and other small vessels properly placed by the commander-in-chief? 'Very judiciously placed,' was the reply. The various signals made by Cochrane were now listed, and the question put to him:

Was it your Lordship's opinion, at the time of making the first-mentioned signal, that it would have been expedient for the Commander-in-Chief to send in half, or any of the ships of the line, to effect the purpose of destroying the enemy's ships, considering the state of the wind and tide at that time, and the shoal-water in the inner-harbour; and, if so, was there a probability, in your Lordship's judgement, that such ships could have got off again safely?

Cochrane then began a detailed answer to this very involved question, referring to hand-held notes. Before he had preceded very far, the President raised objection to this on a point of order: 'Is it not usual, when minutes are referred to by witnesses, to ask whether they were minutes made at the time, or subsequently upon reflection?' The Judge Advocate agreed and Cochrane confirmed that they were minutes made at the time 'which I am willing to swear to'. Cochrane then went on to answer the question in this manner:

> It is my opinion, that a much smaller force than half the fleet would have been sufficient; the signal was directed by the *Caledonia* to be repeated: I ordered the signal to be made that two sail of the line were enough; which I have since understood was not made, but that the officer repeated the previous signal; the fact was, that he thought it would be an insult to make that signal, and that therefore he repeated the signal previously made, leaving it to the discretion of the Commander-in-Chief to send what proportion of the force he thought proper.

Cochrane confirmed that he considered that the depth of water would have enabled even the largest ships to get in and out again safely. The President then asked: 'You say that there was room enough for six sail-of-the-line to lie within the range of shot or shells; do you mean that at any time of the tide?' Cochrane replied in the affirmative and, on being pressed, added: 'When I say six sail-of-the-line, that was the impression on my mind; but I believe you might put a dozen or twenty there.' When the Judge Advocate read over his reply Cochrane qualified this statement: 'That was merely conversation. I should not wish to swear to that, only to the other part.' It was duly struck out.

Cochrane was then asked whether the position the admiral then moved to was a good one for observing what was happening and to make an attack. Cochrane qualified his answer and the question had to be repeated. Again, the reply was:

> I have no hesitation in saying, certainly it was a good position for that purpose – certainly it was a good position for observing the transactions of the enemy; and being near, assistance might have been set to any vessels, *had an attack been made upon the enemy*; that position might have been taken at daylight, when an attack might have been made with advantage to the service.

There was further digression when, in response to another question, Cochrane indicated he would answer from notes. The President interrupted:

I do not know what may be the opinion of the Court, but I confess it appears to me, that the more regular course would be for Lord Cochrane to answer that question, if it is in his power to do so, not by reference to any correspondence he had with any other person, but what is the conviction in his Lordship's mind ...

Cochrane tried to amplify his reasons, but the President responded that:

I still retain the same opinion, that where you can have the evidence stated by word of mouth, you are bound so to take it, and that you cannot with propriety receive as evidence anything which has been thrown together as a communication to another person ...

The Judge Advocate confirmed this view: 'it is the constant practice to refuse the witness leave even to look at those memoranda.' The President added: 'I never, in all my experience, knew the document of a witness permitted to be received when he was present himself to be examined.' Nonetheless, Cochrane continued to refer his notes, which he had made in June, and this caused yet further delay to the proceedings while the legitimacy of this was debated.

Finally, the question that was the crux of the whole affair was repeated – was there any unnecessary delay in making the attack on the stranded enemy? The reply was unequivocal:

... the direct answer is, that there was no delay whatever, to the best of my belief, after the signal for assistance was made, on the part of my Lord Gambier, in ordering vessels to our assistance; but had the attack been made in the morning, when the tide was falling, until past eight o'clock, and when the enemy's ships were all, with the exception of two, fast aground ... it is my opinion, that seven sail of the enemy ... might have been destroyed with facility, by two sail of the line, assisted by frigates and smaller vessels; and that after the hour of half past eleven, when the enemy's two ships remained at anchor , until the British fleet weighed, that the frigates alone, assisted by smaller vessels, might have destroyed the whole of the above-mentioned ships, the rear of which afterwards were attacked.

When the court reassembled the next day, the question was asked, 'Did it appear to your Lordship that there was any unnecessary delay on the part of the commander-in-chief from daylight on the morning of 12 April, when your Lordship made the signal, "... that half the fleet could destroy the enemy's ships," till the Imperieuse and other frigates went in to the attack'.

Cochrane's reply was, again, a firm 'yes'. He added:

> ... the tide and wind were ... both going the same way, and ships of the line by
> passing near to the Boyart and putting their helm-a-lee, their fore and main-top
> sails being to the mast, would have brought their heads to the north east, which
> would have enabled them, at a distance at which the shot of Aix would have
> been of no effect, to have brought all their guns to bear upon the enemy's two
> ships [by which he meant those that remained afloat, the *Cassard* and *Foudroyant*].

More upsets followed. Cochrane's later replies were considered not relevant. The court was cleared and earnest deliberations followed, after which the President issued another warning to Cochrane, 'in all succeeding questions, they must require you to give a short and decisive answer to the question put to you'. Yet still the ding-dong went on and Cochrane was continually pulled up and told to stick to the point, while he argued that his answers were the truth and the whole truth.

Cochrane was later to allege that the French batteries on Aix were no great threat, for he had observed them closely and they seemed to be under repair. He stoutly maintained that Gambier could have made the same deductions regarding the ease of entry to the inner anchorage that he himself had done. 'The Commander-in-Chief had the same charts, I believe, as I was in possession of.'

However, here his lordship was not backed up by any of the other commanders on the spot. Admiral Stopford stated, 'I do not think there was any delay or deficiency on the part of the commander-in-chief, in executing the service entrusted to his Lordship's care.' Stopford later added that, from his long experience in these waters:

> ... the difficulties of the navigation, and our imperfect acquaintance with it,
> with the wind right in, would, I think, have made me unworthy of command,
> if I had risked a fleet or a squadron entrusted to my charge, in a situation where
> our's would have been only the loss, and the enemy's all the advantage.

Captain George Wolfe of the frigate *L'Aigle* was asked whether he knew of any vessels being withheld from the attack that might have been sent in. He replied: 'None whatever ... I mean to say there were no vessels under his Lordship's command with a draft of water that could have further effected the destruction of the enemy's ships.'

Captain John Rodd of the frigate *Indefatigable* was asked: 'From the first attack upon the enemy's ships to the final cessation of hostilities against them, was everything done that could be done to effect their destruction?' He replied, 'I believe everything with safety to his Majesty's ships.'

When asked if the battleships could have attacked without risk of grounding or being risked by fire from the Aix guns, Rodd answered: 'I do not know that they would have grounded, but they must have been wholly disabled by the batteries and two line-of-battle ships in coming in. I counted thirteen guns as we passed the battery.'

Lord Gambier himself gave his defence in a long statement on the fifth day of the trial. He was hurt, he said, by having to ask for the clearing of his name thus but he could do little else in the circumstances:

> I believe there is not a precedent to be found in the naval annals of Great Britain, or an officer of the rank I have the honour to hold, commanding a fleet which has performed so important a service as that accomplished under my direction ... being obliged, from a sense of what is due to his own character and honour, as well as to the profession to which he belongs, to appeal to a naval tribunal against the loose and indirect accusations of an officer, so much his inferior in rank ...

Gambier asked the master of the *Caledonia*: 'Could any more of the enemy's ships than the four that were destroyed have been destroyed, had any of the king's ships been sent to attack them at daylight on the 12th April?' The reply was that, if it had have been attempted, 'I think we should have sacrificed our own ships without making any impression on the enemy or destroying any of their ships'.

Captain Beresford of the *Theseus* backed this opinion: 'Two of the enemy's ships were afloat ... which, in my opinion, would have entirely crippled any ships sent in to act.'

So it continued, with captain after captain maintaining, as did Captain Kerr of the *Revenge*, that everything had been done that could have been done, despite Cochrane's assertions to the contrary. Several witnesses were asked the same question: 'From the time of the Commander-in-Chief's arrival in Basques Road, to the time of your quitting it, can you state any instance of neglect, misconduct, or inattention to the public service, in the proceedings of the Commander-in-Chief?'

Captain Burlton of the *Resolution*: 'I know of none.' Captain Ball of the *Gibraltar*: 'No, I cannot.' Captain Newman of the *Hero*: 'None.' It was a catalogue of affirmations on Gambier's conduct and it was obvious before the court even adjourned to consider their verdict that Cochrane very much stood alone in his criticism, as far as the trial itself was concerned, whatever the mood in the fleet or the country at large might be. Thus it transpired. The court's verdict was read out on the ninth day of the trial, 4 August:

> ... having maturely and deliberately weighed and considered the whole, the charge, 'That the said Admiral the Right Honourable Lord Gambier, on the 12th day of said moth of April, the enemy's ships being then on shore, and the signal having been made, that they could be destroyed, did, for a considerable

time, neglect, or delay, taking effectual measures for destroying them,' has not been proved against the said Admiral ... but that his Lordship's conduct on that occasion, as well as his general conduct and proceedings as Commander-in-Chief of the Channel Fleet employed in the Basque Roads, between the said 17th day of March and the 29th day of April 1809, was marked by Zeal, Judgement, Ability, and an anxious attention to the welfare of His Majesty's service, and doth adjudge him to be most honourably acquitted; and the said Admiral the Right Honourable Lord Gambier is hereby most honourably acquitted accordingly.

The President asked for Lord Gambier's sword and this was duly returned to its owner with the words:

Admiral Lord Gambier, I have peculiar pleasure in receiving the command of the Court to return you your sword, in the fullest conviction that (as you have hitherto done) you will, on all future occasions, use it for the honour and advantage of your country, and to your own personal honour.

However, recorded another historian: 'This verdict was not supported by public opinion, or by the majority of the naval profession, and it would seem that Lord Gambier displayed anything but zeal or enterprise in the destruction of the French ships aground.' Nonetheless, the vote of thanks to Lord Gambier was carried in the House of Commons by 161 votes to 39, and without a division.

An interesting footnote to this affair can be included for it concerned the opinion of Napoleon Bonaparte himself. The emperor later remarked that:

Lord Cochrane could not only have destroyed them, but he might and would have taken them out had your admiral supported him as he ought to have done. For in consequence of the signal made by Allemande to the ships to do the best in their power to save themselves, they became panic-struck and cut their cables. The terror of the fire ships was so great that they actually threw their powder overboard, so that they could have offered very little resistance. The French admiral was an imbecile, but yours was just as bad.

Whether or not the memoirs of the then bitter emperor-in-exile carried any weight in the verdict of history, the verdict of the court martial stood. Cochrane's reputation did not suffer in the least, his earlier deeds of daring had already enamoured himself to the British people and he went on to even greater fame and acclaim, while Gambier's star soon faded.

13 SHIPS THAT GO BUMP (1893)

Three-quarters of a century after the end of the Napoleonic Wars the Royal Navy waxed as mightily and powerfully as it had ever done. It was both the mirror and the supreme and unchallenged defender of the majestic British Empire, which it had done so much to create and preserve. In that unique period of tranquillity and prosperity Great Britain really did 'rule the waves', exercising her long wisdom and knowledge of that responsibility both impartially and tolerantly. No other fleet in the world even began to approach the splendour and size of the Royal Navy, although brash raw newcomers were beginning to aspire to such thoughts – Germany and America – as the old enemies and traditional sea powers, France and Spain, faded away. Full of self-confidence and boosted by 'A tradition of victory', the British admirals led their huge battle squadrons in the supreme knowledge that they wielded more power than most foreign kings and emperors. Untroubled by actual conflict, they devised elaborate exercises and drilled their tars repeatedly. The ships themselves had changed out of all recognition from those of Nelson's day: steel and coal, not wooden walls and sail, thundering compound engines watched over by oil-covered engineers, an alien world below deck to those that controlled them from the bridge. Huge guns that could fire projectiles to the horizon from revolving turrets had replaced close-range broadsides. Yet, incorporated into this vast and awesomely complex fighting organisation was a weapon as old as sea warfare itself, the ram.

Strange that such an antique method of war should be so highly thought of in an age that worshipped technical innovation and embraced change with the fervour of a new religion, yet so it was. The weapon utilised at the Battle of Salamis in 480 BC by the Greeks and the Persians had made a remarkable renaissance in the mid-nineteenth century.

It had been the coming of steam at sea that had first led to this strange re-adoption. With this new power at their command, making them independent of the weather at last, the feeling was that the use of the whole vessel in one powerful thrust into the side of an enemy ship would prove irresistible. Despite the new innovations, sea battles were still expected to be conducted at close ranges, and here it was felt that a reinforced armoured ram, cutting into an opponent below the waterline at full speed, was a quite practical and viable proposition.

It had been the French who had set the pace here, although with no such planned design in mind. Their *Magenta* and *Solferino* battleships of the 1850s had featured a long projecting stem and the British had followed the style with the *Defence* and *Resistance* launched in 1861, both being described as 'steam rams'. Soon, every ironclad was built with this feature, and a hot debate commenced about its effectiveness in combat. Many at this period considered the ram to be the primary weapon, despite the increase in the range of the ships' main armament.

These huge pieces of ordnance were to remain chronically inaccurate for many years, whereas a well-directed ram, it was held, would be decisive. This applied not only to finishing off an already crippled enemy vessel, but as a desirable object of any fleet's 'first strike capability', to put it in modern parlance.

The first tests of the ram in modern warfare occurred during the American Civil War, but proved far from conclusive, the *Merrimac* and *Monitor* duel proving an elaborate stalemate. Directing the ram in action proved more difficult than anticipated. It required an iron resolution on the part of any captain to deliberately steer his vessel full-tilt into another ship. When, on the rare occasions, this was managed, more often than not the angle was wrong or the blow was cushioned by the target's course and own speed through the water. However, the reputation of the *Manassus* off New Orleans heavily influenced worldwide opinion, although her actual achievements were not that great. They influenced the French ship designer de Lome in particular.

However, the greatest acclaim came as a result of the Battle of Lissa in 1866, which took place between the fleets of Italy and Austria. The Austrian commander-in-chief, Tegetthof, issued his ships with just one clear order that day, 'Ram everything grey', his own ships being painted black. That instruction his commanders endeavoured to carry out to the letter. The result was not so much a naval encounter as a series of charges, which usually resulted in nothing more than near misses. By a supreme chance, however, one blow was finally delivered which resulted in a fatality. The *Ferdinand Max*, having previously aimed without success at two different enemy ships, suddenly burst out of the smoke and steam with which the battlefield was veiled and came upon the already damaged *Re d'Italia*. The Austrian ship struck this unfortunate vessel at a speed of 11.5 knots, more by luck than by judgement, and her ram did its work to perfection, penetrating the hull of the Italian ship and suffering no damage in return. Locked together the Italian might have survived, but the Austrian reversed her engines and backed out of the hole, and the doomed *Re d'Italia* quickly filled with water and vanished beneath the waves.

This lucky fluke, and it was little more, set the whole naval world in fervour. The ram was proclaimed as the weapon of war par excellence. Admiral Colomb, acknowledged as an expert on naval warfare, was to comment: '… the ram, and the ram only, need be feared at sea.' The noted constructor Sir E.J. Reed declared: '… the ship itself – viewed as a steam projectile – possessing all the force of the most powerful shot, combined with the power of striking in various directions – will be deemed the most formidable weapon of attack that man's ingenuity has devised.' Others were not so euphoric. Admiral Warden stated that he, for one, 'was not one of those who think that in the next naval war ramming will rank before artillery as a mode of attack'. But even he qualified that statement by adding, 'I believe firmly that it will play a very important and formidable part'.

The limitations of the ram as a weapon of war for a modern navy to employ have been summed up by Admiral Sir Reginald Custance in his volume *War at Sea* in this manner:

> The ram is a weapon peculiar to the sea; its effective use depends upon facility in manoeuvring, which in turn hinges on speed. The higher the speed the greater is the facility in manoeuvring and the probability of ramming successfully or of avoiding being rammed, since the point of the attacking ram on the one side or the attacked ship herself on the other side can be moved through a greater distance in a given small interval of time. And further, the higher the ratio between the speeds of the opponents, the greater the margin for error on the part of the faster attacking ship and the greater her corresponding advantage. This will be made clear by considering extreme cases. If one ship is a rest, the moving ship has an infinitely greater advantage, whereas if both ships are moving at equal speeds the chances of success are equal.

Quite so, and the author was obviously considering two opposing ships in time of war, but by far the greatest number of casualties caused by this fearsome weapon were inflicted by friend upon friend. Reverting to the American Civil War once more, the biggest material loss to ramming had been the *Southfield*, a Federal vessel, which was rammed by another Federal ship, the *Albemarle*. Despite these statistics, by 1893, when a British fleet containing the most powerful battleships of their age was approaching the port of Tripoli in the eastern Mediterranean, every one of these awesome warships boasted a hardened steel ram jutting out below their bows just below the waterline.

Let us turn from the ships and the weapons now to consider the men. At least if progress had changed the face of the fleet the sailors who commanded and manned these giant vessels were still the same reliable breed that had drubbed the enemy time and time again down the centuries. Well, yes, they were. Despite the enormously increased powers of destruction these men had at their fingertips, they were still fallible men. We have seen the many faces of the professional seaman, the good qualities of bravery, determination, heroism and skill, but we have also seen the human foibles of which they were no less prone than any other, pride, hesitancy, inflexibility and blind obedience to orders, any orders, once they had been promulgated by a higher authority. None of these things had changed, as was to be proven one sunny afternoon in the most tragic of circumstances.

The Mediterranean Fleet, comprising eleven battleships and their supporting craft, had sailed from Beirut on 22 June 1893, under the command of Admiral Sir George Tyron, KCB, who flew his flag in the almost new battleship *Victoria*. She was a 10,470-tonner, completed in March 1890. She had run aground in January 1892, during her first commission, and had spent several months in dock at Malta as a result. She had been re-commissioned as the fleet flagship the month before. The entire Mediterranean Fleet had spent five days at Beirut and Tyron was anxious to shake the cobwebs away before they again dropped anchor for a night at Tripoli, just down the coast.

The commander-in-chief was a remarkable man, a 'character' in the true meaning of the word. Tyron's unorthodox leadership was the talk and the reluctant admiration of the Royal Navy. Born in 1832, the third son of a peer and educated at Eton, he had enjoyed an enviable and seemingly effortless career to date. Tyron had joined the service in 1848 as a cadet aboard the *Wellesley* at Plymouth, had been present at the Crimea operations aboard the *Vengeance*, had fought with the Naval Brigade at Sebastopol and returned home a lieutenant. Service aboard the Royal Yacht elevated him to commander at an early age and he then became commander of HMS *Warrior* in 1861. Tyron continued his effortless rise to the top with aplomb, one officer writing that he 'never showed jealousy of any of his brother officers, for it may pertinently be replied that he never had occasion for it!' He was a post-captain by 1866, leap-frogging scores of his seniors, became private secretary to the First Lord in 1871, where he made a reputation as a great reformer, was ADC to Queen Victoria and later returned to the Admiralty, after commanding both the *Raleigh* and the *Monarch*, as secretary. Tyron became C-in-C, Mediterranean in September 1891.

Naturally, such success in all walks of life aroused envy and some resentment among less fortunate officers who had to claw their way upward by more traditional and painstaking methods. One such person was Tyron's second-in-command, Rear Admiral Albert Markham. Son of a naval officer and grandson of an Archbishop of York, Markham was born in 1841 and had scraped into the navy in 1855. A sensitive youth, Markham at first found the service life not much to his liking. However, he stuck at it and was eventually rewarded with promotion to lieutenant after service in China, joining the old ship-of-the-line *Victoria* in 1864 in the Mediterranean. This was followed by service in Australian waters aboard the *Blanche* and Markham became a commander in 1872, later taking part in the Arctic exploration expedition of 1875–76. By 1892 he had received his promotion from captain to rear admiral and he joined Tyron's command, hoisting his flag aboard the 10,600-ton *Camperdown*, one of the famous Admiral class battleships, completed in July 1889.

These two men, Tyron and Markham, therefore appeared almost complete opposites: Markham, big, bluff and hearty, a natural leader, forever delighting in dreaming up new and spectacular exercises for his battle fleet to perform; Markham, the slow plodder, able and capable enough, but lacking any sort of special flair or the inspiration to challenge any instruction with careful deliberation.

In order to arrive at their new port of call in immaculate formation, Tyron had come up with one of his sterling new evolutions for anchoring the fleet.

According to his long-established custom, he planned the manoeuvre but kept it strictly to himself. Tyron delighted in such a practice, giving an order, watching the way his subordinates carried it out and then explaining afterward where they had gone wrong. Today, 22 June 1893, was to be no exception to this policy. The fleet was disposed in two columns, led respectively by the *Victoria* and the *Camperdown*, each column being of some 2 miles in length and made up of the eleven battleships and two cruisers divided into two divisions. The ships were on a course steering east by north at a speed of 8.8 knots, some six cables' length apart. At 1525, the flagship hoisted the following signal: 'Second division alter course in succession 16 points to starboard preserving the order of the fleet. First division alter course in succession 16 points to port, preserving the order of the fleet.'

It was at once obvious to the captains of the battleships that such a turn would be extremely dangerous indeed, in fact, suicidal. All the ships of the fleet had different turning circles and it had been established that the minimum distance for the safe execution of such an evolution was eight cables, not six. Eight cables' length gave a turning diameter of 800 yards, but to turn the two lines into anchoring formation heading west by south at least two cables of clear water were required between each of the columns. Therefore, the ships should have been stationed ten cables apart in order to carry out Tyron's orders with any equanimity.

Rear Admiral Markham realised the dangers all right. He hesitated and then ordered his flag lieutenant to query the signal by semaphore in case a mistake had been made. However, before this could be done, a curt signal came to him from the bridge of the *Victoria*, 'What are you waiting for?' and *Victoria*'s signal was hauled down to execute. Markham was no man to backchat a second summons in the form of such a rebuke. Stung by this, the rear admiral ordered compliance with the order and *Camperdown*'s helm was put over as well; although, still torn between what he knew was wrong and a blind faith in his leader to bring off something unexpected that he had failed to grasp, Markham compromised, to 28 degrees instead of 35 degrees. The time was 1531hrs.

The two juggernauts were now closing with each other and it soon became very apparent that something was wrong, fatally wrong. Tyron stood at the after end of the chart-house deck watching solidly astern to see how the rest of his division was performing. His flag captain, Maurice Bourke, became anxious. 'We had better do something, Sir, we shall be too close to that ship,' he hinted, but Tyron made no reply. Captain Bourke turned to a midshipman and ordered him to take the distance, and to hurry up about it. 'Three-and-a-quarter cables,' came the reply. Two minutes had passed and Bourke, now agitated, tried to draw the admiral's attention forward. 'We are getting too close, Sir! We must do something, Sir! May I go astern with the port screw?' To all of which the admiral remained aloof.

Bourke had to repeat the question twice more before the admiral turned and, for the first time, saw the oncoming *Camperdown* bearing down on them, now terrifyingly close. At last he answered, 'Yes, go astern.' But it was too late for that now. Full astern both was immediately rung down, Lieutenant Heath ordered the watertight doors to be shut and the collision mat prepared. All they could do then was wait. They did not have to wait very long. Just before the impact Tyron cupped his hands and shouted across the water to Markham's ship in a last futile gesture, 'Go astern – go astern!'

At 1534hrs the great steel ram of the *Camperdown* sliced into the *Victoria's* starboard bow some 12 feet below the waterline and penetrated for 9 feet, swinging the flagship around some 70 feet to port. As their sterns swung together, the movement ripped the breached hull yet further, tearing a huge gap some 100 feet square before the *Camperdown* broke free. There had not been time for the full watertight integrity of the ship to be achieved and the ocean flooded into her rapidly. With the *Victoria's* bows filling quickly a desperate attempt was made to steer her toward shallow water, but this only made worse the inflow of water into the ship. The flagship's forward battery door, two forward ports and the turret ports were all still open, and a sudden lurch brought her down to their level. The flooding now became uncontrollable. The *Victoria's* stern lifted, the thrashing screws still churning water and bodies; then she fell over quickly on to her port side and turned turtle, sinking at 1535hrs and taking down with her 358 officers and men. Admiral Tyron was not among those saved. His words after the accident went down into posterity: 'It was all my fault.'

Was it? That was for the court, which assembled aboard the *Hibernia* at Malta on 17 July 1893, to try to ascertain. The President of the court was the new C-in-C, Admiral Sir Michael Culme-Seymour, Bart., and on the court itself sat Vice Admiral Tracy, superintendent of Malta dockyard and seven captains. Henry Rickard was the Deputy Judge Advocate, and Captain Alfred Winsloe the prosecutor. The trial was 'to be held under the 91st and 92nd sections of the Naval Defence Act, to enquire into the loss of HMS *Victoria* and to try Captain the Honourable Maurice Archibald Bourke, and the survivors of that ships, for their conduct on that occasion'.

Accordingly, all the survivors were mustered for the trial who were fit enough to attend, the officers and 235 petty officers, seamen, engineers and Royal Marines were herded aboard the *Hibernia* and accommodated behind a roped-off area on the poop deck. Bourke objected to four of the members of the court as they had been present at the time of the accident. They were replaced, but the calling of the long roll caused further considerable delay before the proceedings could continue.

The first evidence heard was from Markham's letter to the Admiralty. In it Markham had stated that 'Having the fullest confidence in the great ability of the commander-in-chief to manoeuvre the Squadron without even the risk of a collision, I ordered the signal to be hoisted as an indication that it was understood'. Markham's flag captain had also written a statement in which he had stated that, when the collision had appeared inevitable, Markham had ordered full-speed astern, but when he had later seen the engine room register, 'I found, to my astonishment, that only three-quarters speed astern was recorded as having been given'.

Bourke then took the stand and caused something of a sensation when he refused to state just what conversation had taken place between himself and Tyron when they had been alone on the stern walk of the *Victoria* just before the collision. The President remained adamant but only after being asked five times did Bourke give way. 'I reminded the Admiral that our circle was eight hundred yards. He said the columns were to remain at six cables. I then went on deck.' It having already been revealed in the narratives that Tyron had been warned of this before, by his staff, Commander Hawkins-Smith and his flag lieutenant, this third warning caused some raised eyebrows. The court returned to this point the next day without obtaining further elaboration. When asked why the signal for six cables was flying and now eight, Bourke replied that 'I had some idea in my head that the Commander-in-Chief had some way out of it. I had confidence in the Commander-in-Chief, and nobody ever questioned him. I never questioned him.'

Lord Guildford confirmed Tyron's remark that it was his entire fault. 'Did he say it to you or was it a general expression?' he was pressed. 'I believe no one heard the expression except myself,' was the reply. However, it turned out that someone else had. Hawkins-Smith confirmed it: 'There was no conversation, but he made use of an expression. He said: "It is entirely my doing, entirely my fault".' Asked whether he had intervened when the accident was imminent, Hawkins-Smith replied: 'No, I was never asked for my advice ...' 'Did it occur to you to express an opinion on the subject to anybody?' 'No.'

On the third day, it was Markham's turn. The second-in-command revealed that when his flag lieutenant explained Tyron's signal to him his immediate response had been: 'It is impossible as it is an impractical manoeuvre.' Asked why he had therefore complied with it after Tyron's impatient 'What are you waiting for?' signal, Markham repeated, 'I thought the First Division were going to wheel round me, which would have been a manoeuvre of perfect safety, and a feasible one'. How did he arrive at that conclusion? 'Because it was the only safe interpretation of the signal. The other was an absolute impossibility.'

Markham's flag captain was not so certain, however. When he was asked whether he was convinced that Markham's interpretation was what he also though Tyron had intended, he replied: 'No, I was not convinced.' The officer-of-the-watch reported hearing a conversation between Markham and Johnstone, in which the admiral had stated: 'We cannot do it. It is impossible. We are not at the manoeuvring distance.' And later, 'They mean it, Captain Johnstone, we shall have to do it. They have asked me what am I waiting for.' These answers revealed that conditions aboard the *Camperdown* were in a far from clear state just before the fateful turn and it was Markham's future that began to look bleak, not Bourke's. On the fifth day, the captains of the other battleships were questioned on what they had made of the order. Several of the captains agreed with Markham's reading of the C-in-C's signal, others did not. Many displayed that same blind faith in Tyron to produce something out of the hat in order to avert the seemingly obvious disaster that was looming. Thus Wilson of the *Sans Pareil*: 'considering the confidence I had in my leaders, I felt sure that they had made some arrangements which would prevent it.' Moore of the *Dreadnought*: 'I thought we were about to see something unusual in the way of an evolution.'

In his own defence, Bourke stated: 'I must say I think any impressions I did have arose from my absolute faith and confidence in the Commander-in-Chief.' He added, with some significance, that 'no one ever criticised the Commander-in-Chief as to what he intended to do. I do not know to what extent I may go, but I do not seem to think that open criticism to one's superior is quite consonant with true discipline'.

The verdict of the court was delivered on the lines expected. They found that the loss of the *Victoria* was due to collision and that collision 'was due to an order given by the then C-in-C'. The court attached no blame to Bourke or any of his ship's company for the accident, but they were more reserved in their judgement of Markham:

> … the Court feels strongly that, although it is much to be regretted that Rear-Admiral Albert Hastings Markham did not carry out his first intention to semaphore to the Commander-in-Chief his doubt as to the signal, it would be fatal to the best interests of the Service to say he was to blame for carrying out the directions of his Commander-in-Chief, present in person.

What was really in Tyron's head that summer after all will never be known. Did the officers of the Royal Navy learn anything from this disaster? They sounded like robots in their answers and in their blind obedience to an order they knew could not be carried out safely. Surely, the lesson had been brought home? Twenty-three years later, in the darkness of the night that followed the Battle of Jutland, that question was answered. Blindly the battleship captains followed Jellicoe, not even showing the initiative to report the presence of the enemy when they caught glimpses of them attempting to break through, but blandly and silently held their tongues and their course because that was what they had been told to do. Tyron would have been proud of them – or would he?

14 'ON THE KNEE' (1906)

Inflexibility is the common theme running through these pages. Inflexibility in the rules and laws governing conduct and battle; inflexibility at the highest level in judging genuine grievances from below; inflexibility from officers in their conduct towards the lower deck or to each other. It might be assumed to be a fault in the system, widespread, rampant even, in the latter half of the eighteenth and nineteenth centuries, had it not equally been displayed by government above and the men themselves below in equal degrees. The striking of gestures, taking up of fixed stances, the inability to see the other fellow's point of view, they might be current disputes with trade unions, but these faults riddle the history of our nation with its deeply ingrained class system, a system unique to Britain and far less marked elsewhere in the world. This inflexibility should not be confused with pride. Pride in one's country, pride in a service like the Royal Navy, is a desirable element. Pride relates to discipline, both of those administering it and those subject to it. It could be maintained that no great institution can exist without it; certainly it is the most human of traits. However, in a position of responsibility, pride must be tempered with compassion and awareness. The fate of some politicians shows what happens when these two key elements are missing from even the most extreme factions.

In many ways the service life is an artificial one, run on regulations that no civilian would tolerate for a moment. Both sides know this and when a firm but fair stance is maintained both abide by the rules. But there always appears to be those who must stand too much upon their dignity, without consideration of the possible consequences. More often than not they get away with it; on rare and treasured occasions the current feeling in the nation will just not stand for it. The secret is to try to anticipate the mood, some are good at this, others are not. One officer who was certainly not a good judge was Bligh, more recently another was Lieutenant Bernard St George Collard, and it was his misfortune to prove this unhappy fact not once but twice in his career.

Collard had joined the Royal Navy around the turn of the twentieth century, entering the service straight from Clifton College. He was 13 and the son of a Dorsetshire vicar. Collard served as a cadet aboard the old training hulk *Britannia*, moored in the River Dart. Later, as a young 'Snotty' aboard his first seagoing ship, he proved himself to be both brave and capable, earning the praise of the Royal Humane Society for his rescue of a seaman who had fallen overboard in Aalesund harbour, Norway. Collard then went on to serve aboard the armoured cruiser *Drake*, which was commanded by a succession of remarkable captains during his time aboard, Bridgeman, Jellicoe and Sturdee. After undergoing a specialist gunner course at HMS *Excellent* in the years 1899–1901, a period as an instructor at Whale Island followed, under the equally renowned Captain Percy Scott.

There is no need to say more about these years to anyone who has been in the service once that has been stated. To anyone in the 'Old Navy', Whale Island meant the navy at its smartest and most efficient, discipline at its most rigorous, punishment at its toughest. To survive Whale Island you had to be tough, smart and quick, damn quick. Everything was done at the double and with the greatest precision or God help you! Nor was HMS *Drake* any less severe at this time. She became the flagship of Prince Louis of Battenberg, with all the associated pomp and ceremony one would have expected from such a combination. Beresford was not the only commander to think that 'paintwork appeared to more important than gunnery'. Nonetheless Collard, a gunnery man through and through by now, did well in keeping the ship taunt, and was marked down as an up-and-coming young officer. Collard had already gained a reputation for being a strict disciplinarian by the time he returned to the shore as senior gunnery officer at the Royal Navy Barracks, Portsmouth.

For such men with his background, the atmosphere Collard found at the barracks did not enamour itself to him at all. This shore base had finally been completed in 1903 after years of wrangling over its possible siting. It stood on the site of the old convict prison and the sailors were naturally not slow to refer to the similarity and aptness of this. The barracks replaced the old training hulks afloat in what many saw as a long overdue reform, and they were first commissioned under Captain H.D. Barry on 30 September, some 4,000 men marching in after two rehearsals, seamen, Royal Marines and stokers. The accommodation was described in a contemporary journal as being 'a perfect palace, with electric light, lavatories on each floor and water taps in every room, which are lofty and swell lighted'.

The report continued much in the same vein: 'Each block is divided into two sections under a Warrant Officer, and the entire block is under a Lieutenant. When seen with the men sitting at the mess tables, the long rooms (each holds 125 men) had the appearance of the decks of an old-fashioned line-of-battle ship.'

In February 1905, King Edward VII inspected these 'palatial' quarters:

> He spent some time in the recreation rooms, and then crossed over to the Stoker block. Entering the subsidiary block on the ground floor, he visited the bathrooms etc., and then going upstairs he went into the clear cheerful cooking room, and saw the schoolrooms and other divisions of the block. Crossing over to the living block His Majesty went into one of the Stoker's long rooms, and saw for himself the conditions under which the sailors live when in Barracks.

With such vast improvement to the sailors' living conditions, with the royal approval, with brand-new accommodation and with every facility, a greater contrast could hardly be found between the living conditions of the stokers in 1904 and the ghastly, stinking hulks like the *Sandwich* in 1797. Surely, under these circumstances, a more unlikely place to see a fresh mutiny in the fleet of the Nore tradition would be hard to find. Yet, within a short time, mutiny there was, albeit mutiny with a small 'm'.

When Lieutenant Collard arrived at this palatial establishment it may well be that his attitude was just what was required. The holiday atmosphere that comes from moving into brand-new quarters still remained in the air. To a man from Whale Island the whole place must have seemed incredibly lax. It needed a shake up, Collard clearly felt, and immediately began to apply himself to just that. Almost immediately Collard was involved in controversy.

The first incident, as always, seemed trivial enough, and nothing serious was thought of it until the press got hold of it later and blew it up as is their wont. It was an evening in November 1905. Lieutenant Collard was supervising the mustering of a fire party from the duty watch and what he witnessed displeased him more than usual. He considered that the whole procedure had been carried out in a lacklustre manner. Collard therefore halted the calling of the roll and admonished the men to smarten up their responses. What Collard required, he told them, was a smart answer, according to the custom, of 'Here, Sir, please'.

Having thus made his position quite clear, Collard continued with the calling of the roll, but on the name of Seaman Acton being enunciated he received the reply, 'Here'. Collard's hackles rose and he corrected him a second time and then instructed the petty officer to call the name again. Acton again responded, 'Here'. It was now blatant insubordination and Collard was not the man to try such tricks on. Impertinence could not be tolerated by any officer, and Acton was duly charged and punished. All was correct so far but what was later alleged to have taken place was far from so.

The story that later went around the barracks, and then got into the *Daily Mirror*, was that Collard, outraged and furious, had roared at the delinquent seaman, 'Go down on your knees, you dirty dog, and learn your manners!' Acton, it was said, had been to see a solicitor as a result of this, and the solicitor had called upon Lieutenant Collard, with the result that the lieutenant had paid over money to keep the whole thing quiet.

Collard vehemently denied this accusation later. 'I absolutely deny having used any abusive words at all. I am not in the habit of using abusive expressions when addressing men.' However, the expression 'on you knees' was, in fact, to re-occur within a year from this same officer, and with far graver consequences.

Time passed, another bleak November evening fell over the huge barrack square. It was Sunday 4 November 1906, but for Collard the fireworks came a day early. A steady rain was falling at 1600hrs as the seamen, signalmen and stokers were paraded for evening quarters under the watchful eye of Lieutenant Collard. Due to the weather, a heavy downpour continued halfway through the parade,

which was broken up by some of the men running for shelter and being followed
by the rest who thought they had been dismissed. Such was not the case, however;
although it was given immediately afterward.

While the men were still dispersing, the stokers in particular made such noise
and disturbance that Collard was again angered and he determined to issue a
general reprimand. The men, many of them new recruits, were therefore recalled,
while the rain continued to lash down, and were made to form up once more, but
this time inside the gymnasium. The seamen and signalmen were soon dismissed
once more, but Collard retained the disgruntled stokers for further words. Before
he spoke he ordered them all 'on the knee'.

Collard was a short man, and he was later to state that it had been his intention
to have the front rank kneel so all the men could see him while he addressed
them on their conduct. The order itself was an ancient one, largely out of use in
the modern fleet, but still retained on the navy's statute books for drill purposes.
Collard himself had been subject to it during his career as it was particularly
common at the gunnery school. However, many quite senior officers passed
their whole service lives without ever hearing it used and it was hardly surprising that a batch of raw recruits might not understand its historic significance.
Collard should have been aware of this, but still chose to use this archaic term to
get their attention.

It was most unwise. The response from the stokers was hostile. Shouts of 'don't
obey' were heard and Collard was forced to repeat his instructions twice before
they complied, and then only in a sullen manner. The kneeling men were then
lectured and dismissed again. One man, who declared that he would go down
on his knees to God and nobody else, was retained and given a personal reprimand. Then Collard reported the incident on the telephone to the commodore
of the barracks, the Hon. W.G. Stopford. Collard assured Stopford that all was
now under control.

It was far from under control. Resentment among the men, fostered by misunderstanding, ran deep. That evening, the canteen was packed with 300 stokers
quietly drinking and talking over the events of the afternoon. At 2130hrs the canteen was being cleared when a seaman entered and shouted out 'On the knee!'
as a facetious comment on them being ordered out. At once uproar broke out
among the stokers, their feelings boiled over and they began to smash everything
they could lay their hands on; glasses, windows and tables were broken up in a
wild orgy of destruction. The canteen offering no further fuel for their flames, the
men poured out on to the parade ground looking for fresh ammunition to vent
their spleen upon.

The guard was called out by the duty petty officer and the barrack gates were
locked and, amid the babble of noise, the commodore arrived and three of the
apparent ringleaders were arrested. With some considerable courage, Stopford

went into the midst of the mob and, after some considerable time, got them to quieten down and listen to him. Their mood was still angry and they demanded the release of those under arrest.

Stopford informed them, amid renewed shouting and jeering, that he would not consider releasing any of them until order had been fully restored. Gradually the men broke up into small groups and dispersed, making their way to their sleeping quarters. Stopford was as good as his word and the three men were then released from custody. As a precaution, however, the gates were kept locked throughout the night and men returning from leave were sent off to find lodgings in the town. This was to lead to further complications, but, at the time, it seemed the safest solution.

This same procedure was repeated the following evening, Monday 5 November, but with the result that instead of dispersing the men remained in groups outside the gate in Edinburgh Road, where civilians joined them. Gradually the mood changed from frustration to anger. The road was under repair, and the loose granite chippings soon provided ammunition for one malcontent who threw it at the officers' quarters' windows. Within a short time many others had joined in and, before very long, a full-scale riot was under way. The local police joined with the gate guards in attempting to disperse the mob, but failed.

Meanwhile, back inside the barracks, the demonstration outside had rekindled the feelings of the stokers. Guards had been rushed to their block in anticipation of further trouble and the stokers, who were unable to break through, attacked them. They therefore turned their attentions once more to the actual building and a fresh bout of destruction of furniture and fittings took place. Others in the canteen rushed out on to the parade ground area and some scaled the railings to join the crowd outside, until soon some 400 ranting men had assembled there.

By midnight, events were totally out of control and sterner measures were taken. Two companies of Royal Marines were rushed up from Eastney Barracks and men mobilised from the warships in harbour reinforced these. Lines were formed and gradually the rioters were forced back down Queen Street, where they repeatedly tried to rush their way through the cordons. It took a further three hours before some semblance of order was finally restored, and a dozen men were under arrest and in close confinement in the cells.

Never had Portsmouth witnessed such scenes, and naturally the citizens were outraged. Questions were asked in parliament and the reputation of the Royal Navy sank to a low level. Courts martial were ordered on eleven stokers. They were not open to the public, which was to cause yet further trouble. The courts sat aboard HMS *Victory*, the men facing charges of endeavouring to make a mutinous assembly and inciting others to join such an assembly. All were found guilty and sentenced to terms of penal servitude, the severest being five years for Stoker Moody. Press and parliament took up opposing sides, and the Admiralty was slated for picking on Moody and some of the others just to make examples of them. The real cause of the outbreak, it was claimed, lay with an insensitive officer who had turned obedient men in good surroundings into animals by his aggressive attitude.

There was some exaggeration in this charge, of course, there always is in the British press, but there was enough firm evidence that Collard's order had been the origin of the trouble, to ensure that he was also brought before court martial. For good measure the case of Acton was cited and an additional charge was made in that connection. In total the charges Collard faced were three. Firstly, that he gave an unauthorised punishment (Acton's case); secondly, that he used abusive language to a stoker (Acton again); and, finally, that he made improper use of the order 'on the knee'.

The court martial of Lieutenant Collard took place aboard HMS *Victory* on 3 December. Much speculation was heard about the origin and continued usage of that, by now, infamous order. Some witnesses claimed that the order had originated from an old musketry drill book, the front ranks kneeling to fire while the rear ranks stood and shot over their heads. Captain Oliver of the *Dryad* declared that he had never heard of it. One petty officer recalled how, in his youth, a whole battalion had been ordered 'on the knee' for not standing still enough. It was, said the petty officer in the Acton case, an order used for assemblies of men, he had never known it to be applied to a single person, until Collard had so used it.

In his defence, Collard made a long statement, in a firm voice, which impressed many of those who heard it:

> I am not accused of using an illegal order but of improperly using a legal one. It is admitted that it is a proper use of the order to place a number of men on the knee under certain circumstances. The witnesses for the prosecution have spoken as to the state of affairs. For a trivial reason, the men on the parade showed a state of indiscipline which it would have been injurious to the interests of the Naval Service to have overlooked. I ordered them to fall in again. They arrived in a noisy and insubordinate state. They refused to fall in properly. They do not obey the orders of the bugle 'Still'. They're out of control of their Petty Officers. The question is, who is to give way, officers or men? I gave the order 'On the knee'. Men who were already insubordinate refused to obey. I insisted. They obeyed, and as the witnesses for prosecution have said, there was then absolute silence and all the fidgeting stopped. Can you say that this action of mine was to the prejudice of good order and naval discipline? What was to follow later in the day I could not foresee and should not now be held responsible for.

With regard to the Acton affair, two eyewitnesses found themselves giving evidence that in places were contradictory. It was further established that the said

Albert Acton was hardly a model victim. Acton, it turned out, had been drafted to the battleship *Duncan* soon after the incident had taken place and, in April 1906, he had deserted and was never found. References to 'dirty dog' abounded in the press and on postcards sold in Portsmouth, but the court refused to believe such an expression had been used by Collard. The accused was found not guilty on this charge and not guilty on the charge of improper use of the order at the gymnasium. However, the court did find Collard guilty of unauthorised punishment in applying the order to a single person and for this he was reprimanded.

In private, the President advised Collard, 'Don't take it too seriously', a piece of advice that, perhaps, strengthened his conviction that his attitude secretly met with approval in the service. The reprimand certainly did not affect his career in the slightest way. A subsequent successful libel action against the *Daily Mirror* and their reporter, a certain Edgar Wallace no less, raised Collard's stock even higher in the navy, always quick to close ranks against the rabid press and similar outsiders.

However, the court's decisions did nothing to actually end the arguments raging outside the service, and the House rang to cries of 'On the knee' and 'Mutiny'. With regard to the accuracy of the latter allegation, one naval journal was to comment: 'The incident has been largely referred to as a "Naval Mutiny"; we think it would be just as reasonable to refer to riot in Trafalgar Square as "Civil War in England!"' With which, we can most certainly agree.

Nevertheless, the debate continued, until, at last, the Admiralty was forced to issue a statement on 13 December, which made some concession to public opinion. One historian has stated that Collard 'took the blame for everything', but such was certainly not the case. Commodore Stopford, who had wisely closed the barrack gates on the Sunday, but rather unwisely on the Monday, was relieved of his command. Commanders Drury-Lowe and Mitchell were relieved of their appointments. Collard's reprimand stood, but two of the stokers had their sentences reduced, Moody's to three years.

Finally, to lay the bogie once and for all, Their Lordships decreed that the order 'on the knee' was not to be used for any purpose whatsoever, other than drill.

Had Collard and his order been the real reason for the riot? Or was it merely an excuse, the last straw so to speak? Indications are that such was indeed the case. There had been widespread feelings of injustice over the men's terms of service before this incident. Warrant rank had been theoretically open to them but conditions of age etc. in fact excluded the majority. The eleven stokers sentenced all had long records of insubordination, the Judge Advocate of the Fleet writing: 'I am clearly of the opinion on the evidence before me that he (Acton) fostered it and incited others to join and continue it.'

On Collard's use of the order the Judge Advocate was to further state: 'Whether the use of the order was improper or not in the exceptional circumstances which existed at the time, is a matter so entirely of the unwritten law of the Service that I cannot express any opinion as to the finding of the Court on this charge.'

Only one thing remains to be pointed out. If there was already a feeling of discontent among the stokers at this time, a responsible officer like Collard should have been fully aware of it. Collard had already seen the effects that this order had on the sensibilities of the men, whether legal or not. Collard should surely therefore have exercised more discretion on its repeated application at such a sensitive time. Collard did not, and so he cannot really escape all responsibility for the subsequent actions of resentful men as he tried to do. In effect, Collard provoked the men. We shall see whether Collard learnt anything from this affair, whether he was to modify his temper and his language, as he rose in the ranks, later in these pages.

15 SUPERIOR OR INFERIOR (1914)

One of the most difficult decisions for any competent and conscientious naval commander to make is to act against his natural inclinations in order to carry what appear to be the wishes of his superiors. Officers of the Royal Navy are trained to obey their superiors; it could not be otherwise. What might appear, at the time, on the field of battle, to be a golden opportunity to deal a blow to the enemy may in fact result in unforeseen complications of an adverse kind in the wider view of the overall picture. Given a certain amount of discretion, the officer can make his own decision, but, when tied down by firm orders, his scope is severely limited and, no matter how he might feel personally, he must comply with his instructions. Nelson's famous dictum that no officer could do wrong if he placed his ship alongside the enemy was stirring and inspirational, but not every commander since has felt he had the right to do so.

All well and good then, although frustrating to any commander worth his salt and imbued with fight qualities. We have already noted in these pages thus far, however, the fate of some of those who, in thus complying with what appeared to be their superiors' wishes, in fact, and often through no fault of their own, adopted a wrong interpretation. They soon found that the Admiralty or their political masters did not always share Nelson's thinking. Thus Torrington was shut up in the Tower and Byng was shot, while Hardy was greeted with praise for imitating the former and others subsequently forgiven for following the latter. One of the most famous cases of a fine officer being pilloried for obeying instructions to the letter, when those instructions were in themselves ambiguous, was that of Rear Admiral Ernest C. T. Troubridge at the start of the First World War.

Troubridge came from sturdy naval stock and would no doubt – circumstances being kinder – have distinguished himself as much as a forebear, Thomas

Troubridge, had over a century before. Professor Arthur Marder described Troubridge as 'a magnificent figure of a man and a born leader'. He also stated that Troubridge did not have much interest in weapon development. Maybe not, but as British naval attaché in Japan the then Captain Troubridge had a first-hand viewpoint of just what modern naval warfare involved, which is far more than could be said for most of his counterparts in the Royal Navy of 1914.

Hardly a serious shot had been fired in anger by the service for 100 years, during which time warships, weapons and tactics had changed out of all recognition. The majority of naval commanders went to war with only a theoretical idea of what would actually be involved. Troubridge had come much closer to modern sea warfare and had been much influenced by the Russian-Japanese conflict of ten years earlier, when the new weapons had been put to their first prolonged test in combat. Reading the reports that Troubridge sent home after the Battle of Chemulpo in 1904, one thing stands out: his respect for the destructive power of the long-range naval gun of the largest calibre. In the subsequent Battle of Tsushima the following year, Troubridge's opinions had been reinforced. The Japanese commander-in-chief, Admiral Togo, had based his battle plan on the crushing power of his 12-inch guns, pounding the Russian fleet at a range to which they could not effectively reply. The result had been an overwhelming victory. Nor were Troubridge's opinions unique, for the example set by that battle influenced the Admiralty to such an extent that the all big-gun battleship *Dreadnought* design followed very soon afterward. As Troubridge subsequently served as private secretary to the First Lord in 1910–11 and chief of the War Staff in 1912, he was in a good position to know that this was the current thinking and belief at the Admiralty.

Troubridge therefore knew the effects of long-range naval gunnery as well as any man. In the intervening years the ranges had grown enormously and this just strengthened his belief in their power. From 6,000 yards' range at Tsushima, the opening salvoes had commenced at 22,000 yards at the Battle of the Dogger Bank in 1915. Along with this had come the revolution in accuracy. With this, if anything, the respect for the effect of the big guns was even more relevant in 1914 than it had been in 1904. This applied to battleship fighting battleship, each with their massive armour protection to shield them. However, in 1914 the now Rear Admiral Troubridge found himself in command, not of battleships, nor even the more lightly protected battlecruisers, but of a squadron of thinly protected armoured cruisers whose own main weapons, 9.2-inch and 7.5-inch guns, were both outranged by their potential opponent and whose 6-inch side armour and 1 to 1½-inch-thick deck armour offered little resistance to the 11-inch projectiles of the opposition.

The potential enemy vessel in question was the German battlecruiser *Goeben*, of 22,640 tons displacement, armed with ten 11-inch guns, which had an estimated range of 25,000 yards. Although she was a battlecruiser and not a battleship, this should not imply too great a weakness in her defensive capabilities. The Germans built their battlecruisers as tougher ships than their British opposite numbers and the *Goeben* boasted an 11-inch-thick armoured belt, against which Troubridge's armoured cruisers' main weapons would hardly have been effective until they had closed the enemy within their range, which was just 16,000 yards. Nor did these cruisers' traditional advantage of speed count in this instance, for the *Goeben* was credited for being good for 25 knots, while the swiftest of the British armoured cruisers of Troubridge's squadron was 23 knots. In truth, at this time the *Goeben* was suffering from machinery defects that limited her best speed to just 18 knots, but this fact was totally unknown to the British commanders and, by clever and audacious bluff earlier, the German commander, Rear Admiral Wilhelm Souchon, had kept this defect hidden.

Souchon flew his flag in the *Goeben* and was accompanied by a single light cruiser, the *Breslau*. This pair of warships had been playing a deadly game of cat and mouse with the British since before the outbreak of the war. The main pre-war concentration of British naval strength had been made in home waters, naturally enough, to face the German High Seas Fleet. The Mediterranean had been left to the French fleet to police. This, despite the long dominance of the Royal Navy in those waters, had been the result of a tacit agreement, or understanding, reached pre-war but not made public. The French fleet was large, but its principal ships were semi-obsolete and they also had to contend with the possible intervention of both Austria and Italy, both of whom were Germany's potential allies. In the event, Italy played her usual waiting game to judge how things developed before committing herself to what she trusted to be the winning side, but, while her attitude remained uncertain, allowance had to be made for her fleet in the opposing camp.

Accordingly, a strong British naval force had to be made available pro tem, which, in August 1914, was placed under the command of Admiral Sir Archibald Berkeley Milne, with Troubridge as his second-in-command. Milne had at his disposal for a limited period the three battlecruisers of the 2nd Battlecruiser Squadron, *Inflexible*, *Indefatigable* and *Indomitable*; the armoured cruisers *Defence* (flying Troubridge's flag), *Black Prince*, *Duke of Edinburgh* and *Warrior*; the light cruisers *Chatham*, *Dublin*, *Gloucester* and *Weymouth*; and the sixteen destroyers of the 5th Destroyer Flotilla. All in all a well-balanced force, itself as large as most Second World War fleets and more than sufficient, it would be supposed, to annihilate Souchon's two vessels.

As the situation worsened and the threat of war drew closer, both sides shadowed each other warily, awaiting events. By 30 July the whole British fleet had been concentrated at Malta while the German brace were in the Adriatic with their Austrian allies. While they were there Milne received a telegram from the Admiralty, the draft of which was in the handwriting of the First Lord of the

Admiralty, Winston Churchill. Renowned for his less than helpful and continual interventions in operational matters during the Second World War, this was an early example of his ill-thought-out urging. The Admiralty missive laid down Milne's prime duties should war break out, stating: '… your squadron should not be seriously engaged with Austrian ships until we know what Italy will do. Your first task should be to aid the French in the transportation of their African Army by covering, and if possible, bringing to action individual fast German ships, particularly the *Goeben*', but Churchill, typically, then added the rider: 'Do not at this stage be brought to action against superior forces …' Hitler was to shackle his naval commanders during the second great conflict with similar restrictions and with equally disastrous results.

Churchill later claimed that this wording was meant to convey, 'so far as the English language may serve as a vehicle of thought', that he clearly referred to the Austrian battleships, but he did not actually say so and his meaning is no clearer from that communication in 2011 than it was to Milne in 1914, even though Milne was to say in retrospect that this was indeed how he had read it. If this is indeed so, then Milne was to compound Churchill's vague epistle when he passed on the instructions to Troubridge on 4 August, for he merely instructed him '… not to get seriously engaged with superior force'. Merely that and nothing more, as Poe's *Raven* has it. Not surprisingly then, Troubridge took this to mean the *Goeben* herself, and only she and the *Breslau* are mentioned in the rest of the signal, not a word about the Austrian fleet at all. From this initial misunderstanding, promulgated by Churchill and not clarified by Milne, all else stemmed.

Not being formal allies, no communication with the French was possible until after war had been declared. Milne was therefore in the dark with regard to the movements of the French troop convoys which he took to be his main responsibility, with the bringing of the *Goeben* to book secondary. The French had, in fact, delayed the convoys sailing and this further confused the issue and allowed the Germans come considerable latitude before the hunt for them was organised in earnest.

On 2 August, Milne was given different instructions; two of his battlecruisers were to shadow the German squadron, then at Brindinsi, the cruisers were to patrol the entrance to the Adriatic and he himself was to wait at Malta. Milne thus had two separate and widely diverse tasks to carry out that split his powerful force into weak segments. In compliance, Milne sent Troubridge with the *Indomitable* and *Inflexible* and his cruisers, while Milne remained at anchor with his flagship and remainder of the force. Milne was moved to enquire what he should then do if the German ships left the Adriatic, continue the watch or protect the French? Churchill drafted the reply, which was yet again hardly a model of clarity: 'Watch on the mouth of the Adriatic should be maintained, but *Goeben* is your objective. Follow her and shadow her wherever she goes and be ready to act on declaration of war …'

The German battlecruiser and her companion had, in fact, already set sail, reaching Messina the same day at noon. Troubridge, on being so informed, asked Milne the same question the latter had asked the Admiralty, and received much the same answer, do both. However, the Germans had sailed again and both Milne and Troubridge thought that they had gone westward after those juicy French transports bursting with soldiers. All good intentions went by the board and the battlecruisers were hurried off that way also, to watch the Straits of Gibraltar. The Germans had meanwhile signed an unexpected alliance with Turkey, in secret of course, and, after a brief bombardment of the French supply ports of Philippeville and Bône, Souchon therefore turned back to Messina intending to coal and then head for the Dardanelles. En route he met the two British battlecruisers hurrying west and the two squadrons passed each other at close range, but of course Britain and Germany were not yet at war.

The two British battlecruisers now reversed course and commenced to shadow the *Goeben*, but, amazingly, failed to report which course she was steering. Milne naturally assumed that it was still to the west, as did the Admiralty. Souchon risked his engines enough to speed up until he had shaken off their pursuit and was thus lost completely when the time to commence hostilities arrived. Milne then concentrated his big ships to the west, leaving Troubridge and his cruisers to continue the watch on the Adriatic.

Not until late on 5 August did Milne finally learn that the Germans were again coaling at Messina. While the light cruiser *Gloucester* fearlessly tailed the enemy, Milne coaled his own heavy ships and followed, expecting them to either force the Straits of Otranto, where Troubridge was waiting, or turn back into his arms. In the event, the German force did neither, and Troubridge took his cruisers south to intercept them, calling for his destroyers, which were refuelling, to join him as soon as possible. Now Troubridge came to his fateful decision, with his previous instructions clearly before him.

During the early morning of 7 August, as the British cruisers steamed hard toward the expected encounter, Troubridge's flag captain, a gunnery expert, Captain Fawcet Wray, held a discussion with his admiral on the bridge of the *Defence*. He asked Troubridge outright if he was going to fight, if so then the squadron ought to be so informed. Troubridge answered in the true tradition of the service that, 'Yes, I know it is wrong, but I cannot have the name of the whole Mediterranean Squadron stink'. As Troubridge was to acknowledge later, this was a most desperate decision in view of what he understood his orders to be with regard to a 'Superior Force'. It is to the credit of the admiral that his natural instincts were to disobey and go for his enemy regardless of the consequences. Troubridge duly signalled his intentions at 0245hrs thus: 'I am endeavouring to cross the bows of the *Goeben* by 6 am and to intend to engage her if possible.'

Nevertheless, again a misunderstanding led to further misunderstanding. Wray applied his considerable knowledge of gunnery to the probable outcome of such a situation and he took the words 'across her bows' quite literally, whereas Troubridge had really meant 'to intercept'. To Wray's mind such an approach was suicidal and he tackled Troubridge again at 0330hrs with this technical point uppermost in his thoughts. However, Troubridge, already deeply troubled at having to disobey a direct order in order to achieve an honourable outcome, appeared, in his turn, to have misunderstood Wray's subsequent technical point to mean that the latter was opposed to the whole idea of engaging at all. Thus, Wray's tactical argument induced Troubridge to change his strategical plan and, at 0440hrs, he signalled his new and final decision to Milne thusly:

> Being only able to meet *Goeben* outside the range of our guns and inside his, I have abandoned the chase with my squadron, request instructions for light cruisers. *Goeben* evidently going to Eastern Mediterranean. I had hoped to have met her before daylight. (0305)

At the time that Troubridge reached this decision, the *Goeben* was some 67 miles ahead of him and capable of a speed of only 18 knots. Troubridge had all along maintained that he would not engage the German heavy ship by daylight, but had firmed his mind to accept the risks after all, 'to clear his honour and reputation'. Troubridge admitted he had been having second thoughts on this even before Wray had spoken to him the second time, and that the latter's arguments had clinched his change of mind. That Troubridge had hoped to close within telling range of the *Goeben* and use his superior numbers and the faster rate of fire of his smaller guns to smother the enemy, who would have had to split his own armament, before dawn broke, he made clear later, but only after Milne had indignantly signalled back, 'Why did you not continue to cut off *Goeben*? She only going 17 knots and so important to bring her to action.'

Troubridge replied: 'With visibility at the time I could have been sighted from twenty to twenty-five miles away and could never have got nearer unless *Goeben* wished to bring me to action which she could have done under circumstances most advantageous to her. I could never have brought her to action.' He added with some poignancy: 'The decision is not the easier of the two to make as I am well aware.'

Goeben continued on her way eastward, still shadowed by the faithful *Gloucester*. Although Troubridge had fallen away to resume his watch on the Adriatic, Souchon was still in a terrible dilemma. The German admiral was uncertain of his reception at the Golden Horn and was fast running out of coal once more. Souchon had arranged for a collier to meet him in the Aegean, but first he had to shake off his persistent shadower. This was finally accomplished and the German battlecruiser then effected the rendezvous with his fuelling vessel at the island of Denusa, where a frantic coaling took place. Well might it be so, for Milne and his battlecruisers were now on his trail once more. Having wasted time coaling one of his own ships at Malta, Milne had set off eastward, although at a slow pace for he was still uncertain of Souchon's ultimate destination.

Even so Milne's tardy progression might yet have caught up with the *Goeben* and found her in an unenviable position had not yet another glaring piece of British human error intervened in favour of the Germans. Great Britain might now be at war with Germany, but she was not yet officially at war with Austria, although this was expected hourly. While Milne steamed slowly eastward, gradually closing the miles between his ships and the helpless enemy, a signal was received on the bridge of the *Inflexible*. This signal read: 'Commence hostilities at once against Austria.'

Here was a much greater threat than one lone battlecruiser, or so it seemed to Milne, and he at once broke off pursuit and headed north to reinforce Troubridge's squadron in blockading the exit from the Adriatic. It must be remembered that, at the time, it was still not certain that the *Goeben* would find a friendly refuge in Turkish waters, even if it might be a good bet that this would be the case. By the time the Admiralty revealed that this signal had been the result of a mistake in London (a standing signal had been readied for the time when war was declared on Austria, but this had been prematurely sent out early by a clerk at the Admiralty, in error, some four days in advance of the actual event), Milne was well on his way to his rendezvous with Troubridge. The qualifying statement to the Admiralty's correction of this error, that war with Austria was not yet a fact, but that the situation was critical, did not weaken Milne's resolve. It was not until twenty-four hours had passed that the Admiralty themselves realised that Milne had not continued his pursuit of *Goeben* and then they curtly instructed him to do so. Far too late! Milne was to the north of Denusa at midday on 11 August when he learnt that the two German warships were safely in the Dardanelles and had no intention at all of returning west. It was a bitter blow.

Subsequent events took a predictable turn. Although Milne had apparently satisfied the Admiralty as to his conduct initially, the return of Fisher and the belated realisation of just what a sensational coup Souchon had pulled off changed attitudes in Whitehall and Milne was not employed again in a major post during hostilities. The fate of Troubridge was to be more severe than this. Even at the time feeling ran high against Troubridge and he was soon recalled home to explain his conduct before a Court of Inquiry held at Portsmouth on 22 September.

This court declared that Troubridge's argument about a superior force was not a valid one. They considered that the total weight of broadsides from his four armoured cruisers at least equalled the *Goeben*'s firepower, added to which he would have had the advantage of superior speed and numbers, thus splitting her return fire. They also took into account the faster firing rate of the armoured cruisers' smaller guns and the benefits of torpedo attacks by the two accompanying light cruisers, *Gloucester* and *Dublin*, and the two destroyers that had managed to join his flag, the *Beagle* and *Bulldog*. Thus their findings were that Troubridge's failure to engage during the hours of daylight were 'both deplorable and contrary to the tradition of the British Navy', a terrible blow for any naval officer to face.

A court martial was therefore inevitable. Troubridge was duly notified of this fact on 1 October. The rear admiral was to appear to answer charges framed under Section 3 of the Naval Discipline Act. The court duly convened aboard the battleship *Bulwark* at Portland on 5 November under the presidency of Admiral Sir George Egerton, KCB. The court comprised Vice Admiral Burney, three rear admirals, Currey, Heath and Thursby, and four captains, Fyler, Armstrong, Ryan and Sclater. Paymaster-in-chief Krabbe was Deputy Judge Advocate of the Fleet. The prosecutor was Rear Admiral Sydney Freemantle, MVC, while Leslie Scott, KC, MP, a barrister-at-law, and Sir Henry Johnson, solicitor, appeared to assist Troubridge.

The official charge was that Troubridge 'did forbear to pursue the chase of the said ship'. Attempts by higher authorities, incensed at his conduct, to include the charge of cowardice were, thankfully, quashed; they would have been completely unfounded, of course. Nonetheless, the charge still remained a serious one, only two flag officers having been tried thus in the preceding forty years.

The trial itself lasted until 9 November and was very ably conducted on both sides. The prosecutor spent a long while going over the various signals and the logs of the ships involved, discovering several discrepancies with regard to times and suchlike, and the court had to be cleared on several occasions due to their secrecy. The attempt to have the whole trial conducted in camera had earlier been rejected, the decision being that 'only when necessary, in the interests of the State, the public should be ordered to withdraw, otherwise the Court would be open'. It is an interesting decision given while the nation was at war. So, open it was, even then, whereas today all such information remains highly classified almost a hundred years later. A good indication of the restrictive civil service attitude that continues to pervade the Ministry of Defence.

The main points made against Troubridge followed the Court of Inquiry, in that the *Goeben* was not considered to be a superior force and that, on two separate occasions, Troubridge had been instructed that she was his main objective. It was also alleged that the *Goeben*'s guns only outranged those of Troubridge's squadron by a quite small amount. The charge was that, accepting the probable loss of part of his force, he could still have defeated her, if only to damage her sufficiently for Milne's battlecruisers to come up and finish the job.

Not one of these points was conceded by the defence. Far from being his sole objective, Troubridge understood that she was, in fact, secondary to the containment of the Austrian fleet. Troubridge further argued that he only expected to have had to engage the German battlecruiser while he had at least two British battlecruisers originally allocated to him, in company. The rear admiral went further, stating that he had verbally informed Milne that he would not engage the *Goeben* with cruisers alone, and that later his commander-in-chief had said that he fully understood his intentions.

Milne was called to give evidence on several occasions, and he was asked what his own impressions were of Troubridge's probable course of action on the night of the 6th/7th. Milne replied in this manner: 'That he (Troubridge) was going to cut her off at 6 am.' When asked to state why he had formed that impression, Milne itemised his reasons thus:

> The Rear Admiral had been twice told that the *Goeben* was the objective; he signalled to me twice on the 5th regarding the engagement of the *Goeben*; the dispositions given me about midnight showed me he had turned south; that the *Goeben* turned south, or very shortly afterwards; his intercepted signal to the *Dublin*, that he proposed or would endeavour to cut her off at 6 o'clock in the morning; also I should have mentioned before midnight the dispositions about his going north for Fano Island. It all brought to my mind that he knew the objective, and that he was going to attack. The Rear Admiral had not signalled to me that he considered that he was too weak or wanted reinforcements. I saw no reason to interfere with his dispositions.

In turn, Milne was questioned about his own dispositions, particularly with regard to sending back his two battlecruisers to Troubridge's force. Mr Scott had thus widened the whole inquiry, as was his stated aim. However, Scott also went into detail with regard to the crucial point of whether the *Goeben* was superior or inferior. Scott skilfully pointed out that the Admiralty, by asking that two British battlecruisers deal with her, seemed to indicate that one alone would not be enough and that therefore the armoured cruisers alone were even less likely to be able to destroy the *Goeben* unaided. (In view of what was to happen to British battlecruisers and armoured cruisers alike at the Battle of Jutland some eighteen months into the future, these arguments might almost be seen as alarmingly prophetic.)

Scott pressed Milne on whether he agreed that it was for the man on the spot to decide such an issue, which the latter conceded to be the case. Scott then brought up the issue of gun ranges. Milne held that he understood the *Goeben*'s 11-inch guns to have a range of only 15,000 yards, whereas the *Defence* could reach almost as far, 14,500 yards. 'At an elevation of fifteen degrees, is it not entered in the books that the 12-inch gun has an effective range of 20,000 yards?' Milne was asked. 'I am afraid I cannot answer the question of what is in the book,' Milne replied. 'Do you know that the *Goeben* has an elevation of up to thirty degrees with her guns?' 'I don't know that. I know her guns range to 15,000 yards.

I cannot tell the elevation.' 'I put it to you her guns range to something like 25,000 to 30,000 yards?' 'I am not aware of it.'

Scott then attempted to have a letter from Sir Percy Scott, the gunnery expert, read out to confirm this view, but, after some discussion, the President ruled: 'I don't think we want to have this letter.' They had, it was to transpire, their own gunnery expert in attendance. Scott then came up with another clever ploy as he resumed his questioning of Milne. 'Have you based your views on the belief that there is not a substantial difference between the effective ranges of the cruiser squadron and the *Goeben?*' Milne could only answer: '11-inch must be more effective than 9.2-inch.' 'I press for an answer. Have you formed the opinion and hold it today, that there was not a serious or big difference between the effective range of the two forces?' 'There is not a large difference.'

However, within a short time further questions had elicited the opinion of Milne that the range that he considered the cruisers to be effective at was 11,000 to 12,000 yards only. 'What do you put the *Goeben's* at?' 'I believe her guns are ranged to 15,000, but I don't believe she would shoot at 15,000. She would probably get into her best range.' Admiral Milne was not the only British naval leader to receive a rude awakening on that score with regard to German naval gunnery in the years that lay ahead. In practice the German ships usually opened fire, very accurately, at much larger distances than this, and with devastating effect. Nevertheless, this was 1914 and that hard lesson had not yet been driven home. Milne was not alone in his delusion by any means.

Captain Fawcet Wray also came under close examination with regard to the two conversations he had held with Troubridge that fateful night. Wray confirmed that he had gone to Troubridge and told him he did not like it; when asked why, he had told his commander: 'I do not see what you can do, Sir.' Wray gave the two options open to them and then said: 'It seems to me it is likely to be the suicide of your squadron.' For these statements, Wray was to be pilloried, but he explained the context of his arguments later on, which put a new light on what had first appeared to be a defeatist attitude, as we have seen. The result would have probably been another Coronel disaster.

Scott's clever arguments no doubt played a large part in convincing the court that Troubridge had much on his side in the way of justification, and their final verdict was that the charges brought against him were not proved. Troubridge was given a full and honourable acquittal. The court's final point read:

> That, although it might have been possible to bring the *Goeben* to action off Cape Malea, or in the Cervi Channel, the Court considers that, in view of the accused's orders to keep a close watch on the Adriatic, he was justified in abandoning the chase at the time he did, as he had no news or prospect of any force being sent to his assistance.

The Admiralty was not pleased with this verdict. 'A great blunder has been committed,' declared one officer. The Third Sea Lord was of the opinion that: 'The finding of the court martial appears to be correct on the evidence educed, but I am of the opinion that its conclusions are wrong, both from the common-sense viewpoint and technically.' Vice Admiral Hamilton, Second Sea Lord, growled: 'The Court has been entirely led off the track by a clever lawyer.' Fisher and Churchill expressed similar sentiments. Fawcet Wray was so treated generally that he had to issue a Statutory Declaration in August 1917 to clear his honour, in which he reiterated that his advice was not designed to lead to the calling off of the chase.

The fates of both Troubridge and Wray were as follows. Wray went on to command the cruiser *Talbot*, serving at the Dardanelles and being awarded the DSO. He retired as a rear admiral in 1922, rising to vice admiral on the retired list. Troubridge, although honourably cleared, was denied a promised position as C-in-C, Nore, Churchill curtly informing him that 'circumstances have been entirely altered by the war'. Fisher had long held a grudge against Troubridge and this incident only deepened his personal animosity. Troubridge received no active employment and Churchill and Fisher refused his pleas to announce their continued confidence in him. The Admiralty also refused him a further court martial in 1919. Troubridge had meantime been elevated to full admiral and had served in Serbia on the naval mission during the war and on the Danube Commission after it. Troubridge was forced to defend himself yet again, after Milne took objection to the official naval history of the operation.

Marder's summing up of the whole episode was that both Troubridge and the Admiralty shared the blame for the fiasco, with Milne in third place. Marder wrote:

> Whatever the degree of Troubridge's guilt, one can only sympathise with his sentiment, that, 'whichever course an officer's honest judgement dictates, whether it subsequently proves right or wrong, the Admiralty who ask of him to take so great risk to his reputation must, in their turn, take upon themselves the responsibility of his resulting action. No doubt they will.' The Admiralty did nothing of the kind. Nor would they even admit any error on their part, which is perhaps only natural and normal for a government department.

Indeed it is! Like Calder before him and Byng before that, Troubridge got no thanks for having wrongly divined his masters' intentions, nor did he receive much in the way of understanding of his dilemma, save from the court itself. But Captain Stephen Roskill is also perfectly correct and on sound ground in noting that this summary totally ignores 'Churchill's personal share in the Admiralty's contribution to the disaster. It may also be remarked that in the authorised biography of Churchill the author entirely glosses over the latter aspect of the muddle.'

There were to be many, many more similar disastrous interventions by Churchill into naval operations in the years to come.

16 AS THE SPARKS FLY UPWARD (1928)

On 7 November 1927, Rear Admiral Bernard Collard, CB, DSO, hoisted his flag for the first time aboard a British man-of-war, the battleship *Royal Oak*. She was a unit of the Mediterranean Fleet under the command of Admiral Sir Roger Keyes, the fire-eating hero of Zeebrugge, now based at Malta. It was a plum appointment for Collard and a reflection on his meteoric rise in the service since we last encountered him in these pages. Following the affair of the Portsmouth Barracks 'mutiny', and his subsequent court martial, Collard's progress had been both enviable and without further upset. Indeed, if anything, Collard had come through the whole episode with his reputation enhanced in the service rather than marred. The fighting of a successful libel action in connection with the aftermath of that fracas had been highly approved of by Collard's brother officers and he had gone from strength to strength.

Collard had been removed from the barracks to what was considered a more suitable and familiar territory for him, Whale Island gunnery school, for another term and, during his year back there, he had been involved with the original field-gun display for the Royal Tournament at Olympia – just about all that remained until the late twentieth century to illustrate what 'Whaley' was once all about. From here, after a year, Collard moved on to the Mediterranean Fleet as first lieutenant and gunnery officer aboard the old battleship *Glory*, being promoted to the rank of commander at the young age of 33.

After a course at the new War College, Collard returned to sea as second-in-command of the cruiser *Donegal* in the Atlantic and this was followed by a three-year stint back ashore in the Naval Intelligence Division. During the Great War Collard showed himself to be as brave and capable officer as expected, earning his DSO for his services as assistant beach master on 'W' Beach at the carnage of Cape Hellas in the doomed Dardanelles campaign. Collard's promotion to captain duly followed and, with it, command of the monitor *Lord Clive*, serving in a bombardment role in the Straits of Dover under Keyes.

Collard then went on to serve as deputy director at the Admiralty in the post-war period of severe retrenchment and the ghastly 'Geddes Axe', which almost destroyed the navy, following this up as commander of the training battleship *Colossus* at Portland before becoming director of the Gunnery Department at the Admiralty. Collard went back to sea again in command of the destroyer *Valhalla*, and then was appointed the commanding officer of the battleship *Royal*

Sovereign, once more in the Mediterranean. The appointment of Collard as ADC to the king followed in 1925, before his promotion to flag rank and finding himself up the straits once more under his old mentor, Keyes. With this background of gunnery, it is perhaps hardly surprising that his selection for his own flag captain should be another from the same hard school, Captain K.G.B. Dewar, but in fact this had not been his first choice. The similarities of background present only a superficial impression of harmony and like thinking between the two men. In practice, the old law of magnetism applied to their relationship, and the two like poles tended to repulse rather than attract. Both men were just too much alike in temperament, and the inevitable explosion between them was not to be long delayed.

Captain Dewar had followed much the same career path as Collard in his early years. Dewar had joined the old *Britannia* as a cadet from an Edinburgh school, being one of three Scottish doctors' sons destined to achieve high rank in the Royal Navy. Dewar had gone to sea in the cruiser *Hawke* in 1895, and had followed this with service and training aboard the battleship *Magnificent* in the Channel Fleet. Service aboard the corvette *Volage*, commanded by the redoubtable Captain George Cherry, a real martinet of the old school, followed. Dewar emerged, much toughened, and was promoted to lieutenant in 1901 and, after a short period with a destroyer flotilla based at Devonport, went out to the China station aboard the cruiser *Marathon*. Dewar subsequently attended the gunner course at Whale Island with enthusiasm, showing his mettle in daring to question the renowned Percy Scott himself on one occasion. Dewar proved himself a dedicated and hard-working young officer, a trifle dour perhaps and rather impatient with old methods.

Dewar went on to command the destroyer *Mermaid* for a brief period during the 1903 manoeuvres, a real feather in his cap, and was then sent to the gunnery school at Sheerness. A period serving aboard the armoured cruiser *Kent* followed, during which time his stubbornness became a byword, but so did his efficiency, which resulted in that ship topping the 1907 firings table. Aboard the battleship *Prince George*, Dewar visited Japan and was much impressed by what he found in the Japanese fleet. Dewar admired the encouragement of the junior officers and the lower ranks to express opinions, but this was not the mood of the Royal Navy as a whole at the time, although a few officers, Scott among them, approved when Dewar commented on this aspect in a subsequent lecture.

In 1909, Dewar became the gunnery officer of the battleship *Commonwealth* in the Channel Fleet, and was still preaching independent thought to largely deaf ears. This was followed with a similar posting, as first lieutenant and gunnery officer of the battleship *Dreadnought* in 1910. Here Dewar found Herbert Richmond was his captain, and they were so alike in their thinking that they became good friends. These 'Young Turks', as they termed themselves, were very much in the minority and tended to compensate by being overly aggressive in trying to get their viewpoints across to doubters, tolerance of others viewpoints not being one of their strong points. As a commander, Dewar went on to the War College. The outbreak of the First World War found Dewar serving aboard the battleship *Prince of Wales*, as second-in-command, in the Channel Fleet and he went out to the Dardanelles aboard her.

Coincidence continued, for, like Collard, Dewar then served ashore at the gunnery school at Devonport and subsequently took command of a monitor, the *Roberts*, in the Channel. Post-war, Dewar served in the Plans Division of the Admiralty, having been promoted to captain in 1918; attended the Versailles conference, for which he received his CBE; turned down an appointment to a cruiser in the Black Sea and was given a job helping to prepare the official account of the Battle of Jutland, before assuming command of the cruisers *Calcutta* and *Cape Town* respectively on the West Indies station. This was followed by an appointment to the Intelligence Division at the Admiralty before Dewar received the summons to join Collard in the Mediterranean.

Surprising, although the two men had charted similar paths to their final rendezvous, neither was well known to the other. Collard, the stern traditionalist, Dewar the frustrated rebel, still eager to turn the established order upside down. As Leslie Gardiner summarised the position, 'two pig-headed gunnery officers, holding clashing opinions; two who were famous for speaking out of turn'. It was the recipe for a clash and that clash duly followed.

In practice, it was more in the nature of a series of clashes, of a relatively minor nature each time, but gradually building up the tension between the two men until one felt that his position had become intolerable. The catalyst that brought about the final detonation, which many felt was as inevitable 'as the sparks fly upward', was yet another gunnery officer, Commander H.M. Daniel. Daniel had also entered the Royal Navy via the *Britannia*, had served aboard three battleships before specialising in gunnery and arriving at Whale Island, where he completed his course soon after the outbreak of the Great War. Daniel served as the gunnery officer of the light cruisers *Isis*, *Royalist* and *Dauntless* respectively, the latter being part of Cowan's force operating against the Bolsheviks in the Baltic in 1919.

In 1920, Daniel had been appointed first lieutenant and gunnery officer of the battleship *Valiant*, was promoted to commander and then served in the Naval Ordnance Department of the Admiralty. Daniel was noted for having written two books during this period, a history of the *Valiant's* service and a gunnery manual. In 1925, Daniel became gunnery commander aboard the *Iron Duke* in the Mediterranean and then served in a similar capacity aboard the battleships *Barham* and then *Royal Oak*, joining the latter ship on 24 December 1927. Daniel vigorously applied himself to all aspects of his new job, particularly with regard to the many social functions that were such features of naval life on the Mediterranean station then.

Three of a kind then, superficially, but how differing in temperament and outlook. This trio of leading players found that their new ship, the *Royal Oak*, while outwardly a technically efficient unit of the fleet, was in practice a far from happy band of brothers. In particular, relations between the lower deck and the officers in general were soon seen to be far from harmonious. The first indication that all was not well in this respect manifested itself very soon. Three stokers were brought before Daniel after an assault upon a petty officer. Dewar sent all three for court martial, but he then looked deeper into their case, discovering evidence of bullying as some justification for their action. Dewar and Daniel felt that this might not be an isolated incident and probed still deeper. They found the prevalent feeling on board was that it was useless for the men to complain, for they felt nothing would be done. Both officers were shocked at this attitude and took steps to rectify it, Dewar reading the Naval Discipline Act to his crew and informing them that their grievances should be aired in the proper manner and not suppressed in future. Following this, complaints came flooding in, some of them unjustified, many of them trivial, a few quite serious. One of these resulted in the court martial of a commissioned warrant officer. Dewar and Daniel had shown the men they could both be trusted.

This was all well done, but if relations between the new officers and the crew had been improved, relations elsewhere went rapidly in the other direction. Feeling between the captain and the commander, on the one hand, and their admiral soon began to sour. The first indication of this appeared, of all places, during a wardroom dance held aboard the *Royal Oak* on 12 January. In attendance were the C-in-C and Lady Keyes, with their attendant officers and ladies. The dance was held on the quarterdeck and all appeared to be well prepared for a successful evening under the guidance of Daniel.

Collard made an early appearance, and at once began to find fault. The admiral criticised the fact that many of the guests were sitting about without partners and Dewar spoke to Daniel and told him to get things moving. Daniel replied that the dance had only just begun, and that, anyway, things would soon be put right for he had detailed junior officers for just such a purpose. However, Collard, impatient as ever, now intervened personally on other matters. Collard sneered at the music being played and told Daniel to get rid of the Royal Marine band and replace it with a jazz band. The admiral then went over, with Daniel, to the bandstand and began berating the bandmaster, an individual with the delightful name of Barnacle. The conversation, according to Daniel, went on these lines: 'Come here you. Stand here. You call yourself a flagship band? I never heard such a bloody awful noise in my life. Your playing is like a dirge and everybody is complaining. I'll have you sent home and reported to your headquarters.'

This outburst, in front of all the guests, was followed by an apology by Barnacle, to which Collard's response, quite audible to the assembled company, was: 'I won't have a bugger like that in my ship.' Daniel, however, was equal to the moment and, with little fuss and much diplomacy, managed to replace the band, which Barnacle then conducted without apparent rancour, despite what he must have been feeling inside. The evening, therefore, passed off relatively well, but in the aftermath a ground swell of indignation manifested itself against such boorish behaviour by a rear admiral. In particular, Dewar resented the fact that Collard had called the *Royal Oak* his ship. Dewar was the captain, Collard certainly flew his flag aboard her, but she was not his ship but Dewar's.

Although petty in itself, this incident had sown the seed of discord. Further planting quickly followed. On 13 January (ominously a Friday) Dewar was taken up with matters of more serious moment, delivering a tabletop battle and accompanying lecture to a group of the ship's midshipmen. As was his wont, Dewar was explaining his pet theories about the advantages of his own 'divided tactics' system over the established 'single line' system for operating the fleet in a major battle. Dewar also acted as prosecutor for one of the courts martial being held as a result of his earlier enquiries. Collard also attended the course, but reserved his judgement. The following day, having brooded overnight, the admiral delivered it, with Keyes and other senior officers of the fleet listening attentively.

It turned out to be a crushing denouncement of all that Dewar had attempted to demonstrate. Completely and ruthlessly, Collard tore into Dewar's theories, demolishing them shred by shred. Dewar vainly tried to point out certain facts in his defence but Collard rode roughshod over him. Sensing an impending explosion in front of the wide-eyed midshipmen, the senior officers abruptly brought the session to a halt, but not before Dewar had been totally humiliated. Meanwhile, Daniel had to deal with the fall-out from the dance fracas. He saw Barnacle and placated him, advising (in words once addressed to Collard) 'not to take it too seriously'. However, Barnacle continued to brood over the incident, sought out the chaplain and requested to leave the navy, even volunteering to forfeit all his hard-earned pension rights to do so. Other members of the band joined him and Major Attwood of the Royal Marines delivered a formal protest to Dewar citing Collard's rant as 'an insult to the Corps'.

Here was a pretty pass! Daniel was called before both Collard and Dewar, who had just been visited by the chaplain with Barnacle's allegations. Collard wanted Daniel to confirm that he had not, in fact, called the bandmaster a bugger. Daniel replied:

If you ask me whether you called the bandmaster that name, I am bound to answer 'No'. But if you ask me, Sir, whether you referred to him by that name in my hearing, then my answer must be 'Yes'. And nothing will alter my recollection of the incident.

According to Daniel this set Collard off into another tantrum; he raged that it was all lies. The appearance of Attwood, seeking an apology, calmed Collard down for a while, and both he and Dewar agreed to allow Daniel to smooth things over if he could. Daniel's version of events was that Collard stated that an apology might be made to Barnacle, but the admiral later denied this. Some sort of an apology was delivered, however, for the following day Collard was reputed to have thanked Daniel 'for getting me out of a damned nasty hole'.

There followed a lull of two months or more before the next incident widened still further the gap between the three men. The *Royal Oak* had returned to Malta on 5 March after gunnery exercises, during which nearly everything had seemed to go wrong. The whole ship's company was in an irritable mood and the weather seemed to reflect that. A wind whipped up a vicious swell inside Grand harbour and, among the many mechanical breakdowns that day had been the failure of the capstan engine, which had, it was thought, been righted once. This failure led to the jamming of the anchor in the hawse pipe. This, in turn, required a great deal of extra work aboard the battleship as she prepared to anchor in the darkness and in the midst of a wild and turbulent evening. Collard himself was due to act as President for a court martial being held aboard the *Valiant* the following day, and his barge had been called for in order to pick him up at 2300hrs and take him ashore.

The earlier arrival of the *Royal Oak* had changed these plans and Collard had ordered Daniel to have the gangway rigged on the quarterdeck in readiness, but not to lower it until conditions were judged right to allow boats to come alongside. Collard also wanted a boat rope and Jacob's ladder on the boom and yardarm illumination readied. The admiral did not, however, specify which side of the quarterdeck he wished to disembark from. Daniel, quite reasonably, assumed that it did not much matter from which side, but worked out that the starboard side would be the safer option under the prevailing conditions. During the boat's approach the capstan engine jammed yet again and could not be freed.

At 2105hrs *Royal Oak* finally came to rest, using her starboard anchor only. Daniel had been supervising these events on the blustery fo'c'sle, and he now made his way aft to see Collard ashore, but, on the way, was summoned there by Collard himself. On arrival, the rear admiral in a towering rage met Daniel. Collard demanded to know why the port ladder was not yet ready despite him having given the order two hours earlier. Daniel determined not to give his senior officer another chance to make an exhibition of him in front of the men, and meekly accepted the order, although he thought it would result in damage and perhaps also the loss of the ladder in such conditions. This was done and Captain Dewar arrived from the bridge to see his admiral over the side, to find that officer subjecting Daniel to yet another flurry of invective abuse, which terminated with the words, 'And get the Commander's reasons in writing'.

1 Sir Francis Drake (1540–96). *(By N. Hilliard)*

2 The execution of Admiral Sir John Byng (1704–57) aboard HMS *Monarch* on 14 March 1757. (*By Thomas Hudson*)

3 Admiral Augustus Keppel, 1st Viscount Keppel, PC (1725–87). *(By Joshua Reynolds)*

4 Sinking of HMS *Royal George* at Spithead at 0900hrs on 29 August 1782. *(Print by W. Mitchell from an original by Henry Slight, 1839)*

5 The mutineer Richard Parker, President of the delegates, in the mutiny in His Majesty's fleet at the Nore. For which he suffered death on board the *Sandwich* on 30 July 1797. *(W. Chamberlain; published as the act directs 9 July 1797 by J. Harrison & Co., York)*

6 The mutineers turning Lieutenant William Bligh and part of the officers and crew adrift from HMS *Bounty* on 29 April 1789. *(By G. Dance, 1794)*

7 The *Victoria* court martial on board HMS *Hibernia* at Malta: examination of Admiral Markham, 19 July. *(By J. Walter Wilson from a sketch by Captain C. Field, RM)*

8 The battleship HMS *Victoria* makes her final plunge off Lebanon as HMS *Nile* stands by in 1897. *(National Maritime Museum, London)*

9 The light cruiser HMS *Manchester* scuttled prematurely in August 1942 during Malta convoy operation *Pedestal*. *(Author's Collection via C.C. Crill)*

10 Sir Robert Calder's action, 22 July 1905. (*By Thomas Whitcombe*)

This second humiliation, again in itself not too untoward in the fleet, left Daniel in great distress. Later that same evening he poured out his frustrations to Dewar. Collard's personal abuse of him, Daniel insisted, was as nothing; it was the effect the admiral was having on the ship that was worrying. Daniel expressed the opinion that he had had enough and would resign. Shades of Barnacle: 'Don't take it too seriously!' How that phrase would have helped all concerned at this time, but take it very seriously they did, especially Dewar.

The already sensitive position was given a final push by Collard on his return aboard the ship the following day. Dewar, Daniel and the other officers concerned stood at the gangway as Collard was piped aboard. When the rear admiral arrived at the top of the platform he totally ignored this formal reception and addressed instead some of the sailors: 'Men, get down that ladder and attend to the boat-ropes.' Without a further word or gesture, Collard strode away to his quarters, leaving the little party on the deck looking as foolish as they felt.

This was the last straw. To Dewar it was a studied insult, which, coupled with Daniel's outpourings, crystalised his mind into dramatic action. Dewar retired to his cabin and composed a long, formal complaint. Daniel also composed his 'reasons in writing' for the gangway incident. Both men incorporated all the little incidents that had taken place since joining Collard. Daniel concluded his epistle, 'Apologies would serve no useful purpose, but assurance is urgently necessary that discipline, which must depend on respect for rank, will not be undermined in this way'. Dewar's letter ended on much the same note and both letters were dispatched to Vice Admiral Kelly, the 'administrative authority' via Collard. The first steps had been taken; the last stage of this tragi-comedy was beginning. Even at this stage things could have been halted before they went too far, but they were not.

Collard received the two letters on 8 March, retained them for a day, then passed them on to Kelly, who received them by special delivery on the afternoon of the 9th. The Mediterranean Fleet was due to sail shortly for combined exercises with the Atlantic Fleet. Keyes had been busy with his huge staff in meticulous preparation for this event, which was to be the magnificent culmination of his term as commander-in-chief. All the vast plans were ready to be brought into being within the day. Then came the two letters and the whole of the greatest fleet in the Royal Navy was brought to a sudden halt.

Kelly placed the letters in front of Keyes, who considered them very improper. The letters did, undeniably, reveal a deplorable state of affairs aboard the *Royal Oak*. The C-in-C grasped the nettle. The exercises were postponed and a Court of Inquiry was hastily assembled to examine the whole affair. The upshot of this was that, for the good of the fleet, Keyes decided that all three offices should be moved on. Keyes offered Collard the *Resolution* for his flag, but Collard refused. Dewar and Daniel were more icily received and dismissed from their ship. All three officers were then sent home to England, but not before Dewar had told Keyes, 'I shall ask for a court martial, Sir'. 'Then it will have to be on this station. You may go', was the C-in-C's only response. Now it was definitely too late, the dirty washing was to be exhibited to the whole world!

So, indeed, it was. The press, of course, revelled in it all and had a field day. There were questions in the House. The whole nation was treated to speculation on the so-termed 'Officer's Mutiny' at Malta. The affair turned out to be a re-run of the unhappy Keppel-Palliser affair, especially in the extent to which hitherto fairly responsible journalists, if such beasts ever existed, vied with each other to produce more and more absurd headlines. And, of course, the reasons behind all this were, by and large, totally absurd. Both Daniel and Dewar got their court martial in the end.

Their trials took place aboard the aircraft carrier *Eagle* at Gibraltar, the court assembling in one of her hangars, complete with press gallery all abuzz. Commander Daniel was the first in the dock. The President of the court was Captain Burges Watson, with Captain Calvert prosecuting and C. Day Kimball, KC, acting for the defence. The court comprised nine post-captains, among them James Somerville, who was to know the Rock in vastly different circumstances sixteen years later as commander of Force 'H', when Churchill instigated a similar inquiry against him. Paymaster-General Marsham was the Deputy Judge Advocate.

Collard gave evidence, stating that he considered both letters 'insubordinate'. Perhaps, but did he think they were unjustified, Collard was asked, to which the admiral replied, with some force, 'Yes'. When asked whether Daniel had acted honestly or dishonestly, Collard replied, 'Foolishly'. When pressed, Collard answered, 'Dishonestly'. Throughout the trial Collard acted in a contemptuous and impatient manner. He denied acting badly or using the language claimed by Barnacle, Dewar or Daniel. Nor would Collard admit to offering apologies to Barnacle as was claimed.

Daniel, under questioning, commenced confidently, but later made a poor showing. He admitted that he had exceeded his orders in writing of earlier incidents in his letter on the gangway incident, stating that he expected that it would result in either his or Collard's dismissal. The defence concluded: 'Was there not something wrong with the *Royal Oak*. Is it not fair to suggest that the good of the Service is involved here to some extent?' With this the court agreed, and Daniel was found guilty, the verdict being: 'Commander Daniel to be dismissed ... and severely reprimanded.'

Dewar's turn came on 4 April, under the presidency of Rear Admiral Townsend, admiral superintendent at Gibraltar. The court comprised three rear admirals and seven captains. The prosecutor was Rear Admiral W.H.D. Boyd, with Dewar conducting his own defence. Collard was again called and gave similar caustic answers. Asked whether he placed 'implicit confidence' in his flag captain,

Collard replied, 'No, I can't say I did'. Pressed at one point by Dewar, 'Will you answer "Yes" or "No"?' Collard retorted, 'I will not. I will answer as I see fit!'

On being questioned on the gangway incident, whether he had expressed himself dissatisfied with his ship, Collard loftily replied, 'No. I said I was fed up with my Flag Captain.'

Under interrogation himself by Boyd, Dewar denied that he had led 'a Machiavellian conspiracy' to get rid of Collard. He described Daniel's letter as 'expressive'. On the results Dewar stated carefully that 'I do not think my action was ill-advised; though I am sorry for the result'. When asked to sum up the real cause for the whole series of incidents, Dewar replied: 'Uncontrollable fits of temper on the part of Admiral Collard.' Why then, had he not had a heart-to-heart with him? 'I felt any personal protest would have been ineffectual. Admiral Collard would have immediately lost his temper and threatened me with a court martial.'

In his summary, Dewar maintained that stance: 'It was certainly not to my advantage to bring a complaint against my Rear Admiral. I bore no malice against him. I bear none now.' Dewar was to conclude with this plea: 'A great question of justice and principle is involved. I ask the court not only to acquit me, but to acquit me honourably. The case is one, Sir, which affects my personal honour.'

Of the two charges with which he was accused, of accepting and forwarding subversive letters, the court found him guilty as charged of the first but acquitted him of the second, the latter being not proven in their opinion. He received the same sentence as Daniel, to be dismissed his ship and severely reprimanded.

Public opinion at home was firmly in favour of the two officers, Collard's uncontrollable temper being generally held as the principal reason for the whole affair. Naval opinion was more divided, many feeling that Dewar and Daniel ought to have made far less of it than they had. Nothing was resolved by the courts martial, other than the pubic marring of the reputations of the three men involved. In effect, though, justice was done, for Collard paid with his job. In April, the Admiralty considered Collard's position in the affair and found that 'Initial blame rests on Rear Admiral Collard, who dealt with trivial causes for dissatisfaction in a manner unbecoming his position; and showed himself unfitted to hold further high command'. Collard was placed on the retired list. The tyrant was to die at the age of 86, having declined a wartime post, as a vice admiral. Dewar continued to serve, first as captain of the battlecruiser *Tiger* and then of the battleship *Iron Duke*. Dewar later became ADC to the king and entered politics. Dewar was to serve at the Admiralty during the war and he died in 1964. He wrote a book, *The Navy from Within*, which made many excellent points, but which the service and public alike ignored. Daniel retired from the Royal Navy soon after this incident, worked for a while as a journalist, served in the Home Guard during the war and died in South Africa in 1955.

It had all been a storm in teacup, which had ruined the careers of two men and marred that of the third. It had most certainly done the reputation of the Royal Navy no good at all at a crucial time for the service, at very low ebb, run down and under-financed. We can do no more that to follow the example of Captain Stephen Roskill and quote the words of *The Times* on this whole sorry episode: 'An Admiral too much given to the "choleric word" served by officers too dour or too zealous to keep the passing moment in reasonable perspective, too little gravity on one side, and too much solemnity on the other ...'

17 JUDGEMENT OR CONDUCT (1942)

One hundred and sixty-three years after the trial of Boteler, accused of not doing his utmost to prevent his ship falling into enemy hands (mentioned elsewhere in these pages) another British captain, Harold Drew, DCS, was found guilty for doing precisely that. The ship in question was the light cruiser HMS *Manchester* during the Second World War. During the particularly hard-fought battle known as Operation Pedestal, an attempt to resupply the island fortress of Malta which took place in August 1942, the *Manchester* had been torpedoed and damaged at night by Italian MTBs in the Sicilian 'Narrows', close off the coast of extremely hostile and collaborist Vichy-French Tunisia.

Captain Drew's own *Narrative of Events* described the action. After having rounded Zembra Island and Cap Bon, at around midnight a mine was exploded close under the port bow of the *Manchester*, either by the sweep or by paravane. It caused no damage. At 0015hrs an E-boat was sighted on the port beam and it was engaged by gunfire, from the main 6-inch turrets down to the Oerlikons for the space of ten minutes and claimed destroyed. At 0120hrs, whilst those on the bridge were looking for the wreck of the destroyer *Havock*, which had run aground in the vicinity of Point Kilibia some months before, a suspicious object was observed on the starboard bow, under the land. It was assumed, correctly, to be another E-boat and it was stationary. Captain Drew ordered hard-a-starboard, full-speed ahead port, and just as the *Manchester* commenced to swing to starboard came the sound of the discharge of two torpedoes. The E-boat then started her engines and sped off at high speed towards the Vichy shoreline. The tracks of two torpedoes were seen approaching and the first of them passed astern of the cruiser. Unfortunately, the second one ran straight and true, striking the *Manchester* abreast the after engine room.

The cruiser continued under rudder, which remained hard over for a while, and the engines were stopped. The *Manchester* took on an immediate list of about 12 degrees to starboard, 070° some 2 miles from Point Kilibia. After circling right round and then continuing to plane round until losing way, the cruiser came to rest heading 160°, in some 20 fathoms of water on the edge of a minefield off her port side. The night was very dark, there was no wind, and *Manchester* was immobilised some 16 miles from Cape Bon and 38 miles from the nearest enemy soil, the island of Pantellaria.

With the remaining escorts busy shepherding the merchant ships of the convoy through these dangerous waters, the *Manchester* was left for a time to her own devices close to this unfriendly coast and within range of Axis bomber bases in Sicily, and with the sea alive with German and Italian submarines and motor torpedo boats. An unenviable position. Strangely enough, under the same captain, the *Manchester* had been similarly hit and damaged the year before in much the same waters but off Galitia Island further west. On that occasion her commanding officer had managed to nurse his vessel back to Gibraltar and safety. The outcome of the second incident was, however, very different.

Anticipating further attacks that night at any time, not expecting his fellow escorts to be able to spare time to help him, and aware that the morning light would reveal his damaged ship to the eyes of both Axis airmen and naval forces, as well as the Vichy, Captain Drew felt that everything depended on whether or not his engineering staff could centre the rudder and effect engine repairs for a speed of 12 knots within a very short time limit that he set himself. If this could be done then Drew was prepared to make an effort to save his ship, if it could not then rather than have his ship fall into hostile hands he would abandon and scuttle her. There was some confusion in the darkness about just what the state of the ship was when Drew finally made the decision to abandon her. Her engineering officer felt that the ship might be got moving again, but Drew appeared unaware of this, and the decision was made the other way; *Manchester* was abandoned.

Many of the crew had already been taken off her earlier by the destroyer *Pathfinder*. The *Manchester*'s main armament of twelve 6-inch guns in four turrets were considered inoperational, but many of her 4-inch anti-aircraft weapons were thought to be functional, along with her lighter weapons. Captain Drew thought that this would be insufficient defence from the air attacks he expected to be mounted against his ship come daylight. Some other defence positions, like HA directors and the transmitting station, had also been abandoned during the night.

In the event the survivors took to the water and the ship was scuttled. Two destroyers, which had been sent back to assist her, picked up some men, but the bulk got ashore on the Tunisian coast, with the loss of just one man from drowning. These latter were herded up by the Vichy authorities and marched off to prison. Here these unfortunates found themselves treated far more harshly by the French than they would have been by the Germans or Italians they were at war with. The *Manchester* survivors were incarcerated at Laghouat in the vilest and most primitive of conditions, and subjected to every humiliation by the Vichy

authorities could conceive, other than outright torture. Even Red Cross par-
cels were opened and ransacked by their captors. Here they remained until they
were finally released on the surrender of Tunisia to the Allies in 1943. While still
imprisoned, Captain Drew heard that Commander (E) John Robb, his engineering officer, had expressed the opinion that the ship could have been got under
way, which, he stated at the time, came as a great shock to him.

The man in command of Operation Pedestal was Rear Admiral Neville Syfret,
a South African, and was described to this author by the later Captain Richard
Onslow as 'a humourless man'. Syfret knew Drew very well indeed, having
served as the captain of another cruiser of the same squadron in the Home Fleet
previously. Syfret, in *Edinburgh*, had commanded that cruiser squadron during
Operation Substance to relieve Malta in July 1941, when *Manchester* had been hit
by a torpedo, disabled but got back to Gibraltar. In the aftermath of Pedestal Syfret
had requested the courts martial in respect of another lost warship, the destroyer
Foresight. This ship had been hit by an aerial torpedo and attempts were made
to tow her to Gibraltar by the destroyer *Tartar*, under Captain Tyrwhitt. These
had failed and Tyrwhitt had ordered *Foresight* to be sunk. Another very famous
destroyer skipper, Admiral Sir Richard Onslow, later told me that Tyrwhitt's
action was an 'obviously correct decision to anyone who knew anything about
destroyers' and, indeed, Tyrwhitt was honourably acquitted, which, wrote Onslow
to me many years later, 'was as expected'. It certainly revealed that Syfret, who,
on 7 June 1943, became vice chief of Naval Staff, was quick on the trigger and
somewhat unforgiving of any loss. It has been alleged that when he heard of the
scuttling of the *Manchester* Syfret 'went absolutely mad' and yet, at that time, he
could not have known of the full circumstances.

Be that as it may, on their return to England, Captain Drew and certain of his officers and crew of the *Manchester* were called before courts martial under Section 92
of the Naval Discipline Act. The proceedings took place at Admiralty House,
Portsmouth, as no ship was available, and commenced on 2 February 1943, lasting
until 20 February. The President of the court was Rear Admiral Clement Moody
of HMS *Daedalus*, the other members being Commodore Edward Thornton, DSC,
and Captains Thomas Armstrong, DSC, Guy Hamilton, Henry Oliphant, DSO,
MVO, and Robert Oliver, CBE, DSC. Two further captains, Gerald Warner, DSC,
and John Cornall, were objected to and the objection was upheld. The Deputy
Judge Advocate of the Fleet was Captain Archibald Frederick Cooper, OBE.

The proceedings took the form of a Board of Inquiry, with no specific accused.
Captain Drew was the first to be called and he later complained that no defence
in advance could be prepared. Drew was to write that:

> … most of the survivors felt that they were under a serious handicap from the
> fact than none of them had any summary of the evidence, neither were they

in possession of copies of it after it was given. And whereas the Court and the Prosecutor had written copies, the survivors had a blank piece of paper and a pencil, and heard the evidence for the first time when it was read out in Court.

Drew went on: 'In my own case, I attended the court expecting to have to satisfy them that my judgement and reasoning in deciding to sink an immobile and damaged ship if she did not become mobile before a certain time, was justified, having regard to her position and the circumstances then prevailing.' Drew stated that: 'The result for me was, that a question of judgement seemed to have become one of conduct.'

Drew was cross-examined by members of his crew, a fact he did not find agreeable either. As the trial went on, with every movement and conversation being subject to analysis and dispute on what was said or thought to have been said, and what was meant or what was not meant, and what was clear and what was far from clear, the whole case began to crystallise. The crucial point came down to the differing interpretations placed on half-remembered pieces of conversation, which in themselves were continually interrupted by dead-tired men under considerable strain after several days and nights on non-stop action. It had come to light that many men had left their posts prematurely and this affected the further defence capability of the ship. These were dealt with, but the crucial decision was made on whether or not the *Manchester* was able to steam at the deadline laid down by Captain Drew in his own mind.

The court sought to summarise what the captain and his commander (E) knew from the various inspections and verbal reports made during those fateful hours. Captain Drew did not know, they felt, with any certainty as to when power would be available on the steering motors, nor did he know that the rudder had been centred by hand pump. The ship's secret and confidential books were in the process of being destroyed (by burning rather than the usual method of weighted bags over the side). The court felt itself in no doubt that Drew had decided in his own mind that the ship had to be able to steam by 0245hrs at the latest in order to make any kind of escape attempt. Robb, for his part, they felt knew 'fairly accurately' the extent of the damage, and also knew that the forward boiler room and forward engine room were intact, and could both be used. He also knew that the ship could only be steered at that time by the hand pump, and that the port outer engine had to be temporarily stopped. However, Robb did not think that this stoppage was due to any major defect, although he was uncertain about the length of time it would take to fix it.

The crucial time was around 0210hrs when Commander (E) Robb arrived back on the bridge to report to Captain Drew in response to the latter's order. What, in theory, should have been a straightforward exchange of their views on the then current position actually developed into a rather one-sided, and frequently interrupted, monologue by the captain during which, Robb asserted, his own points were hardly heard or taken sufficient cognisance of. Captain Drew asked Robb to confirm that the shafts had stopped, which Robb did. Also, Robb maintained that he then informed the captain that he felt sure that he could get the port outer engine working again, but could not put an exact time on when. The commander (E) therefore asked for a little more time to go back and examine the state of affairs once more and make another report of progress. Robb, it was said, begged Drew to withhold making the final decision until this could be done.

However, Captain Drew was anxious to impress on Robb the parlous state of the ship, and that he could not put off the final decision of whether to abandon her for very much longer. Robb was unable to explain his viewpoint sufficiently to make an impression on his captain, who dominated the conversation, which the court later described as being 'unsatisfactory and inconclusive'. Nonetheless, the view that the scuttling of the ship was firmly in the captain's mind was conveyed to Robb, despite the fact that one of the many interruptions was caused by the torpedo officer reporting, at 0220hrs, that temporary leads had been run to the steering motors. This officer, Lieutenant Russell, was informed by Drew at 0230hrs just what preparations were required to scuttle the ship, but Russell said he replied that Drew should 'wait and see what the ship could do' before making his mind up finally. Robb left the bridge with this knowledge, ten minutes later, in order to make his further survey. However, almost as soon as Robb had left his side, Drew instructed Commander Hammersley Johnston for all hands to be assembled on the flight deck so he could tell them he had reluctantly concluded that the ship had been scuttled.

By the time Robb, having made a further rapid examination, returned to the bridge to report that the port outer engine was now ready and that steering had been supplied to the steering motors, he found that this speech had already been delivered and the decision to scuttle had therefore been made without further reference to the state of motive power. In fact, steering could have been as normal, save that only one outer propeller would have been used. The court concluded that, at 0240hrs, *Manchester*, though crippled, was in a condition to start turning preparatory to proceeding, that the information was available to Captain Drew, but he was not at that time in possession of all the facts.

Too late; the die was already cast. Hammersley Johnston therefore began telling the assembled crew to get warm clothing and to then assemble at their boat stations in readiness to abandon ship. The men at once dispersed and they actually began to leave the ship at around 0345hrs. The rest of the story has been told.

The court deliberated long and hard on the various, confused conversations and part conversations, but finally they reached unanimous verdicts. The findings of the court were as follows: Captain Drew was guilty of negligently performing the duty imposed on him when acting as commanding officer, whereby he gave orders on 13 August 1942 for His Majesty's ship *Manchester* to be abandoned and scuttled when, having regard to the conditions prevailing at the time, it had been his duty to stand by the ship and do his utmost to bring her into harbour. Drew was ordered to be dismissed from HMS *Victory* and severely reprimanded. The gunnery officer, Lieutenant Commander Daniel Duff, was found guilty of negligence in that he ordered the premature abandoning of the transmitting station, permitted other gunnery positions to be evacuated, both without due cause, and that he failed to take the proper steps to restore the fighting efficiency of the ship's gun armament. Duff's punishment was forfeiture of six months' seniority and a reprimand. Temporary Lieutenants Allan Daniels and John Tabor were both reprimanded for leaving their action stations at the starboard and port high-angle control towers. Warrant Ordnance Officer Albert Reddy, with an exemplary record of service, was severely reprimanded for omitting to take sufficient steps to ascertain and report to the gunnery officer the state of the armament and to effect necessary repairs. Finally, Petty Officer Samuel Phillips, chief quartermaster, in charge of the lower steering position, was disrated to leading seaman for leaving the wheel and telegraph in the lower steering position unmanned without reporting to the navigating officer that the port telegraph was showing full-speed ahead and the starboard telegraph half speed ahead.

Commander Gill and Commander (E) John Robb were both formally acquitted and nothing was recorded against them. This despite the fact that the Second Sea Lord and chief of Naval Personnel, Vice Admiral Sir William J. Whitworth, considered that 'under the present case Commander Gill and Commander (E) Robb come under the heading of officers implicated in a lesser degree. In view, however, of the recommendations of the Court, no further action is proposed.' The vice chief of the Naval Staff commented that this should remain the case, particularly in the case of the latter, 'since the higher state of discipline in the Engine Room as compared with that of the remainder of the complement should be credited to him'.

The Board of Inquiry procedure itself was criticised after the trial by the Judge Advocate of the Fleet, J.G. Frapnell. He wrote, on 7 May, that 'This enquiry appears to have been conducted in accordance with section 92 of the Naval Discipline Act and King's regulations and Admiralty Instructions'. He continued: 'As a method of ascertaining with as much accuracy as possible what happens upon such occasions, this sort of enquiry is, no doubt, of great benefit but as machinery for deciding whether a man should be convicted of an offence with justice, it leaves much to be desired.'

The Judge Advocate went on to say that the statements of witnesses that were obtained by question and answer without caution were not 'in the legal sense, "voluntary" statements'. He considered it to be of:

... little value to caution a witness who has already given such a statement when he comes to the book to be sworn. It is well recognised that he is unlikely to make objection; advantage is thus obtained of a statement which as to part would not, any rate, be regarded as admissible on a charge before the civil courts. Moreover, the statements are all those of persons who may turn out to be accessories but no regard appears to be made to the requirement of independent corroboration.

The Judge Advocate felt that as, 'In all other respects the system of naval justice as administered by Courts Martial is of such a high standard that the continued use of this procedure appears regrettable'. Nor did he consider that much time was saved as a result. He added that 'officers and men "convicted" would have had (what every man should be entitled to) proper and sufficient notice of the charge, the opportunity to prepare and put forward a defence and in particular to obtain evidence that might have affected the result'. He submitted that the procedure should be discontinued, 'except as machinery for ascertaining what actually takes place'.

The method used had resulted from a Board of Admiralty decision taken in 1939, that this was the best way of ascertaining the facts about the loss of a ship in wartime, a court martial only being convened if there was prima facie evidence of blame. Admiralty Fleet Order 370/40 laid down that it was not the intention to hold Section 92 courts martial during the war. Other than the *Manchester*, there had been only two other such courts martial held since the outbreak of war, those concerning the loss of the destroyer *Sturdy* by wreck off the Scottish coast in a gale in 1940 and that of the loss of the destroyer *Punjabi*, which was sunk in collision with the battleship *King George V* in the Arctic in 1942. The latter was only convened by the C-in-C, Home Fleet with Admiralty concurrence, because the witnesses were only readily available for a few days and there was no time to hold a Board of Inquiry as well as two courts martial.

It was stated by the head of Naval Law, Commander H.F. Lawson, on 12 May 1943, after the *Manchester* proceedings, that 'It may well be that the occasion for holding another section 92 Court Martial will not arise before the end of the war'. He continued:

In the case of the *Manchester*, the Board decided that it would save time to proceed by section 92, and in spite of the Judge Advocate's remarks it is thought that the object was achieved. No one could have foreseen the length of time taken by the trial (one would probably have to go back to the days of Admiral Byng and Admiral Keppel to find another so long), but in any case the alternative would certainly have taken much longer. It would have been necessary to hold a second Board of Inquiry after the survivors were released from internment (one had already been held when the few who had not been interned returned to this country), and as ten officers and men were finally convicted or blamed, it might have been necessary to hold that number of Courts Martial. Apart from anything else, it would have been difficult to convene so many different courts.

It was also stated that:

The custom of holding a Courts Martial to try the survivors of a lost ship has a tradition of centuries behind it. It is recognised that the procedure is not entirely in accordance with modern ideas on criminal procedure, but in ordinary criminal cases it is never necessary to proceed except on a specific charge. The nearest approach to a section 92 Courts Martial is a formal inquiry under the merchant Shipping Act, in which the court has power to take away an officers certificate.

Vice Admiral Sir Henry Moore, vice chief of Naval Staff, considered these points and conceded that: 'Naval justice should be like Caesar's wife, above suspicion.' Nonetheless, he opined that 'It is unfortunately clear that the *Manchester* was scuttled unnecessarily and that except as regards the engine room complement, there *was* a lack of leadership and dogged effort to save the ship'. The First Sea Lord, Admiral Sir Dudley Pound, acknowledged that 'the officers and men should feel that they had a fair trial, which they certainly did not feel in this case'. Nevertheless, he continued, 'There is no doubt that the trial *was* very thoroughly carried out and much time was spent in deliberating on the Findings'. The First Lord, Albert Victor Alexander, concurred with Pound, as did the deputy secretary of the Admiralty, Sir Sidney J. Barnes. Such unanimity should not be lightly dismissed.

While it was conceded that the procedure was driven by the need for speed, and fully explained, it had led to a feeling of resentment. The Judge Advocate had suggested that what the court had found to be negligence might only have been an error of judgement. Captain Drew in a long statement, submitted after the verdict, stressed just this point, and that the latter charge was indeed what he had thought he was being tried for and not the former. The head of Naval Law, however, was of the opinion that 'one can only say that this question must have been very much in the minds of the court and that their decision was not lightly reached. Apart from the thought they gave to the matter during the hearing of the evidence, they took *four whole days* to consider their findings.'

What is still as true today as it was back in 1943 is that many of the surviving crew of the *Manchester* retain their absolute faith in Captain Drew and his decision. After the trial a deputation, headed by a chief petty officer, waited upon Drew when he emerged from the court room. The deputation presented him with several sheets of signal pad on which had been written a statement that all who had signed it would be most happy to serve under Captain Drew again, at any time. Many remained convinced in their own minds that his sentence had been 'unfair' and they still wish to see his name cleared posthumously. Veterans, whom this author met in the autumn of 2002 at the sixtieth anniversary celebrations of Operation Pedestal held at Malta, repeated these sentiments. They remain loyal to his memory and felt his sentence was somehow a slur on them all. Principally, the veterans felt that they owed their lives to Captain Drew due to his decision, which, they assumed, he had taken in order to preserve the crew. Such feelings are, after almost seven decades, most commendable, but, if based on that assumption, were they somewhat misplaced?

This is what Drew himself actually had to say on the matter at the court martial:

Some witnesses, perhaps out of a feeling of friendship for me, have said that I was thinking of saving valuable lives. Much as I would like to be credited with that *I am afraid I cannot agree.* I have never yet known a precedent for sinking a ship to save life. The only justification for sinking your own ship is to prevent her from falling into the hands of the enemy, or to prevent some other major disadvantage that might result from not doing so.

Part Three

Points From Proceedings

1 MUTINY AND DESERTION

Always one of the gravest crimes in the armed services, and treated as such throughout history, cases of mutiny in the Royal Navy have invariably attracted the attention of the media. In this author's opinion, it is to the credit of the service that there have been so few of these of a serious or violent nature throughout the long history of the Royal Navy, but there is no denying their perennial interest to the general public.

Let us commence with one of the strangest and most tragic mutinies ever recorded, for the sentencing in that case was, to many eyes, one of the most horrible of all in its lack of fairness.

In January 1758, some fifteen sailors from HMS *Namur*, then a very new battleship and not long in full commission, formed part of a group of seventy of her crew who were so driven by conditions aboard that they broke out of the ship. These men had no intentions of conducting a mutiny as such, in the sense that it is generally known, but the word covers a wide field in legal parlance and mutiny their action was deemed to be, although their subsequent actions would seem to belie that description. This desperate band did not at once disperse and lose themselves ashore, but made their way up to London in order to lay before Their Lordships their genuinely felt grievance. They felt they would receive no fair hearing aboard the ship herself.

The reception they got was not a sympathetic one, and the ringleaders were court-martialled en masse on 21 January, charged with desertion. There could be no evading the fact that they had, indeed, deserted, whatever their reason might be, and all were duly and without exception sentenced to death. In fact, there seems never to have been the intention to hang them all, but one had to pay the penalty to set an example.

So, in England, in the year of grace 1758, the fifteen were compelled to draw lots to see which one would die. One Matthew McCann finally drew the marked paper. In front of his fellows, the unlucky seaman was duly executed as a lesson in discipline.

❋ ❋ ❋

Although mutiny is usually a violent and bloody event, or at the very least a sombre one, a few instances might be classified as little more than unusual upsets. One such was the curious affair that took place in the fleet in 1791. This event was subsequently dignified with the title 'The Midshipmen's Mutiny'.

The whole business had its inception, as in so many cases, with a trivial incident and thereafter rapidly escalated. Aboard the battleship *Saturn* one evening strode a certain Mr Shields, the first lieutenant of the ship. He had the reputation of a martinet and he was certainly to exhibit the true colours of a bad-tempered disciplinarian during the fracas that followed. As Shields paced back and forth there came across the water from the flagship the boom of the watch gun, and, as its echoes died away over the anchorage and assembled fleet, Mr Shields summoned the duty midshipman to attend on him.

This worthy was Mr Midshipman Leonard. The first lieutenant asked him coldly why he had not performed his required duty and reported the firing of the gun to him. The answer supplied, with all the obvious but tactless reasonableness of youth, was that as Mr Shields was present on deck within a few yards of Mr Leonard, then he must have quite plainly seen and heard the firing of the gun himself. Our young 'Snotty' therefore assumed that a report in person was hardly necessary.

Mr Leonard was very soon undeceived on that point for the first lieutenant's response was to order him to the masthead. Now, this was a common enough punishment for junior midshipmen who were found guilty of neglecting their duties, in order to impress on them that obedience was the first cardinal of their chosen profession. However, Mr Midshipman Leonard still did not consider that he merited a punishment. To make it clear that the order was such, he asked Shields outright, whether it a punishment or not. Yes, replied Shields, it most certainly was, and for neglect of duty. In that case, Leonard responded, with some temerity, he would not comply, although he was willing to go to the masthead in the execution of any duty.

Both men having struck their postures, there could now be but one ending as neither could withdraw without loss of face. Mr Shields reiterated that it was a punishment and Mr Leonard again refused to go, whereupon the first lieutenant ordered a rope be sent down from the topmast and, to the tune of a pipe, several seamen tied the midshipman to it in a form of sling, and he was then unceremoniously hoisted aloft. Unfortunately, in his anger, the first lieutenant had failed to ensure that the correct fastenings had been made that would have kept the boy's body away from the main top, and Leonard struck hard against it, crying out in agony.

At once Leonard was again lowered to the deck, untied and dispatched to the ship's surgeon to have his injury treated. The midshipman quickly recovered, but the story of his treatment, no doubt suitably enhanced in the telling, quickly spread around the fleet. Leonard's punishment soon became the subject of widespread indignation among his fellow midshipmen, some of whom hailed from the nation's leading families and who professed themselves unwilling to be so treated. Some of the latter urged Leonard to take legal proceedings against Shields, but to his credit the midshipman was not willing to fire bullets others had loaded, and tended to dismiss the whole affair as being over and done with. Perhaps he felt, on reflection, that he had overstepped the mark. Others were not so conciliatory and felt that Shields' unseamanlike conduct exhibited an attitude of mind that should not go unremarked.

In the natural course of events, the whole incident would have been just a nine-day wonder, and so it was, by and large, in the fleet. However, certain midshipmen were still not content to let things rest. Meetings were held in which the whole thing was vehemently denounced, the chief agitator being a wealthy young gentleman named Edward Moore, a midshipman aboard the *London*. As a direct result of these gatherings, circular letters were sent out to all the ships at Spithead, which called upon all midshipmen of the fleet to unite in obtaining justice against Mr Shields for his callous action against one of their number.

One of these letters was delivered to the frigate *Alcide*, where it was given to one of the senior midshipmen, Mr Riboulelau, who read it and at once took it to his commanding officer, who, in turn, hastened to deliver it to Lord Howe himself. That gentleman professed himself astonished at the letter's contents and then passed it on to the Admiralty. Within a very short time, on 16 August, Midshipman Moore found himself facing a court martial charged with 'Being principally concerned in writing and circulating anonymous letters, of a seditious nature'.

It had been an act of supreme folly for Moore to have taken matters so far in the first place; it was even more foolish of Riboulelau to have distributed letters around the fleet in such a haphazard way. Perhaps Mr Shields did need showing up, but it was Moore who paid the penalty. The midshipman was sentenced to be dismissed from the fleet and to serve one month's imprisonment in the Marshalsea prison.

Moore was given a severe reprimand and 'admonished to be more circumspect in his conduct for the future'. Riboulelau was neither charged nor brought to trail.

One of the earliest cases of court martial for mutiny was the series of charges made after the return of the Halley expedition of 1698–99. This was reminiscent of Drake's confrontation in some respects, with the professional seamen rebelling against the directions of their less-experienced leader.

Edmund Halley was a famous mathematician, physicist, diplomat and soldier, as well as the leading astronomer of his day, and after whom the famous comet is named. Halley was rather less knowledgeable in the ways of the sea, although he was a navigator. Nonetheless, sailor or not, Halley was given command of an expedition to make magnetic observations in the South Atlantic. Halley was invested with the temporary commission as a captain in the service and placed in command of a pink, HMS *Paramour*, with a crew of true seamen under him.

The voyage was a long and tedious one, reaching southern waters by way of Madeira and returning along the coast of Brazil to the West Indies and thence home to Plymouth by way of Newfoundland. Confined in their tiny craft through all this period, the professional sailors became increasingly exasperated by some of Halley's 'interference' with their duties. The crew felt that Halley should have confined himself strictly to his own specialised skills and left the day-to-day sailing of the *Paramour* to them. The first lieutenant felt his position most keenly, and, in the end, just refused to listen to Halley's orders at all.

On their return to England, Halley brought court martial proceedings against all his officers, which resulted in their wholesale dismissal from the service. This was the reverse of the Drake incident and established the tradition of unqualified obedience to the appointed leader, whatever his failings.

It was not unusual for charges and counter-charges to be mounted in cases of mutiny, and the records of the 1700–1800 period in particular show a large number of multiple courts martial taking place, of which the following is a typical example.

On 9 January 1775, James Bignall, the gunner aboard HMS *Glasgow*, was brought to trial by his captain, William Malby, for contempt and disobedience of orders. Bignall was given a full hearing, but the charges were only partly proven and the sentence was for the loss of one year's professional pay and a reprimand. The following day it was Captain Malby who was in the dock with Bignall making the accusations, charging his captain with cruelty and oppression.

Once more the charges were adjudged to have been but partly proven, though Malby was dismissed his ship. Reading between the lines, it was a good example of six of one and half a dozen of the other, although Malby's fate was the more severe.

Since the time of the mutiny at the Nore, cases of mass mutiny in the service have, happily, been rare. Two of the most recent took place as comparatively recently as in the aftermath of the First World War. The first of these incidents concerned the Royal Marines, and is unique in the history of that most loyal and proud corps, whose reputation for steadfastness is second to none to any service of the nation. It has to be viewed in the light of the peculiar circumstances of the day.

Following the Armistice, a very confused situation remained on the borders of our former ally, Russia. The 'Red' (Bolshevik) and the 'White' (Tsarist) armies were locked in ferocious combat to decide who was going to rule that vast land, gripped as it was in the throes of violent revolution. The break-away states of the Baltic, Finland, Estonia, Latvia and Lithuania all sought their chance to proclaim their independence, while marauding armies of German troops, undefeated in the field and now plying their trade as mercenaries, answering to nobody but their own commanders, were also roaming the region. In the middle of it all there were the remnants of the various allied forces left over from Russia's previous alliances, which were left to interpret confusing and constantly changeing instructions and condition as best they could. Their instructions from home varied from active participation in the civil war, to total withdrawal, depending on the machinations of Lloyd George and Churchill at the time. The British had, wisely, stood aloft from the French revolution more than a century earlier, but less wise heads in the upper echelons of the political machine took a different course of armed intervention in the Russian one. Churchill, in particular, was seen to be always keen to keep the broth stirring, while the rest of the Cabinet seemed indecisive on which way to jump. Our erstwhile allies, France and the United States, were sanctimonious in their own attitudes, keeping their own troops in the area, but not letting them become involved in the fighting. Into this quagmire was thrown the 6th Battalion of the Royal Marine Light Infantry.

The 6th Battalion RMLI was dispatched in April 1919, to reinforce the interventionist forces operating in the region of Lake Onega, to the south of Murmansk. The marines were far from happy from the very onset, for they had originally been assigned the more palatable (and understandable) task of policing the plebiscite to decide the future of Schleswig-Holstein on the borders of Denmark and Sweden. Therefore, this radically different assignment, far to the north, fighting a war few if any of them (or their commanders) understood and even fewer believed in, the men considered a betrayal of previous assurances.

The first combat engagement witnessed the demoralisation of some of the men after a confused encounter with the enemy in which units went astray and confusion overtook them. The greater part of two companies returned to camp in open defiance of their officers and commander. This was unprecedented in the whole history of the corps. Mass courts martial followed, during which no less than ninety Royal Marines were found guilty and thirteen of these were sentenced to death.

Happily, common sense prevailed, and the commander-in-chief commuted all the death sentences, substituting five-year terms of imprisonment instead. Even these sentences were subsequently reviewed. In mitigation, Captain Stephen Roskill refers to a War Office telegram, dated 4 June 1919, which contains indications as to the men's justifiable grievances at the time. These included the age at which new recruits could be employed in the front line and the length of time they were to serve in this theatre of undeclared war. Nevertheless, many felt that the corps was placed in an unenviable position by the posturing of some politicians and left to sort things out as best they could, and, for their pains, were left with a stain on their proud history.

The second episode, which concerned large bodies of men involved in mass indiscipline amounting to mutiny, was the *Lucia* case of January 1931. The *Lucia* was a submarine depot ship based at Devonport, and her lower deck had been simmering with discontent at alleged injustices for a considerable period prior to this date. The ship was not happily run in many respects, and orders to paint the ship before she sailed proved the catalyst for rebellion. The men were ordered to work long hours and their Sunday leave was cancelled or cut in order to complete the work on time. The men, incensed, simply 'downed tools'.

The subsequent series of courts martial involved no less than thirty-one of the ship's complement, of whom no less than twenty-seven received sentences. These ranged from imprisonment with hard labour for three or six months, through to detention for periods of two months or less. However, the trials revealed much that was wrong in the *Lucia*'s higher echelons also, and her captain, first lieutenant and a divisional officer were all placed on half pay as a result. The Admiralty later reviewed all the other sentences and most were reduced.

The *Lucia* case was later overshadowed by the much larger troubles of the so-called 'Invergordon Mutiny' later the same year, of which so much has appeared (much of it malicious or, at best, speculative) in print since. However, it is a remarkable fact that no courts martial resulted from this major incident, for the whole affair was treated as a special case. Many of the Invergordon 'mutineers' were simply discharged from naval service after a cooling-off period and the

Royal Navy cleansed itself of some real malcontents in time to restore its prestige in full during the Second World War.

Dissatisfaction with conditions afloat and other minor personal irritations erupted once more in the years immediately following the Second World War. The introduction of National Service, although more sparingly used to man the Royal Navy than the other services, gave the opportunity for sullen and resentful draftees to vent their spleen in other ways. Some of the cases involved regular service men also, it should be emphasised. A whole series of 'malicious damage' cases, which again marred the image of the Senior Service at a time of headlong decline, took place in the 1950s. There were many of these cases, but they usually took the form of isolated incidents and were not co-ordinated in an organised or mass campaign.

Typical of the type of thing that took place, and which particularly proliferated in the years 1953–54, was that of stoker mechanic Alexander Robertson serving aboard the aircraft carrier *Ocean*. Again, the basic cause of the trouble was suspension of Foreign Service leave from ratings who had been abroad for a long time. One aircraft carrier that had served long stints conducting air strikes against communist aggressors in Korea, when returning home via the Mediterranean, had been held up by Lord Louis Mountbatten, who wished to use her as part of his force to put on special exercises. A mass mutiny was only just averted in this ship's case, which was mainly brought about by one man's ego.

In the case of Robertson, however, it was a one-man protest. At his court martial, which was held on 8 February 1954, Robertson pleaded guilty to maliciously damaging equipment aboard his ship, to wit fifty-nine pressure gauges, a revolution indicator and two electric light bulbs, in what his defending officer, Lieutenant (E) J. Hammersley, described as 'five minutes of utter folly'. The prosecutor, Lieutenant Commander T.B. Holman, read out a statement by the accused which admitted: 'I found myself in the forward machinery space and realised I had broken a large electric light bulb with an iron bar. I then realised I had broken a number of gauges as well. It must have been the effect of the draught cider.'

The defence stated that Robertson had an unsettled home life and that he had been drafted nine times in four years in the navy. The court, sitting at Devonport, sentenced Robertson to fifteen months' detention.

Naval airman David Carslaw was sentenced to thirteen months' detention at a court martial held aboard the aircraft carrier *Glory* at Malta between 18 November 1953 and 16 January 1954. Carslaw had been found guilty of twelve charges of malicious damage to the ship, including cutting the electrical leads and air leads to Bofors and multiple Oerlikon anti-aircraft guns, navigational radar equipment and telephone cables. Again, strong drink was given as the reason.

Similar such outbreaks occurred in the aircraft carrier *Warrior* at Chatham on Christmas Day 1953; on the depot ship *Forth* at Malta on 18 November 1953; and on the depot ship *Montclare* at Rothesay on 16 January 1954. A Roman candle type firework was found in each of the two diesel engines of the submarine *Artemis* at sea, forcing this ship to return to Rothesay on the Clyde on 2 March 1954. Four other aircraft carriers, four destroyers, a frigate and four other submarines were similarly afflicted by 'malicious damage' in just one year, leading to security officers being appointed to HM ships.

In response to this growing problem and worried questions in the House of Commons, Mr Thomas, the First Lord, gave the usual bland reassurance: 'There is no evidence that recent cases of malicious damage in British warships reflect any organised campaign of sabotage, or any subversive motive.' True enough, these cases still continued, if less frequently, and eventually almost died away.

Mutiny proper, as it is generally understood outside the service, both bloody and dire, is typified by such cases as that of the *Hermione*, aboard which ship occurred one the worst cases ever recorded. The mutiny took place while the *Hermione* was serving in the West Indies.

It was soon after the Spithead and Nore mutinies of 1797, when the crew of the thirty-two-gun frigate finally rose up against the sadistic and brutal Captain Pigot. He had a long history of instability and violence and he flogged his men without mercy and with little provocation. Things came to a head when three seamen fell to their deaths from the ship's rigging after being threatened with more of the same if they were the last men down. Hugh Pigot responded to these tragic accidents with typical callousness, and that same night he, along with nine other officers, was butchered with a fervour that defies belief before the ship was surrendered to the Spanish at La Guaira.

No matter how great (and, in the case of the captain himself, at least, how very much deserved) the justification, such an appalling massacre could not go unpunished. Over the eight years that followed, all the mutineers involved were steadily and remorselessly tracked down and brought to justice by the navy.

The first trials took place within five months of these events. Men who had been members of the *Hermione*'s crew were discovered aboard a captured vessel,

La Magicienne, and one of them, John Mason, immediately went to the captain of the *Valiant* and volunteered information. Four other former members were found aboard the captured ship and these, Antonio Marco, John Elliott, Joe Montell and Pierre d'Orlanie, were subsequently brought to trial aboard HMS *York*, on 17 March, by Admiral Sir Hyde Parker. Captain Bowen was the President and the court comprised Captains Crawley, Dobson, Ferrier and Smith, with William Smith acting as Deputy Judge Advocate. Mason, having turned king's evidence, bore eloquent testimony against the other four throughout the hearing. All four men were accused of being 'actually on board His Majesty's said ship *Hermione* at the time of the mutiny, murder and piracy were committed on board her; and for being taken in arms against His Majesty'.

The first witness called by the prosecution, Lieutenant John Harris, had previously served aboard the *Hermione*, but had, fortunately for him, left her before the last voyage. Harris identified all four men without hesitation, as did another former crew member, John Kelly. A detailed deposition by Mason, who had been the carpenter's mate, was read out and Mason himself called to give evidence. Mason gave a detailed account of events but at no point did he detail the part any of the accused had taken in them.

No further witnesses were called. Instead, the accused were asked, 'Separately or severally', if they had any defence to offer. All replied that they had none.

The fate of this quartet was settled very quickly. After the briefest of adjournments the court found all four guilty and, in its own words:

> ... the court is of the opinion that the charge of mutiny, murder and running away with His Majesty's Ship *Hermione* and delivering her up to the enemy; and being found actually in arms against His Majesty and his subjects, on board *La Magicienne*, a French privateer, are fully proven.

The sentence was equally predictable, that all four were 'to be hung by the necks until they are dead, at the yardarms of such of His Majesty's ships, and at such times, as shall be directed by the Commander-in-Chief'. The court added: 'And as a further example, to deter others from committing, or being accessory to, such shocking and atrocious crimes, that when dead their bodies be hung in chains upon gibbets on such conspicuous points, or headlands, as the Commander-in-Chief direct.'

Of course, the limited evidence given, indeed the charges brought, proved no such thing as alleged in the first part of this finding. However, justice was done, if not strictly legally done, for by all subsequent accounts two of the accused were among the worst of the actual mutineers in word and deed. Thus, on the 19th, the yellow flag was hoisted aloft in the *York*, and the four men were strung up at the yardarms. A confession, written by Montell, and which cleared in some part both Elliott and d'Orlanie, was handed to Sir Hyde Parker. It would have made little difference, for hanging was the fate that awaited them for serving aboard *La Magicienne* anyway, but it tended to emphasise the drum-head appearance of the court martial itself, and how eager the navy was to exact some revenge for what had taken place.

Yet two further mutineers, Leech and William Mason, were found aboard the French frigate *L'Aimable* and detained by Rear Admiral Harvey at Fort Royal. On 11 April, loyal men from the *Hermione's* crew, including the master, Southcott, and Midshipman Casey, arrived at the same port in time to identify and give evidence at the trial of this pair. Their courts martial took place on 1 May at Fort Royal, presided over by Captain Thomas Totty of the *Alfred*. Southcott's evidence was crucial for he firmly identified Thomas Leech as one of the ringleaders. His evidence was confirmed by others: the gunner, Mr Searle; Price the carpenter; Moncrieff the cook; and several Royal Marines. All commented that Mason was not observed to have taken part in the mutiny. Leech offered little or nothing in the way of defence; Mason declared that he was innocent. The verdicts of the court reflected these expressions, Leech being found guilty and Mason not guilty. Leech was duly hanged aboard the *Alfred* on 3 May.

Justice had meanwhile caught up with yet four more men from the *Hermione*, John Brown, William Benives, William Herd and John Hill. Brown made a confession, which Parker used in the same manner as he done with Mason's. The trial took place on 5 May at Cape Nicholas Mole, under the presidency of Captain Bowen once more, with six captains forming the court. Brown's statement threw new and more lurid light on to the whole affair and listed twenty-five of the chief mutineers. Called to give evidence, Brown exonerated Benives and Hill, but confirmed Herd's complicity. Brown also fingered both d'Orlanie and Elliott, which posthumously justified the earlier court's hasty decision (as it was no doubt fully intended to do). Herd tried hard to clear himself and Brown was forced to admit that he had not actually seen him in the captain's cabin or carrying any weapon. Both Herd and Hill were, it later turned out, mutineers; Benives was probably innocent, Brown testifying that the latter was temporarily blind at the time of the mutiny. It made no difference; all three were sentenced to hang and their bodies to be hanged in chains. On 8 May, this trio met their appointed fates aboard the *Carnatic*.

Five loyal men faced court martial on their return to England. These were held aboard the *Director* at Sheerness. Among the members of the court was Captain William Bligh, not directly involved for once. All were acquitted. Still the hunt for the rest continued remorselessly down the years. In total, thirty-three of the *Hermione's* crew faced courts martial; of these twenty-four were hanged and one transported, but several of the true ringleaders and murderers were never brought to justice.

One of the most distasteful features of a court martial held on John and James Holford and James Irwin, which was held aboard the *Brunswick* on 23 May 1798, was the vindictive attitude of Sir Hyde Parker after their acquittal by the court. Parker wrote a letter to the Admiralty bitterly inveighing against the court's President, Rear Admiral Richmond Rodney Bligh, demanding his removal from the fleet. Parker appeared more concerned that any ex-*Hermione* found should swing, guilty or innocent, as an example to the fleet, rather than in any correct administration of justice. Their Lordships, in their wisdom, ignored this outburst and also Parker's own threat to resign.

Harsh though many of the sentences might appear in the *Hermione*, and other cases of mutiny, with the hindsight of more than 200 years such executions did not always have the deterrent effect so fondly hoped for by Sir Hyde Parker and his ilk. Injustice and harshness would still drive men to the extremes. Barely two years after the *Hermione* mutiny, the crew of the fifth-rate *Danae* rose up and carried off the ship to Brest in the same imperious manner. It was not until conditions afloat became more reasonable that mutiny, as it is generally depicted, faded and became increasingly a subject of the history books. The latter half of the eighteenth century will, however, always remain infamous for the frequency and the extremeness of such outbreaks, and the court's resolution to stamp them out, root and branch, by equally fiercesome retribution.

2 COLLISION AND WRECK

It was long common for survivors of peacetime disasters to face a court martial, something which not a few faced with more reluctance than shot or shell. Officially, the principal reason for this was so that the Admiralty could ascertain what had gone wrong and to try to prevent it occurring again. Courts of Inquiry were common in times of war and normally a war loss from enemy action would not require a full court martial as well, unless something particularly untoward had taken place that needed to be justified. The records of the courts martial that did take place in such circumstances are among the most interesting of cases, although access to those of the last hundred years has always been heavily restricted. Mysteries like the blowing up of the *Vanguard*, *Bulwark* and *Natal* in the First World War, and the real stories behind the loss of such ships as the *Glorious*, *Manchester* and *Royal Oak* in the second great conflict would have long ago ceased to be the subject of increasingly wild specula-tion, especially by foreign revisionists in the United States and Europe, had access to the official documents been granted to responsible British historians. Frustratingly, no defence was possible from British historians whose hands are tied. Justification for such a policy by the Ministry of Defence is, as best, nebulous, but Whitehall departments have a long tradition of obsession with the withholding of information on historic events, while leaking like a sieve on current ones. The Naval Library, for many years, refused to even acknowledge, let alone reply, to requests for such access. In 1805, another historian of courts martial, John McArthur, was bewailing the fact that the then Board of Admiralty would not allow him access to records covering the period 1793 to 1804. I wonder what he would have thought if he had learned that, two centuries later, their successors were refusing to let documents subsequent to 1905 be examined. A 100-year ban might have seemed a little excessive to him!

One of the most bizarre revelations to come from a courts martial appeared from that investigating the wreck of one HMS *Nautilus* in the Mediterranean, an event that took place on the morning of 5 January 1807. The courts martial of Lieutenant Nesbitt and some of the survivors of the crew revealed some truly ghastly facts. Out of a total complement of 122 officers and men, only sixty-four survived to reach Malta, among the dead being the ship's captain.

The court found that the loss of the *Nautilus* 'was occasioned by the captain's zeal to forward the public dispatches which induced him to run in the dark, tempestuous night for the passage between the islands of Cerigotto and Candia' (the modern-day Kythira and Antikythera between Greece and Crete).

However, the real sensation was caused by the fact that it became known that this was one of the very few authenticated cases of cannibalism in the Royal Navy. Those who survived the wreck were subjected to a terrible ordeal. For four days, they existed without food or water and many died in terrible pain and anguish. Driven by such extremity, some decided that only one option lay open to them. One of the young men who had died during the preceding night was selected as food for those that remained. Many, it is recorded, had no power left to eat or swallow.

It is rare for a Royal Navy captain to voluntarily abandon his vessel, no matter what the circumstances, whether in peace or war. For a commander to abandon his whole squadron was something unique, but this is the unfortunate experience that overtook Captain Sir Edward Belcher in 1853.

The origins of this event went back some eight years, when Sir John Franklin had sailed from the Thames on his last and ill-fated voyage of exploration to find the North-West Passage. Franklin's whole expedition was embarked in two ships, *Erebus* and *Terror*, with provisions for three years, but after July nothing more was heard from them. At first, anxiety was muted, but as time passed alarm grew for

their safety. Not until 1848, however, did the government bestir itself and authorise the dispatch of another expedition to try to trace them. Both Sir John Ross
and Captain Kellett carried out searches, to no avail. In 1850, yet another attempt
was mounted, led by Captains Collinson and McClure. McClure actually made
the passage, but was iced in for two years. This, in turn, led to the sending out of
yet another squadron to effect his rescue.

A force of four ships was readied under the command of Sir Edward Belcher
aboard the *Assistance*, with the *Intrepid* (Commander McClintock), *Pioneer*
(Commander Richards) and *Resolute* (Captain Kellett). They sailed from England
in the spring of 1852. The *Resolute* and *Intrepid* finally reached Melville Island, and
one of their search parties found a record left by McClure. The ships wintered
and then continued their search the following spring.

Another party, from the *Resolute*, under Lieutenant Pim, reached Banks' Island,
where they found McClure's vessel, the *Investigator*, and saved her crew. The ships
were hemmed in by ice once more, and the decision was made to abandon them
and take passage home in the vessels of another relief expedition. Kellett and
McClintock, who had a wide experience of this type of situation, both maintained that the *Resolute* and *Intrepid* could be safely navigated back to England,
but Belcher, new to this type of work, refused to listen to their advice and ordered
that both ships be left. That he had been too hasty was confirmed by the fact that
the *Resolute* ultimately drifted out of ice and into Baffin's Bay that summer, where
she was salvaged by an American whaling vessel and returned to an embarrassed
British Government later.

On his return home, Belcher was brought before a court martial for the premature
abandonment of his four ships. Belcher, in his defence, claimed that his orders allowed
for this eventuality and the court was forced to accept this argument. However, they
were clearly far from satisfied with his attitude, and the sentence passed on him was a
'bare acquittal'. Belcher never received another command.

One of the greatest peacetime disasters to befall the Victorian navy took place
just after midnight on the morning of 7 September 1870. This was the capsizing
of the brand-new battleship HMS *Captain* in a raging gale in the Bay of Biscay.
Her designer, Captain Cooper Coles, her captain, Captain Hugh Burgoyne, and
471 officers and men went down with her. The resulting court martial raised a
colossal row from one end of the country to the other as to who exactly was
responsible for the loss.

The period was one of great transition for the Royal Navy. Wooden walls had
given way to iron and armoured hulls; sail was supplemented by steam, although
not yet fully usurped; and the old broadsides, rows of small smooth-bore cannon

on trucks, had given way to monster guns, able to traverse in barbettes and turrets. Idea followed idea, innovation followed innovation, and hardly one ship followed another that had similar features. It was, perhaps, inevitable that sooner or later a price would have to be paid for this pell-mell change and experiment, but the price exacted was so heavy and so stunning in its enormity as to leave the whole nation shocked, and not a little outraged.

The whole concept of the *Captain* herself had been the subject of great controversy even before she ever put to sea. Coles was convinced that his turrets were the correct answer to the problem of how best to utilise the great new guns, and, ultimately, history was to prove him correct. The alternative, the barbette, had many champions, and counted among them many senior naval officers. Sir Edmund Reed, chief constructor of the navy, was one of the leading opponents of Coles' design of turret ships. To test the conflicting theories the Admiralty decreed that another battleship, the *Monarch*, be laid down to Reed's specification. Overall, the backing of informed professional opinion lay with Reed. Due to this, a vehement argument broke out in public between the opposing factions, fuelled by both press and parliament. Both sides favoured the turret; it was the manner in which it was to be carried and the type of warship best able to do this where they fell out violently.

As the board itself felt so strongly opposed to the design of the *Captain*, they insisted that an outside contractor should build her, while the Royal dockyard, Chatham, built the *Monarch*. The shipbuilding firm with the courage to take on the job was Lairds of Birkenhead. Both battleships were to carry four of the large 12-inch calibre MLR guns, in two twin turrets; however, whereas *Monarch* carried hers 17 feet above the waterline atop three decks; the *Captain* more resembled the American *Monitor*, with hardly any freeboard at all to her main deck, which was but 8 1 or 8 2 feet above the waterline. Despite this, *Captain* still carried a great spread of canvas. Experts pronounced this combination as potentially lethal, but Lairds seemed quite happy with all the inclination tests carried out, even though it later transpired that *Captain* was actually to float even lower in the water than intended because the wrong weight material had been used in her construction.

Despite all the misgivings, Coles' ship came through her initial trials well enough, and when she accompanied the squadron commanded by Admiral Sir Alexander Milne, C-in-C, Mediterranean Fleet, on a cruise to Gibraltar, all aboard her also appeared confident. Admiral Milne himself actually went aboard the *Captain* in the Bay on 6 September, but left to rejoin his flagship, *Lord Warden*, during the afternoon, when a storm began to brew. It was well for him that he did so. All afternoon and evening, the barometer fell sharply and the sea rose, as only the Bay of Biscay seas can.

The whole fleet prepared themselves for a very rough night: upper sails were furled and topsails double reefed. Despite these precautions, as the gale increased in power, all cohesion was lost in the fleet and soon all the mighty vessels were rolling and battling mountainous waves, with the wind blasting at full gale force. Steadily the wind increased still further and the whole squadron found themselves clawing and pitching in the blackness of the night, although still holding their own, albeit with difficulty. Suddenly, at about fifteen minutes past midnight, there came a blast of unparallel violence, which shrieked through the fleet, shredding reefed sails asunder and throwing the battleships over on their beam ends. All the ships eventually righted themselves from this onslaught, save one, the *Captain*.

The watch had been called aboard *Captain* at midnight, with Captain Burgoyne supervising efforts to clew down the topsail yards in a desperate attempt to reduce sail yet further. However, the battleship herself lay over at such an acute angle that this order proved impossible to carry out. That last mighty blast, which had pulverised yards and brought down spars in the other battleships of the squadron, failed to do likewise to the *Captain*'s stout rigging, and this proved her undoing. Unable to take the additional strain, or relieve it, in an instant the *Captain* lurched over past her angle of recovery. She hung on her beam ends, the water rushed into her funnel and penetrated her superstructure, and she rolled completely over, keel up, before vanishing below the raging seas, plunging down into water some 4,000 feet deep off Cape Finisterre.

Such were the terrible conditions that prevailed through the night that it was morning before it was generally realised by the rest of the force that the *Captain* had gone. Only a few survivors managed to reach safety, Gunner James May and seventeen hands in total. In a pinnace, the only boat to be launched successfully, they rode out the storm and reached land at Corcubion Bay, Spain, where they were later rescued, by the *Monarch* of all ships – a last bitter irony.

Not surprisingly, the subsequent court martial was followed avidly throughout the nation. This soon proved to be but a forerunner of yet more recriminations and allegations as responsibility for the tragedy was denied by all the parties concerned. The hearing lasted for many days, but the turbulence that its findings left in its wake lasted for many months.

For their part, Lairds maintained, throughout, that the disaster had come about through some unknown cause and the company felt that even the extra draught had not endangered the *Captain*'s stability. The Admiralty had also been apparently satisfied with Lairds' assurances on that score at the time. The Admiralty's own tests had not been communicated to Admiral Milne prior to the disaster, unfortunately. Captain Burgoyne had always expressed his own complete confidence in his command, an opinion that was subsequently backed up under questioning of the eighteen survivors of the disaster. Various suggestions were made by the experts called in to advise the court, of the flooding of the starboard bilges or the effect that her unique 'flying bridge', necessitated by the *Captain*'s low freeboard, had on her stability. Some held that this bridge was a dangerous wind trap which had contributed to the night's problems, but the court rejected this allegation.

By far the most damning evidence, of course, was Reed's long record of opposition, culminating in him saying to Captain Burgoyne before he sailed: 'I don't want to say any more against her, but I am glad that it is your fate and not mine to go to sea in her.'

The *Captain* carried the greatest spread of sail (50,000 square feet) of any ship in the Royal Navy at that date, simply because her novel design did not allow for a very large coal bunkerage. The masting of Coles' masterpiece was also unique, being tripods, and this increased her stiffness in any sort of a wind. This great weight aloft reduced her stability angle to 21 degrees, compared with about 70 degrees in other battleships then under construction. This, coupled with her low freeboard, seemed decisive in the tragedy, a point that came out during the court martial in the following exchange.

Captain Commerell, VC, asked Reed:

> Do you think that a diagram together with an official intimation that 21 degrees was the point which would assuredly capsize the *Captain*, would have had a great influence upon the officers entrusted with the experiment, and that in dealing with the *Captain* the same as other ships entailed a grave responsibility? I ask this, as an officer who has had the *Captain* under his orders and who, with that diagram before him, would not have dared to keep the ship under sail one single night.

Reed's reply was illuminating:

> The *Captain* was built to be under the same conditions as other ships and I believe – although I regret to have to state it – that if any such information emanated from the Admiralty it would have resulted in the strongest efforts to prove the Admiralty wrong, and to carry all possible sail …

The Admiralty trial had, in fact, included an inclination test, which judged the *Captain*'s safety angle to be between 15 and 16 degrees – in smooth water. It was revealed in evidence from survivors that, just before the final great squall struck her, the *Captain* was already heeling 18 degrees. The point about the ship competing with more conventional battleships with regard to sailing qualities – in all conditions – was illustrated by another fact. In the 'Standing Orders for Officers of the Watch', which Captain Burgoyne listed in the 'Night Order Book' of HMS *Captain*, was the reminder that this ship ought to compare favourably with other, contemporary, battleships when under canvas. Admiral Ballard speculated that this reminder by the *Captain*'s commanding officer 'was not improbably regarded by them as in the nature of a warning never to shorten sail on their own responsibility unless in very pressing circumstances'.

Reed went on to add:

My belief was that the unseaworthiness of the *Captain* was a cause of anxiety to many who professed to believe in her, and what I though would happen with the *Captain* was this – that she would have the highest possible reports to begin with; that she would be very carefully nursed through her early career until admissions of her deficiencies became slowly admitted, and that before she got through a commission she would be condemned as utterly unfit for Naval Service. That in 1869 I did what I though was right in the matter of resisting to the utmost degree in my power a desire on the part of the First Lord to increase the number of Captains. That resistance I repeated, and again and again repeated, basing my objections on the danger which was involved in the *Captain* herself; and when I found my resistance was useless, I retired from duty and undertook to submit my resignation from my office.

Not unnaturally, this and similar statements made a great impression on the court, and their final verdict contained thinly veiled censure for all concerned that such a vessel should have been sent to sea without far more extensive trials. The court stated:

HM Ship *Captain* was capsized by pressure of sail assisted by the heave of the sea; and the sail carried at the time of her loss (regard being had to the force of the wind and state of the sea) was insufficient to have endangered a ship endured with a proper amount of stability. The Court find it their duty to record the conviction they entertain that the *Captain* was built in deference to public opinion expressed in Parliament and through other channels, and in opposition to the views and opinions of the Controller and his Department, and the evidence all tends to show that they generally disapproved of her construction. It further appearing in evidence that before the Captain was received from the Contractor a grave departure from her original design had been committed, whereby her draught of water was increased by about two feet and her freeboard diminished to a corresponding extent, and that her stability proved to be dangerously small, combined with a sail area under those circumstances excessive; the Court deeply regret that if these facts were duly known and appreciated they were not communicated to the officer in command of the ship, or that if otherwise the ship was allowed to be employed in the ordinary service of the Fleet before they had been sufficiently ascertained by calculation and experiment.

✳ ✳ ✳

A mere five years on from the loss of one battleship, the Royal Navy suffered the loss of a second in a peacetime disaster. The sister ships *Iron Duke* and *Vanguard* were second-rate battleships, intended as cheaper options for use on distant stations like the East Indies or China, where opposition was likely to be limited. These vessels displaced some 6,000 tons, had a crew of 450 officers and men, and were powered by two-cylinder engines, giving them a maximum speed of about 16 knots. Their main armament consisted of ten 8-inch and four 6-inch muzzle-loading guns and, in accordance with the dictates of the era, both had stout rams forward below the waterline. Both battleships also carried a good spread of sail, because stocks of coal on distant stations were thought to be a limiting factor in their endurance and versatility.

The *Vanguard* was completed in September 1870 and the *Iron Duke* in January of the following year. The whole class had undergone modifications to the original design before they had taken to the water, and one such amendment was to lead to the tragedy that followed. It had been customary for the battleships of this period to have their main machinery spaces protected from any rupture of the outer hull by the provision of longitudinal compartments on either side, termed wing passages. In this class, however, as part of the cost-cutting profile, this feature had been omitted. Thus, although the ships were double bottomed, this meant that any penetration of the hull above this area and the upper deck would leave the large lower deck totally exposed. And so it turned out.

Iron Duke, when completed, duly went out east as the flagship of the China Squadron between 1871 and 1875, when she returned home. *Vanguard*, by contrast, never left home waters, serving instead as guardship at Kingstown, Ireland, during the same period.

On 1 September 1875, under the command of Captain Richard Dawkins, *Vanguard* was engaged in the annual fleet manoeuvres in the Irish Sea. Astern of her was stationed the *Iron Duke*, the whole squadron being under the command of Admiral Tarleton, flying his flag aboard the *Warrior*. Captain Henry Hickley, a close friend of Dawkins, commanded the *Iron Duke*. The admiral's intention was to steam with these ships, plus the *Hector*, from Dublin Bay for Queenstown, passing outside the dangerous shoal known as Kish Bank.

The force duly sailed at 1030hrs, in the order *Warrior*, *Hector*, *Vanguard* and *Iron Duke* and, after passing well clear of the Kish Bank light vessel, turned due south. Tarleton then made the signal to form in divisions in line ahead, which meant that the ships were to be, in effect, paired off, with the two rear ships moving up abreast and to port of the two leading ships. The method chosen to effect this manoeuvre was for the rear ships to increase speed and move out, while the leading ships maintained a steady course until the others got into position. As the squadron was already steaming at a speed of 7 knots, and steam had only been made available for 8 knots, this process was due to take a considerable time to complete, at least half an hour. Still, it was a normal procedure, which occasioned no special alarm. Both ships' captains thought so little of it that they retired to the cabins for lunch, leaving their respective officers of the watch to carry on with it. Both vessels maintained full speed, although the *Iron Duke* was lagging one cable's length astern at the start of the manoeuvre.

All would have been perfectly well had not, some ten minutes after commencement, the ships have run into a dense fog that appeared suddenly out of a clear morning sky. At once, all contact between the individual vessels was lost. Here again, this might not have been that dangerous, for the captains were called and all the ships trusted each other to maintain both course and speed rigorously. Unhappily, the officer of the watch aboard *Iron Duke* was not content to do just that, but, being very inexperienced, hedged his bets and ordered his ship's helm to be put over two points to port. When Captain Hickley came up to the bridge and noticed that this has been done, the officer concerned stated that he had felt it would have been safer to keep a little more clear of the *Vanguard* ahead, and so he had steered slightly away from the ordained course of the squadron.

However, this unauthorised variation in course had the effect of opening the gap between the two sister ships still further. Hickley immediately sought to rectify matters, and tried to bring his command back into station, as near as he could judge. Unfortunately, no warning was sounded and the easing of the *Iron Duke* back to starboard was carried out in total silence. Meantime, aboard *Vanguard*, another misfortune had occurred, for Dawkins had found that an unknown vessel was crossing his ship's path dead ahead. Dawkins at once put his own ship's helm hard over to pass astern of the stranger and blew a warning blast on the ship's whistle in warning. Thus it came about that *Vanguard* was turning to port, while *Iron Duke* was turning to starboard, both out of station. The two ships were now crossing courses at almost right angles to each other and the inevitable happened.

At 1250hrs those on deck aboard the *Vanguard* saw, to their dismay, the great bows of their sister ship looming up out of the fog and, within seconds, the ram of the *Iron Duke* had plunged into the *Vanguard*'s side amidships. The battleships were only 40 yards apart when they first sighted each other and no avoidance was possible. Although the ram struck into the *Vanguard*'s double bottom, it did not pierce it. Despite this, the fate of the *Vanguard* was still sealed, because the top plate of the double bottom was ripped open, and the inrushing water penetrated up through that space and into the great open deck above, flooding both engine and boiler rooms.

The *Iron Duke* had also suffered in the collision, but only marginally, apart from the ship's bowsprit, and she immediately backed off into the fog bank, powerless to help, although she quickly had her boats away. Both the *Vanguard*'s carpenter and chief engineer gave gloomy reports on the rising water levels in the open compartments. Dawkins began to prepare his crew for abandoning ship, but meanwhile sent a boat over to the *Iron Duke* to request a tow to shallower water, where the ship might be beached and later salvaged. In the confusion prevailing, this order was never delivered, and the *Vanguard* gradually drifted and filled despite valiant efforts at the pumps. Some seventy minutes after the accident the fog lifted as suddenly as it had descended and the *Vanguard* settled on the bottom in 19 fathoms of water, which just left her topmast heads showing above the waves as mute markers of her fate. Fortunately, there was absolutely no loss of life in either vessel.

The disaster made a large impression at home and, in due course, court martial proceedings were taken against Captain Dawkins and his commander-in-chief, chief engineer, navigating lieutenant and carpenter. By some strange quirk of procedure, nobody aboard the *Iron Duke*, which appeared equally at fault, was court-martialled at all, although the officer of the watch in question was dismissed from his ship.

The court duly assembled at Plymouth and the trials lasted for a total of sixteen days. The proceedings were divided into two parts, firstly, to ascertain the responsibility for the collision and, secondly, to examine what steps had been taken to save the ship after the collision. With regard to the first part the court decided on six points, viz.: 1, that the speed of the squadron was too great in the fog, yet the C-in-C who had ordered this speed and not ordered any reduction was not censured; 2, that Captain Dawkins had left the bridge before an evolution that had been ordered by the admiral had been completed, yet Hickley, who had behaved in exactly the same manner, was not so charged; 3, that the speed of the *Vanguard* had been injudiciously reduced, which was the exact opposite of Point 1; 4, that the speed of the *Iron Duke* had been needlessly increased, which was true due to her efforts to regain station, but, again, her captain was not charged; 5, that the navigation of the *Iron Duke* was at fault, again, as Points 1 and 4; 6, that *Iron Duke* made no attempt to signal her intentions.

With regard to the second part of the inquiry, the court was equally scathing, recording that:

> ... the foundering of HMS *Vanguard*, might have been delayed, if not averted, by Captain Dawkins giving orders for immediate action being taken to get all available pumps worked instead of employing his crew in hoisting out boats. And if Captain Dawkins, Commander Tandy, Navigating Lieutenant Thomas and Mr Tiddy, Carpenter, had shown more resource and energy in trying to stop the breach from outside with the means at their command, such as hammocks and sails.

The verdicts were followed by equally harsh sentences. Dawkins was severely reprimanded and dismissed his ship; he was never employed again. The others were reprimanded and none of them was ever subsequently promoted. There was a strong feeling of injustice in the fleet when these findings were announced, but the Admiralty went on to confirm them all, save Point 1 of the first part. Admiral Ballard attributes the attitudes of the court of the second part to their absolute ignorance in matters appertaining to iron-built ships. Breaches in wooden hulls, to be sure, might be stopped up with hammocks and sails, and frequently had been in the past, but not a 9-foot rent in the *Vanguard*'s hull. Nor could pumps, designed to cope with an inrush of 11 or 12 tons of water per minute, have ever coped with the 50 tons a minute that took place. Also, nor could the captain's concern for the safety of his crew be faulted, for he employed all fit hands in the hopeless task of keeping his ship afloat until almost the last.

As in the case of the *Victoria* and *Camperdown*, already described in these pages, the inflow of the water might have been held back a little had the *Iron Duke* held her ram in to the breach, but this was not attempted either. Hickley was concerned at the damage to his own command foremost. After all, the ships were close to a dangerous shoal in thick fog, but by the same measurement of justice, so was Dawkins, yet only the latter was condemned.

The irony of the whole affair was that it was held, yet again, to represent the efficacy of the ram as an instrument of war at sea, a feeling enhanced by the Battle of Lissa in 1866 and given continued lip service right up to 1914. Yet the main result had been the loss of yet another battleship through accident. In the whole history of the ram on British battleships, the only good effect it ever achieved was when HMS *Dreadnought* rammed and sank a U-boat in the North Sea during the First World War. Damage to our own vessels down the years far outweighed this solitary success.

Perhaps the saddest postscript to this tale was mentioned by Admiral Ballard. The young and inexperienced lieutenant, dismissed from the *Iron Duke*, whose part in the whole ghastly mess was so crucial but also so obviously well intentioned, did not labour long over the cloud of guilt that hung over him. He spent a period on half pay before being assigned to a foreign station. Here he contracted a virulent fever, from which he never recovered and soon expired. It is said that, in his final moment, he raved on, imagining himself back aboard the *Iron Duke* on that fateful morning and that his last words before death took him were, '*Vanguard* ahead!'

A similar melancholy fate befell Master A. De Mayne of HM survey ship *Kangaroo*, which was wrecked on the Hogsties in 1828. De Mayne was brought before court martial on 9 January 1829, charged with being:

… guilty of the most palpable neglect in not shaping a course and regulating the distance run, so as to avoid the danger on which the *Kangaroo* was wrecked; that after she struck the ground the most effectual measures were not taken to get the ship off, the time being consumed in fruitless endeavours to back the ship off, by means of her sails, when it should have been employed in hoisting out the pinnace, and laying out a stream anchor …

It is always easier to be wise after the event of course. De Mayne was sentenced to be dismissed from the service 'and never again to be entrusted with the charge of one of His Majesty's ships or vessels'.

If sailors are often accused of being superstitious, then it may be claimed in mitigation that they have better reason than most to be so. In the case of the loss of the *Captain*, for example, it was said that she was doomed from the very beginning, not because of the host of technical reasons debated and discussed, but because at her commissioning ceremony the White Ensign had been hoisted upside down. Certain nautical beliefs might well be considered too tenuous for most to entertain, but some of these were founded upon coincidences more readily of understandable to even a layman. Take, for example, the aversion of the Royal Navy to the naming of warships after snakes.

One of the worst shipwrecks to involve one of HM ships took place on the night of 10 November 1890. HMS *Serpent* was a new cruiser of the Archer class, small, hybrid vessels which on a modest displacement of 1,770 tons nevertheless managed to cram into her modest hull six 6-inch guns on sponsons and five torpedo tubes, as well as a crew of more than 170 officers and men. In total contrast with today's navy, which appear to be building bigger and bigger ships, with less and less armaments, the Victorians obviously believed in obtaining the maximum fighting value for their money. However, of course, a price had to be paid for such an aggressive visage. In addition to her engines, the *Serpent* carried a light fore-and-aft rig, for the tradition from sail to steam was hard in dying. The cruiser was also lightly constructed to compensate for all this top hamper and gunnery, but for all that she had a top speed of about 17 knots.

Serpent was first commissioned in 1888, but only for the Annual Manoeuvres, her first full commission commencing at Keyham in June 1890, under the command of Commander Henry Ross, when she joined the Channel Fleet for exercises. The little vessel sailed from Plymouth steering a south-westerly course across the Bay of Biscay, tracing a similar route to the ill-fated *Captain*. Tragically, the *Serpent* was to join the fate of the battleship. Again, in the Bay the weather was bad, with half a gale blowing and the night being pitch black. At 2230hrs, the *Serpent*, steaming at 9 knots, struck the rocks north of Cape Trece, Spain, and quickly foundered. In the conditions then prevailing, and although the watertight doors were closed, the ship quickly broke up under the buffeting of the waves, which swept her broadside on to the rocks, which remorselessly ground away at her thin hull. Commander Ross discovered that all the ship's boats had been smashed and, after firing distress rockets, told his crew to take to the rigging to save themselves if they could. Very few did so, just three survivors finally managing to struggle ashore, but the bulk of her crew were smashed and drowned or went down with the wreck of the *Serpent* when she broke up completely. The bodies of 129 of the crew were eventually washed up ashore and recovered, being buried by local villagers in a special cemetery. The gunboat *Lapwing* finally rescued the three men who survived, a leading seaman and two ABs.

When the news broke of the wrecking accusations were made in the press, predictably enough, that the *Serpent*'s loss was another *Captain* scandal. The cruiser was unseaworthy, it was stridently alleged, and should never have been put to sea. Fuel was heaped on the fire by reports from the liner *Peninsular*, which had sighted the *Serpent* some seven hours prior to her demise. Despite the fact that the captain of the liner had stated quite emphatically that, at that time, there had been nothing at all wrong with the *Serpent* (she was, he said, 'as upright as a dish'), journalists chose to ignore him and instead they ran with stories from some of the liner's passengers that, in fact, the warship had been in trouble and had refused help. This was blown up into a total condemnation of the navy's attitude, which otherwise might have prevented the disaster.

The truth was very different (and hardly reported at all). It duly turned out that these passengers, who did not know one end of a warship from the other, had, in fact, been confused. The ship they had sighted that had been in difficulties, which she later resolved very quickly, was the torpedo gunboat *Sandfly* and not the *Serpent* at all. The finding of the subsequent court martial was more restrained. 'Her Majesty's late ship *Serpent* was lost owing to an error of navigation.'

Whether her structural weakness contributed to the *Serpent*'s loss or not, such failings were definitely not held to have been the blame for the next disaster that overtook a British warship with a serpent's name. The introduction of the torpedo boat destroyer into the Royal Navy around the turn of the twentieth century, with the first ever destroyer commissioned in 1894, brought about a revolution in the powering of such small warships, with higher and higher speeds being called for. These demands pushed the frontiers of marine science to new limits. The reciprocating engine just could not be pushed any further, but, fortunately, the introduction of the steam turbine arrived to save the day. Initially, however, there were setbacks, not due so much to the new power plant itself, but to the destroyers that had this type of engine installed.

One of three experimental destroyers built for the Admiralty at this period was HMS *Viper*, a 344-ton vessel constructed by the firm of Hawthorn Leslie and launched in September 1899. The *Viper* had Parsons turbines installed, which were expected to give her a higher speed than existing destroyers. The initial trials of the little ship appeared to vindicate such expectations, 32 knots being attained in November, and this was followed by the then incredible speed of 37 knots being achieved on a full-power run.

The first full test for the *Viper* came in the Fleet Manoeuvres of 1901. The destroyer, commanded by Lieutenant Speke, was dispatched from Portsmouth on 3 August with orders to scout the Channel Islands and 'destroy any enemy torpedo boats found there'. In the vicinity of the Casquets, the *Viper* ran into patchy fog and Lieutenant Speke reduced speed from 22 to 16 knots. Despite the conditions, torpedo boat No 81 sighted her and gave chase. Speke increased speed again to 22 knots in an attempt to escape and steered a course designed to take her through the Swinge Channel. At 1723hrs land was sighted off the starboard bow, speed was at once reduced and the helm put over hard to starboard, but it was too late. Rocks were sighted dead ahead – the Renonquet reef, to the north of Burhow Island – and, at 10 knots, *Viper* ploughed right into them, tearing out her bottom. Her pursuer also came to grief at the same time and, when the fog perversely lifted a few hours later, the sun shone down on both warships high and dry and completely wrecked. Luckily, there were no casualties.

At the court martial that followed, Speke admitted that he had not used the Thomson deep-sea lead nor the patent log, because, as he stated, he found speed as worked out by the ship's engineers to be more accurate. Speke also admitted that 'he had underestimated the strength of the current. At 5.10 pm I thought I was in 25 to 30 fathoms, 6 to 7 miles west of Renonquet Island.' Speke also stated that, just before *Viper* struck, the leadsman had recorded 9 and then 7 fathoms, by the chain. Asked if he did not consider he had hazarded his vessel in taking such a risky course, Speke replied: 'I considered it my duty to take more risks in special duties on manoeuvres than normally.'

Regrettably, the ship's log was the only book salvaged, and there was some confusion between the officers on the exact course that had been steered. The court found Speke guilty, but cleared the others. The verdict reached was that Speke had not made allowance for the tide nor taken sufficient precautions by taking soundings. The lieutenant was therefore found guilty of negligence, but his sentence was a mere reprimand, 'taking into consideration the important nature of the services upon which he was employed', which showed that his defence was largely accepted.

❉ ❉ ❉

Yet a further destroyer was to founder within a year; this time she was the turbine-powered *Cobra*, a 375-ton vessel built by Armstrong's at Elswick and launched in 1899. The *Cobra* seemed already fated for soon after her launch she was involved in a collision with a collier and so badly damaged that repairs took seven months to complete. After a full Admiralty inspection the *Cobra* was found to have been very light constructed: no high-tensile steel had been employed in her; her scantlings were lighter than those used in the *Viper*; she had no longitudinal strengthening whatsoever; the stiffening of bows and the strength of stem were inadequate; and galvanising throughout the ship was found to be unsatisfactory.

Although it would appear from these findings that the *Cobra* was a far from well-found vessel, nonetheless initial sea trials were commenced, which, in turn, found numerous other faults. The Admiralty expressed grave concern but still agreed to take delivery and, on 17 September 1901, a navigating party under the command of Lieutenant Bosworth Smith went aboard and the destroyer sailed from the Elswick yard en route for Portsmouth to have her armament shipped. Also taking passage aboard the *Cobra* on this voyage was an engineering party commanded by Engineering Officer J.G. Percey, as well as representatives of her builders and from the Parsons Company, which had supplied her power plant.

While steaming south and in the vicinity of Flamborough Head, very rough weather was encountered, which badly affected the little vessel. These conditions worsened steadily, so much so that it became almost impossible for the stokers to work at all. Speed was reduced to 10 knots. The wind continued to rise, reaching force 6 from NNW and, pitching and rolling horribly, the *Cobra* was soon in grave difficulties. The evidence of the mate of the outer dowsing light vessel graphically portrayed the *Cobra*'s final moments. Soon after 1900, this gentleman saw the destroyer approaching from the north, plunging heavily, and then steam began to issue from her third funnel and from various parts of her hull. Very quickly, the watcher saw the destroyer was settling amidships and she finally sank, stern first, some 30 feet of her hull remaining above the surface, a mute testimonial to her fate.

In the appalling conditions prevailing, the crew of the light ship could do nothing to render assistance, other than to fire distress rockets. Only a dozen men from the *Cobra* managed to escape from the wreck in a small boat, and these were picked up by a merchant ship some twelve hours later. Naturally, theories abounded as to why the destroyer should have broken up as she did. Some blamed the turbine itself; others claimed that she had touched bottom in shallow water or had fouled submerged wreckage. All this wild speculation was found to be utterly without foundation. A subsequent survey located the wreck lying in 15 fathoms of water. There was no sign of any other wreckage and there were no shoals in the area where she went down.

The survivors were summoned to the usual court martial, which was held at Portsmouth and which lasted for six days. There could only have been one conclusion and the court duly announced it. They found that there was no navigational error, no touching bottom, no wreckage, but that the loss of the *Cobra* was 'attributable to the structural weakness of the ship'. The court also added the telling rider, with which we may all concur, that 'it is to be regretted that she was purchased in to HM Service'.

The *Cobra* was the only destroyer of the Royal Navy ever to be loss by stress of weather alone, but the Admiralty had quite enough of snake names for their ships, three losses in a decade convinced them that, silly superstition or not, there would be no more. Thus it has remained to this day – the closest they ever got after this was the naming of one destroyer *Venomous*.

Experimental battleships, cruisers and destroyers have featured prominently in this catalogue of misfortune, but there were other new types of vessel at the turn of the twentieth century under evaluation, not least the warship that, almost a century later, was due to take over the title of capital ship of the fleet, the submarine. If anything, the hazards faced by the pioneers of these fragile new craft were more extreme than that faced by more conventional sailors. Accidents were common; losses pre-1914 were heavy, with no less than five submarines, A-1, A-3, A-7, B-2 and C-11 being lost in this period. In addition, there were numerous near misses, a typical case being that of that of the A-4 in October 1905.

The A-4 was under the command of Lieutenant (later Admiral Sir) Dunbar Nasmith at the time of the incident, and she was at sea conducting exercises when the wash of a passing ship sent a sudden inrush of water through one of her ventilators. The tiny vessel began to fill and it was feared she must go under for good, but Nasmith kept his head and managed to get his command back up to the surface intact. Despite his cool-headiness and presence of mind, which saved the submarine and her complement, Nasmith was subsequently brought before court martial on a charge of negligence.

The sentence reflected good judgement on the part of the court. Submarines were novel toys to some in the service, but to others, including Jackie Fisher, they held the greatest potential, a potential that today they have achieved beyond all speculation. It would appear that those forced to sit in judgement on Nasmith were of a similar mind, for they quashed the charge, 'taking into consideration his great calmness and presence of mind under exceptionally trying conditions'.

The position of the officers involved with the prosecution or defence of their brother officers during a court martial is a sensitive one, 'there but for the grace of God' being the commonest feeling among them. After all, the Royal Navy has always been a close-knit community, where everybody knows everybody else, having usually served in the same command, fleet or even ship at some period of their careers. This is particularly true during the long periods of peace, when governments invariably cut the fleet to the bone. Personal rivalry or friendship, as well as animosity or jealousy, had to be eliminated as far as was possible, while impartiality and objectivity was always sought (if not always achieved). This balance was helped by the fact that there still remained the uneasy feeling, frequently expressed, even in Pepys' day, that it might well be your turn next. An insight into some of the problems can perhaps be illustrated by the case of Admiral J.H. Godfrey, famous later for his work in Naval Intelligence during the Second World War.

In 1931 Godfrey found himself appointed prosecutor during a court martial held on the navigation officer of the formed minesweeper *Petersfield*. This ship had been converted to the new role of commander-in-chief's yacht for service on the China station, who at this date was the fiery and temperamental Admiral Howard Kelly.

As the trial proceeded, it transpired that the *Petersfield* had been on passage from Shanghai to Hong Kong, with the admiral embarked, and had run aground on Tung Yung Island, where she later became a total loss. The fact that the admiral's wife and daughter were aboard her at the time of her stranding added further complications to the events and did little for the admiral's dignity. Nevertheless, the case presented by the defence affected that dignity even more, for it was alleged that the loss of the ship was entirely due to Kelly himself. The admiral, a former navigating officer, had, it was claimed, issued orders to the commanding officer to steer their course, and so on, and had, to all intents and purposes, taken over virtual command of the *Petersfield* for himself.

The assertion, that he was to blame for the loss of his own yacht, Kelly strenuously denied and it fell to Godfrey to prove him innocent and the hapless navigator of the *Petersfield* guilty. Godfrey's biographer was later to record: 'It cannot have been an easy task for the prosecutor to present a just and fair case without either offending his new C-in-C or arousing the resentment of the accused, but he seems to have managed to do so with a very fair degree of success.' Other historians, however, did not share this sanguine view on the eventual outcome of the trial.

It was revealed that, after leaving Shanghai for Foochow, the ship's navigating officer, who was on his first voyage since taking his navigation examinations, plotted a course that was designed to bring the *Petersfield* to the light on Tung Yung at midnight. The navigator was advised to retire to his cabin and rest, in readiness for the subsequent tricky navigation, but he left instructions that he was to be called at 2300hrs, in good time to carry out this task.

While the navigator slept, the C-in-C went to the bridge and he stopped the bridge messenger from waking the officer at the requested hour, stating that he would assume responsibility and that the navigator could be left to sleep a while longer. When the messenger finally roused the navigator, he was horrified to learn that it was now almost midnight. The officer immediately rushed up to the bridge but, before he could arrive there, the ship had struck.

A court martial was inevitable, but the convening authority decided that the officer of the watch should not be tried because the commanding officer was on the bridge, as was Kelly, who had assumed responsibility. The *Petersfield*'s captain and the navigating officer, however, were both charged and brought before the court, and both were found guilty as charged. Both subsequently left the service soon after this harsh verdict, their careers in ruins. In both cases Kelly was called as a witness, and the whole court rose to their feet every time he entered and left. Remarkably, the C-in-C himself did not have to face court martial, despite the fact that he had publicly assumed responsibility on the bridge that fateful night and that it had been on his specific order that the unfortunate navigator had been left asleep.

Many in the service fleet felt that there had been a grave miscarriage of justice. In those days it would have taken some six to eight weeks to have dispatched an admiral of the required authority out from England to have presided over Kelly's court martial, even should there have been such a worthy readily available. Nonetheless, many asked at the time, and since, was justice really done?

Another case from around the same era is a good example of the Admiralty using their reserved right to reverse the findings of a court martial upon re-examination of the trial. It concerned the collision between two of the most famous warships of the 1930s Royal Navy, the battlecruisers *Hood* and *Renown*. At the time of the incident, the *Hood* was the flagship of the Battlecruiser Squadron, flying the flag of Rear Admiral Sidney Bailey, and was commanded by Captain F.T.B. Tower, OBE. The *Renown* was under the command of Captain Henry Sawbridge and she had only just recently rejoined the squadron (in May 1932) after undergoing a long refit. Bailey had been her captain not many years earlier and therefore knew the ship, and her capabilities, well.

The occasion was the start of the spring cruise to Gibraltar. The time was around 1050hrs on 23 January, and the two ships were steaming parallel courses of 223 degrees at a speed of 18 knots, and preparing to carry out an inclination exercise. At 1135hrs, Admiral Bailey gave the order for the exercise to commence. At this time, the two warships were between 10 and 12 miles apart. Both vessels complied, putting their helms over and converging at a pre-arranged angle, the

Hood steering 254 degrees and the *Renown* closing her from her starboard side on a course of 192 degrees. The intention was for *Renown* to glide smoothly astern of the flagship as the latter turned the squadron on to a new course of 180 degrees and formed line ahead. At least, that is what was at first assumed.

What actually took place was somewhat different. At 1221hrs, the two great ships struck, the *Renown*'s bows hitting the much larger *Hood* amidships, with considerable way still on, despite the fact that the former's engines had been ordered to full astern moments prior to the impact. Fortunately, neither ship was fatally damaged (neither was fitted with a ram), nor were there any serious casualties, although it had been a very close shave indeed.

The *Hood*'s side armour took the shock well, but the stem of the *Renown*, just above the waterline, was crushed in badly. Both ships remained able to steam and at once returned to their home ports. There had been no casualties, either from the first collision or from the second glancing blow that bent the *Renown*'s plates back.

The aftermath of this collision proved to be much more protracted and harrowing for the three officers who were required to face court martial proceedings at Portsmouth at the end of February. The case also caused a good deal of adverse comment and friction between the crews of the two warships, one Chatham-manned and the other Pompey-based; this accident increased the centuries-old rivalry between the two ports.

The Deputy Judge Advocate was Rear Admiral C.G. Ramsey, while the President of the court was Vice Admiral Astley-Rushton, with Vice Admiral JAG Troup, a tactical expert, acting as prosecutor. The court, in total, consisted of five admirals and three captains.

Admiral Bailey was the first officer to be tried, the prosecution alleging that he was to blame for the accident because, 'Having ordered the *Hood* to steer 254 degrees and *Renown* to close her on a course of 192 degrees, he failed to take action to prevent the development of a situation in which risk of collision between the two ships arouse'.

In his defence, Bailey replied: 'My impression at this time was that *Renown* was carrying out the manoeuvre badly; in fact that she was making a bad shot. I have been the captain of her myself, and I know she is a handy ship.' Bailey continued: 'Since the accident I have naturally gone over in my mind whether some other form of signal would have been more appropriate to my purpose, but I cannot think of one, unless I had been prepared to give orders for the movements of *Renown* – in fact, to command the ship myself.'

After a recess, the Naval Provost brought Admiral Bailey back and the court announced its verdict on him: 'The Court finds that the charge against the accused is not proven. The findings are signed by all the officers of the Court.' The President then lifted Bailey's sword from the table, strode across the court-room and handed it back to the admiral with one word, 'Congratulations'.

It was then the turn of Captain Sawbridge to face the court. Sawbridge's own report on the matter, written two days after the accident, was read out:

> I fully realised it was the Admiral's intention to turn both ships to 180 degrees at the proper time to bring them into line of that course. *Hood* was held continuously under observation, and, as 1218-1/2, I decided that although she had ample room and time to carry out the manoeuvre I would take the precaution of turning away.

At 1219hrs Sawbridge had therefore given the order: 'Half speed astern both', immediately followed by, 'Full speed astern'. *Hood* hoisted and hauled down to execute the signal to form single-line ahead. 'Thus,' said Captain Sawbridge, 'even as late as 1220 *Hood* could have taken avoiding action by turning outwards, but apparently she did not do so.'

Lieutenant Commander G.M.S. Stitt of *Renown* had been called to give evidence for the defence and he stated that when the captain had decided to hold on to his course as *Hood* appeared to be late in turning, he had entirely agreed with the decision: 'I was convinced then, and still am, that *Renown* was ordered to steer that course for one reason only, and that was that when the ships got within a mile of each other, *Hood* would turn to 180 and *Renown* would be able to form astern.'

Rear Admiral Bailey was asked by Rear Admiral Troup: 'Would you expect your flagship to avoid *Renown* or *Renown* to avoid the flagship?' To which Bailey replied: 'The Flagship, being the guide, I should certainly not expect her to have to alter course.'

The case continued until late in the afternoon. Lieutenant Commander Stitt told how, when the *Hood* was just seven cables away, he remarked to the captain: 'Now is the time for *Hood* to turn to 180 degrees.' The captain replied that, as *Hood* appeared to be late in turning, he would hold on to his present course to give more clearance when she did turn. At six cables, the captain decided to take action. At three cables Lieutenant Commander Stitt said he saw a signal going up in the *Hood* and the captain remarked: 'It is not much use making that signal now.'

Lieutenant Commander C.B. Hodgkinson, the officer of the watch aboard *Renown*, said that when the ships were six cables apart the captain had remarked: 'I don't like this', and had ordered the wheel to starboard and the engines to be stopped. Later Hodgkinson said, 'What doesn't the *Hood* obey the rule of the road?' The captain then ordered 'Full speed astern'. When a collision appeared inevitable, the commander said he ordered the closing of the watertight doors.

Captain Sawbridge was then asked by Captain Miles, 'Why did you not give the order "Astern" at an earlier time?' To which Sawbridge replied, 'I did not expect to have to go astern at all. I was absolutely certain *Hood* was turning to 180, and that when I put my wheel over, she would do the same thing in a proper seamanlike manner, and when she saw me turn away, she would alter course.' Sawbridge added that he considered his action was effective in extricating the two ships from a collision when one of them did nothing to contribute towards it.

The court deliberated for an hour and twenty minutes before reaching a verdict, which the Judge Advocate rose and read out: 'The sentence of the Court, having found the charge against Captain Sawbridge proved, is that he shall be dismissed His Majesty's Ship *Renown*.'

The trial of Captain Tower was the last, and duly followed that of Sawbridge. Tower stated that on the day of the accident he expected that *Renown* would fall into his wake. About two minutes before the collision, he realised that the *Renown* was apparently continuing on her course and he tried to swing his own ship round. 'I began to get uneasy when the ships were about six cables apart,' he said. 'At that time I expected *Renown* to get in astern of *Hood*.'

Captain Miles then asked Tower: 'Why did you not take action to obey the "Rule of the Road"?' Captain Tower replied:

I might have taken action in the literal interpretation of the 'Rule of the Road' when the two ships were separated by two or three miles. That would have involved using the starboard helm. That I did not consider seriously, for I knew it could not possibly have been defended. Later, keeping in mind the whole of the approach, I had no doubt, and had every reason to believe, that *Renown* would fall astern of me. I considered it was my duty as Guide of the Fleet to continue my course and speed to the last possible moment.

The court duly acquitted Captain Tower. However, nineteen days later, there came the following announcement from the Board of Admiralty:

Their Lordships dissent from the findings of the court martial held for the trial of Rear Admiral Bailey to the following extent: Rear Admiral Bailey adopted an unusual procedure in directing *Hood* and *Renown* to steer definite course to close. Since he had given that order, responsibility for the manoeuvre rested on him, and it was incumbent on him at the proper moment to make a further signal to reform his squadron. His not doing so left in doubt his final intention.

The signal for *Hood* and *Renown* to form single-line ahead was made too late. For these reasons their Lordships are unable to resolve Rear Admiral Bailey from all blame.

Their Lordships agree in the findings of the court martial held for the trial of Captain Sawbridge but they have decided to reduce the sentence to a severe reprimand, Captain Sawbridge will, therefore, resume command of *Renown*.

Their Lordships consider that Captain Tower, should have taken avoiding action earlier, and to that extent they are unable to acquit him of all blame.

Captain Sawbridge's dignified response to his good fortune is worthy of record: 'This is not a time for rejoicing, for whilst some rejoice others suffer.'

※ ※ ※

In compiling this section of my book, it is not inappropriate to mention two incidents, one deeply tragic and inexplicable, and the other bearing a lighter aspect. While neither of them refer to the courts martial themselves, they are, nonetheless, relevant in observing a complete lack of justice, on the one hand, and a case a prejudgement on the other.

The first of these two contrasting affairs concerns the fourth-rate *Falmouth*, launched in 1752. It is an almost unbelievable story of heroism, endurance and misplaced loyalty on the part of her crew, and callousness, stupidity and downright injustice on the part of the Admiralty. If ever a case cried out for a court martial, then it was this one.

In 1757, the *Falmouth* became stranded on a mud bank at Batavia. The vessel was not irreparably damaged, but she could not be refloated. The decision was made not to abandon the ship but to await orders from the Admiralty. Thus, the crew remained aboard, but the months passed with no word whatsoever, and these months became years and still no word came. Incredible as it may seem, London had totally forgotten the *Falmouth* and the plight of her ship's company. The crew scraped a precarious living from whatever they could catch or barter on the mainland; wild animals beset them, even invading the stranded ship herself; they used up all their powder and shot in defending themselves. Tropical storms broke over the ship; many of the crew became struck down with strange illnesses, but still the survivors clung on.

The years passed, the officers all died, one by one; some crew members went mad. Those that died fed the sharks and still no word came from the Admiralty. At last, after almost ten years, the *Falmouth* was sighted by one of HM ships, the *Dolphin*. The captain of the *Dolphin* boarded the pitiful wreck of the *Falmouth* in wonderment, describing what he found thuswise:

The ship was lying on the mud in rotten condition. She had been there nearly ten years. She was worn out and so were her men. She was in such a decayed state that she could hardly have survived another monsoon. Only the mud kept her from sinking at her anchors, while her ship's company consisted of no more than a few men, old and broken. There were no executive officers left, and of the remainder the gunner was dead, the boatswain gone mad, and the carpenter was dying.

Although these pitiful survivors begged to be taken home to England, even volunteering to forego the ten years' back pay they were owed, the captain of the *Dolphin*, again amazingly, refused. The *Falmouth*, it appeared, contained government stores that could not be abandoned without orders from Whitehall, which had years ago forgotten their very existence. Some ten years after the *Falmouth* had run aground, the Admiralty finally issued a statement, which declared that the *Falmouth* was to be written off the Navy List, as she was 'unseaworthy'.

To end this section of a less depressing note, a classic case of the findings of a naval court martial being prejudged instantly concerned the unfortunate collision between the light cruiser HMS *Swiftsure* and the destroyer HMS *Diamond*, which took place during exercises in 1953. The cruiser was one of the newest serving in the navy at that time, although some 8 years old, while the *Diamond* was an almost brand-new ship, and at that time the last word in classic destroyer design. The consequent disabling of both these fine warships was keenly felt.

Both ships had been part of the large-scale NATO exercises being held in the North Atlantic when, on 29 September, they struck at about 1000hrs. The destroyer slammed into the *Swiftsure* with some force, opening up the cruiser's hull above the waterline and injuring thirty-two of her crew, fortunately none of them seriously. The *Diamond* herself came off far worse, her bows being crumpled back almost to her forward gun turret, but she still remained under control.

A small group of destroyers clustered around the two cripples to lend assistance and succour, and after a while things began to be sorted out. The *Swiftsure* steamed off, escorted by the destroyers *Decoy* and *Onslow*, while another destroyer, *Battleaxe*, continued to stand by the *Diamond*.

There were press aircraft overhead by this time, gleefully taking photographs and preparing headlines. There had been few recriminations between the two cripples in the immediate aftermath of the smash – it had, after all, been an accident – and there was little doubt about which ship had actually been at fault.

A court martial was obviously going to be the fate of the destroyer's skipper, but when the *Swiftsure* signalled to him as she drew away, 'What do you intend to do now?' that worthy already seemed resigned to the result; his reply was, 'Buy a farm!'

3 LOSSES IN ACTION

Until the Pilcher Committee's recommendations that it be done away with, it was usual for a court martial to follow on from the normal Board of Inquiry when one of HM ships was sunk or captured, however honourably, in combat. As we have seen, this was as much to ascertain the fact that the crew had fought well and gallantly as to censure them automatically.

Such a court also helped Their Lordships ascertain how materiel had held up in action and both personnel and defensive weaknesses would be highlighted, which could then be rectified. Under these circumstances, such a trial could often be welcomed by those summoned as a means of clearing their names completely. In some of the cases illustrated in this section, indeed it did just that. In others, the findings revealed, often for the first time, particular unforeseen elements or stresses that no peacetime exercise or theoretical hypothesis had hinted at. Of course, it was also the fact that, often as not, such a court was instrumental in revealing the weaknesses of some of the less able Royal Naval personnel and showing them in an unfavourable light, but the effect on the service as a whole could be just as beneficial.

One early illustration of the latter may be found in the court martial of Captain Fox, which took place at Portsmouth between 25 November and 20 December 1847. The trial was held in the aftermath of the Second Battle of Finisterre, and Fox found himself in the dock for his conduct on 14 October. Although Admiral Hawke's victory on that occasion had brought the naval side of the war to a resounding climax of success, Fox's own conduct had somewhat marred that great achievement.

The court found Fox guilty of misconduct and he was dismissed his ship, not because of any lack of personal courage it must be said, but 'from listening to the persuasion of his First Lieutenant and master, and giving way to them'.

Somewhat graver charges faced a certain Captain Williamson of HMS *Agincourt* following the Battle of Camperdown in 1797. Williamson was brought before court martial at Sheerness facing charges of disobedience to signals and of not going into action, and, secondly, of cowardice or disaffection. Some indication of how his fellow officers felt towards Williamson may be intimated by the fact that Admiral Duncan flatly refused to give evidence in his favour.

In the event, after due deliberation, the court found the first charge proven, but the latter, and much more serious charge, not fully proven. The sentence pronounced was that Williamson be placed at the bottom of the captain's list and declared incapable of ever again serving. Even so, it would appear that to many that Williamson had got off lightly. Nelson, no less, later was to comment that he considered the sentence a most lenient one. It ended John Williamson's naval career, nevertheless.

❋ ❋ ❋

An example of the fate that might befall a commander who, although highly successful in one enterprise, might overreach the mark and misjudge events back home, may be found in the case of Commodore Sir Home Popham. Popham found himself a national hero in January 1807 and facing a court martial a mere fifteen months later because he assumed too much.

With the Dutch fighting with Napoleon, the losses suffered by the French and Spanish fleets at Trafalgar and subsequent actions threatened to be made good against us. Quick and firm action was required against the new enemy, which was taken by the Royal Navy, and one of the more important actions was the recapture, and this time for good, of Cape Town. This victory was achieved by the naval squadron under the command of Popham, who, with four battleships and two frigates, covered the transportation and landing of the troops at Saldanha Bay. After a brief land campaign, the Dutch surrendered this strategically vital town and colony on 6 January 1806.

Such a cheap victory tempted Popham, with the willing complaisance of the military commander Sir David Baird, to look for fresh fields to conquer with their tried and tested units. Their choice of objective fell upon the Spanish possessions on the other side of the South Atlantic, which seemed ripe for plucking. Popham, now buoyed and emboldened by the Admiralty's recognition of his fine work at the Cape, grasped the nettle. The combined British force set sail from Table Bay, called in at St Helena for reinforcements, and, on 25 June, landed the redcoats ashore near Buenos Aires. Initially, the campaign ashore seemed another swift and resounding feat of arms, the Spanish garrison at Buenos Aires laying down their arms on 2 July. This happy state of affairs was not to last, unfortunately, and things then started to go very awry. The local population rose up against their British occupiers, who amounted to a mere 1,600 officers and men, and sheer weight of numbers forced a humiliating surrender upon General Beresford. Popham was forced to commence a close blockade of the town, and appealed to London for reinforcements.

Instead of help, what Popham received was a sound ticking off. The admiral, in his eagerness, had acted without any consultation with the government, and they, at this juncture, had adopted a policy of attempting to keep the Spanish sweet and to try by diplomatic means to wean them away from Napoleon's influence. The unfortunate admiral, having put his foot in it, was curtly summoned back to England by an irate Admiralty and, in March 1807, found himself facing court martial charged with 'Unauthorised action'. In Popham's absence, moreover, things at Buenos Aires had deteriorated yet further and a larger army was also forced to lay down their arms. This further defeat did not help Popham's case. The admiral was 'severely reprimanded' by the court, a verdict that once again was to demonstrate that initiative is not always rewarded with either success or praise.

* * *

One result of Gambier's action in the Basque Roads, which we have already described in detail, was the court martial of Captain Sir Elias Harvey. Captain Harvey had greatly distinguished himself at Trafalgar, when captain of the *Temeraire*, and his lust for action had not been slaked by that experience. When Cochrane had been appointed to command the fire ships in 1809, Harvey took it badly, considering himself slighted. While still hot, he presented himself aboard the *Caledonia*, where he then proceeded to acquaint Lord Gambier fully with his feeling on the matter, and in no uncertain terms.

The result was Harvey's own court martial, 'for grossly insubordinate language'. The court found the charges amply proven and Harvey was sentenced to be dismissed from the service. This verdict by the court, coupled with the popular outcry against Gambier's own court martial acquittal, caused further furore. The Admiralty had rapid second thoughts and, the following year, the sentence on Harvey was quashed. Harvey was fully reinstated in both rank and seniority, because of 'his long and meritous services'. It proved to be a mere gesture only, however, for his language when addressing his commander-in-chief could not be condoned. Harvey was never again to be employed on active service.

* * *

It has been recorded in the main body of this book how often the vexed question of 'maintaining the line of battle' brought discomfiture and, worse, disgrace to those who, for whatever reason, found themselves unable to comply. Another instance of this, which resulted in court martial proceedings being brought, was the fate of several captains serving under the command of Sir George Pocock on 29 April 1758. The gentlemen concerned were Captain Nicholas Vincent of HMS *Weymouth*, Captain William Brereton of HMS *Cumberland* and Captain George Legge of HMS *Newcastle*.

At their trials, held at Madras, India, all three captains faced identical charges, viz., 'Keeping back in time of action'. The series of hearings commenced on

20 June and, with various recesses, lasted until 5 July. Gradually the situation as it had fallen out on that fateful day became clear to those listening to the testimony. It quickly appeared that there were no grounds for suspicion of cowardice on the part of these officers, but the villain of the piece was, yet again, that part of the Fighting Instructions which held that the line be kept, regardless of circumstances, once battle had been joined. Admiral Sir Charles Stevens was the court President for all three trials, while Kempenfelt was one of the captains on the court.

The battle itself was insignificant and inconclusive; Pocock's squadron had clashed with a similar strength French squadron, commanded by the Comte d'Ache, in the Bay of Bengal. Combat had been forced in the usual manner and line of battle had eventually been formed, and Pocock had kept the signal to maintain the line flying throughout the whole action. Once more, Sir Charles had been forced to adopt the 'lasking' approach in order to close his reluctant opponent, and again it did not work out as hoped. On this occasion, however, it was the commander who brought charges against his subordinates for the failure.

Thus it was that the court assembled aboard the *Elizabeth* in the sweltering heat of Madras harbour to hear how, as the English squadron closed with the French, the rear of the line was left behind as Pocock led the van into action. As the leading English battleships engaged in the duel with their French opposite numbers, those who paused to glance astern were concerned to note that the last three English ships had not come into the action. Many could not understand why this was so. Harsh things were said, for the van found itself unsupported and outnumbered, and harsher thoughts followed as the situation continued. But why had the *Cumberland*, *Weymouth* and *Newcastle* not followed their leaders closely as they had clearly been ordered to do?

From the long sequence of statements, questions and answers, the facts gradually became apparent. It transpired that the *Cumberland*, not the best sailing ship of the force at any time, was stationed third from the rear. This vessel had not been docked for months and her hull was foul, thus slowing her down even more than usual. The order of battle signalled was for the ships to keep at a distance of half a cable from each other, very close indeed. Too close, as it turned out, because the *Weymouth* briefly ran foul of the *Newcastle* ahead of her. When this contretemps had been sorted out the *Cumberland* was found to be trailing and holding back the two ships astern of her still further. The *Weymouth* attempted to rectify this by leaving her appointed station in line and getting ahead of *Newcastle*, but this breaking of the orders, although undertaken with the best of intentions, and for which Captain Vincent apologised to the court, proved of no avail either. If anything, it added to the confusion. The *Cumberland* still barred the way of the other two ships. Brereton hoisted more sail but his command still failed to respond sufficiently to rectify the position. And so the French sailed away, leaving Pocock frustrated and convinced he had been ill-used by part of his command.

It might have been thought that, as it had been revealed that all these captains had tried their best to come into battle as instructed and had failed to do so through circumstances not entirely of their own making, they would have been acquitted. Not so! The verdict of the court was very different. Captain Vincent, who had attempted so desperately to get into action, so desperately in fact that he had broken the sacred convention, was judged, as were the other two, of being guilty of an error of judgement. Vincent was dismissed his ship; Legge of the *Newcastle* was cashiered. Brereton, whom the court considered should have hoisted even more sail than he did, was sentenced to lose one year's rank as a post-captain.

Not even the submission of a 'Round Robin' by 169 members of his crew could save Vincent. The words expressed in this unofficial and spontaneous appeal from the lower deck demonstrated the feeling aboard the *Weymouth* and the grave wrong they felt had been done to the captain and their honour, and is worth placing on record:

> Being informed by our acquaintances that the sentence of the Court Martial is like to be too harsh upon our worthy Captain Vincent, and we all being very well convinced that he did everything to the utmost of his power to bring the *Weymouth* to close engagement with the French Squadron had not we been hindered by the damned *Newcastle*, and afterward by the cursed *Cumberland* who was the hindrance of our own success that day.

We can, perhaps, be moved some fifty-two or more years later by such sentiments of confidence from the crew of one of HM ships for their captain, especially after studying the conditions that brought about the Nore, *Hermione* and *Bounty* mutinies. In Captain Vincent, here was a man who tried his very best to join battle and here was his crew backing him up to the hilt. It made no difference.

A similar pledge of loyalty and show of confidence toward a well-respected officer, whom his crew considered had done well in trying circumstances, but whose superiors thought otherwise, so much so as to bring him before court martial, occurred during the Battle of Navarino in 1827. Here, on 13 October, Sir Edward Codrington, with a combined fleet of British, French and Russian warships, inflicted a crushing defeat upon the Turkish and Egyptian fleets under Ibrahim Pasha, and thus saved Greece.

One of the Royal Navy battleships present at the battle was HMS *Genoa* (74), commanded by Commodore Walter Bathurst, an exceedingly competent and well-loved officer. The *Genoa* took her place as next astern of Codrington's flagship, HMS *Asia* (84), and her opponent was a Turkish battleship. When the battle commenced *Genoa* was thus in the thick of the fighting and suffered heavily, losing twenty-six men killed and thirty-three more wounded, among the former being Bathurst himself. In reply, her Turkish opponent was left gutted, with 800 of her crew dead or dying.

When Captain Bathurst fell, command dissolved upon Commander Dickson, but, despite the subsequent conduct of *Genoa*, Codrington professed himself highly displeased with Dickson, and severely reprimanded him, appointing another officer to command in his stead. The crew of the *Genoa* submitted their own 'Round Robin' expressing their own confidence in Dickson, and requesting that he be allowed to sail the ship back to England. This request Codrington refused outright. The commander-in-chief went further and Dickson faced a court martial on his return home. The charge Dickson faced was that of mishandling the *Genoa* in such a way as to endanger both the *Asia* and the *Albion*, and of falsifying the ship's log at the time of Bathurst's death.

At the subsequent trial Dickson was acquitted of both these charges, but was found guilty instead of submitting his crew's appeal, which was deemed out of order. The reprimand he had already received from Codrington was, however, adjudged to have been sufficient punishment and no further action was taken.

❋ ❋ ❋

Happily, it is very rare for a Royal Navy vessel to strike her colours in action or surrender herself to an enemy. It was even rarer for a British frigate captain to submit. One famous sailor who was tried for this by court martial was Captain Thomas Pakenham (1757–1836). Pakenham was in command of the frigate *Crescent*, a 3-year-old fifth rate of twenty-eight guns in 1781, when she was sailing in company with the thirty-six-gun frigate *Flora*. Both ships were en route to Minorca, when they fell in with two Dutch frigates off Ceuta, their opponents being the thirty-six-gun *Brill* and *Castor*.

At the commencement of the engagement the two British frigates were separated by a considerable distance and thus, initially, the *Crescent* was forced to tackle both enemies unaided. The British ship was attacked from both sides simultaneously, and when the *Crescent* turned to starboard to engage the *Brill* better, the *Castor* fell astern of her and raked her through and through. Finally, *Flora* managed to come up and she engaged the *Castor*, leaving the *Crescent*, despite being by now badly damaged, with the other Dutch ship. It was not long before the superior weight of enemy fire began to take effect. All the *Crescent*'s masts were brought down and her guns disabled while her rudder jammed to port. At pistol-shot range the unequal contest continued until, both defenceless and powerless, Captain Pakenham was forced to strike his colours.

Command of the *Crescent* then fell upon her first lieutenant, Robert Bligh, for, having surrendered his ship, Pakenham refused to resume command until he had been court-martialled. This decision was adhered to even when the *Flora*, having herself defeated the *Castor*, came up and drove away the *Brill*. It appeared the *Crescent* had now been saved at last, and, with one Dutch ship as a prize, the two British frigates resumed their voyage. Unfortunately, their luck failed to hold, for they shortly came upon yet more enemy ships, in the shape of two French frigates.

The condition of the British men-of-war soon revealed to the French that easy pickings were to be had, and they at once steered to attack. The *Flora*, herself damaged and with a prize to attend to, made off as best she could. She was clearly unable to assist *Crescent* further without risking everything else, thus Lieutenant Bligh had little option but to surrender the *Crescent* for a second time. Both Pakenham and Bligh were eventually duly brought to court martial aboard the *Warspite* at Portsmouth on 20 July 1781.

Not too surprisingly, both men were honourably acquitted, the court going so far as to state:

> The Court cannot dismiss Captain Pakenham, without expressing their admiration of his conduct on this occasion, wherein he has manifested the skill of an able and judicious seaman, and the intrepidity of a gallant officer; and from the great and extraordinary number of killed and wounded on board the *Crescent*, as well as the state she was in at the time of the surrender, the court express the highest approbation of the support given by the officers and the men of the *Crescent* to their Captain, and of their courage and steadiness during the action, a circumstance that, while it reflects high honour on them, does no less credit and honour to the discipline kept by Captain Pakenham.

Pakenham amply fulfilled their confidence, going on to command the *Invincible* at the Glorious First of June and attaining the rank of Admiral Sir Thomas before his death in 1836, a much-honoured seaman.

One of the strangest 'ships' ever to be part of the Royal Navy, and which was forced to surrender to the enemy after a gallant fight, was HMS *Diamond Rock*. She was, of course, not a ship at all, but a tiny islet in the West Indies occupying a position of great strategic importance. This fastness was occupied by HMS *Centaur* in 1804 and commissioned as a sloop-of-war. This tiny islet, literally just a jutting cone of rock, rising sheer from the sea, lay between French-held Martinique and British-held St Lucia. The French considered it unscaleable, but Commodore

Hood of the *Centaur*, then charged with the blockade of Martinique, landed 120 sailors and Royal Marines ashore there in January and fortified the place. HMS *Diamond Rock* was quickly established as a thorn in the side of the enemy. Gun batteries were erected along the eastern side of the rock, with nine heavy guns at water level and another battery at the peak. This latter could command the sea to a distance of 5,000 yards out.

Martinique, with its vital harbour at Port Royal, could now be virtually sealed off, something which the French, who for 200 years had ignored the rock, found highly unpalatable. However, for eighteen months, the French could only sit and rage at British audacity. With the arrival of Villeneuve's fleet in the Caribbean in May 1805, while trying to evade Nelson, events came to a head. The French admiral decided that such an affront to French pride and dignity could no longer be tolerated and he ordered an overwhelming attack to recapture it. Against the 125-strong British garrison under Captain James Maurice, no less than 2,500 French soldiers, mountaineers and marines were disembarked from a convoy of transports and supported by two battleships and a frigate, to throw themselves at the defenders.

For three whole days and two nights the battle raged, before the little garrison was finally overcome, but not before they had inflicted heavy casualties on the attackers (and, incidentally, bringing about a two-day delay to the sailing of Villeneuve's fleet, which probably cost him his total defeat of Trafalgar later).

The court martial held on the survivors of the British garrison commenced on board the *Liace* at Barbados, on 24 June 1805. All were honourably acquitted. In the words of the court:

> Captain James Wilkes Maurice, the officers and company of HM late sloop *Diamond Rock*, did everything in their power to the very last in the defence of the Rock against a most superior force; and that Captain Maurice behaved with firm and determined resolution until he was unable to make further defence for want of water and ammunition …

It still remains the custom in the Royal Navy for passing warships to pipe when passing *Diamond Rock*, saluting a fellow ship-of-war.

※ ※ ※

It is rare for modern British warships to be forced to surrender, and rarer yet for them to be taken intact by the enemy. During the Second World War this happened only to the smallest of craft, other than some submarines and one destroyer. This latter was the 'S' class destroyer HMS *Thracian* at Hong Kong. This destroyer had been converted for fast minelaying and, on the onset of the Japanese assault on 8 December 1941, she was immediately dispatched to mine Port Shelter, in the New Territories. A second minefield was to be laid by her at Tolo harbour, south-west of Mirs Bay, but this was cancelled as it was considered too risky. Instead, on 10 December, the *Thracian* laid mines in Kap Shui Mun, in the north-west approaches. From then onward she reverted to general defence duties as a normal destroyer. On the night of 14/15 December the *Thracian* attacked and sank two river steamers carrying Japanese troops in Kowloon Bay, but during her withdrawal ran aground. Although she got afloat again, her hull had been damaged and she was docked at Aberdeen Yard for repair the following morning.

While in dock, she was attacked by Japanese dive-bombers and damaged yet further. Her position was deemed hopeless by the commodore, who ordered her to be undocked and beached. This was carried out and the destroyer's armament was stripped from her, while her crew joined the outnumbered defenders fighting ashore. On the surrender of Hong Kong, the Japanese navy set about salvaging her, and finally got her patched up and repaired. The Imperial Navy then pressed her into service on 25 November 1942, under the flag of the Rising Sun as patrol boat P101. She later became a training ship. On Japan's defeat in 1945, the Royal Navy took her back and she was finally sold for scrapping in 1947.

More surprisingly, at least to the British public until the true facts became known, was the surrender of two submarines to the enemy in the summer of 1940 – the *Shark* and the *Seal*. Although the subsequent capture of certain U-boats by the Royal Navy later in the war has received wide publicity, mainly due to the capture intact of the German Enigma coding device and Hollywood's subsequent re-writing of history to make this appear as an American achievement (despite the fact that that country had not even joined the war at the time), these British surrenders were hushed up. (Nevertheless, of course, the Germans were to make a lot of them at the time.)

The crews of these submarines became POWs for the rest of the war and so it was not until six years after the event, in 1946, that the courts martial were held, during which the full story finally came out for the first time in Britain and even then the press, by and large, preferred to ignore it. On 10 April 1946, the former captain of the *Seal*, Lieutenant Commander Rupert Lonsdale, faced his court martial at the Royal Naval Barracks, Portsmouth. The court was formed under the presidency of Captain C.F.W. Norris, with many leading submarine experts called.

The length of time that had elapsed since the incidents – almost six years – the great loyalty of the crew and, in particular, the effects of carbon-dioxide intoxication in affecting the rational decisions in exceptional circumstances all weighed heavily with the court. The charges, that Lonsdale had failed to take immediate action to engage the enemy aircraft which had attacked his command, and that he had also failed to prevent the *Seal* falling into enemy hands, were both dismissed and Lonsdale was honourably acquitted, as was his second-in-command, Lieutenant Trevor Beet. A similar happy outcome resulted from the *Shark* inquiry, and her commander went on to achieve flag rank and later became the best, and certainly the most courteous, head of the Historical branch there has ever been.

The misfortunes of war can certainly be said to have brought about the court martial of Captain William Wolseley and his officers and crew on 16 June 1784. They had surrendered their command, the fifth-rate *Coventry*, the year before, after they had encountered a thick fog, which had enveloped them. When this fog eventually lifted, it was to reveal, to *Coventry*'s astonished ship's company, that their frigate had had the misfortune to have sailed right into the centre of the French fleet. Surrounded on all sides, there was nothing to do but submit. Rarely, if ever, can one of HM ships have been so surprised. The court was understanding of nature's impartiality and all were acquitted of the surrender of their vessel.

Perhaps, if any captain might be said to been even more disorientated than the skipper of the *Coventry*, that man must have been Captain Philip Boteler, commander of the sixty-four-gun *Ardent*. The *Ardent* was part of the English fleet hastily assembled by the incompetent Sandwich after the Keppel-Palliser affair, and sent down Channel to face the oncoming French and Spanish fleet then under sail off Plymouth. Due to a decided lack of any other takers, command of the fleet had been given to old Sir Charles Hardy, brought out of semi-retirement as Governor of Greenwich Naval Hospital. Hardy was sent off post-haste, to lead the force of thirty-six vessels that remained to bar the enemy approach to the Thames and the capital.

On 19 August, the combined enemy fleet, variously estimated at having strength of fifty-six to sixty-six sail-of-the-line plus attendant vessels, had passed Plymouth, and Hardy followed the earlier example of Torrington in the face of such odds, but beating a hasty 'strategical' retreat. Hardy was not censured for this move, but praised for it; however, such was the general panic and haziness in the fleet at the time that the *Ardent* became detached. Without being aware of the withdrawal, *Ardent* sailed on, straight into the centre of the vast assembly of enemy warships, under the happy illusion that so great a fleet could only be friendly. She had dropped anchor among her myriad enemies before it was belatedly realised that such was not the case. Hemmed in on every side by such a host, there was little Boteler felt able to do, other than strike his colours.

The officers who formed the court that tried Boteler and his entire ship's company on 2 March 1780, failed to share that view. They considered that the least he could have done was to follow Sir Richard Grenville's example with the *Revenge*,

the 'one against fifty-eight', and totally destroyed his command, rather than allowing her to fall into enemy hands. The sentence they passed on Boteler confirmed
their view, for he was dismissed from the service, 'as it appeared to the Court he
did not do his utmost to prevent her from falling into the Enemy's hands'.

4 MURDER AND OTHER CASES

When one considers the close confines of a warship, which forced men of different temperaments to live cheek by jowl together for periods, in the old days, of
years at a time, and of the stress such enforced conditions imposed, it is remarkable how few cases of murder appear in the records. Also, with the press-gangs, the
fact that a larger proportion of the crews of those days were the sweepings of the
streets, this comparatively low total amazes still more. For this we must be thank-
ful, and only a few of those rare cases need to be recorded here for completeness.

In addition, despite Churchill's sneering and unwarranted slur on the service
– 'Rum, Sodomy and the Lash' – cases of what used to be termed 'Unnatural
Offences' are not as common as he made out. Such cases were, until recent times,
dealt with by the Royal Navy with caution and delicacy, although in former and
less enlightened times, both this and murder were punishable by death. However,
that no longer applies, although the Royal Navy lagged behind public morality
on these issues in some cases.

It must be remembered that it was not always the case that when murder took
place at sea a naval court martial dealt with it. When, in 1741, the captain of
HMS *Ruby*, then at Bristol, was convicted of the murder of his brother, it was the
Bristol Sessions that passed sentence on him, even though the crime was covered
by Article 28 of the existing laws appertaining to the sea.

This despicable crime took place while the ship was within the jurisdiction of that
town, and reference was made to the act of Richard II when the case was referred
to by their recorder. It was found that Captain Samuel Goodere had kidnapped his
elder brother, Sir John Dineley Goodere, and brought him back to his ship, where
he was imprisoned in the pursuer's cabin. While the captain himself stood guard
outside, with drawn sword, his two confederates, members of the crew coerced by
him to carry out the deed, entered and strangled the unfortunate man there and
then. For this act, all three were duly executed together in a triple hanging.

The borderline between justifiable homicide and outright murder can be a delicate one, especially so in cases where the defendant could, perhaps, claim he was merely doing his duty and thus preventing even worse trouble. Such a case was that of Lieutenant Gamage of HMS *Griffon*.

It was on 20 October 1812, that Gamage's lack of self-control brought about his trial by court martial for murder. A Royal Marine sergeant had committed some minor offence, for which Gamage ordered him to walk the gangway with his musket as punishment. The man refused to do so and was grossly insubordinate as well. By now highly incensed, Gamage went below for his sword, and, returning on deck armed and still fuming, repeated the order, but once again the marine refused point-blank to comply.

It was at this point that Lieutenant Gamage's patience broke completely, and with it his honour, for he stabbed the marine to death with his sword. At the subsequent court martial, evidence was heard that appeared to show that this mad deed was completely out of character and had only been brought on by intolerable conduct on the part of the deceased man. Moreover, Gamage, although he had gone too far, could perhaps plead that he only did what he was compelled by his rank and authority to do, make the man obey his direct order for the sake of discipline for the whole ship.

The court took a different view, notwithstanding many statements in Gamage's favour by both officers and men of the *Griffon*. The court held that the law only sanctioned the taking of another man's life in such circumstances if the case was the most pressing and an absolute necessity. In this instance, they did not consider it to be so: there was no danger of mutiny connected with the incident, nor any likelihood of there being any. What they considered Gamage ought to have done was to place the man under arrest and confine him below until the marine himself could have been brought to trial. Gamage was sentenced to death, and this sentence was duly carried out.

✳ ✳ ✳

Sometimes a court could be lenient, especially so when in other cases the mere striking of an officer could be punished by hanging at the yardarm until death. An example of this is the case of Henry Luter, a seaman aboard the *Valiant*, who was brought before court martial on 5 January 1761, on a charge that he did give 'another seaman belong to he a stab, of which he died next morning'. Luter was found not guilty of murder, the court recording that:

> … the death of the man was occasioned by a knife in the hands of the prisoner, when he was attacked by the deceased; but the prisoner was not guilty of wilfully putting him to death, but to receive two hundred lashes for not throwing the knife away at the beginning of the quarrel.

❅ ❅ ❅

On 12 September 1840, Seaman Doyle of HMS *Volage* was court-martialled and charged with 'Shooting a Chinese on board a junk, and thereby causing his death'. Was it murder or not? The court decided that the charge failed to fall under Article 28, so Doyle could not be charged with murder. Instead, they found the accused guilty of the lesser charge that he 'unnecessarily levelling his musket at a Chinese and shot him' – surely the most classic case of hair-splitting on record. Doyle's sentence for this act was 'To be imprisoned two years, mulct of all pay, and discharged, with disgrace, from the service'.

❅ ❅ ❅

Duelling was certainly covered by the act and dealt with harshly. Fortunately, this practice tended to die out over the years, but one of the last cases in the Royal Navy took place in 1845 off the coast of Africa. Here Lieutenant W.J.R. Card of HMS *Hyacinth* quarrelled violently with the ship's surgeon, W. M'Crea. Although both men promised not to duel as a result of their falling out, they subsequently landed ashore and fought one, although both men survived to rue the experience.

At the court martial, conducted on 13 January, they were both charged with quarrelling, fighting a duel and 'for conduct unbecoming an officer in breaking their word, pledged, or so far prevaricating or equivocating as to evade and disobey an order'. Lieutenant C.G. Glinn also faced trial at the same time, he being one of the 'seconds' and charged with having 'also broken his word on the aforesaid occasion'.

Card was found guilty under Articles 2 and 23, and was sentenced to be dismissed from his ship and placed at the bottom of the list of lieutenants, 'from which he is not to rise until the expiration of three years'. M'Crea was also found guilty, 'but under circumstances of great provocation', and he too was placed at the bottom of the list of surgeons in the Royal Navy. Glinn received the same fate metered out to Card, but without any time stipulation.

❅ ❅ ❅

There was an alternative to death for those found guilty of murder, which was, from time to time, exercised. For example, on 7 July 1835, Royal Marine Jenkins of the *Malabar* was found guilty of having stabbed the master's assistant with a bayonet. Although duly sentenced to death, Jenkin's final punishment was transportation. However, this sentence was beyond the power of a court martial to impose. A decision, given in response to a query made by a court held in 1797, gave the opinion that 'we do not think that they can pronounce the sentence of transportation, hard labour, or any sort of imprisonment, except such as had been usual'. In other words, as Blackstone recorded in *Commentaries on the Laws of England*: 'No power on earth, except the authority of Parliament, can send any subject of England, out of the land against his will; no, not even a criminal.'

Blackstone added: 'For exile and transportation are punishments at present unknown to the common law; and whenever the latter is now inflicted, it is either by choice of the criminal himself to escape a capital punishment, or else by the express direction of some modern act of Parliament.'

❊ ❊ ❊

The last man to actually be 'hung from the yardarm' in the Royal Navy, following his court martial, was one John Dalliger. His crime was a particularly nasty one, but he professed remorse afterward, for all the good it did him.

It was on 9 July 1860, during one of Britain's periodic campaigns against the Chinese. Earlier that year the commander-in-chief, China station, Rear Admiral Sir James Hope, had suffered a bloody repulse attempting to storm the Taku Forts guarding the seaward approaches to Peking. The British storming force had been forced to withdraw with heavy loss, and a fresh fleet was being concentrated at the mouth of the Pei-ho River in readiness for a second attempt. A small flotilla of ships was busy surveying the coastline seeking a suitable anchorage for this assembly of shipping. Among the survey craft was the small barque-rigged gunboat HMS *Leven*, built for the Crimea conflict a decade before. Since 1858, *Leven* had been under the command of one Lieutenant Hudson, and had a crew of forty-eight officers and men. The *Leven* was charged with surveying the bays on the Liao-tung Peninsular and, on the day in question, was at anchor in Hulu-shan Bay.

Among the ship's crew was a Royal Marine private, John Dalliger, who had only joined the *Leven* the previous February. His shipmates generally regarded him as an unsavoury character with a reputation that had preceded him. Nonetheless, being a fair man, Lieutenant Hudson gave him ample opportunity to begin afresh, and even made him his own personal servant. Hudson was soon to rue his kindness. Brandy and wine went missing from the captain's cabin and Dalliger was accused of the theft. Disdaining the threat of the cat-o'-nine-tails and the like, the captain duly warned him he would be brought to punishment. Dalliger reacted immediately.

At 0830hrs on 9 July, while Hudson was sitting at his breakfast, Dalliger stole a pistol and crept into the cabin. Here he cold-bloodedly shot his captain in the back of the neck. Hudson fell to the deck in a pool of blood, and Dalliger, certain he had killed him, left the cabin and approached the second-in-command,

Second Master Ashton. Dalliger told Ashton that the captain wished to speak with him and, when the officer descended the accommodation ladder, Dalliger shot him as well.

The marine was at once arrested, clapped in irons and confined below deck. Amazingly, Hudson was still alive and was transferred to the hospital ship *Simoon*, where he eventually made a full recovery and later was sent home to England to recuperate. Ashton also survived the murderous assault and, within a short time, a court martial was convened on the homicidal Dalliger.

On the 12th, *Leven* had joined the rest of the fleet anchored at Ta-lein-wan (later to be known as Dalny, then Darien or 'Far-Away' Bay). The C-in-C flew his flag aboard the frigate *Chesapeake* and it was here, at 0900hrs that the trial commenced. The accused could say little in his own defence in the circumstances, as he had after all been caught absolutely red-handed. His character was such that there could be little sympathy or doubt to help mitigate things. At 1430hrs sentence was pronounced: John Dalliger was condemned to death. He was to be hung at the fore yardarm of the *Leven* within twenty-four hours of sentence being passed, and so he was.

The execution of prisoners in this manner was already something of a rarity, but war was threatening, the fleet was in a tense mood readying themselves to renew the battle, they were all a long, long way from England and the law was still valid. The chaplain, as always, administered what solace he could to the condemned man. In return, Dalliger made a full confession and expressed remorse. The prisoner's statement was read out to the assembled ship's company the day he died. It read, in full, thuswise:

> I wish to tell you all before I die that I confess my crime, and am heartily sorry for it, and regard death as only too little punishment. I beg pardon of all whom I have injured or wished to injure, especially of those two I so nearly destroyed in my anger. I forgive all if there be any who have injured me. I hope that God will for the sake of His Son's most precious death have mercy on me. If you would take a word of advice from such a man as I am, I would say, take warning by me, save your soul. When a man leaves God and accustoms himself to sin, he does not know what he may end up in.

All the warships present that day sent away their boats to witness the execution, while the bowmen of each vessel went aboard the *Leven* to man the whip. At three bells, the signal was fired, the boatswain's pipe sounded and before the assembled officers and men and the circle of boats, the whip men ran down the deck and the hooded figure of the prisoner was jerked abruptly up by the rope noose which ran up through a block at the yardarm, where he kicked briefly and then dangled loosely in dire warning.

At 1400hrs, the dead body was lowered to the deck once more and, enclosed in two hammocks; the corpse was taken aboard the frigate *Actaeon*. At 1630hrs the next day, 14 July, the *Actaeon* weighed anchor and proceeded out of Ta-lien-wan and, two hours later, the enshrouded body of Dalliger was committed to the deep over the frigate's side, with the hammocks weighted by ten round shot, 1½ miles north-west of Cape Rock.

Thus passed John Dalliger, executed for a murderous assault, but yet, for all that, not for murder!

✳ ✳ ✳

It is neither desirable nor palatable to linger on any detailed aspect of the offence known as sodomy or buggery, nor to discuss the law appertaining to consenting adults as it now affects the service. For those wish to study a notorious post-war case of alleged homosexuality, which was thrown out, the book *Smoke without Fire*, concerning the Swabey case, should provide more than adequate detail.

Suffice it enough then, to show by a few examples, how our forebears, in their time, viewed and punished what was then an unlawful act. It should be noted that this 'crime' was always one that had to be approached with the utmost caution because of the many pitfalls of false accusation and its ramifications. As Hickman wrote in 1850:

> This is a horrible crime to contemplate, and one wherein the Court may more readily than in any other case be imposed upon by the testimony of false and malicious witnesses, creating, as it naturally does, so much prejudice against the parties accused of having committed it. It therefore behoves the Court to be extremely minute and careful in the examination of witnesses, and guarded in giving their judgement. However clear against the prisoner it may appear to be, no feeling of delicacy or disgust will justify them in omitting to inquire into all the circumstances of the transaction they are called up on to investigate ...

✳ ✳ ✳

On 21 February 1756, Midshipman Francis French of the *Defiance* was found not guilty of 'Sodomitical practices', but was convicted of 'Uncleanness and scandalous actions'. French's punishment was to be given 300 lashes with a halter round his neck and rendered incapable of serving in the navy.

✳ ✳ ✳

Harking briefly back to the Swabey case, it is also, incidentally, a good example of how not to handle a naval court martial, despite Hickman's wise counsel of a century earlier. It might also be considered an indictment on certain attitudes at the then Admiralty, and its even more remote and bureaucratic successor, the Ministry of Defence, which refuses to admit that it is fallible in any way. It took Swabey no less than sixteen years to clear his name, and even then, he was shabbily treated with regard to compensation. The case, therefore, rates with the Archer-Shee scandal in illustrating that the system, although good, had never been perfect and is open to error.

One recent viewpoint on this subject revealed that cases of homosexuality were still occurring in the 1970s and that, during a two-year period, four 'rings' that involved up to a dozen individuals came to light; the aircraft carrier *Eagle* and the HMS *Nelson* at Portsmouth being among the most noted at that time. About 90 per cent of these cases resulted in dismissal from the service. Very little personal attachment was found in the cases and it was mainly for sexual gratification that the incidents were thought to be taking place. Also found was a considerable amount of corruption by older men, which met with a firm response from the Royal Navy to put a stop to it. Although there still existed, at the time, a provision for any true homosexual to have a legal discharge from the service, this appeared to be little known on the lower deck.

Similarly, cases of lesbianism among WRNS at the same shore base resulted in administrative discharge to avoid unwelcome publicity. Far and away the largest single branch of the service involved in such matters appears to have been the Steward branch. However, with today's acceptance of any sexual preference, the stigma, and certainly the punishment, is comparatively mild to what it was even a decade ago.

5 JOINING THE LADIES

The arrival of the WRNS during the Great War had been both welcomed and desirable, for it freed men for the fighting ships and this pattern had followed during the Second World War and after. While a few diehards might frown, there was general acceptance and no real problems at all. The work carried out by these women was both critical and essential, and they performed it perfectly. It was not until the arrival, some decades later, of two new factors of social life – militant feminism and political correctness – that this happy assimilation began to be questioned and was, eventually, overturned. Despite centuries of not mixing males and females afloat in ships-of-war, the Ministry of Defence quickly adhered to new attitudes, and, although the wives of sailors themselves mounted protests, women were granted the equality they so craved and took their place at sea in the Royal Navy.

The rapid advance of technology had, of course, done away with the essential need for the physical strength of men aboard ships to a large degree. The finger that pushed the button could now be gender-free. Combat experience, with warships actually hit and casualties taken, has, at the time of writing, yet to be witnessed, but with female fire-fighters, jet fighter pilots and armed policewomen on the streets, the transition has taken place nationally with little or no problems. The fact also that, during the Second World War, Soviet women had piloted a few units flying dive-bombers and other aircraft in combat proved that battle was no barrier. On the historic side, the famous case of the female marine, Hannah Snell, was an early isolated precedent, even if an unofficial one, for she had fought in the trenches in India.

There remained just one snag, Mother Nature alone refused to give way to political correctness. Try to will it away as much as they wished to do, a few million years of evolution was not so easy to dispel. Young men and young women, in the prime of life, stubbornly continued to be sexually attracted to each other. This fact alone had brought a new element to the naval court martial and a few examples can suffice to illustrate the complication.

One of the very first WRNS to go to sea when the government gave way on the issue in the autumn of 1990 was Sub-lieutenant Jacqueline Ramsay, who had only joined the navy the year before. As a graduate officer under training she was subsequently described by Lieutenant Commander Penny Melville-Brown as being 'in the front line of sorts' when she joined the frigate *Brilliant*. This ship was the first warship to receive female crew members and, in February 1991, sailed to the Gulf to carry out patrols. The *Brilliant*'s commanding officer, Captain Richard Cobbald, was acutely aware of the difficulties he faced in this new situation. A strict 'no touch' rule was promulgated throughout the ship. Aware of the worries of the wives ashore, the captain reassured them that 'The Wrens will be working so hard they won't have any time to cause Navy wives any concern'.

However, as early as 10 April, the new commanding officer, Captain Tobin Elliott, was having to warn Ramsay and Lieutenant Mark Davies, an observer of one of the *Brilliant*'s Lynx helicopters and a married man, about their standards of behaviour. Captain Elliott had been informed that the pair might have been in Davies' cabin at 0130hrs that day. The commanding officer ordered them both not to visit each other's cabins again. This warning went unheeded.

At 0120hrs on the morning of 6 May, another Wren, who shared a cabin with Ramsay, reported that she had not returned to her quarters. Three senior officers went immediately to Davies' cabin, knocked and entered. They found Davies kneeling naked on one end of the bunk and Ramsay, also naked, on the other end. Ramsay was alleged to have responded, 'Fair enough, you've seen enough. Now please shut the door while I put some clothes on.' Davies' response was similar: 'Shut the door.'

Both officers were confined to their quarters, Davies for four days, Ramsay for only two, before they were flown back to Britain to face court martial, accused of conduct to the prejudice of good order and naval discipline in being naked together on the frigate *Brilliant* without reasonable excuse.

In mitigation for Davies, Lieutenant John Parr recorded the accused's combat record. Davies had flown thirty combat missions over enemy territory during the Gulf War, searching for mines of the coast of Kuwait, sometimes at heights of only 10 to 12 feet above the water and on one occasion had his helicopter fired on. Davies, it was said, played 'an effective and active role' in that conflict. The defence added that the whole episode had been 'truly a nightmare'.

Melville-Brown, defending Ramsay, said that, on the night in question, 'Sexual intercourse had not taken place; they were not even touching'. She also pleaded the effect of the job on Jacqueline Ramsay: 'No doubt members of the court will have imagined or experienced the stresses and emotional pressure, the surges of adrenaline and later exhaustion of people in that sort of situation.' Ramsay was also said to the 'naïve' in the ways of disciplined service.

The court's sentence on both defendants was that they were severely reprimanded and fined £750 apiece, subject to confirmation.

This was the first such case in the Royal Navy, but many others soon followed it. The following year a Wren and a sailor were caught having sex aboard the frigate *Cumberland*, while that ship was visiting the Dutch port of Den Helder in October. After another decade the whole thing was clearly out of hand. By February 2001, the Ministry of Defence was investigating how ten Wrens had become pregnant aboard one warship in just one year, while the destroyer *Sheffield* had four out of thirty-seven women crew members taken off her in a two-month period after becoming pregnant. Admiral Sir Jock Slater, one of the Navy Board initiators of the scheme, continued to champion it and was quoted as saying: 'When we took the decision we recognised that there needed to be very firm rules that were drawn up and are for men and women when they are on board ship.' However, another, anonymous, source revealed: 'The no-touching rule went by the board a long time ago', adding, 'Everybody is at it. The girls use the regulations to get out of relationships. Once they've decided they want to end it, they go and tell the captain and their boyfriend gets in all sorts of trouble.' One

pundit, the editor of a magazine called *Warship World*, Mike Critchley, quoted a
senior officer at the time saying, 'a nation which sends its women to sea is mor-
ally bankrupt', and agreed with him, adding: 'If you put young men and young
women together in a tin box 24 hours a day, 365 days of the year, this sort of thing
is going to happen.' Admiral Sir John Woodward was quoted as saying at the time
that 'There was an instinctive gut feeling that it's the wrong thing to do, that it
hasn't been allowed for hundreds of years and it can't work. But we had to try it.'
Whatever the retrospective viewpoints, Pandora's box once opened, could not
be closed. In order to prevent an endless series of courts martial, which would
have provided the media with an open-ended feeding frenzy of such cases, the
Ministry of Defence policy was alleged to have changed to acceptance of the
inevitable. A spokesman is reported to have said that the navy 'did not know – and
would not ask – where the women became pregnant'.

There is no need here to include any further examples of such courts martial,
but it was not only at sea that the man-woman relationship led to recourse to
the law. Temptation was not always easy to resist and those that succumbed, even
ashore, faced the penalty, and the publicity.

While serving in the aircraft carrier HMS *Invincible*, Petty Officer David Quilter
was brought before court martial held at HMS *Nelson*, Portsmouth, accused of
inflicting 'Actual bodily harm' and 'Assault' on two female members of her crew.
The prosecutor, Lieutenant Commander David Steel, detailed how, when the
carrier was anchored off the Greek port of Piraeus the previous October, Quilter,
who had just got engaged, went ashore to celebrate, and imbibed too well of the
local brew in a bar with colleagues of both sexes from his ship. What resulted, the
defending officer, Lieutenant Commander Nick Hawkins asserted, was the result
of 'drink induced bravado'. The accused had repeatedly pulled at Wren Barbara
Staniforth's top and bit Sub-lieutenant Selina Lamb on her bottom. The court
took the sternest view of this type of behaviour, ouzo or no ouzo, and Quilter
received a suspended sentence of twenty-eight days in a military detention centre.
The navy suffered yet more embarrassing press stories, for two members of the
Invincible's crew, Petty Officers Ian Luff and Sylvia Panter, had, a month earlier,
'jumped ship' to be together.

The combination of drink, high spirits and a lack of appreciation of how times had
changed led to another young naval officer facing court martial at HMS *Nelson*,
when what he had assumed was a harmless prank led to retribution that threatened his naval career almost before it had started. Lieutenant Surgeon Dominic
Ayers was also out celebrating in a bar, this time the occasion was the successful
end of an eight-week training course at the Royal Navy College, Dartmouth, and

the venue was the Royal Castle Hotel. The prosecution was brought by the civilian girlfriend of a Royal Marine who happened to be in the bar at the same time.

Earlier that evening Ayers had been reminiscing about his days as a medical student in Cambridge and a game the undergraduates there termed 'Breast Cricket'. In this, 'runs' were scored dependant on the number of times a 'batsman' could brush up against a woman. In this game, a 'deft touch' might count as a single, while a more 'deliberate stroke' counted as a four. The woman who brought the case overheard two of the group discussing the game at closing time and approached Ayers, asking him to tell her the rules. According to the prosecutor, Lieutenant Commander John Flanagan, Ayers had responded, 'We do this', and had then grabbed the girl's left breast. Ayers continued to explain the rules to her and told her she was supposed to slap his face. The young woman had not seemed upset at the time of the incident, but had continued to talk to the group, including Ayers, until she left with her marine fiancé. Later, on her way home, she expressed resentment and her fiancé confronted Ayers the next day. This resulted in his immediate arrest, charge and subsequent trial.

The defence was conducted by David Lancaster, who told the court that the whole evening had been a 'civilised affair', and the officers were not drunk, but only 'glowing from the effects of alcohol'. He claimed that Ayers had not grabbed the woman, but had just brushed her breast with the palm of his hand, 'and she didn't grab his hand to try to push it away'. On the contrary, Lancaster continued, Ayers' hand 'was taken away quite voluntarily after a very short period of contact. The conversation carried on in the same good humour as it had before.' Ayers had pleaded guilty to the charge, but Lancaster told the court: 'This charge has perhaps been brought because of a world suffering from an over-cautious sense of righteousness. It would perhaps have been some time ago seen as a prank and may have been resolved with a bunch of flowers and an apology.' However, the world had moved on and the court duly reflected that shift in tolerance.

The President, Captain Robert Rowley, pronounced a sentence on Ayers of severe reprimand and a fine of £800. 'The court has given you full credit for your plea of guilty and accepts that you regret this incident,' the President announced. He continued, 'Your conduct on the evening – what you considered to be in good humour – was totally unacceptable for a Naval officer.' The sentence, Ayers was informed, 'is the minimum penalty we can impose'.

* * *

In 1998 naval courts martial featured in another large media story, the Bellingham case, where an officer aboard HMS *Coventry* was cleared of seven charges of sexual harassment brought by four of the female crew members, but convicted on an eighth charge of 'sexually explicit chat', severely reprimanded and fined

'£2,000 and the loss of 25 days' seniority'. Captain Mark Kerr is reported to have said of the case: 'He has been punished and that's the end of it as far as the Navy is concerned', but the press thought otherwise. The same year saw yet further damaging front-page headlines concerning a high-ranking Wren officer, whose affairs on shore with a high-ranking army officer at the Ministry of Defence, and also with a naval officer aboard the aircraft carrier *Illustrious*, gave yet further credence to press stories like 'HMS *LUSTrious*' and did the service no good whatsoever. No doubt this type of story will run and run, but we shall here leave this to the 'Red Top' media and the BBC, and move on to other aspects of the court martial concerning the ladies.

❋ ❋ ❋

The very first WRNS officer to face a court martial was accused of running away to the West Indies to escape the pressures of her new job.

On 21 December 1984, Third Officer Marion Gill was found guilty at a trial held at Portsmouth. Gill had flown to St Lucia on a package holiday for sixteen days, when she should have been at her desk at HMS *Warrior*, the navy's main command HQ in Northwood, London. Third Officer Gill, then based at HMS *St Vincent*, London, pleaded guilty of being absent without leave and she was dismissed her ship and lost sixteen months' seniority as her punishment.

❋ ❋ ❋

The frigate *Brazen* was returning home from a period of duty on Falklands patrol in 1995 when she ran aground off the southern tip of Chile. Attempts to refloat the ship, including a bizarre co-ordinated jumping on the ship's stern by the bulk of the 256 crew, proved unavailing and eventually the *Brazen* had to be towed off by Chilean tugs. Some £100,000 worth of damage was done to the ship, although she managed to sail home eventually.

Courts martial were brought against the person in control on the bridge at the time, Lieutenant Sarah Brothwell. Charges were also brought against the ship's captain, Commander Paul Collins, and her navigating officer, Lieutenant Matthew Payne. During the hearing it was heard that standard navy guidelines in existence at the time of the accident dictated that two officers had to be on the bridge at all times, one in charge and the other navigating. This was complied with, but the prosecutor, Lieutenant Commander Andrew Jameson, claimed, 'Lieutenant Brothwell was considered of sufficient experience by the commander to conduct her own watch, with only occasional help from the navigator, even though she had only had one experience of piloting HMS *Brazen*'. This assumption was an error, the prosecution claimed, and a culmination of an 'ill-considered' navigational

plan for a difficult night passage through unfamiliar waters. Brothwell was on the
bridge just eight minutes before the Type-22 frigate hit the rocks.

In Commander Collins' defence, a whole series of high-ranking officers
spoke of his 'inspirational leadership'. Collins had piloted helicopters during the
Falklands War, for which he was decorated; he had again shown exceptional ability in combat, and had taken a leading part in air-sea actions against the Iraqi
navy during the Gulf War. During the action off Bubiyan Island the Royal Navy's
missile-firing helicopters from the destroyers *Cardiff* and *Gloucester*, as well as the
Brazen, had crippled the bulk of Saddam Hussain's surface fleet. This led to one
admiral describing Collins as a key figure. In the efforts at salvaging the *Brazen*
following the accident his marine engineering officer, Lieutenant Commander
David Lewis, testified that 'My commander's role was essential in saving the ship,
his leadership was impeccable'. Further support came from members of *Brazen's*
crew. It was all in vain, achievements in war counted for naught, and Collins was
sentenced to be dismissed from his position on the flag officer surface flotilla.
Likewise, Lieutenant Payne was reprimanded.

Lieutenant Brothwell was totally cleared of any offence.

6 · UNUSUAL CASES AND VERDICTS

It would be strange indeed should the modern reader not find some cases conducted in days gone by both incongruous and, maybe, inconsequential, though
at the time they appeared serious enough. In judging, also, whether some of the
sentences the courts of that time imposed were either harsh or petty, one always
has to place them strictly and fairly in the context and atmosphere of the time.
Even so, there are many instances that strike the eye as being rather apart from the
norm, and this next selection, will, it is hoped, illustrate my point.

In the aftermath of Cromwell's parliament and the restoration of the monarchy,
it was perhaps natural that the charge of sedition was much featured in the fleet,
itself still unsure of its changing loyalties over the dramatic preceding years. It was
a charge dealt with harshly in many instances, but the accused was sometimes,
surprisingly, given the benefit of the doubt even then.

Gordon Taylor relates one such incident in the book *The Sea Chaplains*.
The tale concerns one Samuel Middleton, 'late Chaplain of His Majesty's ship
Dreadnought', who was brought to trial on a charge of 'speaking treasonable sedi-
tion … touching his Majesty and the present Government'. There were, of course,

many Jacobite sympathisers in the land and not all were silent, although, naturally, it might have behoved Middleton to have been more discreet in his convictions than he had been.

In front of two witnesses, his captain and the ship's purser, Middleton had criticised the death sentences passed on two plotters against William III. The accused, it was alleged, had stated that these two had been 'made of as Tools', and that, after all, they had only done what many would have wished to, 'designed to bring in the late King James again' and that 'if he had so much Policy as Charity, he would be a great Plotter'.

Not surprisingly, therefore, the court found Middleton guilty of 'a high misdemeanour' and he was dismissed from his ship, never again to be employed in the navy, imprisoned for six months and forfeited all his due pay. Middleton's skipper swore on oath that Middleton was 'a very great Jacobite'. That would seem to have signalled the end of Middleton's naval career once and for all, but it is an indication of the looseness of the times that Taylor records that the gentleman was back at sea again within a year, serving aboard His Majesty's ship *Scarborough*, presumably as unrepentant as ever.

A broader view was taken by a court that had tried a lieutenant some years earlier. No doubt he had hoped that a similar fate that had attended Middleton would await his own captain, for he made taunting references to the fact that that worthy had held a commission under parliament from Cromwell himself. How, therefore, the accused had alleged, could the captain now loyally claim to serve the king? It must have come as a nasty shock to the lieutenant to find himself and not his captain on trial. Even more so when the court martial sentence that he, and not the man he had accused of disloyalty, was dismissed from the service. The order of the day at that hearing had very much been 'let bygones be bygones'.

Less fortunate, in all respects, to the captain mentioned above, was one Joseph Paine, who commanded the *Blacknose* in 1667. His ship formed part of a squadron led by Admiral Sir Edward Spragge, a very distinguished officer who had fought in every battle of the Second and Third Dutch Wars, and who was later to be drowned while in the process of shifting his flag at the Texel in 1673. When an attack was made by the Dutch fleet against our forces in the Thames and the Medway, Britain's sea power was at the lowest ebb it ever reached until modern times. Perhaps this fact was reflected in the sentence passed on Paine after being brought before court martial for his bad conduct during that fighting.

The sentence was that Paine:

> … be sent on board the *Victory*, prize, at Deptford on the 18th of the same
> month (November), where he was to have a halter put around his neck, and a
> wooden sword broken over his head; he was then to be towed through the water
> at a boats stern, from the ship to Deptford dock, a drum beating all the time in
> the boat, and to be rendered incapable in future of any further command.

Much the same fate awaited Midshipman Thomas Fuller of the *Chichester* on
10 June 1755, when he was found guilty of 'great misbehaviour to the Lieutenant
when in search of deserters'. Fuller's sentence was that he be degraded 'from the
station of Midshipman, rendered incapable of receiving any preferment, and to be
towed standing up in a boat, with his hands tied up to the sheers, and his sentence
read alongside of each ship in Halifax harbour'.

Such punishments had gone out of fashion by the 1990s, but they might still
be considered suitable for some miscreants. It is an unfortunate fact of life that,
wherever there is the opportunity for some to inflict misery on people over
whom they have charge, schools, workplaces or the services, they will continue to
do so, no matter what the century.

At the shore training base HMS *Collingwood*, near Fareham, Hampshire, four
young apprentices were standing to attention, awaiting the evening inspection.
The inspecting officer, Lieutenant Commander Stephen Kerslake, noticed that
one of the lads, Ben Holland, was standing barefooted. Stepping forward, Kerslake
put his booted heel on Holland's bare foot and then leant forward, throwing his
whole weight on it. Kerslake said to Holland, 'What have I just done?' to which
Holland replied, 'You stood on my foot, Sir'. The pain must have been intense and
the apprentice could no longer stand to attention properly, shuffling from foot to
foot in agony. So Kerslake shouted at Holland to stand to attention properly.

For the defence, Lieutenant Neil Brown stated that Kerslake, a long-serving
officer, had done this in order to teach the apprentice a lesson. Kerslake admitted the assault, but said that he wanted to show the youngsters the danger of not
wearing shoes aboard ship, even though they were ashore at the time. He added
that he now regretted his approach. The court at Portsmouth viewed the matter
somewhat differently, and Kerslake was dismissed from *Collingwood* and severely
reprimanded, but was still able to apply for an alternative job in the navy.

It is a fact that three of the foremost admirals of the eighteenth and nineteenth centuries, Collingwood, Cochrane and Cornwallis, French Revolutionary and Napoleonic War veterans to a man, were all court-martialled at some stage in their long and honourable careers. Cochrane's trial was over a clash with his first lieutenant, Philip Beaver, aboard the *Barfleur* in 1799, and another involved the loss of HMS *Speedy* in 1801. Collingwood's court martial came much earlier in his career and was notable, if for nothing else, in the absolute puerility of the sentence imposed upon him.

It was on 30 September 1777 that Collingwood, then serving as a lieutenant aboard the sloop *Hornet*, was brought to trial at Port Royal on charges of insubordination, disobeying his captain's orders and neglect of duty. The charges, brought by his commanding officer, were a hotch-potch of petty offences, some several months old, and his defence was so scathing, both of the character and feeble vindictiveness of his accuser and the derisory nature of the alleged offences, that the court saw no option but to discharge Collingwood. However, the court felt that they had to say something to justify their time and they gave him the following advice: 'to conduct himself for the future with that alacrity which is so necessary for carrying on His Majesty's service', and they censured Collingwood 'for want of cheerfulness in carrying on the duty of his sloop'.

The case of Cornwallis was rather different, for he found, as many admirals before and since have found to their cost, that Their Lordships always had the last word. In 1796, as a vice admiral, Cornwallis was appointed as commander-in-chief of the West Indies Squadron and he duly sailed for that station, with a convoy under his wing and several warships as escorts, flying his flag in the *Royal Sovereign* (100), to take up his appointment.

The station had a bad reputation with regard to health, but there was little to indicate that Cornwallis was anything other than pleased with his new situation. However, en route and proceeding down the Channel, *Royal Sovereign* was involved in a slight collision with another vessel, which necessitated her returning to harbour to effect repairs before resuming her voyage. Cornwallis returned in her and, on learning of this, the Admiralty dispatched a curt note reminding him of where his duty lay. Their Lordships demanded that Cornwallis transfer his flag to the frigate *Astraea*, in which vessel he was to continue his voyage with all dispatch!

The admiral demurred. He was far from enjoying the best of health, he informed London, and, while he could positively state his own 'readiness to proceed … in the *Royal Sovereign*' once she was fit to sail, he could not see his way clear to make the long journey in a frigate of far smaller dimensions, 'without accommodation or any comforts'.

Lord Spencer and his compatriots on the board were far from impressed with this argument, and forthwith ordered Cornwallis to attend his court martial for disobedience. This was duly conducted. In his defence, the admiral asserted that disobedience was never in his mind, merely a reasonable concern for his own well-being. Cornwallis argued that 'his health would not permit him to go out under such circumstances, and that he would have resigned his command if the order had been made positive, but, as to disobeying, he had not thought of it'.

No doubt the old admiral's distinguished career to date weighed heavily in his favour, for the court found him not guilty of the charge, but they strongly censured him for failing to transfer his flag and continue the voyage nonetheless. Most people would have considered that he got off lightly, but Cornwallis was not at all pleased with this verdict. He requested permission to strike his flag and the Admiralty agreed. Later, when tempers had cooled somewhat, Cornwallis was to serve as commander-in-chief, Channel Fleet, for two periods, in 1801 and between 1803 and 1806.

※ ※ ※

Another famous sailor whose later career was marred by court martial, but still went on to achieve great fame, was William Dampier. Truly one of the 'fabulous' company of seamen, Dampier was born in 1625 and followed a sea calling as a pirate before the poacher turned gamekeeper, going on to become one of the Royal Navy's greatest hydrographers.

Dampier was summoned to his court martial aboard the *Royal Sovereign* on 8 June 1702, at Spithead. The accusation that Dampier faced at that date was of 'very hard and cruel usages towards Lieutenant Fisher, and the Court, under the presidency of Admiral Sir George Rooke, found the charge proven'. Dampier was sentenced to be fined his past three years' pay and the court further recorded the opinion that such a man as he 'is not a fit person to be employed as a commander of any of Her Majesty's Ships'.

Despite this scathing indictment, Dampier was judged very differently by history and at least one of HM ships, a frigate converted into a surveying vessel, bore his name proudly in the 1950s. Incidentally, Dampier's court was notable for the huge number of officers sitting on it. Apart from Rooke, no fewer than three further admirals, including Shovell, and thirty-three captains sat in judgement of the ex-buccaneer, which gives a good indication of how things had got out of hand in this respect, before much-needed limits on numbers were finally introduced.

One of the more remarkable court martial proceedings of all time concerned an occurrence aboard the frigate *Diamond* at Rhode Island on 18 January 1777. While in the process of firing a salute, one the ship's guns discharged a shot, which had been carelessly left loaded. This missile struck the transport *Grand Duke of Russia*, killing five of her sailors. As a result of this tragedy, the first lieutenant, John Duckworth, the gunner, Andrew Wilson, the gunner's mate and crew were all ordered to be tried by court martial.

However, not only the charges of the guns had been carelessly readied, the charges of the accused turned out to be equally slip-shod in their preparation. The wording of these charges only indicated the accused by their rank and qualities, and not by name. Furthermore, the actual charge was framed to read only that they be tried for negligence and failed to mention the resultant deaths of five men. All the accused were duly acquitted on this limited charge but, when the minutes were submitted to the commander-in-chief, Richard, Lord Howe, he was immediately struck by the gross irregularity of the whole thing.

Howe's reaction was to order an immediate fresh trial, a court to be assembled 'to try by name the several persons described for the capital offence, added to the charge of neglect of duty'. When the various officers summoned to form this tribunal were so ordered, they got together in some indignation and, as a body, replied that they declined to do so, on the grounds that 'the persons charged had already been tried and honourably acquitted'. Incensed at this attitude, Howe repeated the instructions to the commodore at Rhode Island, listing the names of the persons involved and threatening that, should they again refuse to comply, he would make 'every captain refusing to perform his required duty in that respect to be forthwith suspended from his command'.

The delinquent captains received this second summons via their commander, Sir Peter Parker, on 20 April and between them conspired to hatch another scheme to thwart justice. The court was duly constituted, the minutes of the first trial were read and 'maturely considered', and then sentence was pronounced. It was that the accused, 'having been acquitted of neglect of duty are in consequence herewith, acquitted of murder or any other crime or crimes alleged against them, relative to the firing of the guns on 18th January 1777'. The court delivered this fresh verdict on 29 May and, amazingly, this time it stood unchallenged, although whether the true ends of justice were correctly served by such conduct remains highly questionable.

We have seen some examples of how sedition was treated in the service at sensitive times in Britain's turbulent history. We may, perhaps, sympathise with the authorities' reactions to such cases, but there were some that ought never to have come to trial at all. The sweepings of the press gangs were totally indiscriminate and among men so pressed were a good number of the mentally disturbed or plain simpletons, who had no business aboard a man-of-war whatsoever. Such was surely the case of a sailor brought to court martial at Plymouth in October 1803.

This man was charged with the grave crime of drinking the health of Napoleon Bonaparte and wishing him success. Though it was certainly a tense time for the nation as a whole, it was widely known that the accused was, from time to time, mentally deranged and not responsible for his actions, even when sober. Despite this knowledge, an unfeeling and insensitive court sentenced him to two years' imprisonment in the infamous Marshalsea at Southwark.

A case in some respects similar to that of the Cornwallis' court martial was recorded in 1814. It concerned Captain James Anderson (1760–1835), who was appointed in command of the *Zealous* (74), in August of that year. Anderson was ordered to sail with stores to Quebec and there to over-winter. The *Zealous* had been launched in 1785 and was feeling her age: she was rotten, badly equipped and indifferently manned but, despite all this, Anderson got her to Quebec as instructed.

Once at this destination, however, Anderson deemed caution the wisest course and decided that to obey his orders to remain was to court disaster, both to his command and his crew. The old girl was just not up to it, about summed his thoughts on the *Zealous* and the Canadian winter. Anderson therefore sailed his command straight back to England, once he had discharged his cargo. Here the good captain was met not with praise for his prudence, but with court martial on the grounds that his return was contrary to his expressed instructions. The trial, which followed, actually acquitted Anderson of all blame once the true condition of the *Zealous* had been revealed, and the ship was broken up in 1816, which many felt had been long overdue.

Despite the apparent vindication of his action, the court's verdict did not go down at all well with the First Lord of the Admiralty, Lord Melville. He confronted Anderson and told him to his face: 'If Canada fall, it will be entirely owing to your not wintering the *Zealous* at Quebec!' Unabashed, Anderson replied coolly, and with complete accuracy, that: 'I rather think it will be in consequence of proper supplies, in proper ships, not having been sent out there at a proper season of the year!' This response was probably even less palatable to his lordship than the court's decision had been, the truth never commending itself very highly to those found wanting in high places. Melville never forgave Anderson for it, and the honest captain never received another command.

The value of expert opinion has always been a feature of naval courts martial. Maybe one of the earliest examples of the way science, in all its forms, was influencing the service came at the court martial of Captain Seymour of the sixth-rate *Challenger* after she had been wrecked off the coast of South America in 1835. The court sat at Portsmouth, and among the evidence that Seymour was able to produce in his defence was a document written by Captain Fitzroy of the survey ship *Beagle*, lately returned from those same waters.

The document concerned contained detailed findings obtained by the *Beagle* of the severe changes in the ocean currents in February due to an earthquake that had occurred in that region and which continued to affect conditions at sea. Armed with this information, Seymour pleaded that, having come from the east coast of the continent before the disaster, he knew nothing at all of the earthquake and, therefore, could hardly be held to blame if the changes it had wrought had subsequently affected *Challenger*'s dead-reckoning estimate of her position from the shore.

This reasoning convinced the court, and Seymour was acquitted from any blame. The members of the court duly paid tribute to Fitzroy's contribution to that decision, adding: 'the high sense it entertained of the conduct of Captain Michael Seymour, his surveying officers and ship's company when placed in the circumstances of the greatest danger as well as afterwards during a period of seven weeks that they remained on a wild and inhospitable coast.'

A famous case involving Horatio Nelson during his period in command of HMS *Boreas* in the West Indies got that officer into even hotter water than the Caribbean he sailed in. One of his sailors, William Clarke, was brought to trial on a charge of desertion and Nelson presided over the court. Clarke was duly found guilty as charged and sentenced to hang. However, Prince William Henry interceded on the man's behalf, asking Nelson to pardon him. This request, Nelson, quite illegally, complied with, compounding his mistake still further by releasing the man to civilian life ashore.

Of course, such a decision was not a junior commander's to make, even if a member of royalty desired it. The correct course would have been for the sentence to have been suspended until the arrival on station of a commissioned flag officer. Nelson, in fact, found himself neither able to hang the man nor set him free.

A case where the royal prerogative was exercised against a man found innocent was that of Sir John Munden in 1702. Sir John was a Rear Admiral of the Red who had been placed in command of a squadron sent out to the West Indies to intercept a French force also bound there. When the two squadrons did meet the resulting skirmish was inconclusive and, when the news reached England, there arose a popular clamour against Munden. Again, the power of the mob had to be assuaged, as so often before and since, and Munden was duly tried by court martial aboard HMS *Queen* at Spithead in July. Several charges were levelled against him, including misconduct and neglect, and the nation waited with baited breath for him to be sacrificed.

Imagine then, the consternation when, far from finding Sir John guilty, the court, after due deliberation, acquitted him and expressed the opinion that, far from disgracing himself, Munden had 'complied with his instructions, and behaved himself with great zeal and diligence in the service'.

Such a verdict was not what the nation had expected, nor wished. The crowds howled their disapproval, the monarchy bowed to their baying and Queen Anne overrode the court and ordered Munden to be dismissed from the service. This order was duly carried out, to the eternal shame of the royal house and of the Admiralty who permitted it.

❋ ❋ ❋

One of the most severe sentences handed out under the charge of embezzlement was that passed on Midshipman John Harvey (or Hervey in some accounts) of the fifth-rate *Defiance* in the West Indies in 1761. Harvey was part of a prize crew sent aboard the polcare *Diligence* and, in the words of the court, he 'sent articles to a considerable amount out of the prize', to wit, 'two trunk cases of iron work, a case of pictures, a case and a cask of Delph ware, and a cask of wine'. How on earth the midshipman smuggled all this loot out of a small ship is amazing; what is not so amazing is that he was caught red-handed doing so. His court martial sat on 16 March, and he faced charges of 'Breach of duty, robbery or embezzlement'. He was found guilty and, for so relatively petty a crime, the sentence was comprehensive.

Harvey was degraded from being a petty officer in a king's ship, received seventy-two lashes alongside the men-of-war in Kingston and Port Royal, 'having a halter put about his neck during the punishment', and had to forfeit his share of the prize and clean the heads (toilets) of the ship for three months.

❋ ❋ ❋

Some trials were held on matters so trivial as to make one wonder what on earth possessed all those involved. One lieutenant was found guilty, and dismissed from the service, at a court martial held at Portsmouth on 18 January 1800. The charge against him had been that 'he did throw a cup of tea in another Lieutenant's face, thereby scalding his nose'.

❀ ❀ ❀

Under the pseudonym Lionel Yexley, Petty Officer Wood wrote many tales of life on the lower deck of the Royal Navy, including this account of how a small irritation, coupled with an insensitive officer, could escalate into something quite serious within a very short time.

Aboard the corvette *Euryalus*, serving in the East Indies in the late 1870s, punishment was hard and rigidly enforced. An able seaman was ordered to muster his bag during his dinner hour, after being reprimanded for some slight flaw in his uniform at 'Divisions'. This sailor failed to hide his contempt and exasperation at this punishment and, because of this, was charged with 'Disrespect to a superior officer', given ten days' punishment and ordered to muster his bag in the dinner hour every day for a week.

For a time the man brooded over the perceived injustice of this and that brooding mounted into a hatred for his small-minded superiors. Finally, what control he had snapped and, in a dramatic gesture that gave vent to his pent-up feelings, he placed a 7-inch projectile into the hated bag, threw it over the side of the ship and watched it sink into the clear depths.

Aghast at such temerity, the officials aboard the corvette moved to inflict yet further punishment. The sailor was court-martialled and sentenced to five years' imprisonment for insubordination.

❀ ❀ ❀

Prior to the passing of the 1749 act, many sentences imposed by court martial involving imprisonment were very harsh indeed, ten to fifteen years' confinement being not uncommon, and sometimes even life.

In May 1744, the third-rate battleship *Northumberland*, commanded by Captain Watson, was engaged with two enemy battleships. During the course of this somewhat uneven struggle the captain was mortally wounded and, before any of his lieutenants could reach the quarterdeck to take over command of the ship, her master ordered her colours to be struck and she surrendered.

At the subsequent court martial of all her officers, everyone was acquitted save for the master, who was found guilty of surrendering the vessel without orders to do so. He was sentenced to life imprisonment in the Marshalsea prison.

❀ ❀ ❀

The law is a complex profession, but so also is a naval career, and the two are not always compatible. It should not surprise anyone if those who followed the vocation of seafaring should sometimes find themselves high and dry when faced with the maze of the laws that they had to navigate. Often the exact requirements laid down for the drawing up or conduct of courts martial themselves were not strictly adhered to, by choice, ignorance or preference. One well-known case involving both these hazards had very wide repercussions on the life of the nation as a whole, and resulted in the total humiliation of several very distinguished naval officers, and even, in part, of the Admiralty itself.

In 1743, a lieutenant of the marines, George Frye of HMS *Oxford*, was brought before a court martial at Port Royal, Jamaica. The charges, raised by the captain of his ship, were that Frye had disobeyed his orders by refusing to assist another lieutenant in bringing a prisoner aboard the ship. Frye, it transpired, had insisted that his captain put the order to do so in writing.

The court sat under the presidency of Admiral Sir Chaloner Ogle, but certain of the evidence produced was, to put it mildly, questionable. Many depositions were made out several days prior to the trial by illiterate persons and transcribed and presented as evidence in court. Frye, quite reasonably, objected to their validity, claiming that the signatures were not known to him. Furthermore, the accused professed no knowledge of such persons involved, nor had he ever heard their names before. How then, Frye asked, could their second-hand evidence bear weight? This was the argument the court refused to consider, Frye was 'browbeaten and overruled'. The charges were considered proven and the sentence passed was for 'fifteen years imprisonment and for Frye to be rendered incapable of serving his Majesty'.

The prisoner was sent back to England to serve his time, but, following his appeals, his case was reviewed by the Privy Council, who subsequently upheld his objections. The king was petitioned to remit Frye's punishment and he was ordered to be released. Justified in the law of the land, if not of the sea, Frye now proceeded to take his revenge against those whom he considered had wronged him. The first target was the late President of the court and Frye brought an action against Sir Chaloner Ogle at the court of the Commons, the case being heard by Lord Chief Justice Willis. Frye was able to prove that he had been kept in close confinement for fourteen months before he had even been brought to trial in 1744. He was duly awarded damages of £1,000 against the admiral in compensation. In addition, Frye was assured by the judge that he was perfectly at liberty to bring additional actions against any other members of the court martial, and this advice Frye proceeded to follow with a will.

Frye's next two targets were Rear Admiral Perry Mayne and Captain Rentone, who had both sat on his court martial board, and were, by May 1746, back in London, both coincidentally at that time sitting in judgement of Vice Admiral

Lestock, with Mayne as the President. When John Willis, as Lord Chief Justice of the Common Pleas, issued his writ of capias against these two worthies, the humour of the whole situation was very apparent to all disinterested parties (among them, Horace Walpole), but the two officers determined to sit on their dignity. However, they could not choose to ignore what next occurred.

While their own court was actually in session at Deptford, both men were placed under arrest and the court martial had to adjourn in considerable disarray. The arresting of the President and one of the members of the court aroused great wrath among the other assembled naval officers, and two very stormy meetings were held that condemned this act as a grave insult to the service. The officers went yet further, drawing up a series of indignant resolutions in which their opinions of Lord Chief Justice Willis, none of them very complimentary, were spelt out in detail. The Judge Advocate of the interrupted court martial was then instructed to take this document to the Admiralty, with a request that it be placed before the king.

The wording demanded 'satisfaction for the high insult on their president, from all persons how high so ever in office, who have set on foot this arrest, or in any degree advised or promoted it'. They claimed that the arrest itself by its very nature, made 'the order, discipline, and government of his Majesty's armies by sea was dissolved, and the statue 13 Charles II ... null and void'.

Their Lordships were equally put out by the humiliation of their court and duly passed on the resolutions to the king as requested. Replying for the latter, the Duke of Newcastle answered the Admiralty thus:

> His Majesty expressed great displeasure at the insult offered to the court martial, by which the military discipline of the Navy is so much affected; and the King highly disapproves of the behaviour of Lieutenant Frye on the occasion. His Majesty has it under consideration what steps may be advisable to be taken on this occasion.

The law was not to be trifled with, however, by either the Admiralty or the monarch. As soon as he heard of the resolution, Lord Chief Justice Willis proceeded to issue writes against each individual member of the court martial for them to be taken into custody, and commenced legal measures to assert and maintain his authority. The Admiralty was unable to shield its officers from this counterattack and a hasty and grovelling apology was quickly drawn up and sent to Willis, signed by each and every member of the court. It read:

> As nothing is more becoming a gentleman, than to acknowledge himself to be in the wrong, so soon as he is sensible he is so, and to make satisfaction to any person he had injured; we, therefore, whose names are underwritten, being

thoroughly convinced tat we were entirely mistaken in the opinion we had conceived of Lord Chief Justice Willis, think ourselves obliged in honour, as well as justice, to make him satisfaction as far as it is in our power. And, as the injury we did him was of a public nature, we do, in this public manner, declare, that we are now satisfied the reflections cast upon him in our resolutions of the 16th and 21st of May last, were unjust, unwarrantable, and without any foundation whatsoever; and we do ask pardon of his lordship, and of the Court of Common Pleas, for the indignity offered both to him and the court.

This unprecedented climb down was dated 10 November 1746 and, upon its receipt four days later, it was registered in the Remembrance Office, a reminder, Willis stated, 'to the present and future ages, that *whoever set themselves up in opposition to the laws, or think themselves above the law, will in the end find themselves mistaken*'.

7 PEACETIME MISDOINGS

Although it was natural that the stresses of a combat environment would provide the most fertile fields for research into naval courts martial, there were some interesting cases to be found during the long periods between conflicts. These were not concerned exclusively with the natural misfortunes of shipwreck or accident, nor with mutiny and other forms of general dissatisfaction. A few of these examples are included herewith.

Court martial being the ordeal it normally is, it is not unexpected that anyone unfortunate enough to have undergone the experience was unlikely to wish to do anything other than forget it as quickly as possible. There were exceptions, and one instance of an officer keeping a souvenir of a trial was related by Sir Charles Beresford, the tempestuous 'Charley B', in his memoirs.

Beresford was in command of the protected cruiser HMS *Undaunted* in the Mediterranean just before the turn of the twentieth century. During the summer of 1891, she sailed from Alexandria harbour, but, while proceeding through the Bogaz Pass, she struck a submerged rock, which made a small tear in her bottom.

Sir Charles duly faced his court martial for a navigational error, but was fully acquitted. As a permanent memento of that decision, he kept in a bottle the preserved remains of a *ditta* fish, which had swum into the ship's hull at the time of the impact, along with a small piece of the ship's keel, which had been broken off by the impact.

On several occasions senior officers have sat as members of courts, only to subsequently find that they had no right to so do. One notorious scandal of this nature concerned Sir Roger Curtis in 1790. The incident took place during the trial of Lieutenant Bligh at Portsmouth in October of that year. Curtis was the first captain to Admiral Lord Howe, and he was sitting at the court in preference to many captains then present, who were actually senior to him on the Navy List. Many of the other captains took offence at this and complained. A formal letter was written and sent to the lord commissioners of the Admiralty, asking for the opinion of the matter of the Crown lawyers. This letter was sent at the behest of Admiral Barrington, who feared that, should the objections be upheld, then the whole proceedings would be declared illegal.

Due to his seniority, Curtis did not, in fact, come within the thirteen members directed to compose a court martial at that time, and the commissioners duly found that 'Sir Roger Curtis was not legally entitled to sit as a member of the Court Martial held on Lieutenant Bligh'.

Flogging, as a punishment, was not finally abandoned in the fleet until as late as 1891. Desertion was the most common crime to be so punished, but the number of strokes inflicted had gradually increased down the years, reaching a ghastly peak in the latter part of the eighteenth century. For example, both Abraham Wrack and George Biggs of the *Hound* were found guilty of desertion at courts martial held on 30 December 1790, and each unfortunate received 500 lashes. Two former convicts, Benjamin George and George Onslow, were sent from HMS *Victory* to the Haslar Hospital after being granted a pardon for their crimes, on condition that they serve in the navy. From there both immediately attempted to desert, were caught and brought before court martial, even though they were still convicts and not sailors. The sentence passed on the pair was that they were to receive 200 lashes apiece.

By 1847, when Seaman J. Savage was brought to trial for desertion from HMS *St Vincent*, things had changed a little. The sentence was for fifty lashes only, but in addition he was to be imprisoned in Winchester prison for twelve months' hard labour.

On 13 January 1843, Captain the Hon. C.G.S. Elliot of HMS *Spartan* was tried by court martial on the charge of flogging a midshipman. The court duly delivered their verdict as proven, but Elliot only received a severe reprimand, due, said the court, to 'the extraordinary and parental anxiety manifested by the prisoner on all occasions for the well-doing and general instruction of all the young gentlemen on board his ship, and looking at the circumstances under which the punishment was inflicted'.

* * *

Having been almost continuously at war with the French for almost 200 years, it appeared that old habits died hard in the years following the last of the campaigns against Napoleon. One Royal Navy officer, with either a long memory or an unforgiving one, was brought to court martial on 31 July 1844. This was Lieutenant E.E. Gray, commanding HM ship *Bonetta*. Gray was charged with various offences against a neutral ship, which, it transpired, was French.

The charges make for interesting reading and deserve to be reprinted again in full:

> Disobedience of orders in causing a French vessel to be detained and searched, she having at the time displayed her proper colours indicating the nation to which she belonged, and no sufficient cause having existed for suspecting such colours to be false, and the said lieutenant, E E Gray, not possessing the necessary French warrant to authorise his searching and detaining French vessels. For neglect of duty in not stopping the search, and ordering the searching parties to return immediately to the *Bonetta* on ascertaining the vessel to be really a French ship. For neglect of duty as commanding office by his permitting a case of wine and other articles to be received in the *Bonetta* from the Frenchman without ascertaining that due payment had been made for the same, and for not punishing a man belonging to the *Bonetta* who had been detected while taking away cigars from the French vessel.

Perhaps the court's members had long memories also. Stopping a 'Frenchie' and helping oneself to cigars and wine was not, maybe, too great a crime considering all that had gone before. At all events, Gray got away with a severe reprimand only and was 'admonished to be more careful in giving his orders in future'. Whether or not this was a hint to be more careful in disposing of the swag next time he stopped a Frenchman on the high seas is not clear; one can, however, imagine that such thoughts may have been in the minds of some of the more senior of his judges who had spent their whole lives and careers combating the French.

* * *

Nothing much can stop a court martial once it is under way, but science is capable of anything. It is on record that one trial being held aboard HMS *Gladiator* in Portsmouth harbour was brought to an undignified halt one day in 1815. What caused this unofficial adjournment was the appearance of one of the first seagoing steamships (possible the *Margery*, built in Glasgow by Archibald MacLachlan in 1814 and transferred to Cortis of London soon afterward). On her way south she called in at Portsmouth and such was the amazement provoked by this unique harbinger of their future that the sitting officers left their seats and their posts to join in the general rush to view this apparition at first hand.

❋ ❋ ❋

Perhaps the loss of the HM sloop *Bulldog* in 1865 might be included in the section under 'Action', possible under 'Wreck', but, as she fits either category, I have included her passing, and the subsequent court martial verdict on her commanding officer, here. For it is a fact that she was not engaged in actual war, but was wrecked, and yet only wrecked as a result of active combat.

This strange affair took place in the West Indies, during the year 1865, when HMS *Bulldog*, a wooden paddle sloop of 1,124 tons' displacement and a length of 190 feet and beam of 36 feet, armed with six small guns, was under the command of Captain Charles Wake. This little vessel had been built at Chatham dockyard, being launched in October 1845, and was serving on the American and West Indies station as a peace-keeping gunboat.

At the time the island republic of Haiti was ruled by President Fabre Geffard, but, as usual, a civil war was raging, with the forces of Sylvestre Salnave endeavouring to overthrow Geffrard and assume power. On 22 October, one of the rebel warships, the *Valdrogue*, attacked a British steamer carrying mail from Jamaica. Captain Wake in the *Bulldog* soon appeared on the scene and warned the rebel vessel that she would be sunk unless she desisted. This was a sufficient enough threat to stop the outrage and the rebel ship slunk back into Cape Haytien. Her commanding officer reported back to Salnave, who, in a rage at having his will thwarted, ordered that fugitives from his rebellion, then taking shelter in the house of the English Consul Mr Dutton, to be seized forthwith. The neutral consulate was attacked, the refugees ran away to the beach and were there massacred wholesale. The consulate was wrecked and the British flag defiled.

Dutton escaped and went aboard the *Bulldog* to relate what had taken place. Wake's response was immediate: he asked Salnave what was the meaning of these further outrages, to which an impertinent answer was received. Wake wrote a letter in reply, demanding full and complete satisfaction within twenty-four hours, but Salnave disdained from replying to this missive.

The following morning, with three loyal steamers following astern, the *Bulldog* appeared off the harbour entrance and, at 0845hrs, commenced shelling Fort Picolet, the fort replying five minutes later against her puny opponent flying the White Ensign. However, if *Bulldog* was small, she was as tenacious as her namesake, and the British ship's fire was very effective. As the sloop steamed closer in to engage better, she came into view of the *Valdrogue* and Wake determined to ram her. Unfortunately, the British ship was in waters strange to her captain, while the young navigation officer, Edwin Behenna, was also new to the area. As a result, the *Bulldog* ran aground before she could ram her opponent and was left in an unenviable position, hard and fast ashore under the guns of the fort, the *Valdrogue* and other ships of Salnave's fleet.

Wake's command still fought back fiercely, so well in fact that within a short time she had sunk the *Valdrogue* with well-aimed shots into her hull at 0945hrs, and dispatched a further enemy vessel at 1010hrs, as well as blowing up the fort's powder magazine, which set the town on fire; she also dispersed, with grape and canister shot, the numerous marksmen who had lined the beach to fire into her.

The United States warship *De Soto* was present in the harbour at the time, but took no part in the action of course. Nor did she tow the *Bulldog* clear despite a request to do so. The *De Soto*'s commanding officer, Lieutenant Sumner, did offer to take off the wounded, but this was declined by Wake as he considered conditions to be too dangerous for the attempt to succeed. In the end the *Bulldog*'s crew were finally taken off in the ship's boats and taken to the Geffradis steamer *Vingt-deux Decembre*, while the gallant *Bulldog* herself was blown up to prevent her falling into rebel hands. From the crew of 175 officers and men, the sloop had lost three men killed and ten wounded in her stirring little action.

On their eventual return home, both Wake and Behenna faced court martial at Devonport. The findings of the court were that both men were to blame for running the *Bulldog* on to the reef and also that the ship had been abandoned and blown up prematurely. Captain Wake was severely reprimanded and Behenna reprimanded. Captain Wake protested to the Admiralty that this verdict was unduly harsh, and received the reply from Their Lordships that they 'did not consider that any imputation was cast upon his honour or his courage'.

The British press and public thought otherwise, and a great hue and cry was raised that one who had so honourably defended the slighting of his nation's flag should be so basely treated. *Punch* magazine summed up the whole furore with a typically patriotic verse thus:

> Then here's three cheers for Captain Wake, and, while we sail the sea,
> May British Bulldogs always find Captains as stout as he,
> That's all for biting when they bite, and none for bark and brag,
> And thinks less about court-martials than the honour of the flag.

Sentiments with which any patriots left might still agree. It evidently influenced Their Lordships a little for the gallant Wake was soon employed at sea once more.

❋ ❋ ❋

With the introduction of the Right of Appeal against a court martial sentence in the aftermath of the Second World War, a new precedent was introduced into the equation. One of the first cases to be heard under the new procedure was that of a popular submarine hero, Alastair Mars. Already a household name from his accounts of his daring exploits in command of HMS *Unbroken* in the Mediterranean during the darkest days of 1942, Mars' original court martial and subsequent dismissal from the service had made headline news in 1952. The charges were that he had, on 28 April 1952, been guilty of an act to the prejudice of good order and naval discipline in wilfully disobeying the lawful command of the lords of the Admiralty, contained in a document issued by the said lords appointing him to HM Ship *Phoenix*. Secondary charges brought against Mars concerned a similar refusal with regard to HMS *Victory*.

The charge of wilful disobedience for turning down an appointment was a new one and Mars rested his argument on the point that an appointment was not an order (or a lawful command) and that, under the Naval Discipline Act, orders as such must be issued by two or more of the commissioners of the Admiralty, which, he maintained, had not been done, but merely issued by a civil servant. The personal reasons behind his taking this stand, which brought him to trial, were varied and complicated. Mars listed them fully and at length in his subsequent book, *Court-Martial*. In retrospect, much of what Mars claimed at that time seems only just and fair. Behind them, though, was the fact that Mars was a fighting man, stifled by the blandness and red tape of the post-war navy. Today, if any consolation might be found after all the years that have passed, many of the undoubted wrongs he and others suffered at the hands of an uncaring Admiralty have been addressed. However, they were a long time in being rectified and the Admiralty of the day acted as stuffily and inflexibly towards his legitimate complaints regarding conditions ashore and afloat, as ever. The subjection of the once proud and independent Royal Navy to the will and usage of the US navy, part of his grievance, has, unfortunately, only increased at an ever-greater pace since that time, and with it the appalling run-down of the fleet appears irreversible.

Be that as it may, the court martial itself, held aboard HMS *Victory* on 24 June, had passed sentence and Mars now determined to try the appeal. This was heard by Lord Chief Justice Goddard, sitting with Mr Justice Hilbery and Mr Justice Havers, on 14 November 1952, at the law courts in the Strand. In the end, Mars had his appeal dismissed. The court held that a letter, although only signed by a civil servant at the Admiralty and not by one or two lord commissioners, was still an order and had to be obeyed. This verdict, Mars protested, appeared to reverse the age-old custom whereby an officer could decline an appointment, if he so wished, without prejudicing his career. He felt that yet another of the old traditions unique to the service had been wiped out.

8 HUMOUR IN COURT

Courts martial would be thought barren ground in which to find humorous anecdotes, after all whole careers and reputations are at stake and the subject matter could hardly be more severe. However, the irrepressible nature of the British matelot can shine through this dour test! Also, inadvertent and retrospective drollness can also be found by the modern reader sifting through some of the weightier pronouncements of our stern ancestors, although the recipients at the time would doubtless have failed to see the funny side. The memoirs of bygone officers can also provide a rich seam of humour, some of which concerned the court martial procedures. From all such sources, therefore, a small but representative selection is included here to bring our review of courts martial to a lighter conclusion.

❋ ❋ ❋

The expression 'Tell *that* to the Marines!' covers a multitude of sins, but certainly that gallant corps features in many tall stories, and some not so disingenuous. Admiral Sir William Kennedy related the following anecdote, and the period is, once more, the late eighteenth century.

It was a hot, sticky day in Hong Kong. A marine was on trial for an act of insubordination, and the opening ceremonies were being conducted. This part of the proceedings was merely a formal routine and nothing untoward was therefore expected. The officers forming the court had stood up in full dress to be sworn in and the Judge Advocate then asked the accused in the usual manner whether he objected to any member of the court. Rarely is an objection made, especially in the case of the lower ranks, but this particular marine had a mind of his own.

'Yes,' he replied at once, 'I object to th' 'ole blooming lot of yer, especially the bald-headed old beggar at the 'ed of the table!'

❋ ❋ ❋

As an author, I can especially appreciate the following true tale.

After being the subject of a court martial, from which he emerged blameless, having been acquitted with honour, Admiral Roddam was eager to ensure that his vindication received the widest publicity. The admiral therefore arranged with a publisher for the complete minutes of the trial to be printed and bound. He gave detailed instructions for the wide distribution of free copies to every member of the court that had tried him, to numerous fellow officers and to other friends. The remainder were then to be sold to the general public.

When, some considerable time later, Roddam met with his publisher, he, like all authors, was anxious to know how well his book was faring. He asked how many had been disposed of so far. When the publisher replied, the admiral was somewhat taken aback. 'Why,' he said, 'that is the number I asked you to give away in my name; how many have you actually sold?'

'Not one,' replied his publisher, no doubt used to such a reaction from authors, 'although I advertised in all the papers'.

'That is strange,' retorted the vexed Roddam, with the wind well and truly taken out of his sails, 'for Admiral Byng's trial went through two or three editions in a week'.

The publisher's reply brought the admiral firmly back to earth. 'That is a different case, Sir. If you had been condemned to be shot, your trial would have sold as well, but people take no interest in an honourable acquittal!'

Looking at today's tabloid press and news reporting, one can see that nothing at all has changed in the intervening decades!

Captain Christopher Craddock told a yarn concerning a trial that took place in the Mediterranean, also in Victoria's day, which, he maintained, should serve as a good example of the uselessness of 'an expression of opinion' being asked for. The prisoner was a post-captain and the witness concerned, another captain, was asked the following question: 'If you had been Captain so-and-so, would you have done the same?' The reply, which was immediate, was hardly enlightening: 'If I had been Captain so-and-so, which I am not; and if Captain so-and-so had been myself, which he is not; – it is within the bounds of possibility that I might have done what Captain so-and-so did *not* do.'

Wigs formed part of the ceremonial gear of all major legal proceedings, adding a further dignity and awesomeness to the judiciary, but, from time to time, they caused more consternation than usual. Two examples of this may be cited.

A court martial was being held aboard the battleship *Hibernia* at Malta, for the trial of a gunner who had recently been discharged from hospital, practically cured, from a long bout of over-indulgence of hard liquor. Now the *Hibernia*, in her day, had been a fine first-rate battleship, but that day was long departed for she had been launched in 1804 and was well into her dotage, having served as a depot ship at Malta for many a long year. Subsequently, her old timber hull admitted all manner of drafts and cold winds and was, to say the least, uncomfortable.

Despite the inconvenience, the trial was proceeding according to custom. Both the prosecution and the defence's evidence had been absorbed, the findings decided upon and the court cleared for sentence to be deliberated upon. When the proceedings re-opened the prisoner was ushered back in, but, to the amazement of the assembled members, hardly had he put a foot over the threshold, as it were, before the man gave forth a wild shriek of fear and threw himself face down on the deck. He remained in that position, all the time pleading in piteous tones for mercy.

The charge had not been that serious – what on earth had brought about this startling display? Suspicion was harboured that the accused's 'problem' might somehow have reasserted itself. Everyone looked toward the President for his reaction, and the reason for the prisoner's emotional display and abject fear immediately became apparent.

The President was a distinguished enough gentleman, but somewhat advanced in years and no longer blessed with the abundance of hair of his youth. In private life he covered his bald pate with a black skullcap. During the long deliberations, with the icy wind playing on his exposed top-mantle, he had therefore replaced this head covering to protect himself from the elements. Inadvertently, the President had forgotten to remove the cap on the court's re-assembly and neither had he replaced his cocked hat, which had hidden the black cap during earlier proceedings.

It was well known that, in pronouncing the death sentence, judges in the civil court adopted this mode of headgear and thus, when the poor gunner, already nervous enough and with the after-effects of his 'drying out' still vividly affecting his demeanour, stepped through the door to face his fate and saw this fearsome vision all his worst fears appeared to have been realised and he fully expected to be hanged.

In 1971, a court martial was under way at the Royal Naval Barracks, Portsmouth, under the presidency of Captain Lancelot Bell-Davies. The trial had gone into its third day and concerned the submarine *Artemis*. All was proceeding according to the book and Lieutenant Commander Brian Rutherford, the defending officer, was commencing his summing up, when he was interrupted by the President. 'Is it not necessary to swear in a new shorthand writer?' the President asked.

'Er, no Sir,' was the reply from the grinning Judge Advocate, 'she's already sworn in'.

The President quickly sized up the situation and, amid laughter around the courtroom, hastily rejoined, 'Oh, I see, carry on'.

It transpired that the shorthand writer, Mrs Christine Stokes, had a collection of assorted shades of wigs for various social occasions, she being at that time the holder of the title 'Miss Solent Secretary'. She had attended court on the previous day without wearing a wig, as a brunette, but had turned into a blonde on day three. She later told the assembled press corps that she was more embarrassed for the captain than anything else. 'I have several wigs and tend to forget when I'm wearing them.'

That the Church and strong liquor were not always incompatible aboard some ships of HM navy was early recognised. Nor were the representatives of the Lord always pillars of virtue in other ways once afloat. This was revealed during the court martial of the chaplain of the *Constant Warwick* in 1656. The chaplain concerned was tried on a charge of drunkenness of 16 November of that year and was found guilty. However, it was the coxswain of the skiff that brought this reprobate aboard after his bender ashore that eloquently described the accused's condition at the time.

The coxswain stated that the chaplain, one Robert Leonard, 'was so drunk they could not get him on board but were fain to hoist him in with the tackles!'

More tolerance was shown to a ship's purser, brought to court martial at the end of the eighteenth century for selling his fellow officers drink under the pseudonym of 'oil'. How 'well oiled' these officers subsequently became is not revealed, but the court took a broad view. The purser was acquitted with only a mild reprimand, on the grounds that 'he only wished to show kindness to his messmates'.

Other examples of what might be termed 'unconscious humour' abound in old documents. For example, a government return, issued on 8 October 1908, stated that during the previous year, 105 courts martial were held on men of the Royal Marines, and that one 1,426 cases of minor punishments occurred, of which 275 were for drunkenness, 'an improvement on last year!'

From the pages of *The Naval Chronicle*, the following strange tale emerged.

On 17 October 1807, a court martial was held aboard the *Salvador del Mundo*, in Hamoaze, on Lieutenant Thomas Beckford Hornbrook of the Royal Marines and Mr William Hamilton, surgeon, both of HMS *l'Aigle*. The charge was that the former pulled the nose of the latter, and the surgeon used 'aggravating means' to induce Lieutenant Hornbrook to do so.

The court, having duly weighed and considered the said charge, sentenced Lieutenant Hornbrook to be severely reprimanded and placed at the bottom of the list of first lieutenants of 1804, and Surgeon Hamilton to be dismissed his situation as surgeon of HM ship *l'Aigle*. After sentence, the President, Sir J.T. Duckworth, 'admonished the prisoners in an able and very appropriate speech'.

Finally, Admiral Sir Charles Dundas related an episode, which reflected to some credit on the tact of a witness when questioned about an officer. It also gave a considerable insight into the lower deck's general opinion of their leaders. The officer concerned was on trial charged with drunkenness. The defence called as a witness his personal servant, a Royal Marine, who was then questioned.

'Was the accused sober?'

'No, Sir.'

'Was the accused drunk?'

'No, Sir.'

'Then what state was the prisoner in if he was neither drunk nor sober?'

There was a moment's silence, then came the reply: 'He was in the state that officers usually are in after dinner, Sir.'

Appendix

The Outline of Justice in the Royal Navy Today

HISTORICAL BACKGROUND

The conduct of English soldiers was for many centuries regulated by the Court of the High Constable and Earl Marshal. From 1521 onwards, it was the 'Court of the Marshal', and after the standing army had been brought into being in Cromwellian times the office of Judge Advocate General was created in 1666 to supervise 'Courts-martial'.

It has been held in continuous succession ever since, being expanded to cover Great Britain and later the United Kingdom, the Royal Air Force, the Royal Navy, and all British land, air and naval forces overseas. Historically the responsibilities of the Judge Advocate General (JAG) were very wide and included oversight of both prosecution and defence arrangements as well as the court.

Since 1948, the role has concerned the court martial process. From 1661 the office of Judge Advocate of the Fleet (JAF) existed to supervise the Royal Navy court martial system separately from the JAG. The two historic offices were amalgamated by the Armed Forces Act 2006, with the role of JAF subsumed into JAG. The Armed Forces Act 2006 repealed the three Service Discipline Acts of 1955/57, established a single system of Service law, and created the Court Martial as a standing court. It came into effect on 31 October 2009.

APPOINTMENT OF JUDGE ADVOCATE GENERAL

The Judge Advocate General is appointed by Her Majesty the Queen by means of Letters Patent, on the recommendation of the Lord Chancellor. He is a Law Officer of the Crown and an independent member of the judiciary and is always a civilian, although he may have served in the armed forces. The JAG is not a General of the Army; the word 'general' signifies broad oversight, as in Secretary-General, Attorney-General, etc. The current JAG (from November 2004) is His Honour Judge Jeff Blackett, who is also a circuit judge and who formerly served in the Royal Navy.

JUDICIARY

The JAG has a team of full-time judges comprising the Vice-Judge Advocate General (Judge Michael Hunter) and seven Assistant Judge Advocates General, and can also call upon the services of up to ten Deputy (part-time) Judge Advocates.

All the judges are civilians, appointed from the ranks of experienced barristers or solicitors in the same way as other District and Circuit Judges. When conducting a particular trial they are formally titled 'The Judge Advocate' and out of court they are generally referred to and addressed as 'Judge'. In court the judges wear legal costume, comprising a bench wig and black gown, with a tippet (sash) in army red with navy blue and air-force blue edges.

The JAG and many Judge Advocates also sit in the Crown Court. It is also possible for a High Court Judge to be specified to preside in the court martial as a Judge Advocate; this is done for exceptionally serious or unprecedented cases, just as in the Crown Court.

ADMINISTRATIVE OFFICES

The administrative staff in the Office of the JAG (OJAG) are civil servants, who are part of the Royal Courts of Justice Group of Her Majesty's Courts Service and thereby form part of the Ministry of Justice. The office is situated in the Thomas More Building, Royal Courts of Justice, Strand, London WC2A 2LL. OJAG staff support the judges in the exercise of their judicial functions.

The Military Court Service (MCS) is part of the Ministry of Defence, and maintains four main Military Court Centres at Colchester (Essex), Bulford (Wiltshire), Catterick (Yorkshire) and Sennelager (Germany), plus further centres at Aldergrove (Northern Ireland), Portsmouth (Hampshire), and Episkopi (Cyprus). MCS arranges, funds and supports trials at these centres and at other *ad hoc* venues in UK and overseas. Communications about particular cases must be addressed in the first instance to the Court Administration Officer at the MCS Headquarters in Upavon, Wiltshire.

SERVICES CRIMINAL JUSTICE SYSTEM

The main elements of the criminal justice system are:

A. The Court Martial

Serious matters, including both offences against the civilian criminal law and specifically military disciplinary offences, may be tried in the court martial, which is a standing court. A Judge Advocate arraigns each defendant and conducts the trial which is broadly similar to a civilian Crown Court trial in all cases, even when dealing with a minor disciplinary or criminal offence.

The jury, known as the board, comprises between three and seven commissioned officers or warrant officers depending on the seriousness of the case. Having listened to the Judge Advocate's directions on the law and summary of the evidence, they are responsible for finding defendants guilty or not guilty.

Following a finding or plea of guilty, the board joins the Judge Advocate to decide on sentence. The court martial has the same sentencing powers in relation to imprisonment as a Crown Court, including life imprisonment. Most of the sentencing powers in the Criminal Justice Act 2003 are also available in the court martial.

B. Summary Hearings by a Commanding Officer

Minor disciplinary and criminal matters are deal with summarily by the Commanding Officer of the accused. The great majority of matters are disposed of in this way, which forms one of the foundations of the disciplinary system of the armed forces. A Commanding Officer has powers of punishment up to twenty-eight days' detention, which may be extended to ninety days' detention with approval from Higher Authority. In all cases an accused person may elect for trial in the court martial rather than appear before their Commanding Officer, or may appeal to the Summary Appeal Court after the event.

C. Summary Appeal Court

The accused, if dissatisfied with the outcome of a summary hearing, always has the right of appeal to the Summary Appeal Court, which is conducted by a Judge Advocate accompanied by two officers. This is modelled on an appeal from a magistrates' court to the Crown Court.

D. Court Martial Appeal Court

The avenue of appeal for a convicted defendant, subject to obtaining permission to appeal, is to the Court Martial Appeal Court (as the Court of Appeal Criminal Division is named when dealing with Service cases), and ultimately to the Supreme Court.

E. Service Civilian Court

Civilians who are officials attached to the Services overseas, or dependants of Service personnel resident overseas (for example in Germany or Cyprus) may be tried for minor offences by the Service Civilian Court (which consists of a Judge Advocate sitting alone) or, for more serious matters, may be tried in the court martial. This is then usually constituted with an all-civilian board acting as a jury; in such cases the Judge Advocate sentences alone.

F. Custody, Search Warrants and Arrest Warrants

If a serviceman or woman is to be detained in custody, or if private premises need to be searched in the course of investigations, or if a person needs to be arrested, the authority of a Judge Advocate is required. The JAG or one of the judges must be satisfied that the continued detention, or the search or arrest, is legally justified. Such cases are often heard by video link and a judge is on duty every day of the year to rule upon urgent applications if required.

Functions of the Judge Advocate General

The duties of the JAG include the following:

To act as the Presiding Judge in the Services criminal jurisdiction and leader of its judges, thereby supervising the jurisdiction

To provide guidance to all stakeholders in the Services criminal justice system on practices and procedures, developments and reforms

To monitor the workings of the Services criminal justice system and to advise on its efficiency and effectiveness

To be a member of the Services Justice Board

To specify judges to conduct specific court martial trials in UK or abroad

To provide judges to conduct Summary Appeal Courts and Standing Civilian Courts, and to rule upon applications for detention in custody and for search and arrest warrants

To act as the trial judge personally conducting some of the most serious, sensitive or controversial trials in the court martial (such as for murder)

To refer to the Court Martial Appeal Court cases involving a point of law of exceptional importance

To keep the record of proceedings for not less than six years after trial in all cases

LIST OF SELECTED STATUTES

Air Force Act 1955
Armed Forces Acts 1976, 1986, 1991, 1996, 2001, 2006
Army Act 1955
Courts and Legal Services Act 1990
Courts-Martial Appeal Act 1951
Courts-Martial (Appeals) Act 1968
Criminal Justice Act 2003
Human Rights Act 1998
International Criminal Courts Act 2001
Naval Discipline Act 1957
Police and Criminal Evidence Act 1984
Reserve Forces Act 1996

CONTACTS

The Office of the Judge Advocate General
9th Floor
Thomas More Building
London WC2A 2LL

All communications by parties and their representatives about current cases are to be addressed in the first instance to:

The Military Court Service
Building 398
Trenchard Lines
Upavon
Pewsey
Wiltshire SN9 6BE

Bibliography

PUBLISHED SOURCES

Admiralty, *Admiralty Memorandum on Naval Court Martial Procedure*. N.L. 1176. London, 1927.

Anon, *Admiral Mathew's Charge against Vice-Admiral Lestock Dissected and Confuted*. London, 1745.

Anon, *Army & Navy Gazette*. London, 1865.

Anon, *Captain Opie's Appeal against the Illegal Proceedings of Vice-Admiral Mathews*. London, 1745.

Anon, *Considerations on the Principles of Naval Discipline and Naval Courts Martial*. Second Edition. London, 1781.

Anon, *Letters and Papers Between Admiral Mathes and Vice-Admiral Lestock*. London, 1744.

Anon, *Officers of the Royal Navy Tried by Court Martial (1880)*. London, 1880.

Anon, *The Tryal of Admiral Byng*. London, 1857.

Anon, *Vice-Admiral Lestock's Recapitulation at the Bar of the House of Commons*. London, 1745.

Anon, *Vice-Admiral Lestock's Account of the Late Engagement near Toulon*. London, 1745.

Atlay, J.B., *The Trial of Lord Cochrane before Lord Ellenborough*. London, 1897.

Barnes, G.R. and Owen, J.H., *The Private Papers of John, Earl of Sandwich, 1771–1782*. London, 1932.

Ballard, Admiral G.A., *The Black Battlefleet*. Lymington, 1980.

Benson, E.F., *Sir Francis Drake*. London, 1927.

Bullocke, J.G., *Sailors' Rebellion: A century of Naval Mutinies*. London, 1938.

Burke, P., *Celebrated Naval and Military Trials*. London, 1876.

Clowes, Sir William Laird, *The Royal Navy – A history*. London, 1903.

Craddock, C., *Whispers from the Fleet*. London, 1907.

Danielsson, Bengt, *What Happened on the* Bounty. London, 1962.

Delafons, John, *Treatise on Naval Courts Martial*. London, 1805.

Douglas, A.D., *The Life of Admiral Sir A Douglas*. London, 1938.

Draper, Alfred, *Smoke without Fire*. London, 1974.

Duckworth, Captain A.D. and Fisher, Commander R.R.S., *An Introduction to Naval Court Martial Procedure*. Devonport, 1955.

Dwyer, D.J., *History of R.N. Barracks Portsmouth*. Portsmouth, 1961.

Ehrman, J., *The Navy in the War of William III*. London, 1953.

Fremantle, Admiral Sir Sydney R., *My Naval Career 1880–1928*. London, 1947.

Gardiner, Leslie. *The Royal Oak Courts Martial*. Edinburgh, 1965.

Gill, C., *The Naval Mutinies of 1797*. London, 1924.

Gurney, W.B., *Minutes of a Court Martial on the Trial of James Lord Gambier*. London, 1809.

Hannay, David, *Naval Courts Martial*. Cambridge, 1914.

Harrison-Smith, F., *Office work in the Navy*. Portsmouth, 1912.

Hayward, R., *The Story and Scandal of H.M.S. Megaera*. Ashbourne, 1978.

Hough, Richard, *Admirals in Collision*. London, 1959.

Johnson, Brigadier R.F., *The Royal George*. London, 1961.

Lewis, Michael, *Spithead; an informal history*. London, 1972.

Lumby, E.W.R., *Policy and Operations in the Mediterranean 1912–14*. London, 1970.

McArthur, John, *Principles and Practice of Naval and Military Courts Martial*. Volumes 1 and 2. London, 1805.

Marsden/Naval Records Society, *Documents Relating to the Law and Custom of the Sea*. Volume 1 1205–1648. London, 1916.

Manwaring, G.E. and Dobree, Bonamy, *The Floating Republic*. London, 1935.

Mars, Alastair, DSO, DSC and Bar, *Court Martial*. London, 1954.

Montague, E., *Celebrated Trials – The Court Martial of Captain John Montray*. London, 1969.

Oppenheim, M., *A History of the Administration of the Royal Navy 1509–1660*. Cambridge, 1896.

Parkes, Dr Oscar, *British Battleships*. London, 1966.

Pope, Dudley, *The Black Ship*. London, 1963.

Pope, Dudley, *Life in Nelson's Navy*. London, 1981.

Senior, W., *Naval History in the Law Courts: A Selection of Old Maritime Cases*. Portsmouth, 1927.

Smith, Peter C. *Petlyakov Pe-2*. Crowood Press, 2003.

Smith, Peter C. *Dive Bombers in Action*. Blandford, 1985.

Smith, Peter C. *Per Mare, Per Terram*. Balfour, 1975.

Smith, Peter C., *The Battle-Cruiser H.M.S. Renown, 1916–1948*. Barnsley, 2008.

Smith Peter C., *Pedestal; the convoy that saved Malta*. Crécy, 2008.

Taffrail, 'The Hanging of John Dalliger', in *The Naval Review*. London, 1946.
Taylor, Gordon, *The Sea Chaplains*. London, 1963.
Tunstall, Brian, *Admiral Byng and the Loss of Minorca*. London, 1928.
Warren, C.E.T. and Benson, James, *Will not we Fear*. London, 1961.
Yexley, Lionel, *Our Fighting Seamen*. London, 1911.

RECOMMENDED FOR FURTHER STUDY

Courts martial registers held at the National Archives, Kew, London:

Chatham Division 1902–05	ADM 194/1
Portsmouth Division 1834–1916	ADM 194/2–17
Portsmouth Division – Royal Marines detachment in HM ships 1836–39 and 1859–74	ADM 194/18–19
Plymouth Division 1854–98	ADM 194/21–32
Plymouth Division: District Courts Martial 1898–1902	ADM 194/33
Plymouth Division: District and Regimental Courts Martial 1902–14	ADM 194/34–38
Royal Marine China Battalion: Chatham, Woolwich and 1st Battalion 1857–60	ADM 194/39
Royal Marine Japan Battalion 1864–65	ADM 194/41
Royal Navy Officers and Ratings 1812–55	ADM 194/42
Royal Navy Officers 1857–1915	ADM 194/43–45

The Naval Chronicle was produced in forty volumes covering the years 1799 to 1819. Some typical courts martial material includes:

1799	Courts martial sentence
1800	Courts martial – (the 'Cup of Tea' incident)
1800	Execution, grim scenes at
1800	Matters of leniency
1801	Courts martial sentence of a pilot
1802	Courts martial of a gunner
1802	Embezzlement – the pillory
1810	Severe courts martial sentencing of a midshipman, etc., etc.

Knight, Dr R.J.B., *Guide to the Manuscripts in the National Maritime Museum, Greenwich*. Volume One: Personal Collections. London, 1972.
Nastyface, Jack, *Nautical Economy*. London, 1836.
Directory of National Biography, Part One to 1900. J.K. Laughton wrote some 900 naval biographies.

Index

A-1, HMS 200
A-3, HMS 200
A-4, HMS 200
A-7, HMS 200
Achille, French ship 114
Actaeon, HMS 223
Actif, French ship 70
Actionnaire, French ship 70
Active, HMS 111
Acton, Albert 139,142–3
Adventure, HMS 42
Agamemnon, HMS 113, 115–6
Agincourt, HMS 208
Agreable, French ship 43
Aigle, French ship 114
Aigle, HMS 122
Ajax, HMS 113, 115
Albermarle, American ship 131
Albion, HMS 213
Alcide, HMS 177
Alexander, First Lord Albert
     Victor 171
Alexander, HMS 105
Alexandre, French ship 70
Alfred, HMS 184
Algesiras, French ship 114
Allemande, Admiral Zacharie
     121–8
Allen, Captain John 81
Ambrose, Captain John 54
America, HMS 70
America, Spanish ship 114
Amphion, French ship 70
Anderson, Captain James 236
Andrews, Captain Thomas 60, 63

Ann, Galley fire ship 45
Anne, Queen 233
Anson, Admiral of the Fleet,
     Lord 58, 66, 111
Antelope, HMS 62
Antoinette, Marie 105
Apollon, French ship 43
Aquilon, French ship 121–2
Arbuthnot, Rear Admiral
     Mariot 74
Archer, HMS 196
Archer-Shee, Cadet George 224
Ardent, HMS 217
Argonauta, Spanish ship 114–5
Armstrong, Captain Thomas
     151, 166
Artemis, HMS 182, 250
Artesien, French ship 70
Ashby, Captain Sir John 37
Ashton, Master Juanne 222
Asia, HMS 213
Assistance, HMS 187
Assurance, HMS 95
Astley-Rushton, Vice Admiral
     Edward 203
Astraea, HMS 233
Atlas, Spanish ship 114–5
Attwood, Sergeant-Major,
     Royal Marines 160
Audacious, HMS 105
Ayers, Lieutenant Surgeon
     Dominic 227–8
Aynon, Shipwright George 78,
     82–3

B-2, HMS 200
Babbington, Anthony 33
Bailey, Rear Admiral Sidney
     202–6
Baird, Captain Sir David 64
Baird, General Sir David 209
Ball, Captain Alexander 105, 127
Ballard, Admiral G.A. 190, 195
Banks, Sir Joseph 86
Barfleur, HMS 113, 115–6, 233
Barham, Admiral Lord 112,
     117–9
Barham, HMS 157
Barnacle, Bandmaster Percy
     158–62
Barnes, Sidney J. 171
Barrington, Vice Admiral
     Samuel 81, 243
Barrow, Sir John 85
Barry, Captain H.D. 138
Bart, Jean, French Admiral 43
Bathurst, Commodore Walter
     212–3
Battenberg, Admiral Prince
     Louis 138
Battleaxe, HMS 207
Beagle, HMS 122–3, 151, 237
Beaver, Lieutenant Philip 233
Beaverbrook, Lord 21
Beet, Lieutenant Trevor 216
Behenna, Lieutenant Edwin 246
Belcher, Captain Sir Edward
     186–7
Bell-Davis, Admiral Sir Lancelot
     250

Belle Poule, HMS 85
Bellingham John 228–9
Bellona, HMS 120
Benbow, frigate 42
Benbow, Vice Admiral Sir John 27, 41–52
Benives, William (aka William Murray) 184
Bentley, Captain Sir John 62
Beresford, Admiral Sir Charles 120, 127, 242
Beresford, General William 209
Berkeley, Admiral Archibald 43
Berthia, HMS 86
Berwick, French prize 114
Berwick, HMS 70
Bettesworth, William St Julien Arabin, Judge Advocate 82
Bien-Aime, French ship 70
Bienfaisant, HMS 70
Biggs, George 243
Bignal, Gunner James 178
Bishop of Salisbury 40
Black Prince, HMS 146
Blacknose, HMS 231
Blackstone, William 221
Blake, Captain Benjamin 11
Blake, Generall-at-Sea Robert 11
Blakeney, General William 63
Blanche, HMS 132
Blenheim, HMS 95
Bligh, Captain William 85, 98–137, 184, 236
Bligh, Lieutenant Robert 214, 243
Bligh, Rear Admiral Richmond Rodney 185
Bonaventure, HMS 42
Bonaparte, Napoleon 113, 116, 128, 209
Bonetta, HMS 244
Booth, Captain William 42, 94
Boreas, HMS 237
Borough, Captain William 33–5
Borrow, Sir John 85
Boscawen, Admiral the Hon. Edward 66, 111
Boteler, Captain Philip 164, 217–8
Bounty, HMS 85, 94, 98, 212
Bourke, Captain Maurice Archibald 133–5
Bowen, Captain Richard 184
Boyd, Rear Admiral W.H.D. 162–3

Boyles, Captain C. 113
Boyne, HMS 55
Brazen, HMS 229–30
Breda, HMS 43–7, 49–50
Brereton, Captain William 72, 210
Breslau, German light cruiser 146–7
Bretagne, French ship 70
Bridgeman, Captain Francis C.B. 137
Brill, Dutch ship 213–4
Brilliant, HMS 225–6
Bristol, HMS 50
Bristol, Lord 68
Brittannia, HMS 42, 74, 77, 137, 156–7
Broderick, Admiral Thomas 62, 94
Brothwell, Lieutenant Sarah 229–30
Brown, Captain W. 113, 115, 118
Brown, John 184
Brown, Lieutenant Neil 232
Browne, Arnold 47–8
Bruix, Admiral Eustace 106, 110
Brunswick, HMS 93, 184
Buceutaure, Spanish ship 114
Buckingham, HMS 59–60, 63
Buckle, Admiral Mathew 74
Buckner, Vice Admiral Charles 97–9, 101
Buffalo, HMS 112
Bulldog, HMS 95, 151, 245–6
Buller, Captain E. 114
Bullocke, J.G. 42, 85
Bulwark, HMS 151, 185
Burghley, Lord 32, 35
Burgoyne, Captain Hugh 187, 189–90
Burkitt, Thomas 90–1, 93
Burlton, Captain Sir George 127
Burney, Rear Admiral James 151
Burrish, Captain George 54
Byng, Admiral George 27, 36, 55
Byng, Rear Admiral John 55, 57–67, 110, 119, 144, 154, 170, 249
Byrne, Seaman Michael 90–1, 93
Byron, Admiral the Hon. John 111

C-11, HMS 200
Caesar, HMS 120, 122
Calcutta, French ship 121–2
Calcuttta, HMS 157
Calder, Admiral Sir Robert 111–20, 154
Caledonia, HMS 120, 123–4, 127, 210
Calton, Mr Paul 42
Calvert, Captain T.F.P. 162
Cambridge, HMS 86
Campbell, Admiral Gordon 123
Campbell, Duncan 86, 123
Camperdown, HMS 132, 136, 195
Cape Town, HMS 157
Captain, HMS 60, 77, 112, 187–91, 196
Caracciolo, Commodore Prince 104, 108–11
Card, Lieutenant W.J.R. 220
Cardiff, HMS 230
Carnatic, HMS 184
Carslaw, Naval Airman David 191–82
Casey, Midshipman David 184
Cassard, French ship 122, 126
Castor, Dutch ship 213–4
Centaur, HMS 70, 214–5
Challenger, HMS 237
Chapman, Captain Eulala 11
Charles I, King 10
Charles II, King 14, 36, 56
Chatham, HMS 146
Cherry, Captain George 156
Chesapeake, HMS 222
Chesterfield, HMS 64, 111
Chichester, HMS 54, 232
Christian, Fletcher 86–7, 89–90
Churchill, Charles 89–90, 92–3
Churchill, Winston S 76, 147, 154–5, 162, 179, 218
Cinque Ports 10
Clarke, William 237
Cleveland, HMS 121
Cnut, King 9
Cobbald, Captain Richard 225
Cobra, HMS 199–200
Cochrane, Admiral Thomas 121, 210, 223
Codrington, Admiral Sir Edward 212
Cole, Boatswain William 91–2
Coleman, Seaman Joseph 90–1
Coles, Captain Cooper 187–9
Collard, Admiral Bernard St George 137–44, 155–64

Collingwood, Vice Admiral
Cuthbert, Lord 233
Collingwood, Colonel
Cuthbert George 43
Collingwood, HMS 232
Collins, Commander Paul
229–30
Collinson, Captain Richard 187
Colomb, Admiral Philip
Howard 130
Colossus, HMS 155
Commerell, Captain John
Edmund 190
Commonwealth, HMS 156
Congreve, Sir William 121
Conquerant, French ship 70
Constable, Captain John 43,
49–50
Constant Warwick, HMS 251
Content, French ship 60
Cook, Captain James 68, 85
Cooper, Captain Archibald
Frederick 166
Cooper, Captain Thomas 55
Cornall, Captain John 166
Cornwall, Vice Admiral
Charles 64
Cornwallis, Admiral Charles
112, 117, 233–5
Courageux, HMS 70
Courier, French ship 78
Couvonne, French ship 59–60,
70
Coventry, HMS 217, 228
Cowan, Admiral Walter 157
Craddock, Captain
Christopher 249
Cranstoun, Captain Lord 75
Crawley, Captain Edmund 183
Crescent, HMS 85, 213–4
Critchley, Mike 227
Cromwell, Oliver 11, 230–1
Culloden, HMS 60
Culme-Seymour, Admiral Sir
Michael 134
Cumberland, HMS 70, 210–2,
226
Cuming, Captain W. 113
Cunningham, Admiral Andrew
B. 71
Currey, Rear Admiral H.P. 151
Curtis, Admiral Sir Roger
123, 243
Custance, Admiral Sir
Reginald 131

D'Ache, Comte Anne-Antoine
211
Daedalus, HMS 166
Dallinger, John 221–3
Dalrymple, Admiral Sir John
81, 95
Dampier, Captain William 234
Danae, HMS 185
Daniel, Captain H.M. 157–64
Daniels, Temp Lieutenant
Allan 169
Danielsson, Bengt 85
Darby, Vice Admiral George 75
Dartmouth, Lord 36
Dauntless, HMS 157
Dauphin Royal, French ship 70
David, Lieutenant Charles 54
Davies, Lieutenant Mark 225–6
Dawkins, Captain Richard
192–5
de Chartres, Admiral Duc 70
de la Galissoniere, Marquis
Roland Michel Barrin
59–62
De Lome, M. Dupuy French
ship Designer 130
de Mayne, Master A. 195–6
de Niza, Contre Admiral
Marquis 105
de Ruffo, Cardinal Fabrizio
106–7, 109–10
De Soto, American ship 246
Decoy, HMS 207
Defence, HMS 129, 146, 148, 152
Defiance, HMS 43–5, 47–9,
60, 70, 74, 113, 115, 120,
113, 228
De Langara, Admiral Don
Juan 77
Deptford, HMS 61
Dewar, Captain K.G.B. 156–63
Diademe, French ship 70
Diamond Rock, HMS 214–5
Diamond, HMS 207, 235
Diana, HMS 112
Dickson, Commander Thomas
Searle 123, 213
Digby, Rear Admiral Robert 75
Diligence, HMS 238
Dilk, Captain T. 54–5
Director, HMS 97–8, 100, 184
Discovery, HMS 85
Dobson, Captain Man 183
Dolphin, HMS 206
Donegal, HMS 120, 155
d'Orlanie, Pierre 183–4

Dorsetshire, HMS 54
d'Orvilliers, Admiral Comte
69–71
Doughty, Thomas 32, 34
Douglas, Admiral William 123
Doyle, Seaman James 220
Dragon, HMS 113, 115, 117
Drake, Admiral Sir Francis
31–5, 178
Drake, HMS 137–8
Dreadnought, HMS 136, 145,
156, 195, 230
Drew, Captain Harold 164–71
Drury-Lowe, Commander
Sidney Robert 143
Dryad, HMS 142
Du Chaffault, Admiral Comte
70
Dublin, HMS 146, 151–2
Duc de Burgogne, French ship 70
Ducasse, Jean-Baptiste French
Commodore 43, 45, 47, 52
Duckworth, Vice Admiral John
120, 123, 252
Duff, Lieutenant Commander
Daniel 169
Duke of Edinburgh, HMS 146
Duke, HMS 70, 72, 90
Duncan, Admiral Adam 75, 81,
111, 208
Duncan, HMS 143
Dundas, Admiral Sir Charles 252
Dunn, Captain Richard
Dalling 123
Durham Lieutenant Philip
Charles 83, 113
Durrell, Captain Philip 65
Dutton, Consul Ernest L. 245

Eagle, HMS 162, 224
Edgar, King 9
Edinburgh, HMS 166
Edward VII, King 138
Egerton, Admiral Sir George
151
Egmont, HMS 70
Egyptienne, HMS 114
Eldon, Solicitor General Lord
John Scot 94
Eleanor of Aquitaine 10
Elizabeth Bonaventure 34
Elizabeth I, Queen 31, 33
Elizabeth, HMS 42, 70, 211
Elliott, Captain the Hon.
C.G.S. 243–4
Elliott, John 183–4

Elliott, Captain Tobin 225
Ellison, Seaman Thomas 91, 93
Elphinstone, Master's Mate 88
Emerald, HMS 122
Erebus, HMS 186
Espana, Spanish ship 114–5
Essex, HMS 55
Ethelred, King 9
Etna, fire ship 121–2
Euryalus, HMS 239
Evans, Vice Admiral E.R. 81
Eveille, French ship 70
Everitt, Captain Michael 63
Evetsen, Johan Dutch Admiral 36, 38
Excellent, HMS 137
Exeter, HMS 70

Falmouth, HMS 43–7, 49, 206–7
Faulknor, Captain Robert 81
Fendant, French ship 70
Ferdinand Max, Austrian ship 130
Ferdinand, King 105, 107
Ferrier, Captain John 183
Fier, French ship 60–1, 70
Firme, Spanish ship 114–5, 119
Fisher, Admiral Jackie 154, 200
Fisher, Lieutenant George 234
Fitzroy, Captain Robert 237
Flanagan, Lieutenant Commander John 228
Flatt, Lieutenant Nicholas 101
Flora, HMS 213–4
Fogg, Captain Christopher 43, 46–7, 50
Foote, Captain Edward James 106–7, 109
Forbes, Admiral John 66
Foresight, HMS 166
Formidable, French ship 114
Formidable, HMS 70–1, 76
Forth, HMS 182
Foudroyant, French ship 59–60, 70, 122, 126
Foudroyant, HMS 107–8
Fox, Captain Thomas 208
Franklin, Sir John 186
Frapnell, J.G., Judge Advocate of the Fleet 169
Freemantle, Rear Admiral Sydney 151
French, Midshipman Francis 223
Frobisher, Admiral Sir Martin 31
Frogmore, Captain Rowland 55
Frye, Lieutenant George 240–1

Fryer, Master John 88–9, 91–2
Fuller, Midshipman Thomas 232
Fury, fire ship 121
Fyler, Captain Herbert A.W.H. 151

Gamage, Lieutenant Richard Stewart 219
Gambier, Lord James 120–8, 210
Ganges, HMS 95
Ganteaume, Admiral Honore Joseph Antoine 112
Gardener, Leslie 35, 157
Gardiner, Captain Arthur 61, 65
Garner, Captain the Hon. A.H. 113, 115
Gaydon, Captain John 41
Geddes, Sir Eric 155
Geffard, President Fabre 245–6
Genoa, HMS 212–3
George II, King 16
George III, King 17, 66
George V, King 17
George, Benjamin 243
George, Prince 50
Gibraltar, HMS 212–3
Gill, Commander Harold Britton Clifford 169
Gill, Third Officer Marion 229
Gladiator, HMS 123, 245
Glasgow, HMS 178
Glinn, Lieutenant C.G. 220
Glorieux, French ship 70
Glorious, HMS 185
Glory, HMS 113, 155, 181
Gloucester, HMS 146, 148–9, 151, 230
Goddard, Lord Chief Justice 247
Godfey, Admiral J.H. 201
Goeben, German battlecruiser 145–54
Golden Lion 34
Goliath, HMS 105
Goodere, Captain Samuel 218
Goodere, Sir John Dineley 218
Gower, Lieutenant Erasmus 55
Grand Duke of Russia, transport 235
Gravina, Vice Admiral Don F. 114
Gray, Lieutenant E.E. 244
Greenwich, HMS 43–6, 49
Greetham, Moses 123
Grenville, Admiral Sir Richard 31, 217
Griffith, Captain E. 113

Griffiths, Lieutenant William 54
Griffon, HMS 219
Guerrier, French ship 60
Guildford, Lord 135

Haddock, Admiral Sir Richard 41
Hall, Captain Basil 123
Hallett, Lieutenant John 91–3
Halley, Edmund 178
Halloran, Revd L.H. 119
Hamilton, Captain Guy 166
Hamilton, Lady Emma 104, 106, 110
Hamilton, Sir William 108
Hamilton, Surgeon William 252
Hamilton, Vice Admiral Frederick 154
Hammersley, Lieutenant (E) J. 181
Hannay, David 39
Hardy, Admiral Sir Charles 58, 217
Hardy, Admiral Sir George 78
Harland, Sir Robert 68, 70–2
Harris, Lieutenant John 183
Harvey (Hervey), Midshipman John 238
Harvey, Captain J. 113, 118
Harvey, Captain Sir Elias 63, 70, 210
Harvey, Rear Admiral John C. 184
Havers, Mr Justice 247
Havock, HMS 164
Hawke, Admiral Lord Edward 53, 57, 62, 77, 111, 208
Hawke, HMS 156
Hawkins, Admiral Sir John 31
Hawkins, Lieutenant Commander Nick 227
Hawkins-Smith, Commander Thomas 135
Hayward, Midshipman Thomas 89, 91–2
Heath, Lieutenant Herbert 134
Heath, Rear Admiral Sir Herbert 151
Hebe, HMS 96
Hector, HMS 70, 192
Henry V, King 31
Henry VII, King 31
Henry VIII, King 31
Herbert, Arthur, Earl of Torrington 36–7, 41–2
Herd, William 184

Hermione, HMS 111, 182–5, 212
Hero, HMS 113, 115–6, 120, 127
Heureux, French ship 43
Heywood, Peter 91–3
Hibernia, HMS 134
Hickley, Captain Henry 192–4
Hickman, William 223–4
Hilbury, Mr Justice 247
Hill, John 184
Hillbrant, Henry Cooper 87
Hippopotame, French ship 60
Hitler, Adolf 147
Hockings, Robert 123
Hodgkinson, Lieutenant
    Commander C.B. 204
Holbourne, Admiral Francis 62
Holford, James 184–5
Holford, John 184–5
Holland, Ben 232
Hollingbery, Lieutenant
    Monins 80–1, 84
Holman, Lieutenant
    Commander T.B. 181
Holmes, Admiral Sir Robert 62
Hood, Admiral Lord 74, 81,
    91, 84–95
Hood, Commodore Samuel 215
Hood, HMS 76, 202–6
Hope, Rear Admiral Sir James
    221
Hornbrook, Lieutenant
    Thomas Beckford 252
Hornet, HMS 233
Hotham, Commodore
    William 81
Hound, Brig 243
Hound, fire ship 121
Howe, Admiral Richard, Earl
    78, 86, 96, 111, 177
Hudson, Captain Thomas 47
Hudson, Lieutenant Joseph
    Samuel 41, 221–2
Huggan, Thomas 88
Hughes, Commodore Sir
    Edward 68, 81
Hunter, HMS 85
Hyacinth, HMS 220

Ibrahim Pasha 212
Illustrious, HMS 120, 229
Imperieuse, HMS 121–3
Incendiary, fire ship 105
Indefatigable, HMS 122, 126, 146
Indienne, French ship 70, 122
Indomitable, HMS 146–7
Indomptable, French ship 114

Inflexible, HMS 97, 146–7
Inflexible, HMS 146, 150
Inman, Captain H. 113
Intrepid, HMS 60–1, 63–5
Intrepide, French ship 70, 114
Investigator, HMS 187
Invincible, HMS 214, 227
Iron Duke, HMS 157, 163, 192–5
Irwin, Captain John 123
Irwin, James 184
Isis, HMS 157

Jackson, George 74–5
James II, King 13, 36–7, 40,
    51, 231
James, Gunner 189
Jameson, Lieutenant
    Commander Andrew 229
Jean Bart 43
Jean Bart, French ship 120
Jekyl, Lieutenant Edward 55
Jellicoe, Admiral of the Fleet,
    Earl 71, 136–7
Jemappes, French ship 121
Jenkins, Marine 220
Jervis, Admiral John 72, 81, 112
John, King 9
Johnson, Brigadier R.F. 84
Johnson, Sir Henry 151
Johnston, Commodore
    Hammersley 168
Johnstone, Captain Charles 135

Kangaroo, HMS 195–6
Keith, Admiral George
    Elphinstone, Lord 106, 110
Kellet, Captain Henry 187
Kelly, Admiral Howard 201, 203
Kelly, Vice Admiral Sir John D.
    161, 183
Kempenfelt, Admiral Richard
    79–81, 111, 211
Kennedy, Admiral Sir William
    248
Kent, HMS 156
Keppel, Admiral Augustus
    17, 23, 62, 67–75, 77, 162,
    170, 217
Keppel, HMS 70
Kerr, Captain Mark 127
Kerslake, Lieutenant
    Commander Stephen 232
Keyes, Admiral Sir Roger
    155–6, 158–9, 161–2
Keyes, Lady 158
Kimball, C Day 162

King George V, HMS 170
Kingston, HMS 60
Kirkby, Captain Richard 43–4,
    46–50, 52
Knight, Captain John 101
Krabb, Paymaster-in-Chief 151

La Magicienne, French ship
    182–4
L'Aigle, HMS 126, 252
L'Aimable, French ship 184
Lamb, Sub-lieutenant Selina 227
Lancaster, David 228
Lancaster, HMS 60
Langridge, Lieutenant Thomas
    49
Lapwing, HMS 197
Lawrence, George 65
Lawson, Commander H.F. 170
le Pelley, Rear Admiral
    Dumanoir 114
Lechmer, Captain W. 114, 118
Leech, Thomas 184
Legge, Captain the Hon. A.K.
    113
Leijden, Dutch ship 36
Leonard, Chaplin Robert 176–7
Lestock, Rear Admiral Richard
    52–9, 241
Leven, HMS 221–2
Leveson-Gower, Commodore
    John 81
Lewis, Lieutenant Commander
    David 230
Lewis, Michael 12, 51, 84
Lewis, Mr Justice 21
Liace, HMS 215
Linzee, Captain S.H. 114
Lion, French ship 60
Lloyd George, David 64, 179
Lloyd, Captain James 55
London, HMS 54, 177
Lonsdale, Lieutenant
    Commander Rupert 216
Lord Clive, HMS 155
Lord Warden, HMS 188
Loughborough, Lord 99
Louis of Battenberg, Prince 138
Louis XIV, King 37
Lucas, Captain George 95,
    210–2
Lucia, HMS 180
Luff, Petty Officer Ian 227
Lumley, Lieutenant Thomas
    Charles 41
Luter, Henry 219

Lutine, HMS 94
Luttrell, Captain James 95

Macdonald, Attorney General 94
Macintosh, Seaman Thomas 90–1
Mack, General Karl 105
MacLauchlan, Archibald 245
Magenta, French ship 129
Magnificent, HMS 156
Magnifique, French ship 70
Malabar, HMS 220
Malby, Captain William 178–9
Malta, HMS 114–5
Manchester, HMS 164–73, 185
Mannasus, American ship 130
Manners, Lord Robert 70
Mansfield, Baron, Lord Chief Justice 67
Marathon, HMS 156
Marchaunt, Captain John 34–5
Marco, Antonio 183
Marder, Professor Arthur 145, 154
Margery, steamship 245
Marie Antoinette 105
Markham, Admiral Albert 132–6
Marlborough, HMS 54
Mars, Alastair, Lieutenant Commander 247–8
Marshall, Rev. 95
Marsham, Paymaster General 162
Martin, Captain G. 113
Martin, Seaman Isaac 89–90
Mason, John 182–3
Mason, William 184
Massaredo, Admiral Don Joseph 110
Mathews, Admiral Sir Thomas 51–9, 61, 64
Matilda, Galley 114
Maurice, Captain James 215
May, Gunner James 189
Mayne, Rear Admiral Sir Perry 54–5, 240–1
McArthur, John 186
McCann, Matthew 176
McClintock, Commander Sir Francis Leopold 187
McClure, Captain Robert 187
McCoy, William 89–90
McKillop, Lieutenant John 80–2
M'Crea, Surgeon W.M. 220
Mediator, HMS 95, 121

Medley, Admiral Henry 58
Melville, First Lord of Admiralty 236
Melville-Brown, Lieutenant Commander Penny 225–6
Mennds, Vice Admiral Sir John 13
Mermaid, HMS 156
Merrimac, American ship 130
Middleton, Samuel 230–1
Milbanke, Vice Admiral Mark 78, 81
Miles, Captain R.B.T. 204–5
Millward, Seaman John 89, 91, 93
Milne, Admiral Sir Alexander 188
Milne, Admiral Sir Archibald Berkley 146–8
Minerva, HMS 108
Mitchell, Commander Francis Herbert 143
Monarch, HMS 27, 70, 132, 188
Monarque, French prize 67
Moncrieff, Carpenter William 184
Monitor, American ship 130, 188
Monmouth, HMS 85
Mont Blanc, Spanish ship 114
Montage, Admiral 74
Montague, Captain John 67, 74
Montclare, HMS 182
Montell, Joe 183
Moody, First Class Stoker Edward Allen 141–3
Moody, Rear Admiral Clement 166
Moore, Captain Arthur William 136
Moore, Midshipman Edward 177–8
Moore, Vice Admiral Sir Henry 171
Morrison, James 90–4
Mosse, Captain James Robert 97, 101, 104
Mountbatten, Admiral Lord Louis 181
Moutay, Captain John 81
Mulgrave, Lord 123
Munden, Rear Admiral Sir John 237–8
Murray, William 83
Musprat, Seaman William 89, 93–4

Naiad, HMS 120
Namur, HMS 54, 175
Nasmith, Admiral Sir Dunbar 200
Natal, HMS 77, 185
Nautilus, HMS 186
Nelson, Admiral Horatio 27, 104–12, 117–9, 129, 144, 209, 215, 237
Nelson, HMS 224, 227
Nepean, Evan 101
Neptune, HMS 101
Neptune, Spanish ship 114
Nesbitt, Lieutenant Alexander 186
Newbolt, Sir Henry 50
Newcastle, HMS 210–2
Newcastle, Lord 67, 241
Newman, Captain James N. 127
Nichelson, William 79
Nonsuch, HMS 42
Norman, Seaman James 90–1, 93
Norris, Admiral John 62
Norris, Captain C.F.W. 55, 216
North, Admiral Sir Dudley 111
North, Lord 67, 76
Northesk, Captain William Carnegie 101
Northumberland, HMS 239

Ocean, French ship 122
Ocean, HMS 70, 121, 181
Ogle, Admiral Sir Chaloner 54–5, 240
Oleron, Laws of/Judgements of 9–10, 32
Oliphant, Captain Henry 166
Oliver, Captain Robert 142, 166
Onslow, Captain Richard 166
Onslow, George 243
Onslow, HMS 207
Orient, French ship 70
Orphee, French ship 60
Oxford, HMS 240

P101, Japanese ship 216
Page, Lieutenant Henry 54
Paine. Captain Joseph 231–2
Pakenham, Admiral Sir Thomas 213–4
Pallas, HMS 121
Palliser, Admiral Sir Hugh 17, 55, 68–73, 75–7, 162, 217
Palliser, HMS 76
Pandora, HMS 91

Panter, Petty Officer Sylvia 227
Paramour, HMS 178
Parker, Admiral Hyde 85, 183, 185
Parker, Admiral Sir Peter 235
Parker, Richard 94, 104
Parker, Ships Master 41
Parr, Lieutenant John 226
Pasley, Admiral Sir Thomas 101
Pathfinder, HMS 165
Patriote, French ship 121
Paulet, Sir Amyas 35
Payne ,Lieutenant Matthew 229–30
Peckover, Gunner William 91
Pendennis, HMS 43–4, 47
Peninsular, SS 197
Pepys, Samuel 36, 40–1, 201
Percey, J.G. 199
Petersfield, HMS 201–2
Pett, Captain Robert 55
Peyton, Lieutenant Joseph 55
Phenix, French ship 43
Philip II, King of Spain 33–4
Phillips, Petty Officer Samuel 169
Phoenix, HMS 247
Pigot, Captain Hugh 182–5
Pilcher, Mr Justice 21, 208
Pim, Lieutenant Bedford 187
Pioneer, HMS 187
Pitt, Prime Minister William 67
Pluton, Spanish ship 114–5
Pocock, Admiral Sir George 210–2
Poe, Edgar Allan 147
Popham, Commodore Sir Home 209–10
Portland, HMS 60, 64
Pound, Admiral of the Fleet Sir Dudley 171
Power, Midshipman Edward 82
Price, Carpenter Richard 184
Prince de Frise, French ship 43
Prince George, HMS 62, 70, 156
Prince of Orange, HMS 55
Prince of Wales, HMS 76, 112–3, 115, 118, 157
Princess Louisa, HMS 60–1, 64–5
Prowse, Captain W. 114
Punjabi, HMS 170
Purcell, William 87–8, 91–2
Pye, Admiral Sir Thomas 74

Queen, HMS 70, 238
Quilter, Petty Officer David 227
Quintal, Matthew 87, 90

Raisonnable, HMS 113
Raleigh, Admiral Sir Walter 31, 34
Raleigh, HMS 132
Ramillies, HMS 59–60, 70
Ramsay, Sub-lieutenant Jacqueline 225–6
Ramsey, Rear Admiral C.G. 203
Re d'Italia, Italian ship 130
Real, French ship 54
Reddy, Warrant Officer Albert 169
Redoubtable, French ship 59–60
Reed, Sir Edmund J. 130, 188–91
Refleche, French ship 70
Regulus, French ship 121
Renown, HMS 202–6
Rentone, Captain James 240
Repulse, HMS 76, 100–2, 113
Resistance, HMS 129
Resolute, HMS 187
Resolution, HMS 85, 120, 127
Revenge, HMS 60–1, 64, 120, 122, 161, 217
Riboulelau, Midshipman Peter 177
Richard I, King 10
Richard II, King 10, 218
Richards, Commander J. 187
Richards, Lieutenant Charles 95
Richmond, Captain Herbert 156
Rickard, Henry 134
Robb, Commander (E) William John 166–72
Roberts, HMS 157
Robertson, Alexander 181
Robust, HMS 70, 74
Robuste, French ship 70
Rockingham, Lord 68
Rodd, Captain John 126
Roddam, Admiral Robert 74, 248–9
Rodney, Admiral George Brydges 27, 54, 77, 111
Roland, French ship 70
Rooke, Admiral Sir George 37, 42–3, 48, 51, 234
Roskill, Captain Stephen 154, 164, 180
Ross, Commander Henry 197
Ross, Sir John 187
Rowley, Admiral Sir Joshua 55
Rowley, Captain J. 113
Rowley, Captain Robert 228

Royal George, HMS 77, 84
Royal Oak, HMS 54, 155, 157–64, 185
Royal Sovereign, HMS 155, 233–4
Royal William, HMS 95–6
Royalist, HMS 157
Ruby, HMS 43–7, 218
Rupert, HMS 54
Russell, Admiral Edward 36–8, 40, 42, 48
Russell, Lieutenant George Vincent Blakely 168
Rutherford, Lieutenant Commander Brian 250
Ryan, Captain Andrew 151

Sage, French ship 60
Saint-Esprit, French ship 70
Saint-Michel, French ship 70
Salisbury, Bishop of 40
Salnave, Sylvestre 245 246
Saltonstall, Captain Dudley 11
Salvador del Mundo, prize 252
San Felipe, Spanish ship 35
San Fiorenzo, HMS 97, 100
San Rafael, Spanish ship 114–5, 119
Sandfly, HMS 197
Sandwich, HMS 70, 75, 95–104, 139
Sandwich, Lord 67–9, 71–3, 75, 77–8, 217
Sans Pereil, HMS 136
Saturn, HMS 176
Saunders, Admiral Sir Charles 68
Saunders, Lieutenant George 80–1
Savage, Seaman J. 243
Sawbridge, Captain Henry 202–6
Sawyer, Captain Herbert 111
Scarborough, HMS 231
Scheer, Admiral Reinhard 52
Schlater, Captain George 55
Scipion, French ship 114
Sclater, Captain Guy Lutley 151
Scott, Captain Percy 137, 153, 156
Scott, Lesley 151–2
Seahorse, HMS 106
Seal, HMS 216–7
Searle, Richard 80–1, 184
Serpent, HMS 196–7
Seymour, Captain Hugh 237
Shark, HMS 216–7

Sheffield, HMS 226
Shields, Lieutenant William 176–7
Shovell, Admiral Sir Clowdisley 37, 42, 234
Shrewsbury, HMS 70
Simms, Carpenters Mate Nicholas (aka Syms) 98
Simoon, hospital ship 222
Sirene, French ship 114
Sirius, HMS 114
Sitt, Lieutenant Commander G.M.S. 204
Slater, Admiral Sir Jock 226
Smart, John 81, 83–4
Smelt, Lieutenant Cornelius 54
Smith, Admiral Thomas 62
Smith, Captain Edward T. 183
Smith, Commodore William 54, 183
Smith, Lieutenant Bosworth 199
Snell, Hannah 225
Solferio, French battleship 129
Solitaire, French ship 70
Somerville, Captain James 162
Souchon, Rear Admiral Wilhelm 146–54
Southcott, Master Edward 184
Southfield, American ship 131
Sovereign of the Sea, HMS 42
Spartan, HMS 243
Speedy, HMS 233
Speke, Lieutenant William 198
Spencer, Lord 99–100, 234
Sphinx, French ship 70
Sphynx, HMS 70, 95
Spragge, Admiral Sir Edward 43, 231
Spurling, Master John 123
St David, HMS 40–1
St George, HMS 58
St Vincent, Admiral, Earl 106
St Vincent, HMS 229, 243
Stanhope, Admiral Henry Edwyn 123
Staniforth, Barbara 227
Steel, Lieutenant Commander David 227
Stevens, Admiral Sir Charles 211
Stirling Castle, HMS 70
Stirling, Rear Admiral Charles 113–4
Stokes, Captain Thomas 123
Stokes, Mrs Christine 251
Stopford, Commodore W.G. 140–1, 143

Stopford, Rear Admiral Robert 120, 122, 126
Strachan, Admiral Sir Richard 120
Strickland, Sir Roger 36
Stitt, Lieutenant Commander G.M.S. 204
Sturdee, Admiral Sir Frederick C.D. 137
Sturdy, HMS 170
Sumner, Lieutenant John 89, 246
Superb, HMS 58
Sutherland, HMS 58
Sutton, Rear Admiral John 123
Swabey, Lieutenant Commander Christopher 223–4
Swiftsure, French ship 114
Swiftsure, HMS 207
Syfret, Rear Admiral Neville 166

Talbot, HMS 154
Tandy, Commander Dashwood Goldie 194
Tarbor, Temp Lieutenant John 169
Tarleton, Admiral Sir John Walter 192
Tartar, HMS 166
Taylor, Gordon 230, 231
Taylour, Captain Richard 11
Tegetthot, Admiral Wilhelm von 130
Temeraire, French ship 60
Temeraire, HMS 210
Temple, Lord 66–7
Terpsichore, HMS 105
Terraine, John 119
Terrible, HMS 70
Terrible, Spanish ship 114
Terror, HMS 186
Thalia, HMS 112
Theseus, HMS 112, 120, 127
Thomas, First Lord of the Admiralty James 182
Thomas, Lieutenant James Cambridge 194
Thornton, Commodore Edward 166
Thracian, HMS 215, 217
Thunder, fire ship 121
Thunderer, HMS 70, 114
Thurn, Commodore Count 108
Thursby, Rear Admiral Sir Cecil Fiennes 151
Tiddy, David 194
Tiger, HMS 163

Tirpitz, German battleship 37
Togo, Admiral Heyhachiro 145
Tonnant, HMS 120
Tonnerre, French ship 121
Torbay, HMS 55, 68
Torpedo boat No 81 198
Torrington, Admiral George, Viscount 37–42, 69, 144, 217
Totty, Captain Thomas 184
Tourville, Admiral Anne Hilarion, Comte De 37–8
Tourville, French ship 121
Tower, Captain F.T.B. 202–6
Townsend, Rear Admiral C.H. 162
Tracy, Vice Admiral Richard Edward 134
Trident, HMS 60–1, 64
Triton, French ship 60, 70
Triumph, HMS 113, 115–6
Tromp, Dutch Admiral Maarten Harpertszoon 11
Troubridge Rear Admiral Sir Thomas 105–6, 144–5
Troubridge, Rear Admiral Ernest C.T. 144–54
Troup, Vice Admiral JAG 203–4
Tunstall, Brian 55
Tyron, Admiral Sir George 131–6
Tyrwhitt, Captain John Reginald Joseph 166

Unbroken, HMS 247
Undaunted, HMS 242
Unicorn, HMS 122

Valdrogue, Haitian ship 245–6
Valentine, Ordinary Seaman James 88
Valhalla, HMS 155
Valiant, HMS 69–70, 120, 122, 157, 160, 182, 219
Vanguard, HMS 77, 105–6, 185, 192–5
Varsovie, French ship 121–2
Vengeance, HMS 70, 132
Vengeur, French ship 70
Venomous, HMS 200
Vesuvius, fire ship 121
Victoria, HMS 77, 131–6, 195
Victoria, Queen 17, 132
Victory, HMS 23, 70, 94, 141–2, 232, 243, 247

Vigilant, HMS 70
Ville de Paris, French ship 70
Villeneuve, Admiral Pierre
112–9, 169, 215
Vincent, Captain Nicholas
210–2
Vincent, Captain Samuel 45–6
Vingt-deux Decembre, Haitian
ship 246
Viper, HMS 198–9
Volage, HMS 156, 220
Voltaire (Francois-Marie
Arouet) 58

Wade, Captain Cooper 43, 46,
49–50
Wadsworth, Captain James 11
Wager, HMS 14
Waghorn, Captain Martin 79,
81–2, 84
Wake, Captain Charles 245–7
Wallace, Edgar 143
Walpole, Horace 241
Walsingham, Captain Robert
Boyle 74
Walton, Captain George 43–4,
47, 50

Warden, Admiral Frederick 130
Warner, Captain Gerald 166
Warren, Captain S. 113
Warrior, HMS 114, 132, 146,
182, 192, 229
Warspite, HMS 81, 214
Warwick, HMS 78
Watson, Captain Burges 162,
239
Wellesey, HMS 132
West, Captain Temple 55,
59–61, 63–4
Weymouth, HMS 146, 210–1
Whetstone, Rear Admiral Sir
William 47
Whitworth, Vice Admiral Sir
William J. 169
William Henry, Prince 237
William of Orange 36–7, 40–1
Williams, Captain Edmund 54
Williams, Thomas 80–1
Williamson, Captain John
208, 209
Willis, Lord Chief Justice
240–2
Wilson, Captain Arthur 136
Wilson, Gunner Andrew 235

Winchester, HMS 58
Windsor Castle, HMS 113,
115–6, 118
Windsor, HMS 43–5
Winslow, Captain Alfred 134
Wolfe, Captain George 126
Wolseley, Captain William 217
Woods, Petty Officer James
(aka 'Leslie Yexley') 239
Woodward, Admiral Sir John
227
Worcester, HMS 70
Wrack, Abraham 243
Wray, Captain Fawcet 148–9,
153–4

Yexley, Leslie (aka Petty
Officer James Woods) 230
York, HMS 42, 183
Young, Admiral Charles Henry
123
Young, Admiral William 100
Young, Captain James 61, 64

Zealous, HMS 236
Zodiaque, French ship 70

Other titles published by The History Press

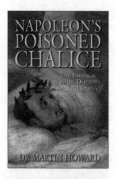

Napoleon's Poisoned Chalice: the Emperor and his Doctor on St Helena
DR MARTIN HOWARD

In this book Martin Howard addresses the political pitfalls navigated with varying success by the men who were assigned to care for the most famous man in Europe, Napoleon. The hostility that sprang up between individuals thrown together in isolation, the impossible situations the doctors found themselves in and the fear of censure when Napoleon finally began to die are all explored in detail.

978-0-7524-4857-2

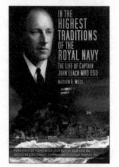

In the Highest Traditions of the Royal Navy: the Life of Captain John Leach MVO DSO
MATTHEW B. WILLS

On 10 December 1941, HMS *Prince of Wales* was sunk by Japanese bombers in the South China Sea. Amongst those who went down with her was her captain. He embodied the best of the service, and truly was in 'the highest traditions of the Royal Navy'. Here is the story of this man, analysing the influences that shaped him and led to his heroic end.

978-0-7524-5992-9

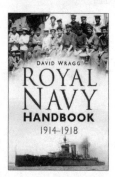

Royal Navy Handbook 1914–1918
DAVID WRAGG

In 1914, the Royal Navy was the largest in the world, as the 'two power standard' meant that it had to be equal to the combined strength of any two other fleets. Yet, the Royal Navy had also suffered from almost a century without war. This handbook tells the story of how the 'Senior Service' adapted to the demands of war.

978-0-7509-4203-4

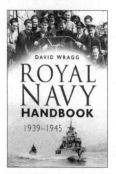

Royal Navy Handbook 1939–1945
DAVID WRAGG

With the coming of the Second World War, the service had to learn fast. The Royal Navy was expected to be active in the North Atlantic and in British waters, as well as protecting Arctic convoys. Meanwhile, it also had to keep control of the Mediterranean, support ground forces and many more duties besides. This handbook explores just how the Royal Navy kept up in such demanding times.

978-0-7509-3937-9

Visit our website and discover thousands of other History Press books.

www.thehistorypress.co.uk